The Cinema of Discomfort

The Cinema of Discomfort

Disquieting, Awkward and Uncomfortable Experiences in Contemporary Art and Indie Film

Geoff King

BLOOMSBURY ACADEMIC
NEW YORK • LONDON • OXFORD • NEW DELHI • SYDNEY

BLOOMSBURY ACADEMIC
Bloomsbury Publishing Inc
1385 Broadway, New York, NY 10018, USA
50 Bedford Square, London, WC1B 3DP, UK
29 Earlsfort Terrace, Dublin 2, Ireland

BLOOMSBURY, BLOOMSBURY ACADEMIC and the Diana logo are trademarks of
Bloomsbury Publishing Plc

First published in the United States of America 2022
This paperback edition published 2023

Copyright © Geoff King, 2022

Cover design: Eleanor Rose
Cover image: *Dogtooth*, Dir. Yorgos Lanthimos, 2009 © Boo Productions
/ DR / Collection Christophel / ArenaPAL

All rights reserved. No part of this publication may be reproduced or transmitted in any form or by any means, electronic or mechanical, including photocopying, recording, or any information storage or retrieval system, without prior permission in writing from the publishers.

Bloomsbury Publishing Inc does not have any control over, or responsibility for, any third-party websites referred to or in this book. All internet addresses given in this book were correct at the time of going to press. The author and publisher regret any inconvenience caused if addresses have changed or sites have ceased to exist, but can accept no responsibility for any such changes.

Library of Congress Cataloging-in-Publication Data
Names: King, Geoff, 1960– author.
Title: The cinema of discomfort : disquieting, awkward and uncomfortable experiences in contemporary art and indie film / Geoff King.
Description: New York : Bloomsbury Academic, 2021. |
Includes bibliographical references and index.
Identifiers: LCCN 2021018237 (print) | LCCN 2021018238 (ebook) |
ISBN 9781501359309 (hardback) | ISBN 9781501359293 (epub) |
ISBN 9781501359286 (pdf) | ISBN 9781501359279
Subjects: LCSH: Discomfort in motion pictures. |
Independent films–History and criticism. | Experimental films–History and criticism. |
Motion picture audiences. | Motion pictures–Psychological aspects.
Classification: LCC PN1995.9.D554 K56 2021 (print) | LCC PN1995.9.D554 (ebook) |
DDC 791.43653–dc23
LC record available at https://lccn.loc.gov/2021018237
LC ebook record available at https://lccn.loc.gov/2021018238

ISBN: HB: 978-1-5013-5930-9
PB: 978-1-5013-8573-5
ePDF: 978-1-5013-5928-6
eBook: 978-1-5013-5929-3

Typeset by Newgen KnowledgeWorks Pvt. Ltd., Chennai, India

To find out more about our authors and books visit www.bloomsbury.com
and sign up for our newsletters.

CONTENTS

List of figures vii

Introduction 1

1 Into the discomfort zone 17

2 'Uncomfortably great': Todd Solondz and *Palindromes* 67

3 Ulrich Seidl: Far from paradise 107

4 Weirdly discomforting: *Dogtooth* and the Greek new wave 149

5 Forces majeure and minor: From existential alienation to personal obligation in the films of Roy Andersson and Ruben Östlund 181

6 A very English discomfort: Joanna Hogg 219

7 The comedy of discomfort: Towards a conclusion 249

Select bibliography 277
Index 285

FIGURES

1. Quietly unbearable tension: Keeping the candle alight in *Nostalgia* (1983) 30
2. Joyless sex: The discomfort of Aviva and Judah after their first encounter in *Palindromes* (2004) 70
3. Camera movement accompanies Aviva's happy mood after the motel sex scene in *Palindromes* (2004) 74
4. Distinctly 'uncool' Christian religious song and dance played straight in *Palindromes* (2004) 81
5. Genuine close-up emotion on the part of Mama Sunshine accompanies the story about the girl who ran away … with no legs in *Palindromes* (2004) 85
6. Spokesman for the filmmaker? Mark's speech about the impossibility of change in *Palindromes* (2004) 86
7. Framing sex in *Import Export* (2007) 111
8. The machinery of online pornography: Olga watching a performance in *Import Export* (2007) 119
9. Less mediated sex: Olga's first online performance to camera in *Import Export* (2007) 120
10. Olga on the ward in *Import Export* (2007) 123
11. The reality of end of life: The final shot of the ward, with English subtitle, in *Import Export* (2007) 126
12. Comical appearance but taken seriously in the narrative: The father after faking attack by a cat in *Dogtooth* (2009) 152
13. Uncomfortable prelude to incest: The son choosing which of his sisters should be his next sexual partner in *Dogtooth* (2009) 154
14. Aestheticized stylization: Water drops on the lens in the play-fencing scene, with English subtitle, in *Dogtooth* (2009) 157
15. Decapitation: Off-kilter framing of the two sisters in *Dogtooth* (2009) 158
16. Awkward kissing at the start of *Attenberg* (2010) 168
17. Silly walks and gestures in *Attenberg* (2010) 169

18 Nightmare colonial 'musical instrument' in *A Pigeon Sat on a Branch Reflecting on Existence* (2014) 184
19 Hyperbolically extended recession in the airport check-in scene in *Songs from the Second Floor* (2000) 188
20 Embarrassing scene framed with characteristic receding depth in *Songs from the Second Floor* (2000) 190
21 Figures in an urban landscape in *Play* (2011) 201
22 Flight rather than fight: Tomas flees the apparently oncoming avalanche in *Force Majeure* (2014) 205
23 Hiding in the herd with downcast eyes as ape-impersonation performance crosses the line in *The Square* (2017) 212
24 Distance in initial shot of Cynthia's lunchtime complaint about her food in *Archipelago* (2010) 226
25 Edward, in background, seeks more contact with Rose, to the annoyance of Cynthia, in *Archipelago* (2010) 227
26 Reducing and abstracting: Christopher talks, reflexively, about his art in *Archipelago* (2010) 229
27 Listening to the off-screen shouting match in pained silence in *Unrelated* (2007) 231
28 Cringe-making: Swanson 'trying to get out of his comfort zone' in the bar scene in *The Comedy* (2012) 255
29 Winfried bursts into the frame in his Toni disguise, startling Ines, in *Toni Erdman* (2016) 262
30 'Hardcore! So Hardcore!' Gerald's reaction to Winfried's giant Bulgarian folk costume during the nude party in *Toni Erdman* (2016) 264

Introduction

A naïve underage girl has anal sex with an unprepossessing truck driver, implausibly declaring the experience to have been 'so beautiful'. A bullying male exerts his (limited) authority on a semi-clad woman in his hotel room, at one point forcing her to crawl around and bark like a dog; other scenes take place in a geriatric ward peopled by real patients, some clearly senile and/or approaching death. An upper-middle-class group sits in embarrassed silence around a restaurant table while one complains to the staff about her food, her tone quiet but nonetheless needlingly irksome. A young man who has been brought up in isolation from society sits naked in the bath choosing which of his two teenage sisters should become his new sexual partner. A vast crowd, including religious and civic dignitaries, watches as a blindfolded young girl is walked up to the edge of a quarry and pushed off, a sacrifice that is unexplained but apparently an effort to avert some unidentified social collapse. A couple's relationship slowly and painfully comes apart after the husband fails to admit to momentarily abandoning his family in panic in the face of an avalanche. A seemingly impervious and well-heeled white male complains about being 'stereotyped' by the occupants of a black-neighbourhood bar, commenting, with a cringe-inducing insensitivity, that he offers a source of diversity. The father of a brittle businesswoman intrudes exasperatingly on her life, disguising himself with a wig and false teeth to pose in front of important clients as a life coach.[1]

These are just a few scenes from what can be viewed as a cinema of discomfort; of the disquieting, the awkward and the embarrassing: the subject of this book. What is involved in the films from which these examples come is usually some form of *sustained* discomfort that characterizes the experience offered to the viewer throughout the navigation of their fictional worlds. I distinguish this from passing moments of discomfort that might more often be found in films in which such a quality is offered only on a local basis, the premise of which is usually that it will soon be alleviated or overcome; in such cases, discomfort is a stage usually founded on the assumption that it will serve to highlight the more comfortable situation to which it leads. The cinema of discomfort, as understood in this book, as a subset of works from the international arthouse and American indie film sectors, is also generally distinct from examples in which significant elements of discomfort are built into the conventional expectations of an established commercial genre such as horror. Such a distinction might not be absolute, however, given the capacity of the kinds of films and filmmakers examined here to generate their own expectations of discomfort.

My focus is on varieties of discomfort that can be characterized by specific terms such as *disquieting*, *awkward* and *embarrassing*, to suggest certain nuances elaborated below, rather than those which are more radically assaultive or extreme in nature. The latter, found in some prominent examples of art cinema, are also sources of discomfort but of a variety different in degree and maybe also in kind. The former is a quality found across a range of films in the institutionalized realms of art and indie film, examined here in case study examples from the work of Todd Solondz, Ulrich Seidl, Yorgos Lanthimos, Athina Rachel Tsangari, Roy Andersson, Ruben Östlund, Joanna Hogg, Rick Alverson and Maren Ade. The art and indie sectors are domains in which varying degrees of freedom are available from the mainstream commercial pressures that tend to drive cinema more generally in the direction of the provision of comfort (or only temporary discomfort) rather than its opposite, and/or where specific institutional contexts actively encourage the production of such material.

Approaches

The Cinema of Discomfort examines this phenomenon at a number of levels. It closely analyses the textual strategies through which impressions of discomfort are created (narrative situations and the formal means through which they are articulated) and considers exactly what kinds of experiences are offered to viewers. What, for example, might be the particular *pleasures*, if any, available from such forms of discomfort? How can we understand their appeal, to at least some viewers, and why might discomfort of this kind often be valued? The challenges posed to viewers by such films are understood in at least two dimensions, sometimes linked. They can offer *cognitive* difficulties, imposed in some cases by a withholding of salient information. But also, and often more importantly, they provide scope for discomfort in what is entailed in the likely *emotional* or otherwise affective responses of viewers, an arena in which some of the films falling into this category also withhold clear indicators of preferred orientation. Films that offer experiences of discomfort can be understood sometimes to be thought-provoking, but they might also often be described (in a less familiar phrase) as uncertainly feeling-provoking, in the sense of leaving viewers without clear cut indicators of how to respond at this level.

This book also examines the institutional foundations of films of this kind: the bases that permit or encourage them to exist within the contexts of particular national or international sites of production and circulation, in the latter case including their appeal within the global festival circuit that usually plays an important part in the life cycle of such work. It analyses viewer responses to such films in most cases, exploring the bases of their appeal to some and rejection by others. Key examples of the cinema of discomfort are also examined as products of either particular or wider sociocultural contexts, to see how they might be understood to reflect or comment on their times and/or places of production. A recurrent theme is the extent to which such films might be read as expressing certain kinds of malaise associated with the experiences of variously defined aspects of contemporary, neoliberal capitalist, late-modern/postmodern, patriarchal, racist or so-called 'western' society.[2]

Discomfort of the kind suggested above can be found quite widely in the art and indie film sectors. This book focuses primarily on close study of a limited number of case studies, but it situates these within a broader arthouse realm in which uncomfortable material has provided one marker of the distinctive status of such material. The films on which I concentrate can be viewed as part of a tendency within the wider art and indie film realms, within which such qualities are brought to the fore. I argue that they share sufficient common characteristics to be situated in this way, broadly, without claiming that they embody anything as strong as a shared essence. As an analytical category, I suggest, the cinema of discomfort is a useful designation through which to capture salient features of certain types of art or independent cinema, although one that remains far from clear cut. Elements of discomfort similar to those I explore in detail here can be found in a substantial proportion of work that circulates in the wider art and indie film sectors, either in the contemporary period or its longer history. My examination of the realm of discomfort is, in this sense, an extension into this particular tendency of some of the approaches to art and indie film included in my previous book, *Positioning Art Cinema: Film and Cultural Value* (2019), and some of my past writing about the American indie sector.

Varying forms of discomfort can be found in many of the major strands of art cinema, including the difficult life situations explored in numerous examples that make claims to the status of realism, from Italian neorealism to its many successors across the globe. They can also feature strongly in films located in the modernist tradition, including various explorations of states of alienation. Discomforting dimensions are central to some of the examples examined in *Positioning Art Cinema*, including many of the films associated with the term 'slow cinema' and the works of figures such as Michael Haneke, Jean-Pierre and Luc Dardenne and Lars von Trier (the latter's *The Idiots* [*Idioterne*, 1988] would be one prime example). The same can be said of the wider salience of discomfort to a significant number of works from the American independent sector, including in some cases the relatively more mainstream Indiewood domain constituted principally by films produced and/or distributed by studio speciality divisions.

Sustained discomfort can also be found on occasion in releases from the major Hollywood studios, although it is much less common and likely to be motivated at least in part by genre location. One notable example is *Mother!* (2017), the oppressively claustrophobic discomfort of which is situated within a psychological horror/thriller context, along with that provided by the auteur signature of Darren Aronofsky (that the film was distributed by the main division of the studio might be explained partly by the fact that Paramount was one of those to have closed its speciality division in the previous decade – an otherwise more likely location for such a production). Less typical studio-released films can also offer difficult relationships with major characters, a feature of some of the case studies in this book; for example *Prisoners* (2013, independently produced but released by Warner), one of the main protagonists of which is driven to disquieting vigilante action following the kidnap of his daughter. Marked discomfort can also be found in other atypical cases, such as some of the films associated with the Hollywood Renaissance of the 1960s and 1970s, examples including *Taxi Driver* (1976) and *Three Women* (1977).

The discomfort offered by the films examined in this book provides a challenge to viewers of the kind often associated with the art or indie sectors, marking such works as distinct from the commercial mainstream but without going as far as the most alienating forms of modernism or work situated at the avant-garde or experimental end of the cinematic spectrum. The particular forms of discomfort involved can give such films a degree of commercial currency or notoriety, albeit within the restricted arthouse and related realms of circulation. Among the most recurrent tropes found in the cinema of discomfort is what can be termed 'the awkward sex scene', as is clear from some of the instances cited above and others explored in detail below. On the one hand, certain treatments of the most intimate of relations provide strong grounds for the experience of acute cinematic discomfort. On the other, such films can participate in the long tradition through which art or otherwise alternative cinema has traded at least partly on its promise of providing representations of transgressive sex.[3]

The cinema of discomfort, as defined here, has not previously been subject to sustained analysis as a phenomenon in its own right. One partial exception is Nikolaj Lübecker's *The Feel-Bad Film* (2015). Lübecker identifies three types of feel-bad film, defined according to the categories of 'assault', 'unease' and 'transgression'. The second of these, 'unease', has much in common with the notions of discomfort I employ here, although the approach and textual examples are substantially different. I focus more exclusively on this part of the discomforting or bad-feeling film landscape, examining it in more detail and at greater length, as a category at least relatively distinct from the more confrontationally assaultive or transgressive instances that constitute the major part of Lübecker's study. The latter body of work, including films from figures such as Catherine Breillat, Claire Denis, Lars von Trier and Gaspar Noé, has been the subject of numerous studies, some of which I consider in Chapter 3. These include Asbjørn Grønstad's *Screening the Unwatchable: Spaces of Negation in Post-Millennial Art Cinema* (2012), the primary concern of which is also with the more assaultive or extreme end of the spectrum. Grønstad includes some consideration of instances of less aggressively discomforting material, but only briefly. *The Cinema of Discomfort*, again, offers a more sustained exploration of this particular terrain, as is necessary to a broader understanding of forms of cinematic discomfort that lie beyond its sometimes more shockingly extreme manifestations.

My approach also differs in some substantial respects from those of Lübecker and Grønstad. The main focus of the former is on a philosophically based reading of the ethical-political implications of such films and the experiences they offer to the viewer. The ethical/moral dimension is also at the heart of Grønstad's approach. Both authors conclude that forms of art cinema that include certain kinds of aggressively assaultive material can be viewed as serving positive ethical purposes, a basis on which they can be accorded cultural value. Such issues are also considered in this book but generally from a different perspective, as indicated above. At the level of textual analysis of either form or content, I often employ a broadly cognitivist approach to the combined dimensions of cognitive and affective engagement, or disengagement, encouraged by examples of the cinema of discomfort. This includes an attempt to evoke the kinds of experiences offered by such films in something closer to a phenomenological manner, as advocated by Julian Hanich in the analysis of films that provoke other affective responses, principally fear.[4] I provide a broader picture of how such films are situated within the art and indie film landscapes, as particular kinds of products that have their own institutional conditions of existence and bases of appeal, rather than just as texts to be interpreted at the level of their ethical valences. *The Cinema of Discomfort* also devotes more attention than Lübecker and Grønstad to an examination of how the cinema of discomfort might be understood in its more general or specific sociocultural contexts.

Social contexts

As far as its broader social-cultural positioning and some stylistic traits are concerned, the cinema of discomfort has points of overlap with US manifestations that fall within the scope of what Jeffrey Sconce terms American 'smart' cinema, a category further explored by Claire Perkins.[5] Smart cinema, for Sconce, includes a range of films from the US independent and Indiewood sectors. Such work, in an account focused primarily on films from the 1990s, is marked by an ironically distanced treatment of a number of issues of 'personal politics' – 'power, communication, emotional dysfunction and identity' – within the arena of white middle-class culture.[6] Notable examples include the work of Todd Solondz, Alexander Payne and Neil LaBute. A particular tone is identified as the vehicle for a critique of bourgeois taste and culture, a tendency Sconce distinguishes from, and sees as having displaced, 'a more activist emphasis on the "social politics" of power, institutions, representation and subjectivity so central to 1960s and 1970s art cinema (especially in its "political" wing)'.[7] Such films are viewed as embodying a particular sensibility or 'structure of feeling', a term drawn from the cultural studies approach of Raymond Williams to suggest a distinct and historically specific cultural phenomenon, although one that makes no claim to be of universal application to any time or place (such things are always easy to overstate in attempts to provide any kind of explanatory context of this kind for cultural products). The sensibility in question is associated in this case with what became known as 'Generation X', a disaffected post-baby-boom cohort seen in Sconce's account as having 'retreated into ironic disengagement as a means of non-participatory coexistence with boomers and their dominance of the cultural and political landscape'.[8] It might also be related to a broader range of complexes associated with the cultural dimensions of a prevalent neoliberal worldview, aspects of which are examined in more detail from Chapter 1 onwards.

As Perkins suggests, one major strand of American indie film can be understood as offering a form of social realism in its focus on a certain contemporary orientation that 'underpins the interpersonal dynamics of the American white middle class'.[9] While middle-class lifestyles and/or ambitions frequently exist implicitly as default assumptions or aspirations in Hollywood, Perkins argues, a key marker of distinction in the indie sector 'is that this middle-class environment of material comfort and financial security is not presented as an invisible backdrop'. Instead, she suggests, in examples such as *Young Adult* (2011) and *Touchy Feely* (2013), 'it is relentlessly drawn to attention through the characters' own self-awareness and/or through varying strategies of satire and critique in which bourgeois identity, taste, and culture is shown to be alienated, absurd, narcissistic, or outright monstrous.'[10] A similar terrain is charted by some of the examples examined in this book, both within and beyond the American context, although much of the work includes a focus broader than the exclusively middle-class arena considered by Sconce and Perkins and entails productions from a decade or so later and up to the present.

A distinction akin to one made within the American indie sector by Perkins can be found in the wider realm of art cinema: between works that can be read as offering a dissection of contemporary middle-class malaise and other varieties in which the focus is on those of working or 'lower' class status. The latter have more often been associated with social realism than the former, examples ranging from the classic case of Italian neorealism to the Romanian 'new wave' of the 2000s, the work of the Dardennes and the films of the Chinese 'Sixth Generation'. As Perkins suggests, a notable feature of dominant discourse in the American context (although not exclusively so) is for the notion of class to be 'othered': for its overt identification in relation to realism to be restricted primarily to an association with these lower-class realms while the characteristics of the middle classes function as a largely taken-for-granted norm.[11]

Perkins cites a number of sources that diagnose particular forms of contemporary middle-class malaise that the films she examines are taken to exhibit, a phenomenon she agrees with Sconce in associating broadly with the 'Generation X' cohort. One component of this reading follows from what Sconce says about the difference between smart cinema and some earlier and more overtly political elements of art cinema, in suggesting a broader cultural retreat: from a sense of political opposition to one in which the culture of neoliberal capitalism has become seemingly all-pervading. A number of sociological and psychological commentators are cited as charting a prevailing tendency in this context, one that continues well into the twenty-first century, in which 'social problems are recast as emotional ones'.[12] Examples include the sociologist Frank Furedi on the expansion of therapeutic language and practices into everyday life; the psychologist Oliver James on the condition of 'affluenza', in which higher rates of emotional distress are associated with the placing of high value on money, possessions, appearances and fame; and Mark Fisher, whose term 'capitalist realism' Perkins adopts more widely, as a signifier of a version of late/neoliberal capitalism 'that colonizes the psyche of contemporary individuals and the horizons of their world'.[13]

Applying such diagnoses to the general context of her examples, Perkins suggests that 'contemporary middle-class indie films appear to turn resolutely inward to personal, emotionalist issues'.[14] She adds: 'They present dominant attitudes of exhaustion, narcissism, depression, dissociation and, even in the most "upbeat" examples, a relentless knowingness that suggests a pervasive cynicism.' Their characters 'are materially comfortable but unable to function effectively, always desiring to do and be something different and better'. The definitive ending of such films 'is the literal or metaphorical cutaway that reveals, with varying degrees of irony and/or pathos, that nothing substantial has changed for them or is likely to, although they may have achieved a measure of enlightenment along the way'.[15] A broadly similar context of neoliberalism and focus on individual idiosyncrasy rather than social malaise is invoked by Kim Wilkins in a study of a subset of indie films she labels 'American eccentric' cinema.[16]

Elements of the reading offered by Perkins can be applied to the non-American examples examined in *The Cinema of Discomfort*, although these include significant differences of orientation or emphasis, including but not limited to the fact that some offer representations of a wider range of social class and generational locations. The latter is the case, for example, in the work of Roy Andersson, which can be read as offering a more general portrait of the existential state of humanity – a familiar component of art cinema – along with more contemporary points of reference. The films of Ulrich Seidl also provide figures from across both generational and class locations, including working-class victims of neoliberal capitalism. A more exclusive focus on an upper- to upper-middle class location is found in the work of Joanna Hogg.

A broader range of social commentary can be added to that cited by Perkins, including similar diagnoses of recent/contemporary 'western' society that have resonances with aspects of the cinema of discomfort, in accounts by sociologists such as Zygmunt Bauman, Anthony Giddens, Ulrich Beck and Richard Sennett, to which I return in Chapter 1. Some caution is again required in the use of sources such as these, which can have a tendency towards rhetorical exaggeration, even where substantial trends are identified. As suggested above, each of the manifestations I consider can be viewed as embodying aspects of broad cultural complexes defined in such ways, along with sociocultural factors more specific to their particular geographical locations. The wider cinema of discomfort often employs variations on what Sconce terms 'blank' style. This is an aspect of the cinema of discomfort elaborated further in Chapter 1, a key source of the withholding of clear cues at the level of the emotional response encouraged in the viewer.

Art and indie cinema

A brief definition is required at this point of what is meant here by 'art' and 'indie' cinema. Each of these can be viewed as part of a broader landscape usually known in the business as 'speciality' cinema, a term that conventionally embraces the realm of feature films that seek or gain some kind of commercial traction but on the margins when compared with that of Hollywood productions or their nearest equivalents in other territories. Indie cinema, as I use the term here and elsewhere, refers primarily to a certain range of American non-studio-based production, of relatively or much lower-budget status than that associated with the commercial mainstream. This is a sector that came to prominence and gained a sustained institutionalized presence from late 1980s and into the 1990s and after. In shorthand, it incorporates varieties of filmmaking associated with events such as the Sundance Film Festival and filmmakers including the likes of Jim Jarmusch, early Steven Soderbergh and Coen brothers, Hal Hartley, Spike Lee, Nicole Holofcener and Kelly Reichardt. The qualities of such films range from radical to more nuanced departures from mainstream-conventional norms. Considerable overlap exists between this kind of indie film and what is included in the more extensive realm of global/international art cinema, as I have argued elsewhere.[17] Some examples of indie film would fit unproblematically into the category of art cinema, although others lean more towards the commercial end of the spectrum. The definition of neither category is unproblematical or clear cut, each being subject to much debate.

The term 'art cinema' is usually deployed in reference to a wide range of types of cinema that present themselves, or are interpreted, as being – in different ways and to varying degrees – more 'serious' or, as the term suggests, more 'artistic' than work associated with the commercial mainstream, issues I discuss at length in *Positioning Art Cinema*. What exactly qualifies for the label can also depend on the contexts in which it is viewed and/or interpreted; one very inclusive definition, for example, would be that art cinema is generally any kind of cinema characteristically exhibited in arthouse theatrical venues. The latter might include films that are radically different at the textual level from those of the commercial mainstream, or relatively less different but where distinctive/niche status is signified or reinforced by being consumed (outside the area of production) in subtitled form. An important part of both indie and art cinema is not only the various bodies of work associated with such categories but the institutional frameworks within which they are produced, distributed and exhibited, contexts including the global film festival network that actively shape the kind of cinema that results. Both are generally viewed as being targeted at relatively distinct niche audiences and their consumption can be understood at least partly on the basis of a kind of distinction-marking outlined below in Chapter 1, although some examples of indie, in particular, have achieved wider commercial success. The art and indie sectors provide considerably more scope to pursue less commercially conventional varieties of filmmaking than is usually associated with more mainstream institutions. Their ability actively to provoke certain kinds of discomfort, among other qualities, is one marker of such status.

Case studies

It is in the American indie territory that the detailed case studies in this book begin, in Chapter 2, with the films of Todd Solondz, a figure of long-standing prominence in this arena. The central example featured here is *Palindromes* (2004). The following chapters focus on films from Austria, Greece, Sweden, the UK, the United States and Germany. The main focus is limited to work from Europe and the United States, but examples can also be found in a wider range of global cinema. An implicit critique of bourgeois alienation creates discomfort and uncertainty in films such as Lucrecia Martel's *The Swamp* (*La ciénaga*, 2001) and *The Headless Woman* (*La mujer sin cabeza*, 2008), for example, from Argentina, to cite the work of just one leading figure in contemporary Latin American cinema. A somewhat different conception of 'films of discomfort' was used by the Brazilian director Glauber Rocha to characterize more radically alternative, anti-colonialist filmmaking from Asia, Africa and Latin America in the 1960s.[18] Discomfort is a major potential factor in the experience of viewing 'slow' forms of art cinema, as suggested above, a phenomenon found in locations from across the globe. To cite just two of many more examples, qualities of awkwardness or discomfort have been identified as defining features of the films of Hong Sang-soo, from South Korea, and other instances of New Argentine Cinema, beyond the films of Martel, including the work of Pablo Trapero.[19] Similar explanatory frameworks might also be suggested in some of these more global locations, especially the growing prevalence of neoliberal worldviews within a middle-class milieu.[20]

The case studies examined in this book also have a particular sociocultural profile that should be acknowledged, skewed towards the work of white and male filmmakers, as is the case in the art and indie sectors more generally. The first characteristic, shared by all nine examples, is partly a consequence of their European or US bases but also related to questions of class and structurally unequal access to practices such as filmmaking. In gender terms, the sample is two-thirds male and one-third female: also unequal but probably including a greater proportion of work by women than the overall output of commercially distributed art and indie film.

The basis of cinematic discomfort is examined more broadly in Chapter 1 (Into the Discomfort Zone). This includes an extended general discussion of notions of discomfort and comfort, establishing key frameworks applied to case studies in the remainder of the book. Comfort and discomfort are considered in film and the wider artistic sphere, and as sociocultural concepts more broadly. A distinction is made between the local deployment of discomfort, as part of a dynamic designed overall to emphasize the comfort generally favoured by works produced in the commercial mainstream, and the more sustained discomfort found in the types of film included in this book. Chapter 1 examines aspects of the cultural history of comfort and discomfort, along with the bases on which the latter has often been valorized as part of a more generally privileged artistic domain. The social-cultural basis of the potential appeal of the cinema of discomfort is situated within accounts of cultural distinction-marking, in the tradition established by Pierre Bourdieu, alongside psychologically based accounts of the particular pleasures available to some viewers from engagement with challenging material. In contrast with some broader and universalized claims made for the artistic or philosophical celebration of discomfort, I argue for the grounding of the cinema of discomfort in more specific sociocultural territory, involving particular forms of appeal to a limited constituency. Central issues outlined here include sources of discomfort relating to both the cognitive and emotional domains and some of the ways qualities such as discomfort, awkwardness and embarrassment have been understood as either general or more particular historical or cultural phenomena.

Chapter 2 ('Uncomfortably Great': Todd Solondz and *Palindromes*) starts with an examination of the key discomforting dimensions of its main example. Central to these is the portrayal of highly uncomfortable sexual encounters involving its underage protagonist, against the background of issues relating to the contentious topic of abortion. A key focus of textual analysis is on the ambivalent relationship the film offers the viewer with its protagonist and other characters, major reference points for the examination of which are Murray Smith's notions of alignment and allegiance.[21] A central argument is that one of the most discomforting aspects of the film is its denial of any overall fixed comfortable point of orientation towards characters and the attitudes for which they stand. The film is shown to shift between ironically distanced and what appear to be more emotionally proximate modes of engagement. The position adopted by the film is likely to provoke discomfort of this kind even – or especially – for the constituency that would be expected to appreciate challenging indie films. Detailed textual analysis is accompanied by an examination of viewer responses and of the industrial context in which the film was produced and distributed.

If underage sex is one of the uncomfortable features of *Palindromes*, Chapter 3 (Ulrich Seidl: Far from Paradise) examines work in which more explicit sexual material provides sources of discomfort, particularly *Import Export* (2007). Close analysis is offered of the manner in which elements of real or explicit sex are framed by Seidl, both in terms of their narrative function and the potential implications of their more direct and discomforting presentation to the viewer. A similar approach is taken to the use of real background settings and figures, particularly in sequences that include footage of very old or infirm patients in a geriatric hospital. A number of critical/theoretical perspectives are employed. These include an initial focus that follows the previous chapter, in considering how far alignment or allegiance is offered with the protagonists, and examination of more general debate about the use of real sex and/or the involvement of bodily as well as emotional and cognitive responses to screened material of this kind. The latter includes the potential such material has to induce uncomfortably or more affirmatively self-reflective thinking on the part of the viewer. *Import Export* is shown to offer an ambiguous perspective on events similar in some respects to that of *Palindromes*, related here to an audiovisual regime that tends to withhold emotional or evaluative cues. Other works by Seidl are also considered more briefly, including *Dog Days* (*Hundstage*, 2001), the 'Paradise' trilogy (*Paradise: Love* [*Paradies: Liebe*, 2012], *Paradise: Faith* [*Paradies: Glaube*, 2012] and *Paradise: Hope* [*Paradies: Hoffnung*, 2013]) and his work in documentary, all of which offer similar dimensions of discomfort. Extensive consideration is given to how far such work can be read as offering sociocultural critique, either specific to the Austrian context or of wider resonance, and as the product of a particular national and international cinematic regime. Some critical and viewer responses are also examined.

Chapter 4 (Weirdly Discomforting: *Dogtooth* and the Greek New Wave) examines discomforting dimensions of films associated with the Greek 'Weird' or 'New' wave of the 2000s, principal examples being *Dogtooth* (*Kynodontas*, dir. Yorgos Lanthimos, 2009) and *Attenberg* (dir. Athina Rachel Tsangari, 2010). These offer further variations on the provision of discomfort, including highly uncomfortable sex and a general capacity for dislocation created by an absence of any clear explanatory frameworks for the discomforting experiences they depict, an effect heightened by a general flatness of presentation. As with those examined in the other chapters, the films are situated within a combination of sociocultural and cinematic contexts. The former includes arguments that relate *Dogtooth* to wider discourses about the state of contemporary society introduced in Chapter 1 – including diagnoses offered by figures such as Bauman, Giddens and Beck – as an embodiment of a defensive and privatized creation of a family-specific local regime of meaning creation and control. The weird/new wave is also examined in relation to accounts that interpret it in the context of the particular socio-economic crisis that hit Greece in the wake of the global financial meltdown of 2007–2008, although I argue that the discomfort offered by the films is also rooted in their resistance to any definitive reading of these kinds.

Chapter 5 (Forces Majeure and Minor: From Existential Alienation to Personal Obligation in the Films of Roy Andersson and Ruben Östlund) examines two in some ways contrasting cinemas of discomfort from Sweden, in the work of Roy Andersson and Ruben Östlund. The films of Andersson, particularly in the trilogy comprised by *Songs from the Second Floor* (*Sånger från andra våningen*, 2000), *You, the Living* (*Du levande*, 2007) and *A Pigeon Sat on a Branch Reflecting on Existence* (*En duva satt på en gren och funderade på tillvaron*, 2014), offer a highly distinctive and stylized aesthetic, while also providing strong potential to be read as a commentary on the status of contemporary alienated existence. The films of Östlund, including *Play* (2011), *Involuntary* (*De ofrivilliga*, 2008), *Force Majeure* (*Turist*, 2014) and *The Square* (2017), supply more familiar art-cinema framings of discomfort. The work of both shares in a wider tendency for discomfort often to be provoked by leaving the viewer to decide how to interpret difficult or awkward material, ranging from the relatively mundane to that which raises heightened and contentious social issues.

Discomfort in what is presented as more 'ordinary' quotidian material than that highlighted at times in the preceding chapters is identified in Chapter 6 (A Very English Discomfort: Joanna Hogg), which examines quietly painful/awkward moments and interpersonal relationships in the films of Hogg, principally her second feature, *Archipelago* (2010). Issues explored include the extent to which this can be seen as a distinctly 'English' understated variety of discomfort and/or one related to particular class locations. Uncomfortable, awkward or uncertain comedy is a widespread feature of the cinema of discomfort, an element in many of the examples examined in this book. The final chapter (The Comedy of Discomfort: Towards a Conclusion) addresses the comic dimension more directly through two principal examples: Rick Alverson's low-budget *The Comedy* (2012), from the American indie sector, and *Toni Erdmann* (dir. Maren Ade, 2016), from Germany. The focus of this chapter draws together some of the major threads of the book, comedy offering a particularly acute arena in which to examine the relationship between the provision of comfort or discomfort on screen.

A word is needed about the role of the notion of the filmmaker as author/auteur in what follows. Most of this book is focused around the work of individual figures, as is very often found in analysis of films from the art or indie sectors. Where this is less the case, that is only relatively so, particularly in Chapter 4, where, as elsewhere to some extent, certain individuals are taken as manifestations of, or leading figures within, what have been identified as broader cinematic movements or tendencies. The unquestioning use of certain auteurist assumptions – that work of this kind issues from on high as the individual vision of privileged filmmakers – has rightly been criticized.[22] Such an approach can elevate the status of the director, or writer-director, to a point that fails to take into account the many other factors that contribute towards the shaping of work of any kind, whether within the collaborative filmmaking process itself or in broader, sociocultural terms. Individual filmmakers never exist within a vacuum, but work of necessity within various contexts, traditions and institutional confines. The notion of the filmmaker as auteur is itself a concept rooted in a particular set of historically and socially specific assumptions, dating back primarily to the separation out of certain concepts of art and craft during the eighteenth century, an historical moment to which I return at some points in Chapter 1.

Certain institutionalized and commodified concepts of auteurism remain key dimensions of the art and indie film sectors, however. The nature of these realms is such that some individual filmmakers can gain much greater freedom to pursue the expression of their own concerns than is the norm in larger-scale commercial contexts, even if this includes their work with regular collaborators. This is not to say they have complete freedom, or that certain kinds of work are not likely to be favoured over others, or that in pursuing their own concerns they might also be mediating issues of broader resonance; but that substantial practical ground can be found at this level for treating films as products of more individual expression than is otherwise usually the case. Auteurist assumptions play a strong role throughout the life cycle of many art or indie films. The identity of the director or writer-director, and the sense that this is a guarantor of a certain kind and quality of product, is a key factor often in the funding of such work. It can also be central to the ability of films of this kind to achieve significant theatrical and post-theatrical distribution. The possessive auteur credit is likely to figure prominently in the marketing of art and indie films and to feature as a major source of attention and focus in critical, analytical and related discourses. Distinctive textual qualities can be associated with each of the filmmakers whose work is examined below, alongside dimensions in which they might also share some material or approaches in common with one another or with some aspects of art and indie cinema more broadly. The individual filmmaker remains a valid framework within which to analyse films such as those considered here, but also requires to be situated within the various informing contexts outlined above and considered in greater detail in the following chapters.

Notes

1. Scenes from some of the case studies examined in detail in this book, in order: *Palindromes* (2004), *Import Export* (2007), *Archipelago* (2010), *Dogtooth* (*Kynodontas*, 2009), *Songs from the Second Floor* (*Sånger från andra våningen*, 2000), *Force Majeure* (*Turist*, 2014), *The Comedy* (2012) and *Toni Erdmann* (2016).

2. I put the term 'western' within scare quotes to acknowledge the complex inheritances that contributed many elements usually associated with the concept. I also use a lower case 'w' throughout, to avoid the reification that can result from capitalization.

3. For more on the latter, see Geoff King, *Positioning Art Cinema: Film and Cultural Value* (London: I.B. Tauris, 2019), chapter 8.

4. Julian Hanich, *Cinematic Emotion in Horror Films and Thrillers: The Aesthetic Paradox of Pleasurable Fear* (New York: Routledge, 2010).

5. Jeffry Sconce, 'Irony, Nihilism and the American "Smart" Film', *Screen*, vol. 43, no. 4 (2002): 349–69; Claire Perkins, *American Smart Cinema* (Edinburgh: Edinburgh University Press, 2012).

6. Sconce, 'Irony, Nihilism', 352.

7. Ibid., 352.

8   Ibid., 355.
9   Claire Perkins, 'Life During Wartime: Emotionalism, Capitalist Realism, and Middle-Class Indie Identity', in Geoff King (ed.), *A Companion to American Indie Film* (Chichester: Wiley Blackwell, 2017), 349.
10 Perkins, 'Life during Wartime', 351.
11 Ibid., 350.
12 Ibid., 355.
13 Ibid. The other sources cited here are Frank Furedi, *Therapy Culture: Cultivating Vulnerability in an Uncertain Age* (London: Routledge, 2004); Oliver James, *Affluenza: How to be Successful and Stay Sane* (London: Vermilion, 2007); Mark Fisher, *Capitalist Realism: Is There No Alternative?* (Winchester: O Books, 2009).
14 Perkins, 'Life during Wartime', 353.
15 Ibid.
16 Kim Wilkins, *American Eccentric Cinema* (New York: Bloomsbury, 2019).
17 King, *Positioning Art Cinema*, chapter 2.
18 'The Tricontinental Filmmaker: That is Called the Dawn', originally published in *Cahiers du Cinéma*, November 1967, accessed online at https://www.diagonalthoughts.com/?p=1708.
19 See, respectively, Kyung Hyun Kim, 'The Awkward Traveller in *Turning Gate*', in Chi-Yun Shin and Julian Stringer (eds), *New Korean Cinema* (Edinburgh: Edinburgh University Press, 2005), 175; Gonzalo Anguilar, *New Argentine Film: Other Worlds* (Basingstoke: Palgrave Macmillan, 2008), 19–20, 114.
20 See, for example, Claudia Sandberg and Carolina Rocha (eds), *Contemporary Latin American Cinema: Resisting Neoliberalism?* (London: Palgrave Macmillan, 2018).
21 Murray Smith, *Engaging Characters: Fiction, Emotion, and the Cinema* (Oxford: Oxford University Press, 1995).
22 For a useful summary, see C. Paul Sellors, *Film Authorship: Auteurs and other Myths* (London: Wallflower, 2010).

1

Into the discomfort zone

The cinema of discomfort can be hard to watch. It might make us squirm in our seats, or make us more *aware* of our seats and of the act of *sitting through* certain kinds of material. What, though, is discomfort, or the comfort against which it is customarily defined and experienced? Neither should be taken as natural or given qualities. If our seats at the cinema or in front of home or mobile screens might themselves vary in their levels of comfort, all chairs are bad for our backs, as we are reminded by the historian John Crowley. Yet we learn to be comfortable in those developed within our own cultural contexts ('episodes of back spasms aside').[1] Comfort is essentially a learned and relative phenomenon, Crowley suggests, although the nature of what is taught can be a suitable topic for the cinema of discomfort. In the opening of *Dogtooth* (*Kynodontas*, 2009), for example, one of the films examined in Chapter 4, three teenagers are taught, among other eccentricities of vocabulary, that the word 'sea' means 'a leather armchair with wooden arms like the one we have in our living room'. Thus defined, 'sea' might be comfortable enough for them, if part of a world likely to be decidedly unsettling to the viewer. In other examples, characters sit or are otherwise positioned uncomfortably, their experiences capable of acting as vicarious proxy for those of the viewer. Chairs are often designed or chosen more for reasons of status or style than for comfort, as Galen Cranz suggests; the act of continuous sitting, as practiced in 'modern' 'western' societies, both culturally specific and damaging to the body.[2] If we can learn to sit reasonably comfortably in chairs that are bad for our backs, however, the cinema of discomfort might be understood similarly: as something that can offer acquired pleasures of its own, for some viewers at least, of the kind that form the basis more widely for the consumption of art and indie film.

Given that *dis*comfort is a negative term, predicated on an absence of something, a full understanding of the phenomenon requires examination of what exactly we mean by the concept to which it is opposed. If it is something of a commonplace that art and indie cinema can offer experiences of discomfort in a general sense, what specifically that entails, in terms of precisely what kind of comfort is missing, is more rarely considered in these terms, beyond a broad sense of the absence of some elements associated with more conventionally mainstream production. What, then, is comfort? The term has two primary usages in English. The older of these is comfort in the sense of the provision of solace or physical support, as in '*to* comfort' someone who is in distress, or 'to be comforted', derived from the medieval French *conforter* or *confort*.[3] Comfort in the sense of material or environmental ease is a more recent usage that, according to Crowley, did not come into widespread use in the English-speaking world until the eighteenth century. Both are germane to the understanding of discomfort employed in this book, although the former might seem more immediately applicable to the sense of comfort or discomfort provided by cultural forms such as film or other media. Certain kinds of film might offer comfort to the viewer, in one way or another, as considered further below. Representational forms do not directly create material comfort or discomfort, we might think, existing as they do at a remove from our physical presence.

The distinction may not always be so clear cut. The experience of witnessing one or the other can have a vicarious impact on the viewer. We might feel at ease, physically, when watching characters at ease on screen or when the forms of cinematic articulation offer comforts of their own. 'Comfort viewing' is a recognizable experience: the pleasurable enjoyment of the familiar and/or the undemanding of certain kinds, akin to the notion of 'comfort eating'. Alternatively, we might experience dis-ease, an unsettling in our seats, in the experience of the opposite, a process considered in more detail below.

What exactly constitutes comfort, in either of these definitions, is historically and culturally specific. Crowley suggests it is impossible to find any general consensus on what qualifies as material comfort. Definitions vary from one culture or period to another.[4] Comfort as understood in relation to material surroundings, signifying a feeling of ease, relaxation or freedom from pain, is dated to historical developments that culminated in the eighteenth century in the Anglo-American world. Physical comfort lacked priority as a value or a problem in the medieval period, Crowley writes, a context in which material culture (dwelling places, furniture and other amenities) was interpreted primarily in terms of social status rather than personal physical comfort. While various forms of architectural improvement were developed in the sixteenth and seventeenth centuries, '*comfort* still referred primarily to psychological and spiritual, not physical, circumstances.'[5] This is still the case in many contemporary uses. A search of book titles containing the term on Amazon.com, for example, reveals that by far the most common context for the employment of the term in this arena is in the context of 'comfort food', a quantity defined through a combination of psychological solace or nostalgia and physical appeal.[6]

No other single category comes close to this in numerical terms, although there are also volumes in which comfort is used in the sense of providing solace for suffering or other negative experiences, often but not always of a religious nature.

Jacques Pezeu-Massabuau also argues, in *A Philosophy of Discomfort*, that comfort is a relative and historically variable phenomenon that 'cannot be conceived as an absolute because it is simply an awareness of well-being that has ceaselessly varied across eras and civilizations'.[7] Comfort is identified at various levels: from the basic requirements of physical and social human existence to sources of convenience and pleasure. The latter includes comfort arising from the consumption of cultural products such as film or other arts and media. Discomfort, in this account, ranges from physical or social privation and constraint to experiences undergone voluntarily, the latter of which would apply to some of the qualities offered by the films examined in this book. A key part of Pezeu-Massabuau's definition of comfort is that it includes a relationship with the prevailing norms of any given society, including 'the décor, the meals, the comments, those anticipated gestures of hospitality whose pleasurable routine we submit to'. All of this 'gently places us in the norms for which our culture has programmed us since the dawn of time'.[8] Comfort, here, is about inhabiting a sense of the familiar and the habitual, a 'reassuring environment'.[9] This is a rather rose-toned picture that does not take into account the many frictions that might also exist between individuals or groups and the societies to which they belong. Social norms can be a source of comfortable familiarity but they can also be constricting or oppressive, either broadly or for particular groups. The concept of familiar norms is a useful one against which to measure qualities of comfort or discomfort, however, in a medium such as film or more generally.

Comfort in cinema

What, then, might be sources of comfort within film, against which the cinema of discomfort can be established? Pezeu-Massabuau's focus on norms is a useful starting point. We can broadly identify what can be termed a 'cinema of comfort', a less marked because more familiar and generally mainstream-commercial phenomenon. This would encompass a range of types of films in which certain customary cinematic norms are likely to be employed, often offering in this domain something akin to the reassuring environment identified by Pezeu-Massabuau. At the level of visual form, for example, this might include the qualities associated with the 'classical' continuity style, developed in Hollywood and subsequently broadly established as a default approach for much mainstream audiovisual material across the world. One of the key sources of the widespread appeal of classical continuity is likely to be the generally comfortable perspective it provides on narrative events. Much the same can be said of the similarly widely employed 'classical' Hollywood variety of narrative structure, among other popular formats, even if they might have more culturally specific origins.

One of the key features of classical continuity is how it usually offers a smooth and, for the viewer, effortless presentation of events. Whatever variety of shot positions and lengths are employed, each is generally made to follow its predecessor according to what is given the impression of being logical progression. The basic ingredients of this system are very familiar. They include long-conventional devices such as eye-line matches, in which cuts are made from characters to approximations of whatever they appear to be viewing, and matches-on-action, in which actions begun in one shot are picked up and continued smoothly in another, a system largely developed by the end of the 1910s. In both cases, the shift from one shot to another is *motivated*, given a rationale, by, respectively, the apparent look of a character or the movement of character and/or object. Another convention is the maintenance of directional consistency during individual sequences through what became known as the '180 degree' system, according to which the camera usually remains on one side of a straight line drawn between any two main points of focus. This generally ensures clear spatial orientation. Within this system, each shot can be seen usually not just to flow smoothly from its predecessor but, in some way, to *answer* or to complete it. Comfort might thus be said often to be created through a constant, local process of resolving any potential tensions that might result from the ongoing shifts of perspective.[10]

As David Bordwell and Kristen Thompson put it, each element can be seen to be *cueing* the viewer to understand the work in a particular way, either at the micro level of shot-to-shot or more broadly across segments or the whole of a film.[11] This is a process at work more widely within artistic-cultural or media products. A key dimension is the creation and satisfaction of expectations. As Bordwell and Thompson argue, this is best understood as a process that entails the active participation of the viewer, in consciously or subconsciously processing the various formal or other components of the work. Within any familiar format, certain conventional expectations are likely to be created. These range from the minutiae of shot-to-shot transitions to the broader narrative or generic frameworks within which these are located. Comfort is likely to be created by the fulfilment of expectations: the expectation that a shot including the gaze of a character is likely to be followed by one that gives us a sense (if far from optically exact) of what they see; the expectation that a particular element of a familiar narrative routine will lead to the usual kind of development or conclusion (an obvious example would be the conventional Hollywood form of 'happy ending'[12]); the expectation that a film more or less clearly located in a specific generic terrain will conform broadly, if with some variations, to its usual conventions; the expectation that tonal soundtrack music will resolve in harmonic closure.[13] Particular kinds of departure at any level might also produce comfortably pleasurable responses, but usually within certain conventional parameters. As Bordwell and Thompson suggest, the creation of such expectations has an emotional component. For example: 'To make an expectation about "what happens next" is to invest some emotion in the situation.'[14] Expectations that are fulfilled, as they often are in products designed to provide mainstream-commercial entertainment, are likely to produce positive feelings: 'satisfaction or relief', as Bordwell and Thompson put it, feelings that can be seen as central components of comfort.

In employing this approach in relation to film style, Bordwell and Thompson draw on a range of broader understandings of the experiences offered by artworks or in perception more generally. These include Ernst Gombrich's analysis of the role of familiar conventions and schemata in all forms of culture and communication: as creators of horizons of expectation than can be either fulfilled (a frequent source of comfort) or from which deviations (more or less comfortable/uncomfortable) can be measured.[15] That the resolving of tensions might be a wider source of the pleasure generated by artistic-cultural works is part of the argument of Rudolph Arnheim, in his classic study of visual perception in the arts and beyond. A search for equilibrium is a widespread component of human striving, for Arnheim, a process often satisfied by sources of balance and completion such as those found in the classical editing style detailed above.[16] The pleasure provided by images of equilibrium is, in this account, part of a broader tendency in organic life and physical systems. This, for Arnheim, is a dynamic process in which the mind is engaged in 'an interplay of tension-heightening and tension-reducing strivings'.[17] If comfort might often equate with a state of low tension, balance and completion, this is not, for Arnheim, a state of inertness or entropy but part of a more active and constructive dynamic. Something similar might be said of the balance between comfort and discomfort found in more mainstream-conventional film, as is suggested below, whether or not we accept the rather universalizing nature of the claims made by Arnheim.

Comfort can be generated by various other dimensions of film, also often associated with the provision of that which is familiar and expected, although such qualities are liable to be combined with elements that are larger, stronger, brighter, clearer or more intense than the usual material of everyday life. These range from examples such as the presence of familiar and attractive star performers to the enactment of activities and behaviours that fit culturally prevailing ideas, ideologies, hopes and expectations. How exactly some of this might work leads us in more speculative directions. Some types of films targeted at a mainstream/popular audience might be said to offer something like idealized versions of certain aspects of life, characters or behaviour, within which viewers might hope or dream of finding themselves in some way or to some degree. Mainstream film, in Hollywood or elsewhere, is often associated with the provision of forms of comforting balm or escapist fantasy, allowing comfortable, luxuriant indulgences in such worlds, generally or as more direct recompense for the shortcomings of real life. Where Hollywood-type films seem to relate to difficult real-world issues, these have often been read as offering what can be viewed as essentially *imaginary* ways of reconciling intractable oppositions, an approach that might be expected to offer potential comfort to the spectator.[18] How exactly any such textual-viewer dynamics might really operate is likely to be complex and nuanced, as is considered further below, but these are qualities often associated with films made within the Hollywood or other popular traditions.

None of this is to say pleasures offered by mainstream entertainment films are entirely those of untroubled ease and familiarity. As Todd Berliner suggests, it is useful to see the Hollywood tradition as providing pleasure through a variable combination of easiness and moderate degrees of challenge, in dimensions such as narrative, audiovisual style, approaches to genre and the ideological valences of material.[19] Drawing on psychological studies, Berliner uses the term 'processing fluency' to suggest the ease with which a particular type of cinematic (or other) material can be perceived, classified and cognitively mastered. Qualities that ease processing have been shown to increase the pleasure of consumption of aesthetic products of various kinds, including film, although other studies demonstrate a preference for 'works that contain moderate amounts of novelty, complexity, incongruity, dissonance, and ambiguity'.[20] Exactly how individual films mix elements that offer comfortable ease with those that represent greater novelty or challenge can vary, either to a moderate extent within the terrain of mainstream Hollywood or popular approaches elsewhere, or progressively more so in less typical studio films (what Berliner calls a 'deviant' studio tradition or what I have elsewhere termed 'quality' Hollywood[21]), or work from different parts of the indie and art-film sectors. Some degree of cognitive demand, a requirement for active processing by the viewer, is made by even the most conventional of mainstream films, however, as Berliner suggests.

Discomfort

If the various dimensions of films outlined above can be seen as offering forms of comfort to the viewer, the negation of any of these is a source of variable degrees of potential discomfort. This might be short-term or more lasting. If the conventions of continuity editing offer a broadly comfortable viewing position, departures can produce the opposite. If a shot of the gaze of a character is not followed by what appears to be the object of the look, without any other rationale being supplied, the viewer's expectation might be frustrated, a potential source of discomfort; or our expectations of how one shot follows another might be more actively undermined in various ways. If directional continuity is subverted by marked departures from the 180 degree system, uncomfortable forms of disorientation can result. The same might occur, on the larger scale, if we are denied a narrative development we have been encouraged to expect. This might be a denial of a conventionally framed 'happy ending', for example, or the lack of closure that results from uncertainty or ambiguity (in my teaching experience, for example, I have found students previously unfamiliar with art cinema to find such qualities distinctly unsettling). Discomfort might also be caused by departure from familiar genre norms and expectations, even if other forms of novelty might be sources of increased pleasure.

The use of atonal music might generate disorientation or anxiety, again based on the absence of familiar tonal reference points.[22] Tonal accompaniment that moves conventionally away from the central note might also fail to make the expected movement back to the tonic. If the synchronization of sound and image is generally another source of comfort, as K. J. Donnelly suggests, an absence or ambiguity of synchronization can make viewers feel anxious or uneasy, a dimension he relates to primal human-perceptual survival needs.[23] A defining characteristic of the cinematic feel-bad experience as examined by Nikolaj Lübecker is precisely the denial of the fulfilment of expectations involved in many of these cases, framed here as the production of a 'spectatorial desire', the satisfaction of which is then blocked.[24] In many of the cases suggested above, the level of discomfort is only likely to be increased where viewers are not consciously aware of its exact source, as is often likely to be the case (proportionally few viewers are likely to be aware of the exact source of discomfort created by the musical effects outlined above, for example), experiencing a more general sense of unease.

In the terms employed by Arnheim, 'an unpleasant effect' can be produced in visual perception by that which is 'equivocal or ambiguous' in such a way as to prevent clear interpretation. This is one source of the particular kind of discomfort or awkwardness on which I focus in this book. A more abstract version cited by Arnheim is the case of a set of grid lines within a rectangular figure.[25] If the lines are centred, comfortable balance and simplicity results. If the lines are clearly off-centre, another stable and balanced dynamic can result. The awkwardly equivocal occurs where the lines are slightly off-centre but not far enough for this to be clearly and unambiguously the case. This is a useful model for what sometimes occurs in the cinema of discomfort: unsettling effects that can result from approaches that are neither classically conventional nor more unequivocally or radically alternative, but that lie in a space somewhere awkwardly in between.

Discomfort might be fleeting or more sustained. It can be a stage in a process designed, overall, to offer comfort: the delaying of an expected shot, narrative development or musical resolution, for example, that can add to the pleasure that results when it is eventually provided. The opening or stretching of a gap can increase the potency of the manner in which it is closed. The heroic ascendency of the protagonists of action or related genres is often increased through the extent of the suffering they experience along the way. The negative qualities of suffering/discomfort in one phase can serve to highlight the more comfortable material that follows. This can be understood as a process akin to the broader tension-heightening/tension-reducing dynamic identified by Arnheim. A spectacle of vicarious discomfort is offered to the viewer in Hollywood examples from *Rambo: First Blood Part II* (1985) and *Unforgiven* (1992) to *Black Panther* (2018). Any real sense of discomfort is likely to be ameliorated in such cases by the strong expectations created narratively and/or generically (or on the basis of star persona) that the heroes will eventually prevail; the extent to which such figures are permitted to suffer, in works designed for popular appeal, seems effectively to be predicated usually on the assumption that they will overcome, and that their triumph will be all the greater for the suffering they undergo on the way. Where heroic central characters die at the end of such films, conflicting with any such expectation, this is likely to be part of an 'heroic sacrifice' trope strongly ameliorated by the survival of others.

Carl Plantinga offers a detailed examination of how such a process works affectively in the climax of *Titanic* (1997), an example that involves the self-sacrificial death of one of the lead characters, Jack (Leonardo DiCaprio). The sadness elicited by this part of the film is likely to generate mental anguish 'and other unpleasant affective experiences for many spectators', Plantinga suggests.[26] How, then, is this explained as a prominent part of a highly successful film generally designed to produce pleasurable experiences? As Plantinga argues, the production of pleasurable affect can be seen as one of the foundations of popular media industries.[27] He rejects any suggestion that painful emotions are themselves generally a source of pleasure, in a masochistic sense. Instead, the inclusion of unpleasure/discomfort is viewed as part of the broader dynamic through which pleasure is created. For one thing, as Plantinga argues, the degree of sadness produced by the death of Jack is likely to be tempered by viewer awareness that it is a fictional individual scenario and, in this case, one located at a historical distance from their own time.[28] The negative dimension is thus attenuated, its probable impact reduced in degree. Material likely to generate uncomfortable emotions is also accompanied by sources of pleasure, in this case qualities such as excitement, exhilaration and awe, encouraged by the manner in which the sinking of the ship and its aftermath are staged. This might include pleasure in the spectacular manner of representation, a dimension in relation to which Plantinga cites David Hume's work on tragedy.[29]

General familiarity with Hollywood narrative conventions is also likely to create expectations that negative emotions 'will be in the end recuperated and/

or transformed into a pleasurable or otherwise rewarding experience', as is the case in *Titanic*.[30] The film ultimately offers pleasurable emotions relating to the sense of what Rose (Kate Winslet) gains through her relationship with Jack, and his self-sacrifice, including a rhetorical impression of love transcending both the social divisions charted in the film and death itself. Painful emotions are attenuated in their effects and mixed with pleasurable emotions and then 'gradually replaced by positive emotions'.[31] The model of transformation involved in the latter is offered by Plantinga as an alternative to theories of catharsis (whether from Aristotle or in psychological accounts), in which the experience of negative affects is understood as a way of purging emotional tensions.[32] In their broader sociocultural or ideological dimensions, Plantinga suggests, such films provide pleasure in the sense of offering a fantasy of mastery and control of the world's miseries, the kind of dynamic involved in the notion of imaginary reconciliation cited above.[33] A representation of irrevocable loss is exchanged for 'a quasireligious, ritual affirmation of the proposed transformative power and transcendence of romantic love and self-sacrifice'.[34] This is a working-through of the material that has distinctly ideological implications in the vision of the world that is promoted; as opposed, say, to one that took the class divisions dramatized in the film as intractable and fundamental rather than existing largely to be transcended at the individual level.

More sustained quantities of discomfort can also be structured into certain types of production other than those that are the subject of this book, most notably horror films. Considerable effort has been expended on seeking to explain the appeal or pleasures offered by horror, given the extent to which its material might be expected to be uncomfortable to experience.[35] Horror is often seen as opening up a space for certain kinds of discomfort but one that is (largely) safely bounded and (often) closed down at the end. This might accord, broadly, with the kind of discomfort suggested above in the case of the suffering of action heroes or in *Titanic*, premised on a deferral of the eventual pleasure that might result from the upbeat form of closure that results at the end. Matt Hills identifies a number of dynamics common to attempts to theorize the appeal of horror, including a focus on this kind of supposed mastery of the range of anxieties or uncertainties typically viewed by theorists as lying behind the pleasures of various forms of horror content, phenomena often articulated in questionable terms drawn from psychoanalytical theory.

Such accounts, Hills suggests, tend to 'explain away' the pleasures of horror rather than engaging with any desire on the part of viewers to be affected by horrific material itself; to, for example, experience an ambiguous mixture of fascination and repulsion at horrific material rather than a separating out of such dimensions into different examples of horror or different phases of individual texts.[36] It is this more complex blending of emotions that is examined by Plantigna in the latter stages of *Titanic* and in Julian Hanich's phenomenological approach to the pleasures of horror.[37] Exactly what the appeal might be of being emotionally affected by horror – of experiencing discomforting feelings such as fear or repulsion – is not something into which Hills goes in any specifics. His primary focus on the experiences of fans leads him to emphasize alternative sources of pleasure such as that which might result from their active articulation of expert knowledge of the field, a variety of cultural capital of the kind considered further below in relation to the cinema of discomfort.

If some forms of discomfort are temporary and can be viewed as part of an overall dynamic that favours the production of comfort, heightened by the overcoming or transcendence of discomforting elements along the way, the focus of this book is on more sustained varieties of discomfort. Where exactly horror might fit in this schema is debatable. Even if horror films have been interpreted as offering an ultimate overcoming of the horrific, discomfort is likely to be figured more strongly in generic territory where it constitutes a substantial part of the running time, rather than being restricted to relatively brief interludes. The same might be said of some anxiety-producing 'jeopardy' varieties of thriller. It is also far from always the case that horror films end on a positive note, with their sources of horror eradicated or contained. A distinct tendency exists for the opposite to happen in some types of horror: for viewers to be left without any such affirmative ending. Horror also appears to be capable of having a more lasting impact on its viewers.[38] Even here, however, any *ongoing* provocation of discomfort can be seen to be generically motivated in horror. As such, it might be expected and thus conform to the anticipated norms at play in examples of this kind, and so be likely to prove relatively less discomforting overall to anyone who chooses to watch such material. This does not mean it significantly loses its impact, however. Hanich suggests that familiarity with genre convention can reduce the creation of fear but that, during the viewing experience, such familiarity is likely to exist only in the background of awareness; only if actively drawn upon, and so put into the foreground, does it 'disentangle' the viewer from a state of 'fearful immersion' in the on-screen material.[39]

Hanich employs a phenomenological approach to examine the ongoing nature of the various experiences offered by horror films and thrillers, seeking to pin down exactly what constitutes the pleasure of experiencing certain kinds of on-screen fear (divided into the separate although overlapping categories of horror, shock, dread and terror). He suggests that the pleasure involved in the experience of cinematic fear itself, rather than some process of overcoming, lies in the creation of moments of subjective intensity that involve shifts at the level of bodily response. A central part of the experience is a dynamic that moves between moments of constrictive immersion in violent or horrific material, a tightening and compression of the viewer at moments of strong interpolation into the fictional universe, coupled with moments of extrication out of the film world.⁴⁰ This is another formulation that has something in common with the tension-heightening/tension-reducing process suggested by Arnheim. A dynamic of this kind might also apply to instances of discomfort more generally, particularly a forcing of the persisting viewer into uncomfortable proximity with disturbing material. The formal means by which such an effect is created is generally rather different in the cinema of discomfort as defined here, however, not generally involving the level of heightened intensity – or, often, camera proximity to the action – more characteristic of horror or the more assaultive brand of feel-bad film. If the pleasure of horror, for Hanich, involves what amounts to intensive *processing* of the experience offered to the viewer, the cinema of discomfort tends to be more distanced and to leave the viewer without such strongly cued responses.

Sustained discomfort in art and indie film

How, then, might we begin to outline varieties of sustained discomfort that have no clear generic motivation of the type found in horror? It might be argued that certain varieties of art and indie cinema generate similar expectations of their own. We might be encouraged to *expect* discomfort in some such works on the basis of their general art/indie status, or that of particular filmmakers, or combinations of such dimensions. Conventions do not have to be as relatively organized and coherent as those of genres – the boundaries of which also tend to be complex and far from clear cut – in order to operate in some such ways within particular film territories. Even if expected, however, or if at least not *un*expected or unfamiliar, discomfort can remain real and substantial (it might also include sources of appeal of its own, to be considered further below). The same probably goes for horror: just because the viewer might expect discomfort, as part of the effective contract entered into when watching such material, does not mean that its potency is eliminated, even if it might be somewhat attenuated.

Discomfort might result from jarring departures from familiar-mainstream norms. If, at the formal level, continuity editing usually takes the viewer through a smooth and comfortable process of articulation from shot to shot, it can be upset in various ways. A classic example is the sequence in Jean-Luc Godard's *Breathless* (*À Bout de Souffle*, 1959) in which the filmmaker creates disorientation by seeming wilfully to contravene the conventions of directional matching during the shooting by the central character of a motorcycle cop. If perceptual discomfort can be created at the level of editing technique, as here, it might also result from a sudden and unexpected shift in the content of images, whether or not classical convention is otherwise maintained. The notoriously discomforting cut to an eyeball being sliced by a razor in the surrealist classic *Un Chien Andalou* (1929) is an aggressive example but one in which classical norms are maintained even with such jarring material, and where the viewer is prepared for what is to come. We see a shot of a young woman with a razor being lifted to her eye in readiness. This is followed by an image of a thin cloud moving in front of the moon. The lateral movement of the cloud matches that begun by the razor in the previous shot and continued through the (stand-in) eyeball in the next, the approximate size and central positioning of moon/eyeball and cloud/razor smoothing over the transition. The overall effect is presumably designed to create acute discomfort, in a sequence many find difficult to watch, but in this case the formal qualities themselves demonstrate overtly fluid continuity. This is an example from the avant-garde end of the film spectrum, a realm that has traditionally provided scope for more extreme departures from familiar-mainstream convention, violently assaultive or otherwise. Asbjørn Grønstad takes this image as metaphorically paradigmatic of 'the unwatchable' in more commercially circulated assaultive art cinema since the turn of the millennium; its offering of *'razorblade gestures*, the emotional, psychic, and ethical slicing open of the gaze of the spectator'.[41]

Abrupt cutting to potentially disturbing imagery is one of many strategies employed to unsettle the viewer in Luke Moodysson's *A Hole in My Heart* (*Ett hål i mitt hjärta*, Sweden 2004), a claustrophobic and viewer-assaulting drama about a trio shooting an amateur pornographic film in an apartment. Images of labial and open-heart surgery are inserted on several occasions into the film, one example of the latter following an extreme close-up shot of an eyeball that perhaps evokes memories of *Un Chien Andalou*. This is an approach that has much in common with some of the means of creating the shocks of cinematic horror examined by Hanich. As well as the discomfort likely to result from the deployment of such imagery in itself, the film encourages perceptual uncertainty at times in its mixture of focus on the bodies of the characters and those of other figures such as dolls and a plastic model of a woman's vagina and anus. In one instance, a cut to real labial surgery, following close-shot images in which dolls and the model are being chopped up, creates a distinctly uncomfortable blurring of perspectives.

Some elements of disorientation can also be created in more mainstream-commercial features by the intensification of continuity regimes identified by Bordwell as a common feature of more recent Hollywood productions.[42] This can involve highly unstable camerawork, sometimes used in combination with rapid cutting, or cutting into camera movement, particularly during action sequences. A general impression of unsettling 'edginess' is confected more widely in some examples – notable instances including the Jason Bourne series (2002–) – through a constant process of slight or more pronounced camera unsteadiness, again sometimes combined with rapid or jarring editing. Such devices can amount locally to a departure from the clarity and comfort of viewing position associated with classical style. The aim might be to create a more realistic impression, through the mimicking of devices associated with documentary or news footage, and a greater sense of proximity to the action. This can create a degree of discomfort, physiological or psychological. The former can involve physical sensations of motion sickness created by unstable camerawork for some viewers, as also potentially experienced in uses of more immersive formats such as 3D or IMAX. The latter might be created by a sense of being closer to, or at times disoriented within, what might be aggressive or otherwise discomforting diegetic scenarios. In most cases, however, any such discomfort here seems likely to be ameliorated or contained by generic or related frameworks. If what I elsewhere term an 'impact aesthetic' is designed to give the viewer a degree of vicarious experience of closer proximity to action sequences, this is both limited in itself and usually balanced by more conventionally distanced perspectives.[43]

Discomfort can be created through juxtaposition of the kind offered by Moodysson or some forms of rapid editing or close, unsteady mobile footage. The latter can become uncomfortably confining and claustrophobic in some works of art cinema, including the films of the Dardenne brothers (examined in *Positioning Art Cinema*) or an example such as Darren Aronofsky's studio-released *Mother!* In the latter, the camera's close attachment to the title character (Jennifer Lawrence) significantly heightens the impact of a narrative in which the intrusive behaviour of visitors to the home of the central couple – at first on a small scale, later amounting to a riotously disruptive invasion – seems designed to be almost as uncomfortable for the viewer as for the protagonists. A close camera combined with a narrow aspect ratio keeps viewers uncomfortably close to the protagonist of the Hungarian Nazi concentration camp drama *Son of Saul* (*Saul fia*, 2015) although (along with shallow focus) it also spares them from having to witness most of the gruesome surrounding detail of material such as scenes in a gas chamber.

Discomfort can also result from the opposite of intensified editing or camera movement: the unflinching holding of a shot longer than would customarily be expected within classical/mainstream-conventional routines. A combination of close and distanced approaches is found in Gaspar Noé's *Irreversible* (2002), from the assaultive end of the discomfort spectrum. The early stages of the film offer a claustrophobic form of disorientation, in which the camera twists and lurches uncomfortably, while the rape sequence central to the film is presented in an unremitting extended static shot. The uncomfortably long-duration shot is a mainstay of certain varieties of art and indie cinema, including many of the examples examined in this book. It is often used in association with, and seeking to evoke, the uncomfortable experiences of characters. It might be employed in conjunction with close proximity, as in an example such as *Son of Saul*, or with longer-shot distance. Extended duration can also create close-to-unbearable tension with quieter material, such as the eight-minute, single mid-shot sequence in

FIGURE 1 *Quietly unbearable tension: Keeping the candle alight in* Nostalgia *(1983).*

Andrei Tarkovksy's Nostalgia (*Nostalghia*, 1983) in which, after a number of failed attempts, the principal character achieves the painstaking (and in the context of the film, highly symbolic) task of keeping a candle alight while carrying it the length of an empty swimming pool (Figure 1).

Discomfort can be premised on the absence of the relief of tension that might be provided by cuts away to other perspectives on the material. This might be identified at two levels. One is the undermining of broader expectations that longer shots will be followed by closer ones or closer ones by longer, and more variety of perspective in general, as is usually the case with material assembled in a broadly classical manner. In this case, viewers might not consciously expect a move into conventional decoupage of this kind, the process of expectation-and-fulfilment usually occurring at a subconscious level. They might not actively become aware of the formal dimension of the discomfort that results from holding a certain kind of shot for longer than usual. Extended duration shots have the potential to draw attention to form, but they might also create a less specific sensation of something being more diffusely and awkwardly different from the generally unnoticed prevailing norm. The second dimension of such experiences involves the nature of the material in the world on screen. Extended shots are often employed to evoke something of the diegetically uncomfortable experience for the viewer. Good examples of this variety of discomfort involving longer shots are found in Sconce's account of the American smart film, along with other manifestations examined in this book.

Blank style

A central feature of smart films, for Sconce, is what he terms their 'blank' style, which enacts exactly this kind of departure from classical norms. Blank style remains distanced and withdrawn from the on-screen action, creating what Sconce terms 'a sense of *dampened affect*', regardless of how disturbing or bizarre the narrative material with which it is associated.[44] While contemporary Hollywood favours a more intensified form of continuity construction, as suggested by Bordwell, smart cinema 'often *de-intensifies* continuity into a series of static tableaux'.[45] This is also akin to an art-cinema style championed elsewhere by Bordwell as a preferred, more nuanced and subtle alternative to the intensified approach.[46] The effect in smart cinema, for Sconce, is to create a matter-of-fact quality that can be seen as a key ingredient in the discomfort offered to the viewer, through an absence of overt moral judgement of what is often disconcerting behaviour, in this case usually situated within a portrayal of middle-class American life. The alienation seen here as characteristic of the latter is signified through what Sconce describes as a number of 'stock' shots in smart cinema that feature in some of the broader range of films examined in this book: 'the "awkward couple" shot (a strained couple shot in tableau form, separated by blank space); the "awkward coupling" shot (a camera placed directly over the bed recording passionless sex); and, in "family" films, the "awkward dining" shot (long-shots of maladjusted families trapped in their dining rooms.'[47]

In each of these cases, one major component of potential discomfort is the fact that, to a significant extent, viewers are confronted with such fictional experiences and left to deal with them for themselves, or without the kind of orchestration that guides the shifts between constriction and expansion identified by Hanich in the case of horror or the violent thriller. It is not that the on-screen materials are not processed at all, which can never be the case for any constructed images, as Sconce acknowledges.[48] 'Blank' shots such as these make points of their own through their very blankness, particularly where they appear to offer an implied critique, as when they seem to signify social alienation. But their temporal extension is such as to open a larger than usual place for viewer interpretation and/or judgement, without offering much explicit guidance as to what this interpretation or judgement should be. Varieties of this approach, with their own distinctive qualities, feature in many of the examples examined in this book, including the films of Ulrich Seidl, Roy Andersson and Joanna Hogg.

Discomfort and awkwardness might also be generated in such cases by a vicarious experience of embarrassment: of witnessing, even if fictionally, that which we would prefer not to witness and certainly not in a painful and temporally extended manner. Strategies of this kind are the most common formal sources of discomfort in the films examined in this book, as opposed to any more radical subversion of the basics of conventional audiovisual form. The latter is more likely to be associated with work at the more marginal avant-garde/experimental end of the film spectrum. If, for Hanich, one way of creating a response of disgust or revulsion in film is the use of close-up shots to intensify what he terms an 'obtrusive nearness' to certain kinds of material, the cinema of discomfort on which I focus tends to deny such emphasis in favour of a more detached refusal to provide clear cut interpretive guidance.[49] If not literally in close-up in formal terms, however, a broader sense of phenomenological proximity to disturbing material from which we would prefer to be separated might remain central to the production of discomfort in many cases.

While discomfort can be generated or enhanced by specific formal approaches, it also lies substantially in the nature of the characters and narrative events depicted in such films. These, too, often entail breaches of more widely accepted norms, at the sociocultural level. One source of discomfort is rooted in what would usually be seen as 'unacceptable' behaviour, but the manner in which this is presented remains central to the particular qualities often found in such work. That which might be seen as socially unacceptable behaviour is common in the broader and unmarked realm of 'the cinema of comfort'. What often changes in the cinema of discomfort is the attitude expressed, or not expressed, towards any such phenomena. In more mainstream-conventional varieties of cinema, 'unacceptable' behaviour is likely clearly to be identified as such, criticized and/or condemned, even if scope might exist for some dispute and complexity about the moral or other rights and wrongs of whatever issues are involved in any case. This is another strong link between the cinema of discomfort and Sconce's notion of smart cinema. Both can entail the presentation of questionable behaviour in what seems a non-judgemental manner, certainly when compared with the kind of moral economy more typical of mainstream institutions such as Hollywood.

It seems reasonably safe to assert that a form of comfort can result from having our sociocultural expectations and assumptions about various kinds of behaviour confirmed and reasonably clear lines drawn between what is or is not deemed to be acceptable. These, in dominant/conventional form, often enable us to separate ourselves from that which is most dark, disturbing or discomforting. They offer reaffirmation. To blur these lines can be a potent source of discomfort, although it is also the case that some viewers might find their own norms affirmed by this more complex position (the latter is another aspect of the potential pleasures of the cinema of discomfort considered further below). Discomfort can result from a refusal of the kinds of reconciliatory dynamics associated with mainstream examples such as *Titanic*. The absence of an affirmative ending in horror might constitute a similar denial of conventional pleasure, although also a potential source of alternative forms of appeal for those who are suitably oriented (the political valences of horror have often been measured along these lines, a more progressive potential sometimes being identified in those which do not offer a comfortable return to a restored 'normality' defined in terms of dominant social-cultural criteria[50]).

Cognitive and emotional dimensions

Comfort and discomfort can be understood at both the cognitive and emotional levels of the film-viewing experience. The denial of certain forms of information and understanding can be a source of discomfort, leaving the viewer struggling at the level of comprehension. As with the other dimensions outlined above, a stage of denial can form part of a more familiar-conventional organization of material that leads eventually to resolution. This might apply particularly to some genres, most obviously the mystery variety of thriller, where the initial withholding is a key part of the pleasure likely to result from its delayed resolution and can be understood as being generically motivated and thus part of the expectations brought to the film; or, in some cases, even where a continuing uncertainty might have a specific appeal of its own. Other forms of denial have potential to offer more discomforting experiences. The viewer might be denied key information in ways for which no immediate motivation is clear and without eventual resolution.

Films of a broadly mainstream-conventional variety can begin with a degree of narrative obfuscation. We might not be clear, at first, what exactly a character is doing, or why, or what the significance of particular actions might be. But this will usually be clarified, often sooner rather than later (unless generic conventions dictate otherwise), as part of the unfolding of a broadly classical dynamic. In other cases, the nature or meaning of activity might remain obscure, either for much longer or without ever being made apparent. The viewer might be left trying to grasp what is going on, or why exactly, without what would usually be seen as sufficient help. One source of cognitive uncertainty can be provoked by questions relating to the reality status of the material on screen, either the main activity or, more often in fictional works, elements of background detail. This is a central feature of some 'mockumentary' films – beyond the focus of this book – that adopt documentary forms so closely with fictional material as potentially to destabilize the response of any viewer not suitably informed in advance. On a first viewing of *I'm Still Here* (2010), for example, a work purporting to dramatize a move into rap singing by the actor Joaquim Phoenix, I felt compelled to pause the film in order to confirm the status of its material online, so uncomfortable was the prospect of continuing without having a clear sense of how to place the content.

Blank or distanced styles of the kind identified by Sconce can contribute to the cognitive dimension of discomfort, if they deny the viewer the fuller audiovisual articulation of detailed information about any given on-screen situation. A camera that sits still and at a distance from characters withholds the full elaboration that can be supplied through a classical variety of scene dissection. The latter is a term that implies precisely the kind of detailed and analytical breakdown of material that tends to be missing in blank style. The effect, at a narrative level, might be a less communicative form of articulation, one that withholds certain nuances of information that might be gleaned by the use of closer shots that highlight particular reactions, gestures or other small but crucial details. A highly communicative approach is one of the central features of the classical Hollywood variety of narrative, except where specific genre conventions motivate departures.[51] Blank style communicates something in its own right, as suggested above, often quite specific meanings relating to the lifestyles of the worlds on screen, but it does so in a broad rather than more finely grained manner. This links directly to the emotional dimension of discomfort, as suggested in Sconce's central reference to a dampening of affect. To deny certain kinds of information can also be to deny the basis on which emotional responses might depend, along with uncertainties at the level of what might be considered to be the moral implications of cinematic material. The withholding of emotional cues is, potentially, one of the strongest sources of discomfort, if it results in uncertainty on the part of viewers at the level of how to respond. This is, again, something that would be expected to be clearly marked in more mainstream-conventional cinema, a key part of which is the orchestration of preferred emotional reactions.

A range of cinematic devices can function as emotional cues, designed to elicit particular kinds of viewer responses. As Greg M. Smith puts it: 'Films provide a variety of redundant emotive cues, increasing the chance that differing audience members (with their differing preferences of emotional access) will be nudged towards an appropriate emotional orientation.'[52] Such cues include facial expression, narrative context, music, lighting and any other elements of film style. In the Hollywood tradition, as Smith suggests, emotional redundancy typically combines with narrative redundancy, in the interests of achieving a clear and largely unambiguous overall effect. In Smith's account of the film-emotional process, occasional strong bursts of expression constitute 'emotion markers', 'configurations of highly visible textual cues for the primary purpose of eliciting brief moments of emotion'.[53] These, for Smith, are sufficient to sustain a more ongoing and diffuse emotional mood. Plantinga argues similarly (although in somewhat different terms, disagreeing with Smith's definition of mood) for the centrality in Hollywood of 'a mode of filmmaking designed to elicit strong emotions',[54] largely through the use of clearly identifiable conventions.

Discomfort can be generated by the use of the same process to encourage uncomfortable emotional responses, such as sadness, anxiety, disgust or loathing. As Plantinga suggests, antagonist characters are sometimes given physical characteristics or deformities conventionally (often perniciously) marked as 'disgusting' as part of the dynamic that encourages the viewer to take pleasure from their elimination.[55] This can be seen as another example of localized discomfort, potentially generated by the appearance, presentation or activities of human or inhuman/alien/monster antagonists, playing a part in the overall generation of comfort in mainstream-conventional work, with various associated ideological implications. A potent form of discomfort might also result from the denial of clear emotional cues, however, a variety more specific to the films examined in this book. If films can be less communicative in cognitive terms, the same can apply to the emotional domain (the two are seen as being closely linked in the accounts of theorists such as Smith and Plantinga, as in contemporary neuroscience more generally[56]). Smith illustrates the difference with a comparison between the studio production *Raiders of the Lost Ark* (1981) and the less mainstream *Local Hero* (1983). The former is densely informative, in the emotional as well as the narrative realm, making frequent use of redundant cues (as does Plantinga's example, *Titanic*). *Local Hero*, in contrast, is more sparsely informative on both levels, its emotional cues less redundant or clear cut. This, as Smith argues, is one useful basis for understanding what constitutes a 'subtle' approach to filmmaking, a quality often associated with the indie or art sectors but not always so clearly pinned down in specifics. The same could be said of the use of blank style considered above. It is largely the reduction of clear or redundant emotional cues that constitutes the dampened affect identified by Sconce.

If music plays a key role in the provision of emotional cues in films made within the Hollywood or other popular traditions, it can also be a potent source of such ambiguity or withholding, as indicated above. This is suggested in Michel Chion's distinction between music, or sound more generally, that is empathetic, matching or helping to orchestrate the mood of the action, and that which he terms 'anempathetic': exhibiting 'conspicuous indifference' to whatever is happening within the diegesis.[57] Where emotional cues of this or any other kind are reduced in density, or where they might conflict awkwardly or be largely absent, the viewer might be left in a state of emotional uncertainty that can be distinctly uncomfortable. While atonal music can be a more active source of disorientation, merely to leave certain cinematic situations to unfold in silence, without any steering of suggested viewer response by the soundtrack, can be a source of heightened discomfort. Not being sure how to feel, particularly when this is in response to certain kinds of 'difficult' narrative material, might be potentially more discomforting than uncertainty about on-screen events of a more cognitive nature, as is suggested in some of the case studies examined in the rest of this book.

An absence of emotional guidance might create a particularly unsettling dissonance in the experience of material that would usually be expected to be accompanied by an interpretation commensurate with its magnitude of discomfort. The cognitive and emotional can also be closely linked, however, our feelings playing a key role in more cognitive processes such as moral evaluation and judgement. Both are encompassed by Douglas Pye's use of the concept of tone as a key dimension of the overall cinematic articulation found in any example: the manner in which a film 'addresses its spectator and implicitly invites us to understand its attitude to its material and the stylistic register it employs'.[58] As Pye suggests, we are encouraged to respond 'almost instinctively', through learned and habitual processes, to the various formal and other aspects of a film that signal its tone, a quality usually established with some clarity from the start. An absence of such an understanding can be a significant component of the cinema of discomfort, or might constitute part of a discomforting tone. As Pye puts it: 'When these habitual processes are disturbed, as they sometimes are when we watch films from a culture other than ours, or when a film makes it difficult immediately to say what kind of thing it is, it can be an uncomfortable or disorienting experience.'[59]

Embarrassment

Uncertainty at the level of affective response might be particularly strong in instances of the cinema of discomfort that have potential to generate embarrassment. One facet of embarrassment can be a sense of anxiety and uncertainty about how properly to respond to certain awkward social situations. This is a dimension that seems especially likely to feature in instances in which clear emotional signposting is absent or reduced. Embarrassment is included by Plantinga in a list of emotions (along with disgust, guilt and shame) that can, more conventionally, be invoked as part of the moral-ideological economy of films. A character who provokes embarrassment for others within the fictional world might serve, like one who generates disgust, to reinforce the encouragement of aversion to that for which they are made to stand. If that embarrassment is also transferred to the viewer, the effect might be heightened. As Plantinga suggests, such emotions can serve as 'a primary means for the internalization of cultural prohibitions and thus for socialization'.[60] The psychologist Rowland Miller argues for a similar cultural basis for embarrassment in general, which he identifies as a basic human emotion that can be considered to have both an everyday social role and a broader evolutionary/adaptive function as a way of reinforcing the adherence to social norms.[61]

Among various dimensions of the phenomenon, Miller includes the possibility of 'empathetic' embarrassment that can result from witnessing the embarrassment of others, a process that suggests the extent to which the basis of the emotion is often widely shared.[62] Embarrassment is usually associated with certain kinds of awkward experiences in public, in front of an audience imagined to judge the embarrassing behaviour negatively. But it can also be experienced in private, Miller suggests, as a result of the internalization of the norms on which it is based. We might feel in private a sense of what would have been involved had the same occurred in public. Such arguments suggest that embarrassment can also be experienced vicariously, through witnessing not only actual instances of embarrassment on the part of others but their fictionalized representation, numerous examples of which are examined in this book. Some blurring of lines might also be possible here. Embarrassment might be created in some cases by a sense for the viewer of what was involved at the pro-filmic level, that of the experiences undergone by performers or others in the process of staging and shooting a discomforting sequence. The degree of embarrassment generated by any material is likely to be variable, depending on the circumstances of viewing, as is generally the case in many of the studies of first-hand or witnessed embarrassment cited by Miller.

Discomfort might be increased by the presence of others, a sense of shared witnessing that can exacerbate the impact of the awkward or the cringe-inducing, although this is likely to depend on the circumstances or the nature of the group involved. Some material might seem more embarrassing if watched in public, at the cinema (or on a mobile screen visible by neighbours), rather than in private. Alternatively, the level of discomfort might be reduced if such material is watched with others who can be expected to be of broadly like mind. This might include the regular constituency at a particular arthouse venue, for example, or individual fellow viewers with broadly similarly structured tastes. Discomfort might be increased by differences of viewer orientation, particularly among intimates. One example would be the embarrassment that can result from shared viewing of such material across generations that might occupy different positions in terms of their sense of what is admissible for public consumption, the outcome sometimes of historically changing boundaries between the public and private realms. A classic source of discomfort is that experienced by younger people when watching with more traditionally oriented older or parental figures. In such cases, the response is likely to be not just to the screened material but also to an imagined or expressed sense of the (probably different, maybe disapproving) response of others. One empirical psychological study suggests that the principal source of cinematic discomfort lies in the content of the film material but that the presence of others can be a secondary source, the most heightened instance for a student-age group unsurprisingly being the viewing of explicit sexual content with parents.[63] Material that generates discomfort can be a source of bonding between viewers who share a broad orientation to the way certain norms are being challenged, but it can also be divisive, as is clear from some of the viewer responses included in the chapters that follow.

The political-ideological valences of vicarious embarrassment can also vary. If the chief social function of embarrassment in social life is to reinforce prevalent norms, its cinematic equivalent can function similarly, when deployed as part of the moral judgement of negatively coded characters. But a different impression might be created in cases in which embarrassment is produced, diegetically or extra-diegetically, by material in which such judgement is withheld, a key feature of some instances of the cinema of discomfort, including the aspects of blank style considered above. Here, the production of embarrassment might be viewed as part of a more critically open or questioning approach of the kind associated with such work more generally.

Some similar distinctions can be made about the relationship between embarrassment and sources of comedy. Tarja Laine suggests that pleasure can be provided by the embarrassing comic performances of Jim Carrey, for example, through a number of mechanisms.[64] Where Carrey's film characters offer an embarrassing performative spectacle, she suggests, this could create discomfort through some degree of identification with the character. One viewing strategy to avoid any such uncomfortable proximity is to laugh at the material, a process that generally often involves a distancing from any sense of implication in the actions of fictional protagonists. This is a feature of comic modality more widely, as I have argued elsewhere, a topic to which I return in the final chapter of this book.[65] For Laine, the viewer faced with embarrassing character behaviour is likely to feel 'an intense desire to see the character respond to the situation'.[66] This is what we would experience in a real-world situation of witnessing embarrassing behaviour, Miller argues, where some ameliorative response is usually expected. It does not happen in the examples Laine cites. Viewers are clearly not themselves able to intervene in the situation on screen and so are left, she suggests, with no alternative but to watch, and to laugh with what amounts to a defensively distancing response.

Laughing should be a relatively unproblematic reaction in most examples such as those cited by Laine, in which the texts themselves and the performances are usually clearly pre-coded as occupying the realm of broad comedy (although a darker edge is found in one case, *The Cable Guy* [1996]). A response involving laughter is encouraged from the start by a range of modality markers that generally establish comic status. These might also be likely to reduce the extent of any allegiance with exaggerated characters such as those played by Carrey in these instances. What might happen, though, in cases where such markers are absent or ambiguous, as seems often to be the case in moments of potential but uncertain comedy in the cinema of discomfort, examples of which are examined in the rest of this book, particularly in Chapter 7? Laughter might still result, as a similarly defensive distancing response, but it might fit the category of 'nervous' laughter, one of the potential responses associated with experiences of embarrassment. This might indicate an uncertainty about how to respond and/or an attempt to enact a distancing conversion of the material into the comic realm; perhaps to will it into being more unambiguously comic and thus potentially less painful. As Laine suggests, citing Ed Tan, pleasure can result from the very freedom from ability to intervene that also prevents any usual external-world response to embarrassment. Viewers can experience strong emotions, including embarrassment, disgust and horror, from what remains a relatively safe distance in film and other media.

Laine suggests that part of the pleasure offered by the comic performances of Carrey lies in the fantasy of a carnivalesque freedom from usual social norms, in an environment in which this can be experienced without the kind of embarrassment or shame that would result from its experience in reality. This, again, seems more likely to be the case with the clearly exaggerated comic modality and excess involved in such examples than with the more uncertain valences of much of the cinema of discomfort. Distance might play a role in both the clearly comic or more uncomfortable, however. As Laine suggests, pleasure might be entailed in the witnessing of some fictional scenarios of embarrassment on the basis of our relief that we are not the ones guilty of the embarrassing acts in question. This might be one basis of the appeal of discomforting material more generally. Modality can be understood here as a dimension in some respects similar to tone, in being broadly established, or in some cases left uncertain, by the combined effects of textual qualities and extra-textual expectations brought to the experience of viewing. Pye makes a distinction between tone and his own understanding of mood, which draws on that of Smith. Mood is seen as a preparatory state of expectation and anticipation, based on factors such as our apprehension of the mode or genre within which a film is placed in advance of viewing, and also a source of 'pervasive orientation' during viewing: 'More specific tonal qualities are implied scene by scene and even moment by moment by the network of decisions that create the fictional world, its characters and events, and present them to the spectator.'[67] These can include a number of strategies that have potential to create discomfort, including uncertainties at the level of tone itself.

The valences of embarrassment, as experienced by individuals or groups, might also vary according to prevailing constructs of gender, an issue worth considering more generally. If the cinema of discomfort often entails a withholding of emotional cues, this might be seen as making it a male-oriented form, within the definitional machineries of gendered subjectivity in patriarchal culture, given the greater expression of outward feeling associated with what are conventionally defined as supposedly more 'feminine' products such as sentimental varieties of melodrama. The cinema of discomfort is one of the elements of art cinema associated with patriarchally defined 'male' qualities such as being 'tough' and 'challenging', concepts the definitions of which exist in opposition to supposedly female-gendered and 'weak' or 'easy' notions of emotional display. Such oppositions remain very particular and pernicious cultural constructs that are ripe for deconstruction, as Robyn Warhol suggests in the case of popular culture more widely, where she seeks to rehabilitate supposedly 'effeminate' and often devalued qualities that have no essential connection with biological sex.[68] They might contribute to the general value sometimes attributed to certain cultural forms such as the cinema of discomfort, however, within the wider arena of cultural valuation to which I turn below.

Theorists of film and emotions such as Plantinga and Smith also help us to address the question of how exactly discomfort (or comfort) on screen might translate to that of the viewer, a key issue in relation to the different historical definitions of comfort outlined at the start of this chapter. Films can offer discomfort in the sense of the opposite of solace, in terms of what they effectively say to us: implicitly or explicitly undermining any more affirmative understanding of the world, for example, through what they depict. But they can also offer a vicarious form of physical and affective discomfort, one that can involve bodily response as well as uncomfortable psychological states. In Plantinga's account, the affective power of films involves a combination of feeling/affect and cognition. He draws upon work that defines emotions as 'concern-based construals', feelings that are related to thought-based appraisals of situations, whether in reality or within fictional worlds.[69] Affective responses also involve bodily experiences, however, as Plantinga suggests, ranging from reactions such as laughter or tears to flinching, various forms of verbal exclamation, screaming or yelling, depending on the nature of the stimulus.[70] Images presented in a manner that conventionally signifies realism in any context offer a form of perceptual realism that draws on real-world perceptual responses for its effects. A significant contribution to this approach was the discovery of mirror neurons in the brain that appear to fire when a person observes another performing an action, as well as when the action itself is performed directly. From a psychological perspective, as Plantinga puts it, watching something 'becomes something like doing it'.[71]

This process, for Plantinga, helps to account for the affective power of audiovisual media. Types of acting designed to create viewer empathy for fictional characters seek not just to *reveal* emotion, as enacted on screen, he suggests. Their effectiveness is based also on the fact that 'they have the capacity to *elicit* emotion through processes such as facial feedback, affective mimicry, and emotional contagion'.[72] The discomfort of screen characters can, in this way, be translated effectively, if inevitably in reduced form, from the world of the fiction to the experience of the viewer. The viewer can share the discomfort of characters at this psychological level. This might work, variously, either instead of, or in combination with, textual approaches that reduce emotional cues and so make the likely responses less certain or clear cut. If, as Plantigna suggests, close-ups of facial expressions or bodily gestures are key ways in which classical style frequently communicates emotion, it is precisely these closely tuned details that are absent from blank style or other variants of this approach often found in art and indie film. A closer consideration of the kinds of character-viewer dynamics that can result from such approaches is given in Chapter 2.

Pleasures of discomfort: Distinction marking and challenge

If a major theme of some accounts of horror is an attempt to understand what pleasures might be taken by viewers of such works, how might we answer such a question in relation to the types of art and independent cinema examined in this book? If the discomfort they can generate is neither a passing phase of a broader dynamic designed to create comfort nor defined in conventional generic terms, what kinds of specific pleasures might be on offer to the viewer who chooses such films? This question has generally not been addressed by commentators on the more assaultive or transgressive forms of cinematic discomfort such as Lübecker and Grønstad. A entirely clear separation cannot be made from what is entailed by generic expectations, as in the case of horror, as was intimated above. The cinema of discomfort, as part of the wider art and indie realms, is likely to generate expectations of its own, often associated with the work of individual filmmakers. These might include the anticipation of the likelihood of some forms of discomfort, even if not as clearly or explicitly as would be the case if the category I have defined here were in more general film-going use, which is not the case. Viewers of some varieties of art and indie film might certainly be cued *not* to expect the kinds of pleasure/comfortable dynamics typical of the Hollywood-style tradition, among other distinguishing features of such work. It is with this kind of viewer expectation and effective positioning that we can begin to consider the appeal of the consumption of films of this kind.

Types of cinema that display significant differences of certain kinds from what is associated with the more commercial mainstream offer potential pleasure at the level of the distinction marking they permit, consciously or otherwise, on the part of viewers. An understanding of this dimension can be combined with a consideration of the more positively defined and specific satisfaction that might be available, for some, from the consumption of challengingly discomforting material. Pleasure that results from the marking of distinction on the part of the consumer is a process theorized most notably by the French sociologist Pierre Bourdieu, one that has been applied to the consumption of art and indie film at greater length elsewhere, by myself and others.[73] The gist of the idea is that the ability to take pleasure in the viewing of such work is rooted at least partly in the possession of the requisite cultural capital: the learned and/or inherited understanding of particular kinds of cultural forms.

Products customarily located at the 'higher' end of dominantly prevailing cultural hierarchies generally require greater resources of cultural capital in order pleasurably to be consumed. In the terms used by Berliner, material of this kind is likely to reduce the component of ease and increase that of potentially discomforting challenge, and thus to require a particular viewer orientation in order to become a source of pleasure.

A degree of challenge can be a source of heightened engagement in works designed to be accessible to much larger audiences, as Berliner argues. Disruptions of narrative unity or genre expectations of a moderate variety can provide a specific pleasure based on the requirement for the viewer to contribute more actively or creatively than usual to finding a source of resolution.[74] This seems a useful way to understand the greater intensity of engagement that can be involved in some instances, as Berliner suggests, such as the enthusiastic adoption of some films that gain cult or similar status. Within a mainstream cinema such as Hollywood, pleasure of this kind is premised on such disruption being limited in extent and seeming at least resolv*able* (if not always resolved in strictly logical terms). Art and indie films, dependent on much smaller and more specific audiences, have scope to push further and sometimes to remain irresolvable in various dimensions, including the cognitive and the emotional. This can offer its own form of pleasure to suitably oriented viewers, based on their learned preparedness to engage in a stronger version of the kind of process involved in relatively challenging aspects of some studio-type films. Abstract or experimental work, for example, usually requires substantial extra-textual knowledge and experience to be understood in a manner likely to provide scope for pleasurable viewing. Art and indie film occupy a realm in which less expert understanding or specific orientation is required but generally more than that associated with works designed for the most widespread popular appeal.

From this perspective, we can challenge the assertion by Grønstad that, in what he terms the cinema of the unwatchable, 'unpleasure stays unpleasure'.[75] This is contrasted by Grønstad with more commercially oriented manifestations of extreme material (such as that found in the Saw franchise [2004 onwards]), in which he suggests aesthetic form is used to produce pleasure as a more conventional variety of entertainment (a position in some ways closer to the bases of pleasure explored in more detail by

Hanich). The latter is characterized here, in clearly hierarchical, distinction-marking terms, as the provision of 'cheap thrills'. Highly discomforting unpleasure also has the potential to provide a source of certain forms of intellectual and/or distinction-marking pleasure, of precisely the kind that might be involved in the manner in which it is differentiated from other manifestations characterized in this negative manner.

In Bourdieu's account, and/or those which have drawn on his approach, a key source of pleasure comes from the expenditure of cultural capital during consumption. The consumer who has invested time and effort in learning about something, for example, would be expected to gain satisfaction from the opportunity to put such investment to use. This is one way to elaborate the broadly unsurprising findings of psychological studies cited by Berliner to the effect that those who have more 'expert' knowledge and experience of the arts tend to prefer more challenging and difficult-to-process works than those favoured by novices in any particular field. This is not just a question of experts desiring to work harder than novices, in the accounts cited here, although this might sometimes be the case. The point is that experience and familiarity with challenging materials gives experts a higher level of ability to process them: a greater challenge is therefore required by experts for them to receive the level of stimulation that would be offered by easier experiences to the more typical viewer.[76] If, as Berliner concludes, *'people prefer artworks that are challenging in accordance with their own coping potential'*, this can also be interpreted in the more sociocultural terms employed by Bourdieu.[77]

A key aspect of this approach is the differential valuation often attached to the consumption of products at different positions in prevailing cultural hierarchies. Consumers of products that are conventionally accorded higher status are understood to be able to gain a particular distinction-marking pleasure through the process of comparing themselves (consciously or otherwise) with those who consume products to which lower status is attributed. Thus, viewers of art or indie film might, at some level, take pleasure from the process of distinguishing themselves from those who consume (or only consume) the products of mainstream cinemas such as Hollywood or other sources of 'cheap thrills'. Class or other forms of status ranking play a central role in such accounts, distinction marking of the kind most likely to involve viewers of art and indie film generally being associated with certain sectors of the middle classes. Similar pleasures can also result from the activation of forms of cultural capital associated with traditionally less-valued products, as in the case of the horror fans considered by Hills.

Many qualifications can be offered of this account, as I have suggested elsewhere,[78] but the broad idea that pleasure can result from a sense of superiority or specificity gained through consuming certain kinds of products in comparison with others seems plausible. One dimension of the pleasure that might be gained through the viewing of discomforting films could, therefore, be identified at this level. If the actual process of viewing might remain thoroughly uncomfortable in some cases, without necessarily any direct pleasures of its own, the fact of viewing, or of *having viewed*, such films might be a source of pleasurable satisfaction; a compensation, even, for what might sometimes be an un-pleasurable viewing experience. We might also be able to identify more specific and localized pleasures, during the viewing experience, as well as at this broad scale. If distinction-marking can operate in general, in relation to the consumption of more or less broad types of films, it might also take effect at a more detailed level, in relation to the treatment of specific material, in particular film sequences, potential for which is identified in the case study chapters that follow. This might be, variously, in relation to narrative developments or their absence, formal qualities, the presentation of character or any other aspects of the work.

If a pleasure rooted in distinction marking is defined at least partly in negative terms, a more positive version can be understood through the approach employed by Berliner: the pleasures available, to those suitably equipped, from engaging with, trying to untangle or revelling in the substantial challenges posed by that which is more difficult than usual to resolve. That is to say, pleasure might be gained from the specific qualities of the text rather than just, or in addition to, any that might result from the satisfaction generated by the mobilization of cultural capital and differential positioning (a criticism often made of work in the cultural studies tradition that focuses on the latter is that it fails to account for the particular appeals of actual texts or objects to those who consume them, especially in the realm of popular culture[79]). Two central sources of pleasure identified by Berliner, again drawing on psychological studies, are 'pleasingness' and 'interestingness'. Pleasingness offers 'hedonic value', the basis of which includes a desire for immediate recognition and easy understanding. Interestingness appeals to a desire for cognitive challenge, the arousal of thinking and comprehension.[80] Hollywood filmmakers, Berliner suggests, generally seek to provide maximum pleasingness and a moderate degree of interestingness.[81] If these terms have some similarity with more traditional and questionably universalistic approaches to aesthetics, such as that of Kant, in which high art is viewed as requiring reflective thought and the popular is associated with the production of pleasing emotional-bodily responses, it is notable here that elements of each are seen as being involved in the consumption of mainstream-popular work. A deconstruction of any fixed binary opposition of this kind is also suggested by the fact that the experience of the 'higher cultural' cinema of discomfort is likely to include a bodily emotional as well as cognitive dimension.[82]

In Berliner's account, to increase the level of interesting challenge beyond a certain point is to risk decreasing the pleasure quotient for the majority of viewers. A stage is reached 'at which point subjects start to become overwhelmed, and their pleasure diminishes and eventually turns into displeasure'.[83] But such a challenge can offer its own satisfactions to those who are suitably oriented, in the realm where 'an object grows less pleasing and increasingly interesting'. Miklós Kiss and Steven Willemsen explore sources of fascination available to viewers from otherwise unsettlingly unresolvable basic cognitive dimensions of what they term *Impossible Puzzle Films*, in examples ranging from the art and American indie sectors to some Hollywood productions.[84] Approaches based on an acceptance and appreciation of productive forms of confusion are offered by Dominic Lash, in what he labels *The Cinema of Disorientation*.[85]

Berliner's approach offers a useful way to elucidate the otherwise rather blandly general notion that works of art and indie cinema might be judged to be more 'interesting' to certain viewers than the tendencies of the mainstream/conventional.[86] For Berliner, the interest potentially provoked by more challenging films can be a source not just of coolly rational engagement but qualities such as excitement and exhilaration.[87] This is particularly the case when viewers are experiencing material that lies towards the far end of, but not beyond, their coping potential. Such a conclusion is supported by some of the viewer responses considered in the chapters that follow, as is a sense of some forms of discomfort pushing to a point at which viewers become uncertain how to react. Berliner expresses a positively evaluative appreciation of that which is defined in this way to be interesting, on the basis that this can be a source of more sustained and enduring appeal. In the stronger variants found in art and indie film, however, this remains an appeal likely to be socioculturally specific rather than a general basis on which to ascribe notions of quality or value, a dimension not addressed in Berliner's account. This is not to say that evaluative judgements cannot be made about how effectively any particular examples might mobilize particular qualities but to locate this as involving particular, acquired bases of appreciation.[88]

The sense of exhilaration identified by Berliner suggests that a source of pleasure can be found in discomforting material that goes beyond the realm of the cognitive and the intellectual. As with the responses to horror considered by Hanich, a bodily dimension also seems sometimes to be implied, in reactions expressed in terms such as 'skin crawling' or 'cringe-making'. Such terms imply an aversive repulsion rather than what would usually be understood to be a source of pleasure, but some form of the latter might result from the heightened level of engagement involved, if here usually at the level of diegetic material rather than intensified cinematic articulation. Such content has potential to exert a fascination on the part of the viewer, a desire to keep watching that which would usually be hidden or conventionally unacceptable material, or the kind of simultaneous pull between the repulsive and the fascinating identified by Hanich in instances of cinematic disgust.[89] More can be at stake than simply a cool cognitive-rational level of appeal to those who gain pleasure from such work, given the intimate bodily nature of some of what is entailed. It seems possible for a certain kind of delight to be taken by some viewers in being pushed into places that provoke strong if uncertain feelings, even if this is combined with more negative emotions, a kind of testing of the viewer within the relatively safety of the bounds of the cinematic. If the cognitive dimension can include a requirement to untangle or resolve matters of narrative or meaning, a similar challenge can be posed by the cinema of discomfort at the level of uncertain emotional responses, as suggested above. The two might also be combined, in cases where viewers gain the opportunity to mobilize distinction-marking cultural capital or cognitive interest while remaining unsettled in their emotional responses and sometimes challenged in their ability to resolve their overall attitude towards the material.

In broader film-theoretical terms, the various responses that might result, including discomfort, fit with Vivian Sobchack's phenomenologically based challenge to textually determinist approaches that constituted an orthodoxy in an earlier period of film studies.[90] Different viewers might experience a range of degrees and kinds of congruency or disjunction with or from cinematic material, as Sobchack argues, based on their own particular material situations. At times when difference becomes explicit – as a result of examples including breaches of cultural taboo or radical formal innovation, such as a camera that digresses from central human subject matter, as in some forms of art cinema – the viewer 'can refuse, partially share, or become rapt in the film's vision'.[91] As she continues: 'I can look in my lap, peek through the fingers with which I cover my eyes, or fully engage the film's vision and the intentional and ethical interest and trajectory it takes in relation to a world and others.' Her experience of the difference between herself and the film's embodiment and situation 'may cause me discomfort. But this experience of difference can also be liberating. It can cause me to restructure my visual address, to transcend its present location in the reformulation and imagination of where it might locate itself in the future.'[92]

Viewers might, then, in different ways, be able to take pleasure or positive forms of challenge from what would otherwise be expected to be sustained sources of cinematic discomfort. The fact that this remains within a fictional context is an additional way of qualifying the discomfort that results, as Plantinga suggests of negative emotions more generally. This might remain a key factor in establishing the overall valence of the experience. In some cases, however, as will be seen, discomfort can also relate to a potential blurring of the broadly comforting line between fact and fiction. The basis of pleasure involved in these various forms of distinction marking is closely linked to the manner in which certain kinds of materials are accorded particular forms of cultural value, an issue I examine at greater length in *Positioning Art Cinema*.

Valuing discomfort

A key framework within which to understand the appeal of discomforting material is its association with notions of 'higher' art. As Pezeu-Massabuau suggests, somewhat rhetorically: 'Hasn't the true function of the artist at any given moment been to disturb our everyday life [...]?'[93] The notion of art, in its strongest sense, has often been distinguished from that of popular entertainment or craft on the basis of its potential to offer challenge to established/conventional varieties of comfort, at the levels of either form or content.

Aesthetic types of discomfort are viewed as sources of the 'making new' or estrangement often associated with the higher arts, particularly, although not exclusively, work in the modernist tradition. A similar stance is implied in the suggestion by Sobchack that material that is challengingly uncomfortable can be a source of potentially liberating changes in perception. Discomforting art is often valued on this basis, as is suggested by Frederick Aldama and Herbert Lindenberger in their book of conversations, *Aesthetics of Discomfort*. Each medium offers its own distinct forms of potential for discomfort, they suggest, film being cited alongside music as a realm in which discomfort can be produced in an ongoing rather than a more temporary manner.[94] That which is discomforting 'is part and parcel of the aesthetic domain', suggests Lindenberger, 'central to the way we experience art'.[95] If discomfort became central to art only after the modernist 'revolution' of the early twentieth century, Aldama and Lindenberger argue, 'it has always been with us', in earlier examples such as the disconcerting dissonances of the music of Claudio Monteverdi.[96] Arnheim suggests similarly that, while the perceptually equivocal and ambiguous can produce unpleasant effects, these are likely to be sought out in some kinds of artistic practice, including the visual clashes and contradictions found in cubist works.[97] Expensive designer furniture that gains or aspires to the status of art often does so at the expense of sitting comfort.[98]

Many of the general examples of discomfort outlined above can be understood as offering the potential to refresh the perceptions of the viewer through a deliberate frustration of customarily more conventional expectations. If we are denied the usual and comfortable, effectively invisible, rhythms of editing, we might be invited to see anew, to some extent at least, if only within the confines of the experience of the work. We might be encouraged to pay greater than usual attention to the process of representation itself, when its normally unnoticed routines are made visible through being breached; or such departures may create a general impression of discomfort or disorientation without the source being so clearly identifiable in most cases. At one extreme is highly modernist work, in which the focus is shifted to the plane of the artistic materials rather than their representational contents. In film, this would be avant-garde or experimental material and some of the weightiest products of relatively more widely circulated art cinema. But considerable space also exists for the more subtle departures and discomforts found in the primary territory examined in this book.

Aldama and Lindenberger take an approach similar in some ways to mine above in identifying sources of discomfort that can be part of a broad process of creating feelings of comfort as well as discomfort in its own right and in emphasizing both the cognitive and emotional dimensions. In the cognitive realm, Lindenberger adopts a clear positively evaluative approach, asserting that artistic discomfort that causes consumers to think about their responses is 'a way of contributing to our intellectual growth'.[99] This is an approach characteristic of a broader set of established ways of attributing special value to a 'higher' notion of the arts, including assumptions about their potential to have a transformational effect on audiences, an issue I examine at greater length in *Positioning Art Cinema*. Such assumptions are rooted in a particular historical context, the formulation of a set of distinctions between notions of 'art' and 'craft' that became institutionalized in the eighteenth century and have since become widely taken for granted in such discourses.[100]

Pezeu-Massabuau offers a similarly positively evaluative approach, in an account that tends to make rather sweeping claims in general. The experience of voluntary discomfort, of the kind involved in choosing to watch films such as those that are the subject of this book, offers pleasure on the basis of creating a sense of mastery, he suggests. Since he is not a masochist, he argues, he expects 'to be recompensed' for choosing to experience discomfort (his focus here is on its physical dimension).[101] He adds: 'My initial pleasure arises from feeling I am the master of my choices, and the more difficult they are, the greater the pleasure.' This might be said, for example, of the viewer who chooses to sit through a film known in advance to offer an experience of otherwise unmitigated discomfort. Pezeu-Massabuau goes on to put this in rather grand terms. By choosing to suffer discomfort, he suggests, he satisfies his sense of free will. His 'humanity is displayed in these accomplishments, since, unlike animals, we want (and do) even the things we do not desire'.[102]

Social and historical contexts

This conception of discomfort can be related to a broadly puritan, 'hair-shirt' basis of valuation of the uncomfortable, a dimension that has some resonance with the historical development of notions or valuations of comfort explored by Crowley. Comfort in the sense that leans towards material luxury has a long tradition of being distrusted within classical and Christian philosophy,

Crowley suggests, where it was seen as violating sanctioned divine or social order.[103] It was viewed as morally questionable, a sign of corruption. By the early modern period, luxury was allowed to nobles, as a means of upholding rank and thus contributing to the maintenance of social order. Comfort increasingly came to be applied to 'a middle ground between necessity and luxury'.[104] During the eighteenth century, Crowley suggests, both luxury and comfort became more neutral terms and discomfort was seen as something that could be averted through progressive rational correction (in cases such as the conditions of slaves, prisoners and the poor).

By the turn of the nineteenth century the denunciation of discomfort in Anglo-American social thought was such that a desire for physical comfort became naturalized.[105] In the early decades of that century, Crowley adds, 'the ideal of comfort provided values, consumption patterns and behaviours crucial to the formation of a middle class'.[106] No longer being disavowed, the search for comfort could effectively function as an engine for domestic consumerism. It seems notable that a key phase in this dynamic is a period similar to that identified by Larry Shiner for the institutionalization of the conception of 'higher' art as a distinct realm. The two appear to share roots in broadly congruent historical trends relating to the growth of commerce and the increased commodification of social life, the notion of a 'purer' higher art having been developed specifically in reaction to the increased commodification of cultural production.

In the inheritance that follows from this historical context, a choice for the experience of discomfort seems much more specific than is implied by Pezeu-Massabuau. To interpret opting to experience discomfort as a marker of something as broad as 'being human' is a generalization that seems unhelpful to the task of explaining the more particular dynamics that might be at work in choices such as viewing the cinema of discomfort. The latter is better seen as involving options likely to be taken by much more specific constituencies, rather than 'humanity' at large, which is where a sweeping account such as this needs to be supplemented by a more sociological approach of the kind associated with Bourdieu. It seems a widespread tendency for particular investments or pleasures to be universalized by their advocates in this way. Most film viewers, it can safely be assumed (from box-office or other sources of viewing data), do *not* choose to view products that offer sustained forms of discomfort, which suggests that more specific dynamics are at work where such choices are made. It seems more likely that the exercise of will outlined by Pezeu-Massabuau is widely applicable to the consumption choices and patterns of specific constituencies only, often those which occupy particular positions in the kinds of distinction-marking hierarchies mapped by Bourdieu and others. The same would apply to the valorization of discomfort suggested by James Harold in the case of films that offer potentially unresolvable conflicts at the emotional level, his main example of which is the highly ambivalent treatment of the child murderer in Fritz Lang's *M* (1931). Such discomfort, akin to some of that considered in the main case studies in this book, is likely to be avoided by most viewers, as Harold argues, although he suggests it is of value as a reminder of our 'epistemic limitations and of the messiness of moral and social life'.[107] This is a statement with which I would agree, but it suggests a very specific rather than wider basis of appeal, one strongly consonant with prevailing definitions of the 'higher' arts.

Something similar can be said about the choice of material that includes potential for embarrassment, as a particular variety of discomfort likely to be among the qualities expected – or not unanticipated – in the cinema of discomfort. Embarrassment is identified by Miller as another capacity that marks our status as human, rooted in the development of self-consciousness and a desire for social belonging (even if exactly what provokes embarrassment can be culturally variable). It is associated with 'higher' brain functions than many other emotions, involving the operations of the prefrontal cortex, the location of conscious thought processes.[108] Although usually unpleasant, the experience of embarrassment is broadly positive in most cases, Miller suggests. It is a desirable process (unless taken to excess) that helps us to negotiate cultural norms and that usually generates positive responses from others, as a way of signifying our awareness of, and appropriate response to, certain kinds of transgression.[109] It remains an experience that is generally seen as negative, however, and to be avoided as a source of discomfort. This begs the question why some viewers actively seek out works that offer or include such an experience, vicariously or more directly, which again suggests that its appeal in this form has a socioculturally specific rather than more widespread basis. The fact that embarrassment relies on what are usually seen as among the higher and more distinctly human capacities might provide grounds for its valorization, when provided in certain forms in particular kinds of cultural products, as part of their questioning/difficult artistic status; but this remains something likely to consumed only by a limited constituency and therefore not a basis for universal acclaim.

If a desire for material comfort became widely sanctioned through the historical shifts outlined by Crowley, the appeal of the discomforting at the cultural level, including film, has persisted within certain circles, if not within the majority film-viewing population. This is notable, for example, in discourses surrounding some valorizations of certain forms of American indie film. A distinctly puritan tone can be identified in some attempts to make distinctions between works seen as of 'true', 'authentic' or more pure indie status and others viewed as having 'sold out' in various ways, as I have argued elsewhere.[110] Such notions of selling out tend to involve the provision of broadly more comfortable material, closely combined with the pursuit of increasingly commercially oriented marketing and/or release strategies. Similar discourses have also been mobilized in relation to works associated with the wider realm of international art cinema, where certain versions – usually the most stripped-back, challenging, minimalist and/or opaque – are often valorized in favour of others seen as less demanding.[111] A key component of such discourse is the distrust of certain forms of comforting pleasure, including that widely associated with mainstream-conventional forms of cinema. This is a central feature of what Plantinga describes as 'estrangement' theories of screen media, in which a superior position (politically, ideologically and morally) is attributed to attempts to deconstruct pleasurable forms of viewer engagement.[112] A wholesale negative judgement of conventional forms of cinematic pleasure is unwarranted, as Plantinga argues, on broad moral or ethical grounds. Forms of positive viewer engagement can serve morally approvable purposes in various ways, as he suggests, if in far from all cases; but the denigration of such approaches remains a potent element in the discursive complexes within which alternatives such as the distanced, alienated and/or discomforting are customarily valorized.

The devaluation of comfort in this sense can be linked to a wider contemporary and broadly 'western' social context, in which the notion of a 'comfort zone' is often denigrated or seen as a negative other against which to define more positive qualities. We are often urged to move out of our personal comfort zones in order to embrace the challenges of life. A distinct category of works found in the Amazon search cited above takes this position, in self-help books of assorted persuasions that share titles or subtitles that include variations on 'stepping out of your comfort zone' as a prescription for a more fulfilling life.[113] The comfort zone tends to imply something narrow, safe, unchallenging, limited and/or self-indulgent. To risk discomfort is seen as part of a bold, adventurous and worthwhile approach, one that opens the individual to new experiences or perceptions in a manner akin in some respects to what is implied by challenging works of art or culture. In her popular psychological account, *Cringeworthy: How to Make the Most of Uncomfortable Situations*, Melissa Dahl suggests that such experiences are often based on gaining a sense of how others see us and, as a result, a route towards better self-understanding.[114] Broader prescriptions for exiting the comfort zone might be understood to be as socially specific as those involved in the consumption of discomforting cultural products, often rooted in fears of settled bourgeois complacency and related qualities. A similar sense of denigrating that which is identified as overly comfortable, familiar and unchallenging is a widespread tendency in some critical or viewer responses that express a preference for more uncomfortable work.

Late modernity and neoliberalism

If discomforting departures from established-conventional norms in cinema can create potential for a refreshing of vision at the formal level, a more prominent dimension of the types of films examined in this book is the use of discomfort – thematically and/or formally established – as part of what is seen as a broader social critique. This can be assumed to be a major basis of the appeal of such work to particular constituencies, and another central source of any cultural value it is likely to be accorded. Many examples of the cinema of discomfort can be read as offering implicit criticism of certain aspects of the contemporary societies they represent, as suggested in the Introduction through the analysis of American indie examples by Sconce and Perkins. Such films tend not to offer explicit analysis of the causes of the problems they dramatize (in the family or the workplace, for example), focusing instead on the creation of a broader sense of social malaise, more or less socially historically specific.

This is a cinema that tends to highlight implicit effects rather than causes, a point made by Bordwell about art cinema more generally.[115] One of the central sources of discomfort can be precisely the absence of any clear larger process of cultural diagnosis or explanatory framework. If such films often leave the viewer to work out how to respond emotionally, they also tend to leave open any source of social explanation for the uncomfortable experiences they chart. Viewers might still be encouraged to search for such readings, however, by protocols that tend to surround the consumption of art and indie cinema. Interpretation of this kind can provide another way of taking pleasure from, or to some extent potentially displacing, certain forms of discomfort, offering a sense of mastery of the material at another level for sufficiently attuned viewers. What is involved here is a form of cognitive frame switching.[116] Engagement might be displaced from more immediate (and often discomforting) diegetic matters to other levels often characteristic of the consumption of art cinema, such as appreciation of either formal qualities in their own right or potential for 'higher-level' allegorical readings of one kind or another.

One useful attempt to diagnose a broader, socio-historical context for a turn to the discomforting in film and television is offered by Adam Kotsko's study of contemporary cultural awkwardness.[117] That which is defined as 'awkward' is closely related to the production of discomfort, a tendency identified by Kotsko in examples such as 'cringe' comedy. This territory has also been explored by Jason Middleton in a study of awkwardness in spheres including documentary film and TV comedy.[118] The literal definition of awkward cited by Kotsko – 'awke-ward', meaning turned in the wrong direction – is one that fits with some of the aspects of discomfort considered so far.[119] Middleton offers a definition of awkwardness similarly congruent with that which can produce discomfort. It is created, he suggests, 'by unexpected shifts and ruptures in representational systems', in this case further defined in the case of documentary as 'moments when differing perceptions and investments among filmmakers, social actors, and spectators are forced into view.'[120] Among other examples, the latter is applied to the ambiguity of the reality status of *I'm Still Here*, which, as Middleton suggests, remains unresolved in the text itself.[121]

Kotsko traces the origins of contemporary awkwardness in America to social upheavals broadly associated with the 1960s, a process he suggests called into question supposedly 'traditional' values without being able to develop a stable replacement.[122] This is another account that usefully defines qualities such as discomfort and awkwardness in terms of challenges to prevailing norms, the maintenance of the latter often providing sources of comfort to some, at least. The period in question, particularly from the 1970s to the 1990s, maps closely onto that of the 'Generation X' sensibility identified as a key ground of American smart cinema by Sconce and Perkins, an era to which many contemporary trends have been traced by a wide range of social commentators. In Kotsko's account, as with others, the challenges of the 1960s were to a set of norms rooted in large-scale institutions such as a Fordist corporate economy, racism and patriarchy. A number of progressive gains were made as a result of challenges from directions such as the civil rights movement and feminism, but this was not sufficient to overturn the forces of cultural conservatism: 'It is here, I claim, that we find the ultimate origin of contemporary awkwardness: the events of the 1960s threw the normative social model significantly off-kilter, making it impossible to embrace that model wholeheartedly – and yet they did not produce any viable positive alternative.'[123] By the 1970s, Kotsko argues, awkwardness had become the new 'default setting' of American culture. An attempt to reassert the values of unfettered capitalism and supposedly 'traditional values' was made during the Reagan era in the 1980s. A turn towards irony followed in the 1990s, Kotsko suggests, a position of detachment from commitment to values. This was rooted, for Kotsko, in the undermining of economic certainty for many people, and accords to some extent with elements of the social context suggested by Sconce for the ironic address central to his concept of smart cinema. The events of 9 September 2001 were claimed by some to mark an 'end of irony', as Kotsko recalls, but rather than a return to earnestness he suggests that what followed was a re-emergence of awkwardness as a cultural default setting.[124]

Kotsko's is a suggestive account, his argument grounded in specific economic and social developments, although it also seems too sweeping, as is likely to be the case with any diagnosis that operates in such very broad trend-spotting terms. The extent to which irony was ever a dominant feature of American culture in the 1990s, as has often been suggested, seems questionable, for example, even if it had distinctive manifestations or relative prominence in this period.[125] This tendency to exaggerate might be understood in the context of a much longer-term split in the definition of irony charted by Claire Colebrook: between its use as a particular rhetorical device involving a gap between apparently expressed and intended meaning – the primary usage considered here – and an understanding of irony as a marker of a broader 'modern'/'western' consciousness that understands all meanings ultimately to be contingent and contextual in nature.[126] The latter version, the origins of which are traced by Colebrook to Socrates and to a revival in nineteenth-century Romanticism, is key component of notions of the postmodern that became prevalent in certain circles in the 1980s and 1990s, a period in relation to which some slippage might occur in certain diagnostic uses of the concept. In this variety, the ironic as a rhetorical tool is a means of signalling the necessary limitations of *all* forms of discourse, while the other tradition has often taken irony to presume some more stable and shared basis against which to be measured.[127]

We might also question Kotsko on the degree to which awkwardness of the kind to which he refers *dominated* either in the 1970s, or more recently. As with some of the experiences of choosing discomfort suggested above by Pezeu-Massabuau, this is best seen as something likely to be more specific to particular constituencies than as generally prevalent as is sometimes claimed. The same might apply to ironically distancing discourses more generally: that they all depend on some particular context or social formulation (a potential source of comfortable orientation) for their recognition as such. As Linda Hutcheon argues, irony is always culturally specific and rooted in particular discursive communities.[128] Kotsko also seems to exaggerate what he suggests is the pervasiveness of awkwardness when he suggests, hyperbolically, that it is 'everywhere, inescapable' and 'dominates entertainment to such an extent that it's becoming increasingly difficult to remember laughing at anything other than cringe-inducing scenes of social discomfort'.[129] Kotsko makes some useful distinctions, however, including one that would separate certain more mainstream manifestations of the cinematic comedy of discomfort from the kinds of films that are the subject of this book. He cites examples such as films associated with Judd Apatow (as writer, producer or director) in which the awkwardness of figures of the overgrown adolescent is combined with affirmative sentimental coming-of-age narratives of a kind that mark their more broadly mainstream-commercial status.[130]

Although much of his account of the history of contemporary awkwardness is based on interpreting it as a result of an inability sufficiently to establish new and more progressive norms, to replace conservative notions of 'traditional values', Kotsko is another who also finds positive potential in such discomforting phenomena. What he terms 'radical awkwardness' involves situations, often cross-cultural, in which no 'meta-norm' is available to govern encounters between those adhering to two different norms. Despite 'the obvious discomfort associated with awkwardness', he suggests, there is 'a tendency for awkwardness to become a site of utopian hope'.[131] The possibility exists of 'dwelling in awkwardness', a concept Kotsko develops in the context of a reading of the TV series *Curb Your Enthusiasm* (2000–). 'Rather than attempting to cover the gap introduced by the eruption of awkwardness', he suggests, 'one should endorse it by redoubling it', as an alternative form of opposition to the existing social order.[132]

A similar phenomenon is considered by Melissa Dahl, in relation to workshops in which discomfort is provoked as a way of encouraging participants to confront their own hidden bias and misconceptions on issues such as race or class.[133] A requirement to accept discomfort of this kind is a recurring theme of Robin Diangelo's *White Fragility: Why It's So Hard for White People to Talk about Racism*: a productive acceptance of the discomfort involved for all white people (however avowedly anti-racist) in acknowledging their own implication within and benefit from pervasive structural racism.[134] Something of this kind might conceivably result from some manifestations of the cinema of discomfort, at its most acute, although, as Kotsko concedes, there is always a danger that any such radical approach can be co-opted by the system it seeks to challenge. Exactly what potential any such tendency within forms of representation might have to bring about actual change also remains highly open to question and impossible to gauge.

The context of post-1960s uncertainty cited by Kotsko can be situated as one phase in the much longer-term development of modernity to which Colebrook's account is related, as can others that focus on this particular era. Key features of the broader historical process undergone in the societies to which this applies include forms of social fragmentation, alienation and moral disorientation associated with the undermining of more traditionally established and institutionalized sources of meaning, order and hierarchy. Diagnoses of heightened more recent developments of this condition are found in the writings of sociologists such as Zygmunt Bauman, Anthony Giddens, Ulrich Beck and Richard Sennett. Common themes of this work, along with some of those cited by Perkins, include the widespread creation of discomforting forms of anxiety and uncertainty. These are seen as resulting from the increased exposure of individuals to overwhelming and largely incomprehensible social and economic forces, in a context in which more collective forms of solidarity and meaning-creation have often been undermined.

Such phenomena are, for these commentators, products of a particular phase of modernity, although they are elsewhere sometimes labelled as postmodern (exactly where, if anywhere, the boundary exists between these two categories remains a topic of much debate). Similar potential sources of anxiety and uncertainty have been associated more specifically with the culture of neoliberalism. Examples of the cinema of discomfort join other artistic-cultural forms, including earlier traditions of art cinema, that can be read as expressions of either the very broad modernizing context or specific manifestations associated with particular and often more recent/contemporary periods. The accelerated modernity of the first three-quarters of the twentieth century is, for example, the background against which

Amos Vogel celebrates various departures from dominant convention found in 'subversive' works of art and avant-garde cinema up to that time.[135] These range from examples of discomfort cited above, such as jump cuts in Godard and the slicing of the eyeball in *Un Chien Andalou*, to the ambiguities of the films of Michelangelo Antonioni and the bolder challenges found in many instances of the avant-garde or otherwise radically alternative.

Individual films can be understood in the context of either a broad and undefined sense of discomforting malaise, or in relation to more specific aspects of the dynamics identified by particular commentators, as will be seen in some examples in the chapters that follow. To suggest such an interpretive basis is one key way in which cultural value is effectively ascribed to products of this kind, if often only implicitly, particularly in the case of work that highlights rather than seeking to provide solace for any such social phenomena. Hanich locates one of the sources of the pleasure of fear or horror within a similar context of 'advanced modernity', although here the argument is that the appeal of such experiences is based on the compensation they offer for certain aspects of contemporary existence. These include bodily stimulation said to counterbalance an increasingly disembodied way of life and the creation of forms of collectivity (particularly in the theatrical experience of such films) that compensate for a broader loosening of social bonds.[136]

The contemporary cultural complexes diagnosed by figures such as Bauman, Giddens, Beck and those drawn upon by Perkins, including Furedi, vary in some details but with a number of recurring themes. These tend to combine a broader modern undermining of traditional sources of authority with dynamics specific to a more recent and contemporary period, dated back usually to somewhere around or from the 1970s or 1980s. Within the economic, political and ideological spheres, this is the era that witnessed the institutionalization of the neoliberal form of capitalism, largely displacing a postwar 'western' consensus around social democracy.[137] For Bauman, the cultural diagnosis is what he terms 'liquid' modernity, an updating of the famous 'all that is solid melts into air' characterization of the radically destabilizing dimension of capitalism highlighted by Karl Marx and Friedrich Engels in *The Communist Manifesto*.[138] This is a heighted stage of the modern dynamic, in which social structures that help to limit individual choices and establish familiar patterns of behaviour are said to decompose at a rate faster than they can be cast. The result is that they are said no longer to be able to serve as reliable long-term frameworks for human action.[139] Like Kotsko, Bauman identifies a broadly Fordist worldview as a key component of an earlier and more solid phase of modernity, one in which traditional frameworks were replaced by an emphasis on a supposedly enlightened rationality.[140]

Beck's influential concept of 'risk society' is one in which a range of 'inscrutable' threats (especially those relating to global environmental, financial and 'terrorist' sources, resulting specifically from the successes of modernity) are said to create a mood of anxiety and pressure at the individual level.[141] A more positive interpretation of risk, at this sociological level, includes a focus on voluntary risk-taking behaviour that might be seen as part of self-development or self-actualization, a framework within which the less acute risks entailed in viewing products such as the cinema of discomfort might be embraced along with more physically hazardous varieties.[142] This is itself a discourse implicated in the culture of neoliberalism, however, one that celebrates exploitative notions of individual flexibility and self-entrepreneurship. These are component parts of an ideology that has become deeply sedimented into understandings of everyday life and that can be seen as a context that explains the proliferation of the 'getting out of your comfort zone' variety of self-help exhortations cited above.[143] It is hard to resist the conclusion that the cinema of discomfort, along with the broader art and indie sectors of which it is a part, can also be seen as implicated within the almost all-consuming purview of the neoliberal economy as it operates in the realm of cinema, in this case in its globalized niche markets, whatever potential any of its products might have to generate critical discourse.

Another common theme of this kind of work is that, with the crumbling of faith in traditional sources of orientation combined with the precepts of neoliberalism, individuals have come under greater pressure to take responsibility for various aspects of their own lives, including the intimate realm of interpersonal and sexual relations. This is a source potentially of greater freedom from earlier constraints but also of discomfort, anxiety and uncertainty resulting from what Giddens terms the involvement of everyone in '*everyday social experiments* with which wider social changes more or less oblige us to engage'.[144] A similar focus on the intimate domain, and the rival pulls of older ideals and attempts to find new solutions to relationship issues, is found in what Ulrich Beck and Elisabeth Beck-Gernsheim term, in the title of their book, *The Normal Chaos of Love*, a context in which the domains of the family and notions of love are viewed as troubled areas in which security is sought after the loss of faith in religious or other traditions.[145]

For Furedi, the contemporary situation of pervasive anxiety, moral disorientation and therapeutic intervention is, in a similar fashion, a response to an individualist undermining of political and ideological allegiances that had previously served to temper the fragmenting tendencies of modernity.[146] This can be viewed as another product of the neoliberal turn within capitalist societies. Among other developments, the impact of neoliberal ideology is widely agreed to have reduced the salience of social class as a basis for self-identification in 'western' societies, if not the relevance of class itself as an analytical category. The latter has also been argued by many commentators, for whom social class has been displaced by a wider and more diffuse range of 'identity' formations, although some such interpretations can themselves be viewed as a product of neoliberal orientation.[147] Furedi's argument is also consistent with the diagnosis of contemporary anxiety-inducing instability and fragmentation of life identified in particular but influential economic and social sectors by Richard Sennett.[148]

A central dimension of many such accounts, as in those of Bauman, Giddens, Beck and Sennett, is the role of globalization – a key component of contemporary neoliberalism – as a force for the weakening of certain social bonds and the creation of pervasive individual pressures, anxieties and perceptions of risk. As Giddens suggests, the destabilizing tendencies of such widespread social phenomena exist in a dialectical relationship with the maintenance, imposition or re-imposition of various types of reactionary fundamentalist authority, giving rise to potentially complex combinations of the two.[149] This argument is a useful way to avoid a frequent tendency found in sweeping sociocultural diagnoses of these kinds, as with Kotsko, which is to slip into a rhetorical exaggeration of certain dynamics, however substantial they might be up to a point (this is also the case, I would suggest, with Furedi and Fisher, two key sources for Perkins, as well as in some of the language employed by Bauman). To whatever degree more established-traditional frameworks of gender, class or ethnicity might be said to have lost salience in some areas, it is clear that this is far from entirely the case. As John Tulloch and Deborah Lupton argue, perceptions of the kind of risk highlighted by Beck themselves continue to vary significantly along 'traditional' cultural lines such as class, gender, ethnicity and geographical location.[150]

The concept of 'structures of feeling' developed by Raymond Williams offers a useful way to capture a sense of the lived 'meanings and values' that might be said to be expressed or participated in by the kinds of films examined in this book.[151] That is, as something perhaps less fixed than some of the social tendencies diagnosed by the commentators listed above; an impression of something of the experience of certain recent/contemporary social phenomena, while remaining more complex and actively in process, as Williams suggests, than 'more formal concepts of "world view" or "ideology"'.[152] This might fit with a sense of the lack of any more overt sociocultural diagnosis in most of the examples considered below, in which the viewer tends to be confronted with discomforting material often without any immediately obvious or specific basis on which to interpret its valence. Structure of feeling is also a useful notion through which to address the dimensions of form and tone, as is central to its use in Sconce's reading of smart cinema. It is, for Williams, 'specifically related' to the evidence provided by 'forms and conventions – semantic figures – which, in art and literature, are often among the very first indications that a new structure is forming'.[153]

If the cinema of discomfort can offer an implicit critique or manifestation of certain prevailing social norms, this seems likely to remain of a broadly affirmative nature to the primary target constituencies of such films. This is another dimension in which a nuanced understanding of discomfort is required, and where a form of comfort-within-discomfort can be identified that is particularly germane to this kind of cinema. For a viewer who shares the general worldview of such work, a significant component of comfort might result from having it confirmed. This has potential to act as a further source of distinction marking on the part of such viewers: a self-confirming indication of their sense of belonging to a presumed like-minded group of consumers, characteristically likely to be seen by themselves as superior to those who do not view this kind of material. The dynamic involved is akin to what Sconce identifies as the role of irony in American smart cinema, a quality that requires a certain understanding on the part of the viewer: a recognition that the opposite might be meant of what is explicitly stated. Belonging to such a group constitutes a process of 'getting it' that implies the existence of others (often negatively coded) who might not get the point.[154] The viewer is offered a form of what Pezeu-Massabuau more generally describes as 'intellectual comfort',[155] founded here on the reconfirmation of a sense of 'superior' critical-intellectual engagement with the text and what it is taken to say about the world (even if the diagnosis implied by the latter might remain discomforting to such an audience in its implications about their own lives or those of others). This is what might be mobilized by the sense of being able to cope with, or take some form of pleasure or satisfaction from, the stronger challenges offered by discomforting films, or works of art or indie cinema more widely, as opposed to the moderate departures from pleasingness identified by Berliner within the Hollywood tradition.

One possible reaction to discomforting material can be a split between the responses of the viewer at the intellectual/cognitive and emotional levels. This is an experience I can vouch for on a personal basis: one in which I have often viewed material of the kind examined in this book and found myself intellectually willing the work to remain challenging and unsettling while, at an emotional level, wanting narrative material to work out in a more happily conventional manner as part of my personal experience of affective engagement. That it is entirely normal to be able to consume films or other media in so contradictory a manner is key to the cognitive-perceptual approach taken by Plantinga, a quality he attributes more generally to the modular structure of the brain: the same phenomenon that enables us both to be aware of the fictional nature of the events and to become engaged personally-affectively in their emotional valences.[156]

Any reading of the cinema of discomfort in terms of wider sociocultural dynamics of the kind explored by the commentators cited above always needs to be accompanied, and often qualified, by an understanding of such phenomena as the product of more specific institutional factors. If the cinema of discomfort can be seen in some ways as reflecting concerns about the nature of certain aspects of the societies within which it is produced, it is also shaped by the infrastructural frameworks of art and indie film. These can offer space, if often limited, for the pursuit of the kinds of approaches examined in this book, as is suggested in particular examples in the chapters that follow.

Notes

1. John Crowley, *The Invention of Comfort: Sensibility and Design in Early Modern Britain and Early America* (Baltimore, MD: Johns Hopkins University Press, 2001), x.
2. Galen Cranz, *The Chair: Rethinking Culture, Body and Design* (New York: Norton, 1998).
3. Crowley, *The Invention of Comfort*, 3.
4. Ibid., x.
5. Ibid., 69.
6. Search conducted 8 November 2017 at https://www.amazon.co.uk/s/ref=nb_sb_noss_2?url=search-alias%3Dstripbooks&field- keywords=comfort. My quick survey covered the first 65 pages of results, a total of 1,040 items.
7. Jacques Pezeu-Massabuau, *A Philosophy of Discomfort* (London: Reaktion Books, 2012).
8. Ibid., 27.
9. Ibid.
10. A strong version of this process asserted in some psychoanalytically based theory is the notion of *suture* as a means of (supposedly) producing the subject position of the spectator.
11. David Bordwell and Kristen Thompson, *Film Art: An Introduction*, sixth edition (New York: McGraw Hill, 2000), 39.
12. For an analysis of the varying degrees of 'happiness' and 'ending' actually to be found in Hollywood, see James MacDowell, *Happy Endings in Hollywood Cinema: Cliché, Convention and the Final Couple* (Edinburgh: Edinburgh University Press, 2014).
13. See Emilio Audissino, *Film/Music Analysis: A Film Studies Approach* (London: Palgrave, 2017).
14. Bordwell and Thompson, *Film Art*, 45.
15. Ernst Gombrich, *Art and Illusion: A Study in the Psychology of Pictorial Representation* (London: Phaidon, 1977).

16 Rudolph Arnheim, *Art and Visual Perception: A Psychology of the Creative Eye, The New Version* (Berkeley: University of California Press, 1974), 37.
17 Arnheim, *Art and Visual Perception*, 411.
18 For one classic account of this phenomenon, see Thomas Schatz, *Hollywood Genres* (Austin: University of Texas Press, 1981).
19 Todd Berliner, *Hollywood Aesthetic: Pleasure in American Cinema* (Oxford: Oxford University Press, 2017).
20 Berliner, *Hollywood Aesthetic*, 16.
21 Geoff King, *Quality Hollywood: Markers of Distinction in Contemporary Studio Film* (London: I.B. Tauris, 2016).
22 Audissino, *Film/Music Analysis*, 96.
23 K. J. Donnelly, *Occult Aesthetics; Synchronization in Sound Film* (Oxford: Oxford University Press, 2014), 74.
24 Lübecker, *The Feel-Bad Film*, 2.
25 Arnheim, *Art and Visual Perception*, 22, Figure 7.
26 Carl Plantinga, *Moving Viewers: American Film and the Spectator's Experience* (Berkeley: University of California Press, 2009), 181.
27 Plantinga, *Moving Viewers*, 2.
28 Ibid., 181.
29 Ibid., 182–3.
30 Ibid., 181.
31 Ibid., 187.
32 Ibid., 177–9.
33 Ibid., 190.
34 Ibid., 173.
35 For a summary, see Matt Hills, *The Pleasures of Horror* (London: Continuum, 2005).
36 Hills, *The Pleasures of Horror*, 61.
37 Hanich, *Cinematic Emotion in Horror Films and Thrillers*.
38 Ibid.
39 Ibid., 207.
40 Ibid., 22, 24 and elsewhere. Hanich draws here on the phenomenological work of Hermann Schmitz.
41 Grønstad, *Screening the Unwatchable*, 6 (emphasis in original).
42 David Bordwell, *The Way Hollywood Tells It: Story and Style in Modern Movies* (Berkeley: University of California Press, 2006).
43 Geoff King, *Spectacular Narratives* (London: I.B. Tauris, 2000), chapter 4.
44 Sconce, 'Irony, Nihilism', 359; emphasis in original.
45 Ibid., 360; emphasis in original.

46 David Bordwell, *Figures Traced in Light: On Cinematic Staging* (Berkeley: University of California Press, 2005).

47 Sconce, 'Irony, Nihilism', 364.

48 As Sconce suggests, 'there is no such thing as truly blank style or narration – only a set of strategies employed to signify the *idea* of blankness.' Ibid., 359.

49 Julian Hanich, 'Dis/liking Disgust: The Revulsion Experience at the Movies', *New Review of Film and Television Studies*, vol. 7, no. 3 (September 2009): 293–309 (296).

50 See for example Robin Wood, *Hollywood from Vietnam to Reagan* (New York: Columbia University Press, 1987).

51 For a classic account, see David Bordwell, *Narration in the Fiction Film* (London: Routledge, 1988).

52 Greg M. Smith, 'Local Emotions, Global Moods', in Carl Plantinga and Greg M. Smith (eds), *Passionate Views Film, Cognition and Emotion* (Baltimore, MD: Johns Hopkins University Press, 1999), 116.

53 Smith, 'Local Emotions', 118.

54 Plantinga, *Moving Viewers*, 78.

55 Ibid., 213.

56 For a popular account, see Daniel Goleman, *Emotional Intelligence: Why It Can Matter More than IQ* (London: Bloomsbury, 1996). See also George Lakoff and Mark Johnson, *Philosophy in the Flesh: The Embodied Mind and Its Challenge to Western Thought* (New York: Basic, 1999).

57 Michel Chion, *Audio-Vision: Sound on Screen* (New York: Columbia University Press, 1994), 8.

58 Douglas Pye, 'Movies and Tone', in John Gibbs and Douglas Pye (eds), *Close-Up 02* (London: Wallflower Press, 2007), 7.

59 Pye, 'Movies and Tone', 7.

60 Plantinga, *Moving Viewers*, 218.

61 Rowland Miller, *Embarrassment: Poise and Peril in Everyday Life* (New York: Guilford Press, 1996).

62 Miller, *Embarrassment*, 34–6.

63 Richard Jackson Harris and Lindsay Cook, 'How Content and Co-viewers Elicit Emotional Discomfort in Moviegoing Experiences', *Applied Cognitive Psychology*, vol. 25 (2011), 856. For a more general account of the role of fellow viewers in theatrical viewing, see Julian Hanich, *The Audience Effect; On the Collective Cinema Experience* (Edinburgh: Edinburgh University Press, 2018).

64 Tarja Laine, 'Jim Carrey: The King of Embarrassment', *Cineaction*, July 2001.

65 Geoff King, *Film Comedy* (London: Wallflower, 2002).

66 Laine, 'Jim Carrey', 54.

67 Pye, 'Movies and Tone', 30.

68 Robyn Warhol, *Having a Good Cry: Effeminate Feelings and Pop Cultural Forms* (Columbus: Ohio State University Press, 2003), 10.

69 Plantinga, *Moving Viewers*, 55–6. See also summary in 'The Affective Power of Movies', in Arthur P. Shimamura (ed.), *Psychocinematics: Exploring Cognition at the Movies* (Oxford: Oxford University Press, 2014). The relationship between emotion and cognition is much debated. For an argument for the large extent to which emotions are also generated at a more basic, pre-cognitive level, see Joseph Ledoux, *The Emotional Brain: The Mysterious Underpinnings of Emotional Life* (New York: Phoenix, 1999).

70 Plantinga, 'The Affective Power of Movies', 97.

71 Ibid., 101.

72 Ibid., 101. My added emphasis.

73 Pierre Bourdieu, *Distinction: A Social Critique of the Judgement of Taste* (London: Routledge, 1984). I have drawn upon this approach particularly in *Indiewood, USA: Where Hollywood Meets Independent Cinema* (London: I.B. Tauris, 2009) and *Positioning Art Cinema: Film and Cultural Value* (London: I.B. Tauris, 2018).

74 Berliner, *The Hollywood Aesthetic*, 20–1.

75 Grønstad, *Screening the Unwatchable*, 16.

76 Berliner, *The Hollywood Aesthetic*, 191.

77 Ibid., 29, emphasis in original. See also, among the studies cited by Berliner, Paul Silvia, 'What Is Interesting? Exploring the Appraisal Structure of Interest', *Emotion*, vol. 5, no. 1 (2005): 89–102 and Silvia, 'Artistic Training and Interest in Visual Art: Applying the Appraisal Model of Aesthetic Emotions', *Empirical Studies of the Arts*, vol. 24, no. 2 (2006): 139–61.

78 For example, King, *Positioning Art Cinema*, 36–9.

79 See for examples various contributions to Michael Bérubé (ed.), *The Aesthetics of Cultural Studies* (Oxford: Blackwell, 2005) and Alan McKee (ed.), *Beautiful Things in Popular Culture* (Oxford: Blackwell, 2007).

80 Berliner, *The Hollywood Aesthetic*, 27.

81 Ibid., 28.

82 For a summary of the traditional approach criticized by figures such as Raymond Williams and Bourdieu, along with arguments about the role of thought and discrimination in the potential pleasures of popular cultural forms, see Alan McKee, 'Conclusion', in McKee (ed.), *Beautiful Things in Popular Culture*.

83 Berliner, *Hollywood Aesthetic*, 26.

84 Ibid., 28. Miklós Kiss and Steven Willemsen, *Impossible Puzzle Films: A Cognitive Approach to Contemporary Complex Cinema* (Edinburgh: Edinburgh University Press, 2017).

85 Dominic Lash, *The Cinema of Disorientation: Inviting Confusions* (Edinburgh: Edinburgh University Press, 2020).

86 A judgement that, however, might often fail to appreciate dimensions of more popular cultural products with which they are less familiar, as argued by McKee.

87 For a psychological account of the basis of this dynamic, cited by Berliner, see Thomas Armstrong and Brian Detweiler-Bedell, 'Beauty as an Emotion: The Exhilarating Prospect of Mastering a Challenging World', *Review of General Psychology*, vol. 12, no. 4 (2008): 305–29.

88 For a useful discussion of these issues in relation to complex television, see Jason Mittell, *Complex TV: The Poetics of Contemporary Television Storytelling* (New York: New York University Press, 2015).

89 Hanich, 'Dis/liking Disgust'.

90 Vivian Sobchack, *The Address of the Eye: A Phenomenology of Film Experience* (Princeton, NJ: Princeton University Press, 1992).

91 Sobchack, *The Address of the Eye*, 289.

92 Ibid.

93 Pezeu-Massabuau, *A Philosophy of Discomfort*, 91.

94 Frederick Aldama and Herbert Lindenberger, *Aesthetics of Discomfort: Conversations on Disquieting Art* (Ann Arbor: University of Michigan Press, 2016), xiii.

95 Aldama and Lindenberger, *Aesthetics of Discomfort*, 1.

96 Ibid., xii.

97 Arnheim, *Art and Visual Perception*, 14, 302.

98 For one of many illustrations available online, see Tom Morris, 'Why Is Uncomfortable-Looking Furniture So Desirable?, *The Financial Times*, 2 December 2016, accessed at https://www.ft.com/content/332bd73c-b16c-11e6-9c37-5787335499a0. See also Cranz, *The Chair*.

99 Aldama and Lindenberger, *Aesthetics of Discomfort*, 7.

100 See Larry Shiner, *The Invention of Art* (Chicago, IL: University of Chicago Press, 2001).

101 Aldama and Lindenberger, *A Philosophy of Discomfort*, 58.

102 Ibid., 59.

103 Shiner, *The Invention of Comfort*, 149.

104 Ibid.

105 Ibid., 168.

106 Ibid., 292.

107 James Harold, 'Mixed Feelings: Conflicts in Emotional Responses to Film', in Peter French Howard Wettstein and Michelle Saint (eds), *Film and the Emotions, Midwest Studies in Philosophy*, vol. XXIV (2010): 293.

108 Miller, *Embarrassment*, 17.

109 Ibid., 151–2.

110 Geoff King, *Indie 2.0: Change and Continuity in Contemporary American Indie Film* (London: I.B. Tauris, 2014), 9–19.
111 An issue I address in *Positioning Art Cinema*.
112 Carl Plantinga, *Screen Stories: Emotion and the Ethics of Engagement* (Oxford: Oxford University Press, 2018).
113 A dozen were found with titles or subtitles of this kind. Only one used the term to suggest positive qualities.
114 Melissa Dahl, *Cringeworthy: How to Make the Most of Uncomfortable Situations* (London: Corgi, 2019).
115 Bordwell, *Narration in the Fiction Film*, 207.
116 For how this might work in the case of narrative-based cognitive challenges, see Kiss and Willemsen, *Possible Puzzle Films*, 130.
117 Adam Kotsko, *Awkwardness: An Essay* (Winchester: O-Books, 2010).
118 Jason Middleton, *Documentary's Awkward Turn: Cringe Comedy and Media Spectatorship* (London: Routledge, 2014).
119 Kotsko, *Awkwardness*, 6.
120 Middleton, *Documentary's Awkward Turn*, 1.
121 Ibid., 103.
122 Kotsko, *Awkwardness*, 17.
123 Ibid., 19.
124 Ibid., 24.
125 I address some of these issues with reference to various commentators on the balance between the qualities of irony and sincerity in this context in *Indie 2.0*, 55–62.
126 Claire Colebrook, *Irony* (London: Routledge, 2004).
127 Colebrook, *Irony*, 41.
128 Linda Hutcheon, *Irony's Edge: The Theory and Politics of Irony* (London: Routledge, 1994).
129 Kotsko, *Awkwardness*, 1.
130 Ibid., 48–66.
131 Ibid., 68.
132 Ibid., 88.
133 Dahl, *Cringeworthy*, 79–88.
134 Robin Diangelo, *White Fragility: Why It's So Hard for White People to Talk about Racism* (London: Penguin, 2018).
135 Amos Vogel, *Film as a Subversive Art* (originally published 1974, republished C.T. Editions, 2005).
136 Hanich, *Cinematic Emotion in Horror Films and Thrillers*, 25, 221–51.
137 For a useful overview, see David Harvey, *A Brief History of Neoliberalism* (Oxford: Oxford University Press, 2005).

138 Karl Marx and Friedrich Engels, *The Communist Manifesto* (Harmondsworth: Penguin edition, 1967), 83.
139 Zygmunt Bauman, *Liquid Times: Living in an Age of Uncertainty* (Cambridge: Polity, 2007), 1.
140 Zygmunt Bauman, *Liquid Modernity* (Cambridge: Polity, 2012), 56.
141 See, for example, Ulrich Beck, *World at Risk* (Cambridge: Polity, 2009).
142 See John Tulloch and Deborah Lupton, *Risk and Everyday Life* (London: Sage, 2003). For more on this understanding of risk-taking in contemporary society, see also John Tulloch and Belinda Middleweek, *Real Sex Films: The New Intimacy and Risk in Cinema* (Oxford: Oxford University Press, 2017). Tulloch and Middleweek argue that a range of films that feature 'real sex' sequences, among others, can be read as manifesting certain aspects of what is diagnosed as 'risk' society at the level of personal-intimate relations, drawing on sources including those by Giddens and by Beck and Beck-Gernsheim cited below.
143 See Philip Mirowski, *Never Let a Serious Crisis Go to Waste: How Neoliberalism Survived the Financial Meltdown* (London: Verso, 2014), 89–155, for an account of what he terms 'everyday neoliberalism of this kind'; specifically, on risk, 119–20.
144 Anthony Giddens, *The Transformation of Intimacy: Sexuality, Love and Eroticism in Modern Societies* (Cambridge: Polity, 1992), 8; emphasis in original.
145 Ulrich Beck and Elisabeth Beck-Gernsheim, *The Normal Chaos of Love* (Cambridge: Polity Press, 1995).
146 Furedi, *Therapy Culture*, 86–91.
147 For numerous arguments to this effect, see various contributions to Deidre O'Neill and Mike Wayne (eds.), *Considering Class: Theory, Culture and the Media in the 21st Century* (Boston: Brill, 2018).
148 See, for example, Richard Sennett, *The Culture of the New Capitalism* (New Haven, CT: Yale University Press, 2006).
149 Anthony Giddens, *Runaway World: How Globalization is Reshaping Our Lives* (New York: Routledge, 2003).
150 Tulloch and Lupton, *Risk in Everyday Life*.
151 Raymond Williams, 'Structures of Feeling', in *Marxism and Literature* (Oxford: Oxford University Press, 1977), 132.
152 Williams, 'Structures of Feeling', 132.
153 Ibid., 133.
154 Sconce, 'Irony, Nihilism', 352.
155 Pezeu-Massabuau, *A Philosophy of Discomfort*, 27.
156 Plantinga, *Moving Viewers*, 66.

2

'Uncomfortably great': Todd Solondz and *Palindromes*

Palindromes (2004) is, in many respects, a model example of the cinema of discomfort as defined in this book. A desire to examine the qualities it offers, and some of the responses it can provoke, was one of the starting points for this project. The cinema of discomfort is a label that could be given to the entire oeuvre of Todd Solondz, from his feature debut *Welcome to the Dollhouse* (1995) onwards, but it seems to apply particularly strongly in this case. The film offers numerous individual dimensions of discomfort, ranging from highly awkward sex scenes to a number of characters, sequences and/or scenarios that seem designed to make members of even the most likely target audience cringe with embarrassment. Beyond specific details, however, it seems to go further than usual, even for the work of a figure such as Solondz, in its refusal to allow any comfortable position of alignment for the viewer. This chapter begins with close analysis of how such dynamics operate across the film, with particular attention to the nature of the relationship encouraged between viewer and text. It then considers some viewer responses before examining the limited nature of the space available for such work within the contemporary American indie sector.

The film employs one central device that marks a distinctive status within the indie and art film sectors, the dimension for which it is probably best known. The principal character, Aviva, thirteen years old in the main portion of the narrative, is played by eight different performers of varying age, skin colour and build (one, appearing only briefly, is a teenage boy). At the start, we are introduced to a younger-girl version, pre-teenage and black (with no explanation offered for the fact that her parents turn out to be white). 'Some years later', as a title informs us, she is played by one of a series of performers who fit a white, young-teenage identity (old enough to become pregnant but below the age of consent), standing out from which is one who is older, black and of overweight build. Another incarnation of Aviva (the only widely recognizable performer, Jennifer Jason Leigh) is also clearly considerably older than the character is supposed to be. The shift of performers is a radical departure from convention, although exactly how it might best be interpreted is far from immediately clear. It offers a potential destabilization of character, or of the kind of character-performer bond expected in film fictions, including most works of art or indie cinema. This can be interpreted up to a point as a Brechtian type of alienation device, one that keeps reminding us of the constructed nature of the text.

A strong sense of emotional character-led narrative is sustained across these transitions, however, as we are led through the story of Aviva: impregnated by a young contemporary, Judah (Robert Agri); browbeaten by her parents into having an abortion against her wishes; leaving home as a result, her parents lying to cover up the fact that she is now sterile following complications that led to a hysterectomy; taking up with, but soon abandoned by, a truck driver, Earl (Stephen Adly Guigis), with whom she has anal sex; being taken in by a Christian fundamentalist religious extended family and its matriarch Mama Sunshine (Debra Monk); leaving them with Earl, who turns out to be involved in a plot to assassinate the doctor who carried out Aviva's abortion; helping Earl to kill the doctor and witnessing his consequent suicide-by-police; attending a party to mark her return home; and finally having another assignation with a now-older Judah (John Gemberling). The extent to which a strong impression of character survives the changes of performer can be taken as testament either to the potency of such figures, as conventional sources of narrative-based orientation for the viewer, and/or the commitment of the filmmaker to sustain this dimension despite the choice of so otherwise unconventional an approach.

If the use of multiple performers in the role of Aviva is a radical departure from the norms even of independent and art cinema (if by no means unprecedented[1]), it is not the most awkward or potentially discomforting feature of the film. *Palindromes* proceeds relatively conventionally, in character-led narrative terms, once the fact that such changes are going to occur has been established, even if they might cause confusion for viewers. Aviva remains a consistent character in terms of her central drives and motivations, across her various incarnations, a factor that balances the otherwise destabilizing nature of this shift from the norm. Within this framework, however, *Palindromes* offers a regular supply of uncomfortable material and a number of implicit challenges to the viewer. We can start with the awkward sex, highlighted particularly in two instances. First is the initial coupling of Aviva and Judah. The sequence is a classic, and quite straightforward, example of the awkward-coupling trope as identified by Sconce.[2]

Uncomfortable sex

Aviva and Judah both appear to be alienated from their parents. Not 'attractive' by stereotypical standards, they bond to a limited extent in

Judah's bedroom but in a manner filled with hesitancy and awkwardness, the more so as the sequence develops into sexual territory. Judah talks of his attempt to make a film, something 'totally original', complaining that no one has any faith. 'I know', agrees Aviva, in her small and hesitant voice, moving closer to kneel at his side, while his gaze remains averted. She seems to be seeking a connection at this point, with little reciprocation yet from Judah. A dissolve takes us to a shot of the pair leafing through a photo album that includes pictures of Judah as a small child. 'Too bad you had to grow up', comments Aviva. 'I know', says Judah, 'I was so happy then, and I didn't know it', an interchange during which a degree of connection seems established both ways.

Another dissolve takes us to a shot of the two, blankly facing a screen from which we hear the sounds of a pornographic video. Dissolve to the pair lying on his bed in silence in a mid-shot that is quite spatially confining and provides the principal framing for the awkwardness to follow; she on her back, he at this point on his side. Her head is turned rather awkwardly towards him while he looks only towards her body. Expressionless, he places a hand flatly and tentatively on her breast. 'Please take it off', she says, after a pause just long enough to increase the awkwardness quotient. He complies. She suggests they should get under the covers, which they do, as we are taken to a longer shot that reveals posters of semi-clad women on the wall behind them.

They lie down, side by side, each facing the ceiling with hands clasping the top of the bed covers, an image held in silence for a couple of beats. Cut to a closer mid-shot view of the pair, their faces now displaying apparent discomfort (his in particular) as each avoids looking in the direction of the other. His body posture is stiff and awkward, more so than hers. Aviva asks if he thinks about sex a lot, to which he replies 'I don't know … I guess.' She says she never thinks about it just about having a baby (thus establishing her agenda, introduced to the viewer in her previous incarnation). She says she wants one, to which he replies: 'OK then' and 'are you ready?' At this point she turns to face him and concurs. He says 'here goes' and they reach down under the covers to remove or adjust their lower garments. A cut is made to a closer shot from the side as he mounts her and proceeds to thrust a number of times, during which her expression remains blank.

The process seems entirely mechanical and joyless and is short-lived. Behind Judah's head we can see one of the pin-ups on his wall, the nude idealized body of which, and the promise of eroticism, provides an clear contrast with the figure of Aviva and the experience in general. A cut to the previous shot from above shows his highly discomforted expression and posture. He faces away from her with his arms folded across his body in a manner that suggests acute discomfort and embarrassment (Figure 2). A moment of silence is followed by her saying, with a pained expression, she thought he had done this before (clearly implying lack of competence on his part). 'I did', he claims, adding, rather too quickly to be convincing, 'You

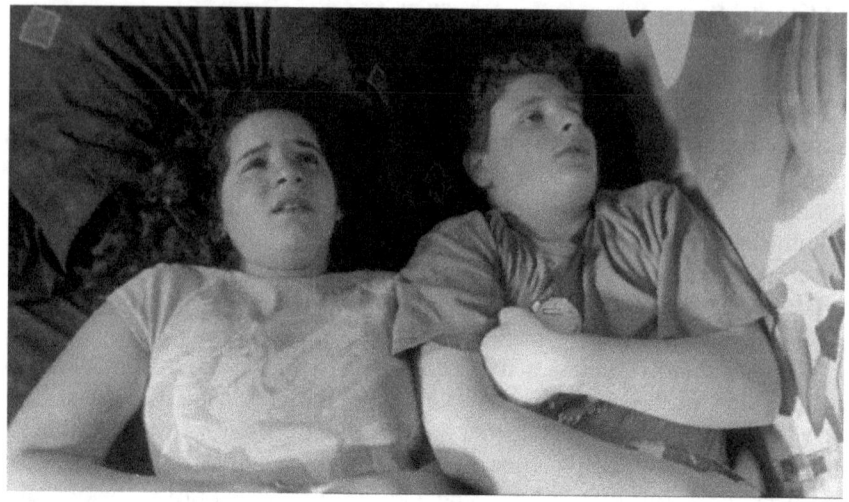

FIGURE 2 *Joyless sex: The discomfort of Aviva and Judah after their first encounter in* Palindromes *(2004).*

were supposed to move your hips more.' 'Huh', she says sceptically, turning to face him, eventually asking if he can try again, following comments that suggest he has so far failed to achieve insemination. 'I don't know', he says, after which the shot is held for a few beats longer before a dissolve to the film's next chapter-title heading and a cut to a new version of Aviva vomiting, which suggests the eventual success of the impregnation.

This sequence displays a number of key ingredients of the awkward sex routine. The couple are underage and their efforts fumbling and lacking any indication of pleasure. Their expressions and body postures are consistently uncomfortable, a dimension often emphasized through framing and via silence more than dialogue. There is just enough attempt to make some personal connection, at the start of the sequence, to make its overall lack seem all the more painful as the events proceed. The sequence seems clearly designed to make the viewer cringe in a vicarious manifestation of some of the discomfort experienced by the characters.

Certain general aspects of the awkward-sex trope might be familiar from the lighter context of the mainstream teen coming-of-age sex comedy, in examples such as *American Pie* (1999) or some of the Judd Apatow films cited by Kotsko, but there are also notable differences in these cases. *American Pie*, for example, includes sequences that are highly embarrassing for characters, and potentially also for viewers, including the main protagonist being caught masturbating by his parents and, most famously, being interrupted while attempting coitus with an apple pie. Some localized discomfort can be created by material of this kind, along with a number of 'gross out' effects offered by the film, but it is surrounded by other material that establishes a more clearly comic modality in which a certain proportion of cringe-inducing material is established as part of a pleasurable generic routine. The viewer is meant, generally, to laugh at such material when provided in this context, even if laughter might sometimes be mixed with a local quota of discomfort. Viewing context might also be an important factor, with such material likely to be more uncomfortable for a teenage viewer (the primary target market) watching with parental figures rather than peers, as suggested in the previous chapter. Overall, however, a number of factors add up to what is designed to offer a more comfortable effect, from general lightness of tone to factors such as the affirmative and sentimental narrative structure within which such incidents are situated.

Any laughter generated by the first sex sequence from *Palindromes* seems likely to be of the distinctly nervous and embarrassed variety identified as an expression of discomfort in Chapter 1. The viewing situation can again be a factor in how we might understand such responses, given its importance to potential experiences such as feelings of embarrassment (an emotion associated most strongly with the presence of witnesses, as suggested by Rowland Miller, even if it can also be experienced in vicarious, empathetic form). This material is capable of creating such a response even for the solitary viewer, however, as I can attest from my own experience of the film and that of others I have polled at an individual level, as well as the online viewer responses cited below. There is no sense here of providing sexual material of a kind likely to offer seductive/erotic pleasure to the viewer, even if any such quality were later to be undermined. The sounds of the porn video and the sight of the pin-ups on Judah's wall underline the difference between such fantasies and the painfully awkward, fumbling and largely incompetent reality suggested by the experience of the characters. This is not the kind of sexual feel-bad effect in which viewers are tempted along by the provision of what is initially designed to be erotic/salacious material that is only subsequently turned against them as a form of discomfort, often implying moral judgement, a feature of some uses of explicit material in art cinema.[3] The sequence is built around a sense of awkwardness and uncomfortable relationship from the start, consistently emphasizing such characteristics and lacking any conventional sources of potential erotic heightening, either in what is shown or the style employed.

The characters are presented as being uncomfortable themselves, physically and emotionally, and their experience seems designed to be uncomfortable to witness at close quarters. When Solondz holds certain shots, most notably the mid-shot above the characters on the bed, the effect is to imprison not just the characters but also the viewer, if relatively briefly. Viewers are confronted with a vicarious sense of the experience of character awkwardness, increasing the likelihood of a transfer of some degree of uncomfortable, embarrassed affect to the spectator. This is a variant of a formal approach found more widely in the cinema of discomfort, as discussed in Chapter 1. A widespread source of discomfort is provided by formal qualities such as blank distance and framing that leaves much of the interpretation to the viewer, as in Sconce's variety of smart cinema and as seen in some of the examples examined in subsequent chapters. In this and other sequences from *Palindromes*, the style is somewhat different, however, not relying on long-shot distance for its effect. We mostly see the characters in mid-range two shots, with their gazes usually elsewhere than at the other (looking at the photo album, the pornography screen, the ceiling). The style mixes relative proximity (only one longer shot) with a flat and deadpan approach that leaves an important dimension of emotional or other forms of processing to the viewer. No musical cueing, extra-diegetic or otherwise, is supplied to help steer the response, the level of discomfort only being increased in this instance by the incongruous background chatter of the couple's parents outside.

A rather different orchestration of uncomfortable experiences surrounds the second sex scene, involving Aviva and Earl. When Aviva stows away in the back of Earl's truck, the immediately following sequence offers a conventional-seeming impression of freedom and escape, in what appears to be a familiar American road-movie guise. Non-diegetic music plays an important role here, a gentle and plaintive female voice supplying narratively apt phrases such as 'take me please now help me please, get me please, far, far away'. This is accompanied by images of the truck crossing a highly elevated bridge over a river (and so suspended in a vast space) and further shots from high above the vehicle on the road. If the film here seems to evoke familiar road/escapist tropes, the mood is halted, deflatingly, by the silencing of the music and a cut to a head-on view of the two characters, framed either side of the strut that divides the truck's windscreen, each at first looking blankly ahead. We are left to imagine what happened in the ellipsis, when Aviva's presence in the truck became apparent. Aviva invites Earl to play a game, but his visage displays no reaction before a cut is made to the sign of the motel at which they will spend the night. The next sequence begins with a lavishly romantic Tchaikovsky piano concerto playing on the soundtrack. The image is dark, but we can make out Earl's body moving on top of Aviva, who remains motionless and apparently unresponsive. The action continues for some more seconds before we hear her voice, small and fragile, asking 'Can you still get pregnant ... when it goes in there', before the image brightens into a white-out transition to the next scene.

The effect here is markedly different from the treatment of the earlier sex sequence. The music adds a strong dimension of irony, in the incongruous mismatch between its richly romantic tones, and what they conventionally imply, and the decidedly unromantic nature of the physical encounter. A clear separation is made between the experience of the characters and that offered to the viewer, one that more explicitly invites a particular interpretation on the part of the latter. This is precisely the kind of distancing irony identified by Sconce as a key component of his notion of smart cinema. It can be understood, as Sconce suggests, as a strategy designed to mark a difference between the target audience of such films – those who 'get' the ironic point – and anyone, actual or imagined, who might not.[4] This process entails two key dimensions of cinematic irony identified by James MacDowell. One is dramatic irony, in which we are 'granted information or perspectives pointedly denied to one or more of the story's characters', a form that often applies to the treatment of the naïve Aviva.[5] The other is what MacDowell terms 'communicative' irony, in which a text creates such a juxtaposition between different perspectives by 'feigning to possess precisely the limited point of view that is being ironized'.[6] This would apply to the use of devices such as the brief adoption of the road-movie/escapist trope and the deployment of the Tchaikovsky during the sex sequence. In each case, the film employs a style that superficially implies a more straightforward adoption of a conventional romantic articulation than appears to be the intention. Ironic distance is also encouraged by the nature of Aviva's question to Earl: first, in indicating that the sex is anal, and potentially even less romantic than might possibly be implied; second, in displaying the naïveté of any uncertainty about such facts. Both kinds of irony are sustained in the following scene, although the character–viewer relationship encouraged here seems here to be complicated by other strategies.

A cut takes us to a shot of Aviva lying in bed, off-screen sounds indicating Earl's nearby presence in the bathroom on the following morning. Aviva talks in a manner that suggests the adoption of the blandishments of a standard romantic script that has no apparent relation to the reality. 'I had a good time last night. I mean I never knew it was so beautiful', she says, her face remaining largely blank. She adds, rather pathetically, 'do you think next time you could try coming inside me … I mean, the regular way?' 'Sure', he replies, after a brief pause, appearing in his usual discomforted state, before bustling outside without at any point appearing to look in Aviva's direction, saying he will meet her in the coffee shop. Cut to Aviva happy and smiling while taking a shower, to the accompaniment of jaunty music. We see her exiting the motel room from the outside, as the music continues, almost skipping along in happiness. The camera moves with her, quite speedily and a little unsteadily at times, sharing in both her movement and the evocation of her mood, and thus encouraging some degree of translation of this to the viewer. A closer shot has her moving towards the camera, smiling in pleasant anticipation (Figure 3). A cut is made as she turns towards the door of the diner building – only for both her and the camera to be brought up short, abruptly, by a 'closed' sign and the boarded up entrance, revealing that she has been tricked and abandoned. As the music recedes and Aviva turns away, we hear the throaty sound of a semi-distant truck departing. A blank-faced close-up of Aviva is followed by a high long shot that situates her forlorn figure in the drab margins of an empty car park.

FIGURE 3 *Camera movement accompanies Aviva's happy mood after the motel sex scene in* Palindromes *(2004)*.

Alignment, allegiance or ironic distance from character

Aviva's comments about her sexual experience with Earl sustain the previous heavy layer of irony. We seem strongly encouraged not to take these at face value but to see them as a somewhat desperate attempt on her part to maintain an affirmative romantic fiction in the face of the evidence provided by seedy reality. Viewers are thus urged to differentiate themselves from what appears to be the naïve world view of the character (or, potentially, that of any spectator, real or imagined, who might fail to get the irony). When it comes to Aviva's response to the prospect of joining Earl for breakfast, however, the cinematic articulation puts the viewer in a position much closer to hers. We are given a position of close *alignment*, in the terms in which these relationships are explored by Murray Smith. The film moves closer to an evocation of character experience and the irony to a communicative form. Terms such as alignment and allegiance, as Smith argues, are generally more useful for a close-grained analysis of the complex nature of film/viewer dynamics than broader and often oversimplified concepts such as identification.[7] They offer a useful way to articulate the sometimes complex range of positions encouraged by *Palindromes*.

In place of the often rather crude and vague notion of 'identification', Smith suggests a flexible and nuanced three-part 'structure of sympathy' that offers different levels of engagement between the viewer and fictional characters. The first of these, preceding alignment and allegiance, is the more basic level of *recognition* of a character, as 'an individuated and continuous human agent' within a narrative.[8] This is a base level dimension, usually entirely unproblematic in films made within both the broadly classical and the arthouse traditions but challenged in *Palindromes* through the use of multiple performers in the central role. Recognition, as Smith puts it, usually depends on 'a legible and consistent representation of the human face and body, a fact which becomes clearer in those films which refuse to follow this practice'.[9] A number of factors still encourage us to recognize a single character across the changes of performer in *Palindromes*, however. These include the continuance of the basic narrative arc, in which she is involved from one embodiment to the next, and her basic attitudes, along with the establishment of some specific consistencies in the clothing worn by the various incarnations of Aviva. Narrative progression from one manifestation to another is in some cases a little elliptical but clear enough (for example, the cut from Aviva and Judah's sexual exploits to Aviva vomiting as a result of what quickly turns out to be her pregnancy) but sometimes more direct (the version of Aviva who takes off on her own after being abandoned by Earl floats down a river on a toy boat, while another is found on the bank of what is presumably the same waterway the following morning). Most of the incarnations of Aviva are clothed similarly, in crop tops and jeans. What is probably the most jolting performer transformation in the main narrative, from one of the slim white girls to the large-bodied black woman at the waterside (Sharon Wilkins), is bridged by the fact that they wear identical-seeming outfits. This is a clear encouragement to the viewer to interpret a continuity of character across the change of performer.

The second dimension identified by Smith, alignment with character, has two interlocking dimensions. The first is 'spatio-temporal attachment' to character.[10] This can vary from a general sense of following the experiences of a major protagonist throughout a film – a position created in relation to Aviva by *Palindromes*, if recognition is maintained – to a closer engagement in any specific moments that might be created through particular formal means. Close spatio-temporal attachment can contribute to the establishment of Smith's second dimension of alignment, the creation of 'subjective access' to character. While the former provides access to the actions of characters, the latter suggests 'what they know and feel'.[11] It is this that is often denied or attenuated by the use of blank style. *Allegiance*, in Smith's account, is a quality that comes from the viewer's response to what is presented, centrally involving a process of moral evaluation and judgement of character. Alignment, in this scheme, often contributes to the creation of allegiance but this is not necessarily the case. We can be given positions of alignment, spatio-temporally and/or subjectively, with characters of whom we do not approve, at all or entirely. As Smith suggests, such judgements may be relative rather than absolute, a question sometimes of evaluation of certain characters in comparison with others rather than in unequivocal terms. We might expect the complexity of the judgements on offer to increase in examples from the art or indie film sectors. This can be a key component of their more generally complex or challenging status.

If a broad sense of spatio-temporal attachment to Aviva is created across the film, simply by the process of following her experiences across the running time (assuming, again, that recognition is achieved in this case), the morning-after sequence at the motel offers an example of closer attachment that also contributes strongly to the evocation of subjective access. While we do not experience in any specifics whatever internal mindset or emotion might have led Aviva to conclude that sex with Earl was 'beautiful', apart from a general sense of her naïveté, we are given subjectively expressive access to her high spirits during this interlude. This is achieved especially through the music – conventionally expressing character emotion, here upbeat – and visuals that also seem to echo her mood: a pair of jump cuts during the shower, maybe signifying eager impatience, and particularly the way the camera moves speedily with Aviva on the way to the diner.

Our orientation is here aligned in a more specific and close sense with that of Aviva than is the case in many other parts of the film. An impression of subjective access is created visually, not through a literal point-of-view perspective but by the camera moving broadly in synch with her to the point of contributing to the expression of her mood. The cinematic norm for creating alignment generally is to employ positions close to those of characters rather than via optical point of view (one notable instance of the latter is the blurry imagery and distorted sounds used to convey a sense of Aviva's perspective as she awakens from her abortion and surgery, although the effect here is not an entirely or literally subjective one, as the viewer is given more information about the consequences of the treatment than ever seems to be known by the character). Close subjective alignment seems in this part of *Palindromes* designed to create at least some degree of empathy with Aviva. We seem encouraged to share her positive expectations to some degree, in this moment, even if this might fall well short of the moral approval entailed by allegiance as defined by Smith. We are probably unlikely to expect all to be gloriously romantic at breakfast, given what has gone before, but we might at least anticipate Earl still being on the premises. The abruptness of the revelation that the diner was never open, and therefore that Earl was probably being flagrantly dishonest rather than having decided to leave in a more opportunistic manner, appears designed to be experienced by the viewer as well as the character, although a clear separation of positions is then enacted in the cut to the high overhead angle.

The effect in this sequence is similar to the mobilization of the 'road/escape' trope examined above. In both cases, the viewer is offered an experience of being carried along, briefly, with the more positive feelings of the protagonist, through the process of subjective alignment. Music plays a crucial role in both cases, as it does on numerous other occasions during the film, in establishing a mood that seems to come broadly from the perspective of Aviva (the principal other manifestations of this are the employment of a soft lullaby theme that expresses her childlike naïveté). The experience of subjective alignment increases the sense of deflating let-down that follows: first, by the awkward realities of the two characters juxtaposed in the cab of the truck; second, and more strongly, by an abrupt realization of betrayal and abandonment by Earl. The viewer might also become to some extent inoculated against the effect of such positive interludes, however, once a pattern of disappointment is established as a recurrent strategy; or as a result of broader expectations created by either the film up to this point, the previous work of Solondz or this kind of indie film more generally.

That *Palindromes* at times offers a position of mainstream-conventional alignment with character, rather than exclusively remaining more ironically/critically distant, is a measure of the blending of its overall strategies more generally. The adoption of a more conventional form of articulation in moments such as these gives the film potential to draw viewers into greater proximity with character emotion than might otherwise be expected in such a work. Rather than simply viewing her from the superior position of ironic distance, as often seems encouraged, such material invites us to share more closely, at least for certain moments, some aspects of Aviva's emotional experience. To mix this and a more clearly distanced approach is probably to enhance the impact of the latter, the distance involved being measured out and itself experienced in the shift from one register to the other. The approach of the film might also be consonant here with Linda Hutcheon's suggestion that the production and interpretation of irony can generally be a complex and multifaceted business, with a range of possibilities at the level of the nature of any ironic intent – critical, distanced, or more affectionate, for example – and in the degree to which it is attributed in reception.

Degrees of sympathy

This leads us more generally to the question of how viewers are likely to be aligned or experience allegiance, or otherwise, with various characters in *Palindromes*. Beyond its various incarnations of Aviva, the film offers a number of characters with whom the viewer seems encouraged to have uncomfortable or mixed relationships, an issue that goes to the heart of some of its most distinctive features as a product situated at the more challenging end of the indie spectrum. A key issue here is the degree of sympathy we are encouraged to feel for various characters, including the dimension of moral approval central to Smith's concept of allegiance. If the film offers a cognitive challenge in its early stages – as a result of the initial shifts of central performer – it can also offer challenge at the moral and emotional levels, in terms of how much of exactly whose feelings and perspectives we might be inclined to share. As Plantinga suggests, the elicitation of emotion by narratives involves not just feelings but also ways of thinking and valuing. The emotional dimension is, thus, inseparable from the ethical and the ideological.[12]

Any consideration of this question raises issues relating to whatever assumptions we might make about the primary or most likely target audience for a film of this type. My working assumption is that this would involve the kind of constituencies usually associated with the art or indie film sectors in general, chiefly comprised by certain groups of middle- to upper-middle class, often higher-educated urban viewers with moral and sociopolitical leanings of a broadly liberal nature.[13] We might expect such viewers morally and emotionally to distance themselves from the world embodied by Mama Sunshine and her extended family, the ardent sunny religious optimism of which might be considered to range between the mildly grating and the full-scale cringe-inducing (particularly during their song-and-dance routines). A world of difference exists between their outlook and the more ironic or otherwise critical perspectives associated with some products of the indie or art film sectors, or a broader notion of the 'cool', 'hip' or ironic dimension of indie culture.

A key marker of difference is the brand of naïve sincerity embodied by the figuration of certain aspects of the Sunshine community, a ground against which a more sophisticated indie 'knowingness' might readily be established or reconfirmed as a distinction-marking strategy. A more clear cut opposite of that which is associated with 'cool' indie culture would be difficult to imagine. If a certain form of ironic distance has sometimes been viewed by critics as an emotionally defensive cultural formation, such ardent sincerity as found here might be embarrassing to an indie constituency, or some of its members, in its vulnerable and unabashed openness of expression and the religious fundamentalist discourse within which it is situated.[14] None of what the Sunshine children say is delivered within defensively ironic quotation marks issuing from the characters themselves, even if some of the material might encourage an ironic mode of consumption. *Palindromes* can be situated within the framework of quirkiness explored in several essays by James MacDowell.[15] For MacDowell, the quirky quality associated with a particular range of indie films is a product of the line they tread between ironic detachment and the offering of sincere emotional engagement. As I have suggested elsewhere, one measure of the relative degree of commercial/mainstream or alternative status achieved by indie films, or the 'Indiewood' productions of studio speciality divisions, can be the relative balance they offer between these qualities.[16] Works nearer the mainstream end of the scale are more likely to combine any irony with larger components of sincere emotional engagement, often increasingly so as the narrative develops. More persistent ironic distancing is often likely to be a marker of stronger indie or art film status, with a range of possibilities available in between (other varieties of art or indie film exhibit a strongly sincere modality, however, including many that work within neorealist traditions).

Palindromes seems to complicate this schema, to some extent, creating discomfort through the very process of combining approaches rather than specifically through consistently favouring one (irony) over the other (an offer of sympathetic engagement). If a key dimension of the quirky for MacDowell is an element of childlike naïveté, the variety of this quality offered by *Palindromes* seems more awkward and unsettling than what is usually connoted by the indie-quirky. 'Quirky' generally suggests something lighter and less discomforting, rooted often in a relatively gentle comedy of incongruity rather than the stronger disjunctions that characterize Solondz's film. The blank-faced and often pitiful Aviva has none of the endearing characteristics associated with the eponymous protagonists of considerably more crowd-pleasing examples such as *Napoleon Dynamite* (2004) or *Juno* (2007), for example, even if manifestations of the quirky can include their own sources and degrees of awkwardness.[17] The naïve tone struck by Aviva, and by the film as a whole when offering subjective access to her world view, offers a discomfort that seems to extend beyond the realm of what is usefully encompassed by the notion of the quirky, even if it displays shifts of tone of a kind similar in some ways to those explored by MacDowell. In this case, tonal uncertainty seems generally to be strong, with potential for the discomfort or disorientation suggested by Pye.

If some indie films have been criticized for being seen to pander to certain notions of 'cool' hipsterdom (in dimensions such as narrative, character, general attitude and music), *Palindromes* seems to invoke such a cultural realm primarily through the representation of its opposite.[18] A cool/hip viewing position is implicit to some extent, as a component of the broader indie film culture within which the work is most likely to circulate, but viewer discomfort might be cued by a number of ways in which the film shifts between a more or less distanced orientation towards the naïve outlooks of figures such as Aviva or the Sunshine children. Liberal/indie-oriented viewer antipathy might also be fuelled more directly by material such as the explicitly anti-abortion lyrics of one of Sunshine group's songs. The particular nature of this community is very loaded, given the prominence of the Christian evangelical right as one of the poles in the broader 'culture wars' from the 1990s onwards against which qualities such as liberalism, relativism and ironic distance are often rhetorically pitched. It is here that the sociocultural dimension of the film can be situated within the context elaborated by commentators such as Sconce and Kotsko, or broader considerations of the state of a late modernity in which oscillations occur between the undermining of traditions and their fundamentalist reassertion. There is, in this case, a specific point of political reference, although one of the central sources of potential discomfort results from the far from straightforward manner in which it is handled. It remains possible, of course, for a film such as this to be consumed by viewers with orientations very different from those associated with liberal, urban bohemia – or more subtle gradations of difference – in which case their responses might also vary considerably. Some outright rejections of the film found in the sample considered below might fall into this category.

Plenty of comic irony can be found in this segment of the film, a key basis on which to establish or reinforce likely target audience distance from the Sunshine characters. When Aviva is being welcomed to the family, for example, one of the children questions her revelation that she was never taught to cook. Not even with a microwave, she is asked, to which Aviva responds: 'My mum didn't believe in microwaves. She was organic.' The latter is expressed in a tone that suggests it was something bad and of which to be ashamed. This is a clear reversal of the positive interpretation more likely to be made by an indie-oriented constituency, on the implicit grounds of the moral superiority (from what remains a class-based position) of organic food over what is implied by cooking via microwave, and thus an invitation to an ironic mode of consumption by suitably oriented viewers. Further irony is implied in the manner in which some of the children trot out their life histories, including the various pat religious expressions with which these are larded. The impression is, again, that these are meant to be viewed critically rather than taken at face value. They sound like a rote-learned routine, to be morally disapproved even if the individual characters might not be blamed for this, rather than the substance of a more individually inhabited belief structure. There are occasional moments of potentially laugh-aloud comedy. One comes in an anecdote told by Mama Sunshine when she fears that Aviva might leave the group. She refers to another child, their 'special daughter', who 'ran away' the previous year, 'and … she didn't even have … any legs'. Sunshine's voice breaks here, in what is presented as genuine upset at the memory, combined with what appears to be obliviousness to the comic potential of the concept of someone running away without having any legs (and of the deadpan manner in which the reference to the absence of legs is left hanging at the end).

This is another moment in which the film seems to articulate a multilayered dynamic. The joke, presumably unintended by the character, seems to invite critical distance on the part of the viewer. This might be expected, for a typical indie constituency, given their likely moral attitude towards one of the leaders of a socially reactionary fundamentalist community; the more so when we discover that her husband and their doctor friend are involved in a conspiracy to murder physicians who carry out abortions (how much she knows about this is not made clear). At the same time, however, Mama Sunshine is expressing what is presented as real and heartfelt emotion and is positioned as a source of genuinely good works. Whatever any religiously sceptical viewer might make of the Sunshine community, including what appears to be the indoctrination of the children into a conservative world view, no clear grounds are provided for any doubt as to the morally approvable nature of her commitment to the variously damaged youngsters for whom she has provided a stable home within this fictional universe. One of the higher-level ironies of the film is that she is probably its most positively coded character in this sense. The Sunshine children are also presented as being individually pleasant, sincere and well-meaning, qualities not conspicuously undercut in themselves, even for viewers (among which I would include myself) for whom they constitute overly 'straight' cringeworthy material.

An archetypal indie-oriented audience is obliged to spend more time than might be comfortable in the company of these characters, including witnessing the performance of their distinctly 'uncool' Bible-bashing musical numbers. Some ground is given for marking ironic – that is, superior – distance from this world, but what makes *Palindromes* relatively distinctive within the indie realm is that this is not the only, or even necessarily the dominant, note struck during this part of the film. No noticeable irony is suggested, for example in the presentation of the ardently delivered musical numbers, shot in a standard mixture of long, medium and closer perspectives (Figure 4). As far as we can tell, Mama Sunshine is separated out from the harder-line attitude expressed by her husband Bo (Walter Bobbie) and Dr. Dan (Richard Riehle). The latter are exposed as more clearly suitable objects for dislike and moral disapproval, from what remains a particular sociopolitical position, when we join Aviva in overhearing their comments about her, which follow the revelation of

FIGURE 4 *Distinctly 'uncool' Christian religious song and dance played straight in* Palindromes *(2004).*

the plot in which Earl is to murder Dr. Fleischer (Stephen Singer). Having examined Aviva while she was unconscious after arrival at the Sunshines, Dan describes her as a 'child whore'. Bo declares, coldly, that he never had a 'slut' in his house before, indicating no sympathy or likelihood that she would have been allowed to stay if she had not run away later that night. Earl, for his part, questions this verdict, saying 'maybe she's not a slut,' indicating a relatively more positive potential to his character.

The shifts between ironic and more sincere registers give *Palindromes* an element in common with the strand of American eccentric cinema identified by Kim Wilkins, although the overall balance is different. Like Claire Perkins, Wilkins interprets such films within the context of responses to the conditions created by a state of neoliberal individualism. The American eccentric mode, for Wilkins, is one in which existential anxieties created by 'unanchored cultural belonging' – a condition of the type examined in relation to the work of various commentators in the previous chapter – are given expression through being mixed with sources of irony and reflexivity.[19] Distancing forms such as irony and self-consciously fabricated dialogue and settings are employed, Wilkins suggests, to create a safe space for the expression of sincerely felt anxieties, allowing the latter to be both articulated and masked or deferred. This seems to fit to a certain extent with some of the aspects of *Palindromes* examined above. In watching a sequence such as that containing Mama Sunshine's comments about the girl with no legs, the viewer can maintain a sense of ironic distance while also appreciating the sincere emotions and anxieties that are being expressed; and the former might create a space for the latter, which might otherwise be more uncomfortably exposing.

In the films highlighted by Wilkins, one key exemplar of which is the work of Wes Anderson, the blending of the ironic and the sincere appears to function as a way of reducing (if not entirely removing) the level of discomfort that might be generated by a recognition of contemporary existential anxieties. Blatantly artificial, reflexive and meta-cinematic dialogue and settings put limits on the impact of what is presented, while still allowing bounded scope for sincere expression. Such devices 'explicitly tell the viewer that what they are watching is not real, and thereby create a space for the spectator in which it is safe to engage with the thematic content of the film during screen-time, precisely because of her awareness that the film will end'[20] (the latter is a point that might be made of fictional narrative more generally, however). One element of the 'blatantly artificial' is also clearly found in *Palindromes*, in the changing of the performer in the central role, although in general the balance offered by the film seems rather different from that attributed to the eccentric mode. As suggested above, the ironic and the sincere seem to clash in this case more than to operate in balance or for the former generally to create a more comfortable space for the latter.

Complexity of character engagement

A key factor in how we interpret the overall stance of the film is what we are supposed to make of Aviva's parents, especially her mother – as an implicit rival to Mama Sunshine – who plays the lead role in pushing Aviva into having the abortion that results in the destruction of her ability ever to achieve her desire to bear children. Solondz seems again to toy with the kinds of perspectives that might generally be expected to be favoured in work from the indie sector. We might expect a liberal pro-abortion position to be treated more positively than that of those who either campaign against abortion generally or conduct terrorist attacks on those involved in the process. In another prickly indie treatment of abortion, *Citizen Ruth* (1996), the title character is positioned as a 'difficult' maverick individual pitched against organized camps on both side of the debate, but it is unsurprising that the anti-abortion lobby is in this case presented the more negatively of the two.

What then should we make of the presentation of the mother, Joyce Victor (Ellen Barkin)? At first, her arguments against keeping the baby are made quietly and reasonably, along the lines that Aviva should not allow her life to be ruined. A moment of comedy intrudes, when Joyce at one point mistakes Aviva's comments for an indication of lesbianism, but this enables the former to display her liberal credentials, saying she will accept her daughter whatever she is. This suggests an initial position we might expect morally to be approved by a characteristic indie constituency. Gradually, though, her tone turns harsher and she ends up describing the baby as a 'tumour' and telling Aviva she will have to leave home if she has the baby, none of which seems either liberal or laudable. The father, Steve Victor (Richard Masur), also starts gently, when Aviva locks herself in her bedroom, but a façade of niceness also seems to crack when he ends up violently trying to force the door. Joyce shifts into a rather insidiously more subtle argument at one point, saying she had an abortion years earlier after becoming pregnant during a difficult financial time, when Aviva was young. It is only because of that decision, she says, rather meanly, and thus another ground for moral disapproval, that Aviva was able to have various extras in her life.

Later, after Aviva's return from her odyssey, Joyce talks about how hard she tried to be a good mother and how she will attempt to change. This might be viewed as a laudable element of self-awareness, but it could also come across as somewhat self-serving. Joyce, then, is not a very positive representative of the liberal values that might be expected to be set in opposition to the world of Sunshine fundamentalism. She does not actually support 'pro-choice' in any literal sense, in relation to abortion, given how little effective option she leaves to her daughter. She is not a very comfortable source of allegiance for the likely target audience. But neither does the film present her entirely negatively, giving considerable space for the expression of her emotions, generally without any overt encouragement of ironic-critical distance. Solondz follows general classical convention in moving into closer shots for the sequences in which the emotional stakes are raised, including those in which Joyce tries to talk Aviva into having an abortion and when she later says she had tried to be a good mother. In both cases, more time is devoted to close, head-and-shoulders shots of Joyce than to Aviva, giving intimate access to the character as she expresses her views and feelings. The staging is such that her face is oriented towards that of her daughter, also visible at the edge of the frame, but at the same time opened outwards in the direction of the viewer.

This is the kind of framing likely to maximize potential for what Plantinga terms 'emotional contagion' from character to viewer in 'scenes of empathy, in which the face of a favoured character is dwelt upon for some length in a close up.'[21] If Joyce is not an entirely favoured character, the use of a device associated with such figures is another example of the way the film complicates the use of such conventions. A cut is made to a medium-long two shot of the characters at the point where Joyce asks if Aviva is a lesbian, which might indicate an interlude of ironic withdrawal (the viewer is encouraged not to share her misapprehension on this point), but this is followed by a return to further close shots. The latter are sustained as the conversation continues, although a move is made out to a two shot as the argument gains a harsher edge (including Joyce's use of the word 'tumour'). When Joyce voices her final word (that it is a choice of having the abortion or leaving home and that an appointment has already been booked), she is standing in mid-shot, the two having parted. The viewer is placed at a greater distance when Joyce becomes more adamant, but this remains consistent with the norms of a more general classical style that modulates according to the emotional temperature of the exchange.

One of the basic values often attributed to art and indie films, or some critically favoured films from the commercial mainstream, lies in the presentation of complex, ambiguous or conflicted characters such as these. The very fact of awkwardness and complexity in dimensions of this kind can provide strong grounds for distinction-marking approval. On balance, *Palindromes* seems to paint Mama Sunshine some degrees relatively more positively than Joyce, which can be seen as a deliberate attempt to complicate what might more usually be expected in an indie production. A similar visual style to that used in the closely shot sequences involving Joyce and Aviva is found in material of equivalent valence between the latter and Mama Sunshine, again offering close access to the emotive expressions of the maternal figure, whatever reservations any viewers might have about the character or the group to which she belongs. The scene in which Mama Sunshine expresses her anxiety about the possibility of Aviva leaving is perhaps notable for including no cut back to a greater distance at the

FIGURE 5 *Genuine close-up emotion on the part of Mama Sunshine accompanies the story about the girl who ran away ... with no legs in* Palindromes *(2004)*.

moment of unintentional humour relating to the girl with no legs. The close shot is held, as she becomes tearful, the viewer being offered simultaneously both the close emotional proximity created by Mama Sunshine's reaction and the ironic distance implied by the humour (Figure 5). This sequence also ends with a longer shot, of the two embracing, but marked as a way of leading out of the scene rather than establishing emotional distance from the characters.

If we ask who else is represented at all positively in the film, as a potential source of any degree of allegiance, we might also partly have to include Earl, despite his status as a haplessly unappealing statutory rapist and murderer. The film creates the impression that some real heart comes to exist in the relationship between Earl and Aviva, amid whatever naïve or exploitative dimensions are involved. This comes out particularly in their last moments, after the murders (Earl shoots both the doctor and, accidentally, his young daughter), where he is wracked with remorse. Earl declares a pitiful desire to start again and live a good life, making no mistakes this time, but says he wants to die. 'How many more times can I be born again?' he wails, a line that conjures up an entire lifetime of inadequacy and despair, one that invites some sense of sympathy for his plight. Earl and Aviva are held in a medium two shot during this sequence that emphasizes the bond that has developed between the two (closer-shot access is provided to both Earl and Aviva in an earlier dialogue sequence in a diner).

Both Joyce and Earl declare a desire to change themselves, an issue raised more generally in what seems a clear statement of position on behalf of the film and/or the writer-director himself. At the party that marks her return home, Aviva makes a point of talking to her shunned cousin, Mark Wiener (Mathew Faber), who has been accused of child abuse. Mark gives a speech in which he suggests nobody ever changes, that we all remain as we are and that there is no such thing as free will. We are all robots, he declares, programmed arbitrarily by nature's genetic code. All there is, he says, are genes and randomness. Asked if he is going to get married and have children, he replies that he has no idea and no control and that it does not really matter given the dismal environmental prospects of the planet.

Mark's speech amounts to a denial of key American and/or Hollywood-narrative tenets, in its refusal to accept the possibility of transformative change or individual freedom. He appears to be a spokesman for the filmmaker, all the more so given that when he was seen earlier in the narrative, giving Aviva a lift before her meeting with Earl, it was Mark who spelled out the link between her name – a palindrome – and the title of the film. A palindrome, he says, stays the same whether spelled backward or forward; it 'never changes' and thus seems an encapsulation of his broader philosophy. If this is embodied in the title, it might seem reasonable to interpret Mark's as the vision of the film itself. It also the case that the experiences and attitudes of Aviva, across her various incarnations, seem to confirm the argument against character change. Added to this might be the fact that the performer – presented as somewhat 'nerdy', narrow-faced, with glasses – bears more than the slightest resemblance to Solondz (Figure 6). His generally intellectualized attitude might also seem akin to that associated with certain kinds of indie film.

FIGURE 6 *Spokesman for the filmmaker? Mark's speech about the impossibility of change in* Palindromes *(2004)*.

Even here, however, the filmmaker seems to pull the rug at least partly from under the viewer who might make such an interpretation or find this speech potentially something of a relief, as a direct statement of a thesis that helps to explain the basis of a challenging work. Mark tells Aviva he is not a paedophile. She says she believes him, adding, flatly, 'because paedophiles love children'. This is a rather destabilizing barb. Mark cannot be a paedophile, according to this reading, because he lacks the dimension of human emotion required to be even so reviled a figure. He is presented, that is, as worse than a paedophile, on this score, a judgement with potential to undermine any clear cut basis of character morality. He is *not* something nobody would want to be accused of, but the basis for this conclusion is another lack, which makes this an uncomfortably paradoxical double negative. This is a return to a territory also treated in a discomforting manner by Solondz in *Happiness* (1998), in which one of the characters is a paedophile who is not demonized in any conventional manner and in some of whose efforts the viewer is formally encouraged into uncomfortable moments of alignment.[22] If films generally offer cues to viewers as part of an 'on-going process of moral orientation', as Smith puts it, *Palindromes* seems often to encourage moral *dis*orientation, a major source of its production of potential discomfort.[23]

We might have expected Aviva and Mark to bond at this point, as two figures each alienated from their suburban world, but any such comfortable alliance is avoided. Something similar happens between the main protagonist and another rejected outsider figure in *Welcome to the Dollhouse* and can be seen as another marker of indie distinction from more comforting mainstream narrative norms. In the final sequence, Aviva meets and again has sex with Judah, a figure also caught up in the discourse of change, although his claims to have 'matured' do not seem very convincing and little appears to have altered in the limited competence of their sexual encounter. The impression that not much has changed, and the explicit thematic reference to such a situation in Mark's speech, locates *Palindromes* within the strand of indie film examined by Perkins, as cited in the Introduction; although without, in this case, anything to suggest the achievement of even a 'measure' of enlightenment. The film ends with Aviva shifting back to her youngest guise and declaring 'I'm going to be a mum!', an unsettling maintenance of naïve delusion, all the more so for being voiced by so juvenile a performer, the awkwardness of which is hardly alleviated by being followed by an end-title religious song from the Sunshines. The use of this music can be taken as ironic, as can be seen in the closing themes employed in some other indie films (examples such as *Blood Simple* [1984] and *The Evil Dead* [1981], each of which uses end-title music that seems strikingly incongruous with the tone of what has gone before), but it remains noteworthy to give this voice so prominent a place at the end.

Such strategies seem characteristic of the overall level of discomfort offered by the film, the status of which, as a particular variety of indie production, seems largely a product of the types and degrees of engagement offered to the viewer. In the terms employed in another work by Murray Smith, *Palindromes* can be seen as creating a distinctive 'field' of emotion – a combination of that which is offered by the text and the manner in which this might be taken up by viewers – the complexity of which is a marker of difference from more straightforward narrative treatments of familiar paradigm scenarios.[24] The emotional field is one major dimension within which the particular qualities of art or indie cinema are often grounded, as suggested in the Introduction and Chapter 1, an arena of particular importance to the constitution of qualities such as comfort or discomfort.

We are offered varying degrees of sympathy for some characters in *Palindromes*, and some moments of significant subjective alignment with the figure(s) of Aviva, the latter as would be expected for any main protagonist and a quality that survives the periodic changes of performer. Aviva remains the character with whom we are most closely aligned because of the basic fact that it is through her presence that all the events of the narrative are focalized. Whether we are likely to feel the stronger sense of allegiance suggested by Smith's notion of moral approval for Aviva seems much less clear. We might be asked morally to approve her attempt to escape her family after the abortion, to some extent, or a more general sense of 'escape' and 'freedom', as familiar American ideological tropes, although these are short lived and undermined. But it is notable that the manner in which we are offered subjective alignment is generally one that also underlines her naïveté and is combined on some occasions with strong markers of ironic distance. Something akin to a programmatic message, with its own moral stance, seems explicit in Mark's speech, but the ground is also pulled partly from under this – and it is notable that this is done in emotional terms, from the character with whom we have the greatest emotional proximity, which seems to increase its potential to undercut his position. Yet, at the same time, devices that encourage considerable ironic distance from the position of Aviva continue, up to the final moment. We end with a denial of any clear cut or more conventional position of sustained character alignment or allegiance. This can be seen as a marker of a modernist form of distance to some extent, but *Palindromes* does not offer this modality as a consistent or one-dimensional approach. It shifts, instead, between more and less critically ironically distancing modalities, as if seeking to wrong-foot the viewer, even (or especially) those coming to the film with a clearly established indie-cultural orientation.

Plantinga offers a typology of five varieties of viewer alignment with the concerns and understandings of characters, starting with a mode of 'congruence', in which the two are broadly matched. Of the other options, *Palindromes* seems to combine two: 'mixed, ambiguous, and conflicted congruence', which quite readily encompasses the various and sometimes shifting relative degrees of alignment offered with all the major characters

(Aviva, Joyce, Mama Sunshine, Earl), and 'distanced and/or ironic observation', a mode into which the film moves at some moments but far from entirely.[25] The degree to which the film employs some conventional structures of engagement, across a range of awkward characters, makes all the more challenging the nature of its departures. Rather than being entirely distanced, a position that might be uncomfortable but less emotionally implicating, viewers are likely to be left unsure exactly in whom, or how much, to invest their feelings.

Elsewhere, Plantinga suggests another chart of varying stances offered towards fictional characters that seeks further to nuance the territory that exists between stronger poles such as antipathy and allegiance. This ranges from 'dislike' to 'neutral interest', 'liking' and 'sympathy'.[26] Sympathy, as defined here, involves a sense of care and concern for characters who suffer or are treated unfairly, but without necessarily involving any personal liking (elicited by qualities such as attractiveness, similarity or affiliation) or requiring the moral approval central to Smith's concept of allegiance. This would appear to be the most likely orientation encouraged towards Aviva in much of the film, one that permits movements between mixed and more distanced engagement.

The uncomfortably ambiguous stance offered by the film is the kind of quality generally associated most often with the art or indie film sectors, although this is not exclusively the case. Some similar complexities of tone or modality have been identified in Hollywood examples, although this usually involves works that have been privileged by critics as more 'sophisticated' than is considered to be the mainstream norm. Douglas Pye finds a complexity of overall orientation to characters and events in some instances of studio melodrama, for example, his main case study being *Some Came Running* (1958), directed by Vincente Minnelli. He also draws upon the work of Bruce Babbington and Peter Evans in relation to the films of Douglas Sirk, the figure most often cited for the use of critical irony within the genre. Babbington and Evens offer the term 'critical pathos' to describe what they see as a mixture of empathy and detachment found in such films, a phrase that captures a sense of the combination of feeling and ironic distance also found in relation to some of the characters of *Palindromes*, although in a rather different overall register.[27]

As Plantinga suggests, ironic distance is often seen from an evaluative perspective as a more critical and therefore more sophisticated approach than that which encourages sympathetic engagement. This is a point made more generally by Colebrook in relation to the wider tradition in which irony has been embraced as an elitist marker of quality by literary critics.[28] This remains the case, despite the point made by Hutcheon that irony is best seen, more analytically, as marking *differences* at the level of discursive communities rather than relations of superiority/inferiority.[29] Plantinga suggests that irony can have problems of its own, from an evaluative point of view. Distance and detachment discourage emotional involvement in on-screen material. In its effort to avoid a naïve form of sentimentality that can be self-deceptively simplistic in its moral economy, Plantinga argues, an ironic approach 'is prone to a smug sense of superiority'.[30] It is this kind of smugness, a comfortable position of its own, firmly distanced from its characters, that *Palindromes* might seem largely to avoid at the textual level, in any sustained form, through its blend of approaches.

The suitably oriented viewer is offered plenty of more comfortable localized elements, such as the clearly marked moments of ironic distancing that can provide a viewing position which might be characterized as one of smug (or more general) superiority to character(s). But the film does not offer a settled position of this kind. It is possible that another form of satisfaction and pleasure might result from viewer appreciation of exactly the kinds of destabilizing shifts enacted by the film, as a marker of distinction entailed in the consumption of such material. This might be seen as constituting another level of smugness for those who appreciate this aspect of the overall texture of the film, a comfort-with-discomfort that remains a distinctive kind of viewing position overall, although the viewer responses considered below suggest that uneasiness often persists even for those who most admire the work. The potential effect of this use of irony, without a fixed, stable point of orientation, is akin in some respects to that propounded by some advocates of Romantic irony examined by Colebrook, in which the purpose of irony is not to establish a firmly unstated alternative position but precisely to avoid falling into any such 'smug self- recognition.'[31]

A similar dynamic can be found in other Solondz films, as in some of the other examples of the cinema of discomfort examined in subsequent chapters. In *Happiness*, for example, the viewer is offered a withdrawal from character on numerous occasions in which a barbed irony – of which the protagonists remain unaware – is offered to the audience (for example, when the smug Trish [Cynthia Stevenson] airily compares herself to one of her sisters who 'doesn't have it all', just after the viewer has been shown that her husband is a paedophile, on the basis of which her 'perfect' world will be shattered[32]). We might be lifted out of the diegetic situation to some extent by this effect, one that asserts a position of superiority on our part and that of the filmmaker, based on the fact that we are led to understand more than can be grasped by the characters. This can be seen as a way of reducing the discomfort that might result from unbroken emotional proximity to the kinds of experiences undergone by figures such as those who populate *Happiness*. But the approach of Solondz here, as in *Palindromes*, is to mix such distancing strategies with a more prolonged and often unironic confrontation with sustained painful diegetic situations.

An element of greater distance is also encouraged in some cases through more reflexive gestures, but these are also often mixed in what they might imply. One of the three sisters in *Happiness*, the writer Helen (Lara Flynn

Boyle), declares herself to be living 'in a state of irony', a line the viewer seems encouraged to take ironically itself, rather than as an expression of honest self-understanding. Questions of textual modality are also voiced within the fictional world in *Storytelling* (2001). In a session of group criticism by students taking a creative writing class, one declares of the work of another that 'its earnestness is a little embarrassing'. This is a position that would seem to favour some ironic distance, although it is far from clear that this is the stance of the film, here or as a whole. In the second half of *Storytelling*, featuring the attempts of an aspiring documentary filmmaker to chart the travails of the contemporary teenager, his editor finds some of his material glib and comical. She comments: 'You're showing how superior you are to your subject', to which he replies with an earnest declaration that this is not the case and that he loves his subjects. When a rough cut goes down hilariously with an invited audience, it is comic distance that seems to have ensured its appeal. Rather that criticizing this, however, Solondz presents its central teenage protagonist as happy with any basis of success that might help to propel his seemingly fatuous dreams of making it in show business. Dimensions of reflexivity such as these add further grounds for distinction-marking approval of films of this kind, but Solondz seems, characteristically, to avoid using them to stake out any single or simple basis of settled orientation for the viewer.

Viewer responses: Embracing or contesting discomfort

How, then, do viewers respond to *Palindromes*, particularly to the discomfort it can produce? To get some idea of the nature of responses that can result, I examine three samples of user-generated online reviews, posted on the Internet Movie DataBase (IMDb), the Rotten Tomatoes review aggregation site and in the pages of the leading retailer, Amazon.[33] The numbers involved are relatively modest for such forums, reflecting the limited reach of a film of this kind: 114 in the case of the IMDb, a more substantial total of approximately 800 for Rotten Tomatoes and 49 on Amazon.[34] A number of caveats have always to be issued in relation to the use of such materials. The respondents are self-selecting and in no way constitute anything like a scientifically based or representative sample. But they can give us an idea of the manner in which at least some viewers respond to such films when they choose to communicate their opinions in this way, and such fora are open to relatively broad potential constituencies and so tend to provide a reasonable range of orientations even towards a niche product such as this. My initial focus is on how the uncomfortable dimensions of *Palindromes* are articulated positively, for viewers who are approving of the film as a whole.

The basis on which the film is most often strongly approved in general is that it offers a challenge to the viewer and/or is deemed to be thought-provoking, as might be expected from the prevalence of the kinds of discourses about the value of the arts considered in the Introduction. These are familiar terms in which to praise 'difficult' works. The production of discomfort is seen by many as a key dimension of this process.

On the film's treatment of the abortion dispute, for example, one of a number of reviewers who suggest that the film refuses to offer a clear position on the issue (which is far from all of them) suggests that 'it challenges you on your moral outlook on life'.[35] It shows extremes on each side 'and makes you feel uncomfortable that you can't side with either. The film has scenes that will make you very uneasy'. *Palindromes* is declared to be a 'masterpiece of film making that is bound to offend everyone who sees it and then make them think again about their views'. This is a valuation that matches my reading of the film as not offering any comfortable position on such issues. Another respondent makes a similar point more generally. A number of elements of the film 'will unnerve, maybe even horrify some viewers', but 'if you are in the mood for a challenging film that will bring about strong emotions and give you some food for thought, by all means, see it. Just don't expect to be extremely happy once it's over.'[36] For viewers such as these, the film seems to offer not pleasure in any usual sense of 'feeling good' but an alternative form of satisfaction in the shape of being challenged and, it seems, proving up to such an experience. In the terms employed by Berliner, as cited in the previous chapter, the coping potential of such viewers is sufficient for them to be able to find cognitive and/or emotional interest in the material rather than a hedonistic form of pleasure.

The films of Solondz 'are uncomfortable to watch', for another reviewer, 'Because they are more truthful and honest then [sic] we expect a movie to be.'[37] That the sequences featuring the Sunshines are likely to be particularly discomforting to the primary constituencies for indie films is overtly confirmed by some responses. This part of the film 'is the creepiest and most disturbing thing I've ever seen (and you feel trapped there)', suggests one, the sense of entrapment suggesting a strong aversion to being forced into the extended company of such characters.[38] For another, this is 'the hardest stretch to sit through – but also the most entertaining' with 'some of the funniest/skin-crawlingest scenes'.[39] In this case, the response suggests an acute mixture of pleasure, in the comedy, and marked discomfort. A similar combination of the comic and the painful is identified by many other positive reviewers. In one account the filmmaker is 'so unrelenting, so unmerciful, and so true that it hurts. Painful, yes, but still funny as hell. […] Jokes taken so far to the point of uncomfortableness that they can only be genius, or otherwise pure madness.'[40]

Respondents such as these, who admire the film, remain discomforted by some of the material, even when this is seen as part of a positive dynamic such as provoking thought or challenge. Discomfort might be rationalized positively in this manner, but it does not seem to be a quality that can easily be rationalized *away*. It remains a key part of the experience. Some respondents express what seems a more unambiguous sense of pleasure, or at least admiration, within their discomfort.

Palindromes is 'beautifully uncomfortable' for one and 'uncomfortably great' for another.[41] One reviewer says it 'should leave you feeling wonderfully uncomfortable. Yes, you heard me, discomfort can be wonderful.'[42] This poster adds, as a rationale: 'Life is uncomfortable. Get comfortable with it.' The entire review of another is: 'the more uncomfortable i am after watching a flick, the better.'[43] Somewhat more specifically, and suggesting a real pleasure in the way the filmmaker articulates such qualities, another suggests that 'Solondz makes you uncomfortable with a grace and skill that no one else has.'[44] We find in some of these reactions a manifestation of the kind of positive exhilaration in being challenged identified by Berliner as a part of the pleasure entailed in the consumption of films that are difficult but, again, within the bounds of the coping potential of those involved.

Some responses suggest a real element of challenge that stays in force and can destabilize aspects of the reaction, as in the case of the respondent who seems unsure where the line might exist between genius and madness in the work of a figure such as Solondz. Some are unclear exactly what value to attribute to the film. As one puts it: 'Actually this film may be brilliant, I just can't get my head completely around it.'[45] This suggests the experience of material beyond the coping potential of the viewer: specifically, beyond their ability entirely to handle the cognitive challenge by getting their head 'completely around it'. One positive reviewer who indicates a familiarity with the director says: 'I found myself enjoying and hating this movie at the same time ... just the way I like my Todd Solondz films.[46] Another highlights more explicitly a key basis of discomfort outlined above, suggesting that one of the things that qualifies a film such as this as a 'masterpiece' is 'generating conflicting emotions in the viewer, largely ones that that cannot satisfactorily be resolved [...], including the way the film blurs the lines between ' "good people" and "bad people" '.[47] For some viewers, the inability to resolve is itself a source of appreciation, on the basis of what is implied to be a sophisticated way of understanding the world.

A number of positive responses in these samples also embody a clear process of affirmative distinction-marking of the kind highlighted in the tradition associated with Bourdieu. When it comes to articulating oppositions between this type of film and notions of the mainstream, numerous reviews include the kind of phrases often found more widely in responses to indie or art films, familiar components of the discourse through which particular kinds of films are considered to be suited to certain categories of viewer. Respondents typically situate themselves at the favoured discursive pole, whether implicitly or explicitly. *Palindromes* is emphatically 'NOT for the average moviegoer', as one asserts, clearly distinguishing himself from this position.[48] 'If your idea of a good movie is "Roadhouse", please do not watch this,' a comment followed by a characteristic 'however' that leads to the 'if you are in the mood for a challenging film' form of recommendation quoted above. When another reviewer says they 'recommend this to anyone with a sufficiently open mind to appreciate' it, we can again assume that they include themselves in that category.[49] Another comment of this variety that clearly aligns the film with a certain kind of viewer, including the respondent, concludes: 'If you are the type of person who likes to be troubled and challenged, then this is definitely the film for you.'[50] Such formulations are common currency in the articulation of these structures of cultural distinction-marking, as is also seen in responses to other films considered in this book.

Far from all respondents who find the film uncomfortable do so in an appreciative manner, however, as might also be expected given the nature of the material. Some are directly critical of Solondz for, as one puts it, 'the lengths to which he'll go to make his audience feel uncomfortable'[51]. This, as with some others, constitutes a direct rejection of what is perceived to be the approach employed by the filmmaker, as opposed to being a more general rejection of discomforting material per se. One reviewer goes further in seeing this as a deliberate strategy on the part of Solondz, identifying it more substantially as involving 'Brechtian-style audience alienation'.[52] Another describes those who enjoy such films as 'masochistic audiences hungry for more of Solondz's patented abuse.'[53] The film is described as an 'attempt to make people squirm in their seats and twitch with uncomfortable laughter'. Viewers in these samples appear divided overall on whether or not the film invites emotional engagement. Those who admire the film tend to find more of this than some of its rejecters. The reviewer who cites Brecht above objects that: 'I don't want to have to sit there very uncomfortably whilst watching two pre-teens indulge in very bad, very offensive sex, and then get told it was my fault for doing so!' For this respondent, the film seems to be guilty of something like the kind of ironic smugness identified in some cases by Plantinga.

It is also worth noting that those who express dislike for the discomfort generated by the film include a number who indicate a taste more generally for indie films or other works by Solondz. Those who respond negatively to this dimension are far from limited to the constituency conjured up by those admirers who suggest that *Palindromes* is not a film for those who only like mainstream fare. The previous example is one of numerous instances of dislike for *Palindromes* being articulated by commentators who declare admiration for other Solondz films, *Happiness* in particular. 'I know Todd Solondz is capable of making movies that are full of edgy, dark humour', says the reviewer, in the processes positioning himself as someone with appreciation of such qualities. 'But the line to [sic] which you should not cross has been completely lost in the sand in "Palindromes." '[54] Such a view could be taken as confirmation of the sense that, in this film in particular, Solondz has undermined even the relatively more comfortable indie-oriented viewing position offered by his earlier work. One approving reviewer makes another point akin to mine above, identifying the film as 'aimed squarely at a liberal audience' but adding that it 'absolutely refuses to pander to liberal prejudice'.[55] The suggestion here is that 'Solondz is challenging his own opinions on the issue, as much as ours.'

Some less positive reviewers find the film uncomfortable without identifying this as part of any more positive dimension or process. One judges the film to be 'A mostly uncomfortable experience that doesn't carry a compensating degree of insight or impact'.[56] Another, who says they 'utterly hated this film', finds it 'so totally perverse and uncomfortable to watch'.[57] For another, 'my skin was crawling the whole time', with no indication that this had any redeeming quality.[58] This also comes from a source who comments positively on previous Solondz films. Something similar is said by another admirer of *Happiness*. In response to the comment by Mama Sunshine about the girl who ran away despite having no legs, this viewer 'didn't laugh; I averted my eyes from the screen in embarrassment.'[59] This might be exactly the response the line seems designed to provoke, but in this case it results in explicit rejection of the effect, part of what this viewer interprets as a lack of empathy created for any of the characters, a point on which it is distinguished from *Happiness*. The aversion of the eyes suggests a response similar to that identified by Julian Hanich as common to the experience of being confronted with more overtly repellent or disgusting screen material, as a way of creating distance from discomforting content.[60] In this case, it seems the experience is one of being pushed away without the dynamically orchestrated switches between immersion and extrication seen by Hanich as characteristic of the more generically conventional pleasures of horror.[61] Views such as this appear to confirm that the uncertain structure of sympathy offered by the film provides a particularly acute form of discomfort in some cases, less easily accommodated to a positive overall response.

The film creates 'a sense of uneasiness throughout' for another critical reviewer, but this has 'nothing to do with what Solondz was saying, but the queasy sense of a creator' unable successfully to pull off a satirical treatment of the subject matter.[62] Any sense of discomfort is here shifted onto another level, that of the supposed competence of the filmmaker. More generally, if admirers often enact a distinction-marking gesture, in the way they oppose such films (and their viewers) to more mainstream productions, a frequent basis of contrary opinion from less sympathetic sources, also found more widely in viewer responses to art or indie films, is that *Palindromes* is pretentious or 'artsy', the latter a term usually employed in this context with negative connotations. Some viewers reject the film more broadly in terms that suggest a distance from the kind of liberal-oriented constituency often associated with the indie sector, objecting to what are seen as 'horrible' or 'vile' aspects of the content. This remains a minority view overall, however, among these responses.

Positive user ratings outnumber the negative in all these samples. Rotten Tomatoes reports a total of 8,906 providing numerical ratings (including the 800 who provide textual comments). The overall 'audience score' is 69 per cent 'liked it', a considerably higher rating than the 43 per cent approval rating recorded for a total of 117 professional/journalistic reviews (the latter a low score for a work by a filmmaker of established repute). Among the Amazon reviews, 25 per cent give the top rating of 5 stars with 41 per cent 4 star, 16 per cent 3 star, 8 per cent 2 star and 10 per cent at the lowest 1-star rating. No overall data is provided for the IMDb ratings but 52 of the 114 are in the 'loved it' category, awarding the maximum 10 out of 10, while only six give the lowest 'hated it' 1-star ranking. The broadly positive verdict seems likely to reflect the self-selecting nature of such samples rather than what might result from a broader public survey were a wider audience to be shown the film.

Finding (and losing) space in the system

The final part of this chapter considers what space is available at the industrial level for uncomfortable films such as *Palindromes*, particularly within the American indie and arthouse economy. A wider snapshot of the situation faced by such work can be gained through an examination of the circumstances of one example of this kind. Two aspects of the industrial context of the film are examined here: how it was funded and the nature and fate of its theatrical distributor, Wellspring Media, including how the latter was interpreted more broadly within American indie circles at the time. Funding is obviously a key issue faced by difficult or challenging films, as for independent and art films more generally. Theatrical distribution remains the primary initial goal sought by the makers of such films. The state of the theatrical market tends to be seen as the most important barometer of the broader health of the indie or arthouse sectors. That was true when the film was released and remained so at the time of writing, even while a number of other alternatives or hybrids including theatrical release were being explored.

The story of the funding of *Palindromes* is a very simple one. No one would fund the film. In interviews, Solondz says he approached a number of potential backers but could not get any of them interested. He refers in one of these accounts to the television market in Europe having lost its previous interest in American independent filmmakers.[63] He also suggests that the subject matter made the film scary for anyone connected with any sort of corporation, which is not surprising. Solondz famously ran into difficulties with *Happiness* when Universal blocked its then-subsidiary October Films from releasing the film because of its treatment of the paedophile character. He also had difficulties with *Storytelling* three years later, when another studio division, Fine Line Features, tried to get cuts made to a sex scene.

The films of Solondz had been relatively challenging up to this point but had previously found investors. Solondz was at this stage a filmmaker with a solid and established reputation, created particularly by *Welcome to the Dollhouse* and *Happiness*, and a great deal of critical regard, even if his films were not known for setting the box office alight. He was generally recognized as an important indie filmmaker; and yet, it seems, no one wanted to invest in this film. Solondz ended up funding the production himself and appears to have invested most of what he had into the project. He was reported effectively to have used his life savings to get the film made.[64] Exactly how much it cost has not been reported, although some indication can be gained from details elaborated below. It may be that some of the more challenging aspects of the film were enabled or strengthened by this situation, as the filmmaker had no one to answer to during the production process, but this suggests a rather precarious situation as far as production is concerned.

The film fared much better when it came to distribution, however, often the major stumbling block for independent features. *Palindromes* found a theatrical distributor quite readily, it seems, Wellspring Media, based in New York. According to *Variety*, there was even a 'bidding war' for the film, involving two other companies (the US branch of Tartan Films and Roadside Attractions).[65] Wellspring bought North American rights for what was reported to be 'a mid-to-low six-figure sum',[66] which appears to have covered the filmmaker's costs, as he was said to have broken even at this point.[67] We can approximate some idea of the budget on this basis (mid-to-low six-figures suggests something in the region of £300,000, perhaps). This seems a more positive story. New York's Observer.com described Wellspring as a 'safe haven' for Solondz, and as a 'scrappy company', suggesting appropriate indie credentials.[68] Solondz released a statement quoted by this source saying he was 'happy to be working with such smart, hard-working and nice people – and also because they always distribute my favourite movies'.

It is worth a closer look at Wellspring, which has a history in some ways typical of what is often found with indie distributors of this kind, one that is quite complicated as far as its backstory and subsequent fate are concerned. The company was founded in 1994, originally as a producer of health and wellness videos. It was bought by Winstar New Media in 1998 and later merged with Fox Lorber Associates, a home-video company with a substantial library of film titles, under the name Winstar TV and Video. The Winstar parent company went bankrupt in 2001, but the TV and video division was saved and spun off as Wellspring Media, which included a theatrical arm.[69] Wellspring was subsequently bought in 2004 by American Vantage, a Las Vegas investment group, with the declared aim to turn it into a significant indie player.[70] The intention was said at the time to be to create a 'mini-Miramax', something that could fill the space occupied by Miramax before it was perceived to have turned away from 'cutting-edge independent film' at some point under its ownership by Disney.[71]

This is a situation often typical of the emergence of a new independent distributor, having come about through a somewhat convoluted process of takeovers and reinventions. It also includes one key source of commercial underpinning, Wellspring's library of more than 700 titles being the kind of asset that can significantly increase the stability of operations of this kind. The collection included strong arthouse representation, with films by major established figures such as Truffaut, Godard, Rohmer, Fassbinder, Greenaway and Almodóvar.[72] The company's reputation as a new, 'edgy' player in the indie landscape was established by its distribution of films such as Vincent Gallo's controversial *The Brown Bunny* (2003) and Jonathan Caouette's almost no-budget *Tarnation* (2003), followed by *Palindromes*. It also handled a number of overseas art films, both new titles theatrically and new and classic art films on DVD. *Palindromes* was given a modest-scale US theatrical release of the kind we might expect for a film of this variety. It opened on seven screens in April 2005, widening to twenty-four in its third week and reaching a maximum of forty-six the week after, eventually running for twenty-two weeks, the latter half of which was on between one and three screens. Its domestic gross was $553,368, plus just $153,901 from overseas, making a total of $707,269.[73] This is clearly a modest performance, the weakest of Solondz's films at the time, but might not be considered particularly bad given the challenging nature of the work.

Up to this point, this is at least a positive story in that the film found a distributor and achieved a theatrical release and the attendant critical coverage, despite its distinctly difficult qualities. Wellspring was a distributor that seemed welcoming to exactly this kind of material. As so often seems to be the case in the American indie landscape, however, the story took a turn for the worse following further changes of ownership during this period. Wellspring's owner American Vantage was bought by Genius Products, a Santa Monica company specializing in home-entertainment distribution on DVD and other platforms. This deal was closed in February 2005, before the release of *Palindromes*.[74] Wellspring continued to release other indie and overseas films during the months that followed, including Claire Denis's *The Intruder* (*L'intrus*, 2004) and the documentary *Unknown White Male* (2005). It maintained a reputation for being filmmaker friendly. The Wellspring team was described in *Indiewire* as 'a quirky, passionate group of likeable, young cinephiles'.[75] It was said to have run a profitable business based on limited theatrical runs followed by release on DVD.

Genius was, in turn, taken over, by The Weinstein Company, the outfit created by Harvey and Bob Weinstein after they left the Disney-owned Miramax in September of the same year, 2005. The Weinstein Company (TWC) was a vehicle through which the Weinsteins maintained their focus on a certain kind of relatively commercial prestige film, although on a lower scale than during the latter part of their time at Miramax. Genius then effectively became the DVD and home entertainment division of TWC.[76] The deal also involved TWC becoming the exclusive theatrical distributor for any future Wellspring releases.[77] The much-lauded theatrical division of Wellspring was closed and its celebrated acquisitions and distribution team lost their jobs. This produced an outpouring of dismay in the indie-oriented media, with the name of Wellspring added to a list of companies that had met a similar fate after trying to carve out a niche for the distribution of art-house films, including examples such as The Shooting Gallery, Lot 47 Films and Cowboy Pictures.[78]

The fact that it was the Weinsteins who were held to blame added to the level of anger in some responses, given the existing reputation of Miramax as a previously dominating force in the indie or studio speciality sector (this was long before the Harvey Weinstein sex scandal that eventually scuppered TWC itself). The rhetoric found in some cases is a familiar part of the discourse that surrounds anything seen as a threat to more challenging indie or art film. Anthony Kaufman, a prominent figure in indie-oriented journalism, a regular contributor to *Indiewire* in particular, referred to TWC as 'gutting' Wellspring, which he described as 'one of New York's best loved art house theatrical divisions'.[79] As so often happens in the world of independent film, he wrote, 'corporate forces arrive to squash risk taking for the sake of the bottom line'. 'While the Weinsteins get richer, film lovers get poorer', he concluded. It was ironic, to say the least, that a company that had sought to fulfil something of the role of the earlier Miramax was effectively destroyed as a theatrical distributor by the Weinsteins, who clearly formed a suitable target to blame.

The reaction to the fate of Wellspring is worth dwelling on, as it seems symptomatic of broader expressions of concern about the viability of more challenging indie films or works of overseas art cinema in the American marketplace and beyond. Just a month before his piece about Wellspring, Kaufman wrote an article in *The New York Times* lamenting the difficulty of releasing foreign-language films in the United States, noting a decline in numbers and in their box-office takings.[80] One of the sources cited was Marie Therese Guirgis, then still the head of Wellspring (sister of Stephen Aldy Guirgis, who plays one of the lead roles in *Palindromes*). The blame for this situation was placed on various factors, including lack of media attention, although that was interpreted as part of a vicious cycle, reflecting a perceived lack of general public interest in such films. The studio speciality divisions were, unsurprisingly, another object singled out for blame. What are described here as 'major pseudo-indie productions', such as *Brokeback Mountain*, released the same year as *Palindromes*, are seen as competing unfairly for the limited arthouse audience. 'Every studio now has a speciality division', Guirgis is quoted as saying, although that was to change a few years later, with the disappearance of Miramax and the closure of such divisions by Paramount and Warner Bros, moves that prompted a fresh round of soul-searching about the state of the indie landscape.

Some hope is expressed here in the continued availability of overseas films on DVD, to which Wellspring was destined to be limited after the Weinstein takeover. Netflix was also seen at this point as offering a more level playing field for smaller films. But the key issue at stake in this discourse is the presence of such films in cinemas, a dimension they are often thought to require fully to be appreciated and to gain critical attention. In another piece, in *Indiewire*, Kaufman suggests that the film business was either 'fleeing art – or looking for new business models to distribute it'.[81] The latter included a move by IFC Films to deliver some art films through a combination of select theatrical release and a new video-on-demand service, which has since become an increasingly used option for some releases of indie or arthouse titles.

Apart from Sony Pictures Classics, the only studio division generally to have had any real commitment to overseas art films, some of the other companies cited more positively by Kaufman, in terms of their potential orientation towards overseas films, also subsequently folded. These included Tartan Films USA (2008) and New Yorker Films (2009). Of those singled out most strongly, only one was still going at the time of writing: the Film Movement, most of the releases of which were said by Kaufman to be direct to DVD.[82] The list of closures, then, included one of the other companies reported to have bid to distribute *Palindromes* (New Yorker). The other, Roadside Attractions, remained in operation, having been strengthened by the sale of a minority stake in 2007 to Lionsgate, still at this point the largest distributor unattached to any of the major studios and a company that had tended to focus on more commercial independent niches. Under this deal, Roadside Attractions retained its autonomy, subsequent releases including *Manchester by the Sea* (2016).[83] A number of other distributors continued to handle small or difficult indie and art films, some of which had been in operation for decades, including First Run Features, Strand Releasing, Kino International and Zeitgeist films (the latter formed an alliance with the parent company of Kino, Kino Lorber, in 2017).

It is unsurprising, given the general nature of the market for films of this kind, that the picture is one of insecurity, change and, often, eventual demise. These are familiar patterns, both in the sequence of events and the manner in which they are customarily articulated within indie circles. It is quite clear that the business of supporting or releasing difficult or discomforting indie or art films is a challenging one, even when some elements of relatively greater stability exist. Wellspring had one of these, in its large catalogue, a source of strength for many larger media players. It is ironic that its strength here, and in home-entertainment distribution more generally, was a major attraction for The Weinstein Company that led to its closure as a theatrical operation. It is also typical for relatively larger forces such as TWC to have a hand in the fate of such companies, and for this to be interpreted as part of a state of crisis facing certain kinds of indie films or the broader category of global art cinema within which some can be located.

If the role of studio speciality divisions has often been singled out as one of the threats to smaller, more specialized operations, it was notable how the closure of several of these in 2008 was celebrated by some commentators, a phenomenon on which I have commented elsewhere.[84] If that was seen as potentially clearing more space for what are viewed as 'true' indies, or works of art cinema, either in the United States or more widely, this is an arena that tends always to be seen as deeply embattled and challenged, particularly in the theatrical realm. As far as subtitled films are concerned, for example, even the biggest and most sustained player in this market in the United States, Sony Pictures Classics (SPC), said in 2006 that the proportion of its slate comprised by such works had fallen from two-thirds in the past to between a half and a third.[85] US box-office returns for the top five foreign-language films were reported in 2014 to have dropped by 61 per cent over the previous seven years, with SPC saying it would take fewer risks on subtitled works in the future.[86] SPC reported continuing difficulties in 2020, exacerbated by a collapse in the numbers of local newspaper critics (along with an oversupplied market), the surprise scale of the success of the Oscar-winning *Parasite* (2019) being seen generally as an exception to the norm.[87] The conclusion of many figures from indie companies after the closure of Wellspring was that theatrical was always likely to be a loss-leader, at best, for smaller indies, overseas films or documentaries, as a supplement to some form of home-viewing release.[88] The question that emerges is whether the costs of theatrical release can be recouped by the still-limited revenues usually achieved by such films on DVD, Blu-ray or video-on-demand, one that remains still very much open today.

Notes

1. Another example is Todd Haynes' *I'm Not There* (2007), although in this case the use of multiple performers playing Bob Dylan is motivated by the conceit of exploring different dimensions/faces of a notable real-life figure. A classic instance is the employment of two performers in a central role in Luis Buñuel's *That Obscure Object of Desire* (*Cet obscur objet du désir*, 1977).
2. Sconce, 'Irony, Nihilism', 364.
3. See King, *Positioning Art Cinema*, chapter 7, and Lübecker, *The Feel-Bad Film*.

4. Sconce, 'Irony, Nihilism', 352.
5. James MacDowell, *Irony in Film* (London: Palgrave Macmillan, 2016), 38.
6. MacDowall, *Irony in Film*, 59–60.
7. Murray Smith, *Engaging Characters: Fiction, Emotion, and the Cinema* (Oxford: Clarendon Press, 1995). For a useful account of more nuanced uses of terms such as identification, one that seeks to pluralize some of the more polemical debates about the possibility of emotional identification or empathy with fictional film characters, see Berys Gaut, 'Empathy and Identification in Cinema', in Peter French, Howard Wettstein and Michelle Saint (eds), *Film and the Emotions, Midwest Studies in Philosophy*, vol. XXIV (2010): 136–57.
8. Smith, *Engaging Characters*, 82.
9. Ibid., 75.
10. Ibid., 83.
11. Ibid.
12. Plantinga, *Moving Viewers*, 191.
13. See, for example, the argument about indie audiences in Michael Newman, *Indie: An American Film Culture* (New York: Columbia University Press, 2011). Sconce also evokes a similar kind of urban 'bohemian' constituency.
14. For more on the critique of irony in this context, see Sconce, 'Irony, Nihilism'.
15. Starting with James MacDowell, 'Notes on Quirky', *Movie: A Journal of Film Criticism* 1 (2010): 1–16.
16. King, *Indie 2.0*, 61.
17. *Punch-Drunk Love* (2002), for example, one of the cases cited by MacDowell.
18. On the questioning of some indie films on this basis by some critics, see Michael Newman, 'Movies for Hipsters', in Geoff King, Claire Molloy and Yannis Tzioumakis (eds), *American Independent Cinema: Indie, Indiewood and Beyond* (Abingdon: Routledge, 2013).
19. Wilkins, *American Eccentric Cinema*, 5.
20. Ibid., 18.
21. Plantinga, *Moving Viewers*, 126.
22. For more detail, see Geoff King, *American Independent Cinema* (London: I.B. Tauris, 2005), 197–9.
23. Smith, *Engaging Characters*, 191.
24. Murray Smith, *Film, Art, and the Third Culture: A Naturalized Aesthetics of Film* (Oxford: Oxford University Press, 2017), 202, 208.
25. Plantinga, *Moving Viewers*, 152–4. The other varieties suggested by Plantinga are 'benign incongruence' and 'movement from incongruence to congruence or vice versa'.
26. Plantinga, '"I Followed the Rules and They All Loved You More": Moral Judgment and the Attitudes Towards Fictional Characters in Film', in Peter French, Howard Wettstein and Michelle Saint (eds), *Film and The Emotions, Midwest Studies in Philosophy*, vol. XXIV (2010): 43.

27 Babbington and Evans, 'All that Heaven Allowed: Another Look at Sirkian Irony', *Movie* (1990) 34–5; cited by Pye, 52–3.
28 MacDowall, *Irony in Film*, 19.
29 Hutcheon, *Irony's Edge*, 94–8.
30 Plantinga, *Moving Viewers*, 192.
31 MacDowall, *Irony in Film*, 50.
32 On this and other such examples in the film, see King, *American Independent Cinema*, 185–6.
33 IMDb reviews accessed 23 November 2017 at http://www.imdb.com/title/tt0362004/reviews?count=114&start=0; Amazon reviews accessed 23 November 2017 at https://www.amazon.com/Palindromes- Jennifer- Jason- Leigh/dp/B000A1IOGG/ref=sr_1_1?ie=UTF8&qid=1511440167&sr=8-1&keywords=palindromes+dvd; Rotten Tomatoes accessed 30 November 2017 at https://www.rottentomatoes.com/m/palindromes/reviews/?page=5&type=user.
34 Rotten Tomatoes reports a total of 8,906 user ratings making up its overall 'audience score'. Actual review-type responses constituted forty-one pages of twenty responses per page, of which approximately a dozen or so were of no relevance to the film, making a total of about 800.
35 Shan Jayaweera, Amazon, 9 August 2005. Details provided for each reviewer are given here as in the original, in this and subsequent chapters.
36 Steven Adam Renkovish, Amazon, 11 January 2008.
37 Rich Dunbeck from United States, IMDb, 22 July 2005.
38 TBJCSKCNRRQTreviews from Earth, IMDb, 6 November 2010.
39 match-3 from United States, IMDB, 20 September 2010.
40 bastard wisher from Hawaii, IMDB, 13 November 2005.
41 Matt B, Rotten Tomatoes, 5 May 2008; Kamilah J, Rotten Tomatoes, 26 August 2008.
42 Merkley M, Rotten Tomatoes, 15 January 2013.
43 A.D.O., Rotten Tomatoes, 28 November 2011.
44 Cheryl C, Rotten Tomatoes, 21 June 2010.
45 Michael B, Rotten Tomatoes, 19 May 2012.
46 Maxwell D, Rotten Tomatoes, 15 August 2008.
47 Nathan F, Rotten Tomatoes, 16 May 2010.
48 Steven Adam Renkovish, Amazon, 11 January 2008.
49 TBJCSKCNRRQTreviews from Earth, IMDb, 6 November 2010.
50 C.D. Shisler, Amazon, 11 May 2006.
51 Jamesdamnrown.com/movies from jamesdamnbrown.com, IMDb, 3 June 2005.
52 James Alex Neve from London, UK, IMDb, 22 April 2006.

53 Frankenbenz from Sydney, Australia, 6 December 2008.
54 James Alex Neve from London, UK, IMDb, 22 April 2006.
55 Chris Bright from London, IMDb, 28 October 2004.
56 Robert F, Rotten Tomatoes, 11 March 2010.
57 Amy K, Rotten Tomatoes, 16 December 2007.
58 ultra kid from Birmingham, England, IMDb, 30 April 2007.
59 Adam Whyte from Scotland, IMDb, 18 March 2005.
60 Hanich, 'Dis/liking Disgust'.
61 Hanich, *Cinematic Emotion in Horror Films and Thrillers*.
62 scorseseisgod-1from San Diego, IMDb, 12 November 2005.
63 Matthew Ross, 'The Divided Self', *Filmmaker* magazine, Spring 2005, accessed at https://filmmakermagazine.com/archives/issues/spring2005/features/divided_self.php.
64 Ross, 'The Divided Self'.
65 Ian Mohr, 'A Home for "Planindromes [sic]"', *Variety*, 12 October 2004, accessed at http://variety.com/2004/film/markets-festivals/a-home-for-planindromes-1117911891/.
66 Jake Brooks, 'Solondz Fares Well; Wellspring Gushes for Palindromes', *Observer* (website), 18 October 2004, accessed at http://observer.com/2004/10/solondz-fares-well-wellspring-gushes-for-palindromes/.
67 Ross, 'The Divided Self'. Another source suggests that Solondz 'recouped his "nest egg" as a result of foreign sales: Geoffrey Macnab, 'I hate my job', *The Guardian*, 15 April 2005, accessed at https://www.theguardian.com/film/2005/apr/15/2.
68 Brooks, 'Solondz Fares Well'.
69 Ibid. and Eugene Hernandez, 'As Wellspring Closes, Examining the State of Art House Distribution', *Indiewire*, 24 February, 2006, accessed at http://www.indiewire.com/2006/02/as-wellspring-closes-examining-the-state-of-the-art-house-distribution-77107/.
70 Brooks, 'Solondz Fares Well'.
71 Ibid.
72 Eugene Hernandez, 'Major Changes for Wellspring as Weinstein Controlled Genius Pulls Plug on Existing Theatrical Distribution', 21 February 2006, accessed at http://www.indiewire.com/2006/02/major-changes-for-wellspring-as-weinstein- controlled-genius-pulls-plug-on-existing-theatrical-distri-77127/.
73 Figures from Box Office Mojo, at http://www.boxofficemojo.com/movies/?id=palindromes.htm.
74 Hernandez, 'Major Changes for Wellspring'.
75 Ibid.

76 Jeremy Kay, 'Weinstein Co forms US DVD venture with Genius', *Screen Daily*, 6 December 2005, accessed at https://www.screendaily.com/weinstein-co-forms-us-dvd-venture-with-genius/4025404.article.

77 Hernandez, 'Major Changes for Wellspring'.

78 Hernandez, 'As Wellspring Closes'.

79 Anthony Kaufman, 'Good Morning Night', *The Village Voice*, 21 February 2006.

80 Kaufman, 'Is Foreign Film the New Endangered Species?, *New York Times*, 22 January 2006, accessed at https://www.nytimes.com/2006/01/22/movies/is-foreign-film-the-new-endangered-species.html.

81 Kaufman, 'The Evaporation of Wellspring, cont'd', *Indiewire*, 28 February 2006, accessed at http://www.indiewire.com/2006/02/the-evaporation-of-wellspring-contd-135107/

82 Kaufman, 'The Evaporation of Wellspring'.

83 Jeremy Kay, 'Lionsgate takes minority share in Roadside Attractions', *Screen Daily*, 26 July 2007, accessed at https://www.screendaily.com/lionsgate-takes-minority-stake-in-roadside-attractions/4033769.article.

84 King, *Indie 2.0*, 9–10.

85 Kaufman, 'Is Foreign Film the New Endangered Species?'

86 Kaufman, 'The Lonely Subtitle: Here's Why U.S. Audiences Are Abandoning Foreign-Language Films', *Indiewire*, 6 May 2014, accessed at https://www.indiewire.com/2014/05/the-lonely-subtitle-heres-why-u-s-audiences-are-abandoning-foreign-language-films-27051/.

87 Akiva Gottlieb, 'After "Parasite", What's Next for Foreign Films?', *Variety*, 26 March 2020, accessed at https://variety.com/2020/film/features/after-parasite-whats-next-foreign-films-1203545054/.

88 A number of such figures are quoted to this effect in Hernandez, 'As Wellspring Closes'.

3

Ulrich Seidl: Far from paradise

Whether varieties of art or indie film such as the cinema of discomfort are best interpreted, in sociocultural terms, as a product of their place of origin or as a wider implicit statement about contemporary society remains a topic of much debate. *Palindromes*, along with other films by Solondz, might be viewed in the light of the particular American milieux examined by figures such as Sconce, Perkins and Kotsko, or it might be seen as having wider resonance for certain kinds of societies; or, perhaps most usefully, some combination of the two dimensions. The general sense of middle-class malaise or broader (late)modern/postmodern disorientation and anxiety diagnosed by some writers could clearly be applied more broadly than just within the US context. Similar debate has surrounded the films of Ulrich Seidl. For some commentators, the works of Seidl, and others with whom he is associated, display tendencies specific to the context of early twenty-first century or late twentieth-century Austria, a country with a distinct inheritance in both the broader social and more specifically artistic or cinematic realms. Others have argued for their wider resonance, whether in sociocultural terms or as products of the international/global institutional landscape of art cinema. This chapter will consider both dimensions, including a closer consideration of the dynamics that can support or encourage the production of work of this kind.

The primary focus is on discomforting material in Seidl's second fiction feature, *Import Export* (2007), an exploration of the lives of two principal characters involved in crossings of borders between Austria and parts of eastern Europe. Other examples examined more briefly include his fictional debut, *Dog Days* (*Hundstage*, 2001), and the 'Paradise' trilogy, *Paradise: Love* (*Paradies: Liebe*, 2012), *Paradise: Faith* (*Paradies: Glaube*, 2012) and *Paradise: Hope* (*Paradies: Hoffnung*, 2013). Some notable points of overlap are identified with the uncomfortable qualities of Seidl's work in documentary, including *In the Basement* (*Im Keller*, 2014). My consideration of *Import Export* follows the previous chapter in focusing initially on the structure of sympathy offered to the viewer in relation to the two main characters. This leads into analysis of the uncomfortable use of explicit sex in the film. The other main point of focus is the setting of part of *Import Export* in the real-world environment of a geriatric hospital, in sequences that raise various issues about the discomforting mixture of factual and fictional realms.

The orientation towards central characters offered by *Import Export* is generally more straightforward than is the case in *Palindromes*. The film is structured around the parallel narratives of Olga (Ekateryna Rak), a Ukrainian nurse who moves to Austria in search of work, and Pauli (Paul Hoffman), a bristling young man who loses his new job as a security guard and becomes involved in an excursion across the border in the other direction, to Slovakia and the Ukraine, while working for his stepfather. Olga offers a conventionally straightforward and unproblematic source of both alignment and allegiance. She is presented as a caring and well-intentioned figure, worthy of the moral approval of the viewer. Our sympathies are encouraged by the numerous injustices and sources of ill-treatment she faces. The one moment she might appear to act in a questionable manner is when Olga attempts to leave home in secret, abandoning her baby to the care of her mother. This is presented effectively as the product of circumstances, however, and no recriminations follow from the mother when she awakes and catches Olga about to leave, implying that few should come from the viewer either.

Prior to this, our sympathies for Olga are encouraged by the fact that she is paid only part of her wages, a situation presented as ongoing rather than a one-off, and her experience attempting to boost her income by performing in an online sex parlour. She finds employment in Austria, as a cleaner in a coldly middle-class home, only to face arbitrary and blameless dismissal. Her next job is cleaning in a geriatric hospital, where her low status is made clear by a nurse, Maria (Maria Hofstätter), who insists on enforcing the letter of the law which decrees that a cleaner not be allowed any of the human contact Olga attempts with the patients. Maria further accuses Olga of seeking to find a 'victim' among the elderly men to marry in order to stay in Austria. Olga is offered such an arrangement by one of the patients, Erich Schlager (Erich Finsches), who subsequently dies, although she is presented as in no way seeking to solicit any such business. The film would, in fact, be a good deal more challenging were the unambiguously positive status of Olga questioned in any such way.

Pauli is a more ambiguous figure, at first presented as a distinctly uncomfortable source of allegiance, although his position changes as the film progresses. Pauli can also be viewed as a victim of circumstances, in his not-so-convincing macho posturing, but he is a considerably less appealing figure. The tall, dyed-blond Olga has the benefit of being presented as conventionally attractive at the level of physical attributes, in gendered patriarchal terms, even if her Austrian household employer responds sniffily to her brash (lower-class signifying) clothing. This dimension remains a significant ingredient in the structure of sympathy more generally, as Plantinga reminds us. Pauli is something of an essay in attempted masculine swagger. On the short side, he cuts a partially ridiculous figure when we see him engaging in activities such wrestling with an aggressive dog and shadow boxing. He appears proud of his masculinity and strength, as a source of self-avowal, but it seems as much a pose and performance as anything more substantial. He is seen acting in what seems a particular crass manner in an early sequence in which he takes the dog to the flat of a girlfriend, mocking and dismissing her sustained complaints, her evident fear and discomfort.

Pauli also suffers what seems unfair treatment, however, and is offered substantial redeeming qualities in later sequences in which he separates himself from the discomforting behaviour of his stepfather, Michael (Michael Thomas). He loses his job in security after being stripped and mocked by a group of men. He continues to act in a manner that makes him an awkward source of allegiance. This includes attempting an unlikely scam involving accosting strangers in a station concourse and claiming they owe him money for a bar bill he supposedly met when they were drunk. Immediately after this, he is accosted in similar fashion by a figure to whom he really does owe money. A sense is created of Pauli being a somewhat hapless figure, constantly attempting to dodge from one minor misadventure to another. He seems primarily to be naïve and lacking in perspective, however, rather than mean or actively mendacious, as seems to be demonstrated in the latter part of the film. When Michael seeks Pauli's help to chat-up a woman in a bar in Slovakia, the stepson demurs, objecting to the attempted betrayal of his mother. Given some of his earlier behaviour, we might be encouraged to respond sceptically when Pauli refers to having his own values, of 'harmony, with myself and my surroundings.' But Pauli's position seems more closely aligned with that encouraged for the viewer in some key scenes, most clearly in a subsequent sequence in the Ukraine in which Michael seeks to demonstrate to his stepson 'the power of money' when it comes to the sexual acts he can procure from an unnamed woman he has paid to join him in their hotel room (Anastasia Sergeyeva, the character credited as a hotel sex worker). This is one of the strongest sources of potential discomfort in the film.

Framing uncomfortable and more explicit sex

If sex is a frequent source of the central quality of the cinema of discomfort, the uncomfortable sex in *Import Export* is very different from that of

Palindromes. While we might be encouraged to squirm in embarrassment at what we witness in the Solondz film, here we are confronted with far more explicit representation. This begins in the sequences depicting Olga's experiences with live online pornography. Along with her, we witness a number of workers displaying and manipulating their bodies in front of cameras, following the instructions of their viewers. We then see Olga engaging in one such encounter. A more direct, in-person variation on such dynamics occurs in the sequence involving Michael and the sex worker in the hotel room. When Pauli walks in on the scene, it seems notable that the latter is on the floor with her naked rear facing the camera, a position broadly the same as that which features most prominently in the earlier Ukrainian sequences. Michael's demonstration of the power of money, and the assertion of his own relative dominance in this situation, consists of instructing the woman to act in various ways such as displaying herself while sitting and moving her legs in the air in a cycling motion and repeating self-insulting words in German that she does not understand. The peak of humiliation is suggested when he tells her to get onto all fours and to crawl around and bark like a dog. This is followed by a striptease and an act of fellatio.

Michael encourages Pauli to watch and enjoy the spectacle he conducts, but Pauli resists. 'Sit and make yourself comfortable', Michael insists, but Pauli is clearly experiencing the opposite reaction, his discomfort signalled most clearly by an aversion of his gaze, along with his bodily orientation, and his remainder at a distance from the woman. Pauli seems unambiguously positioned here as a surrogate for the viewer, his discomfort standing in for that likely to be experienced by the audience. The staging of these sequences plays an important role in whatever effect might be created, although it has considerable potential for ambiguity, as either an additional source of intended discomfort or something that might be beyond the limits of control for the filmmaker in the deployment of such material.

The staging of the scene starts with a device used on several occasions during *Import Export*, in which Seidl presents an activity viewed through the frame-within-a-frame created by a doorway or similar aperture between one room or space and another. One such occurrence earlier in the film, for example, shows us Pauli's mother dancing, seemingly alone, in her living room, viewed through a doorway from a hall. A cut follows to a classic blank distanced shot of the type highlighted elsewhere by Sconce: a square-on shot of a sofa on which sit Pauli and Michael, watching without any noticeable expression. Such images feature prominently in Seidl's oeuvre, particularly in his documentary films. A cut takes us back to the perspective from the hall, as Michael joins the dancing. Distanced shots such as these can imply an ironic and/or slightly mocking attitude towards such material, broadly along the lines suggested by Sconce. In the case of the hotel sex sequence, the distance seems more strongly critical, without the droll impression sometimes created elsewhere in this and other works by Seidl. It marks a clear separation between Pauli and the uncomfortable action. At the start of the sequence, he remains in an ante-chamber space outside the main part of the bedroom. The woman is positioned across the threshold, into the bedroom. When Michael later leads her to crawl out, closer to Pauli, the latter responds by moving into the bedroom space, although he is then followed by the two others. Pauli eventually acts in a manner that actively undermines Michael's bluster, as Nikhil Sathe suggests; he pushes his stepfather to get on with having intercourse with the woman, if that is his intention, exposing what appears to be his impotence.[1]

The staging of the acts of sexual display directed by Michael has potential for a more ambiguous reading than that which simply seeks to mirror the discomfort of Pauli, raising issues concerning the implications of what is presented both within and beyond the fictional space – to the diegetic audience and to that of the film itself. A key question is what happens when sexual display is offered by the film to the viewer as well as within the narrative world. When we first see the woman, she is kneeling with her rear raised at middle distance, close to the lower edge of the frame. Narratively, she is presented towards Michael, whose figure occupies the closer far right-hand side of the screen, while Pauli stands back and to the left.

But the sexual spectacle is also oriented more or less directly to the viewer (areas of shadow serve to cover the most intimate modesty, a distinction the film consistently maintains from the close-up detail associated with hardcore pornography or some instances of more explicit sex within art cinema). A cut then gives us a closer view of the woman's rear and Michael, the latter now filling most of the right-hand part of the screen (Figure 7).

FIGURE 7 *Framing sex in* Import Export *(2007).*

A similar set-up is employed for some time in the sequence that includes the woman sitting with her legs in bicycle motion. Her gaze is towards Michael, at screen right, but her body is oriented directly towards the camera, slightly more so than in the previous longer shot that included Pauli.

This is a form of orientation not uncommonly found in the cinematic framing of certain kinds of fictional performance more generally, including the staging of the exchanges between Joyce and Aviva examined in the previous chapter. The performative antics of comedian comics are sometimes presented in this manner, for example, as I have suggested elsewhere.[2] A comedian doing the kind of routine familiar to their persona will rarely do so directly to camera, but sometimes a position is adopted that is directed only *slightly* to one side. The fictional frame is maintained in literal terms, that is: the performance happens, strictly, within the diegetic universe, towards other characters. But a strong sense is also created of the performance being directed substantially towards the viewer. It is the serving up of the performance to the viewer that is likely to be a primary motivation for the existence of, and pleasures provided by, such a film. The ideal, in comedian comedy, is usually to achieve a balance between the two dynamics, the fictional frame providing a licensing for the performative acts and a more sustained context than might be available from sequences of such performance alone.

What happens when this kind of framing is employed with material of the kind found in *Import Export*? The presence of Michael in the frame seems important as a way of mediating the material. It might help the viewer to maintain a higher level of comfort than if he were absent and the sexual display presented more directly to the audience. This assumes, of course, that the sexual display in question is interpreted negatively and a critical attitude taken towards Michael's behaviour. This seems clearly to be the intention of the filmmaker, as reinforced by the response of Pauli. We have plenty of potential reasons to distance ourselves from Pauli at times, if with some sympathy for him as a somewhat hapless victim in his own way; but, it might be inferred, *even he* at his worst can see that this is an unpleasant abuse of power. Pauli expresses concern about the fear and discomfort being expressed by the woman, which Michael disavows. There is some irony here, given Pauli's insufficient comprehension of the real fear his girlfriend experienced during the earlier scenes with the dog. Both male figures appear wilfully blind to the responses of women in these situations, even if Michael's behaviour might be considered to be more extreme because of its sexual focus.

If we are meant to share Pauli's discomfort in the hotel room scene, however, no film, or any other cultural product, can guarantee to control the manner in which its content might be interpreted. It is quite possible for a viewer to be sexually stimulated by this material. How such a response might work is subject to potential variety. A viewer might gain sexual arousal from the display offered by the sequence, if potentially mixed with a complex range of other responses, as is suggested by the findings of a large-scale analysis of audience responses to a group of in some ways similar films that include sequences of explicit sex and/or sexual violence.³ The study, commissioned by the British Board of Film Classification and led by Martin Barker, finds such sequences to provide strong sources of viewer discomfort, as might be expected, in a sample including *À Ma Soeur* (translated as *Fat Girl*, 2001), *Baise-Moi* (*Rape Me*, 2000) and *Irreversible* (2002). A perspective expressed by many of those whose views are reported is that the material of such films, particularly the representation of rape, is uncomfortable of necessity and as it should be: represented as loathsome and shocking, and the better so the more discomforting the effect.⁴ Some viewers report discomfort on the basis of feeling arousal to some extent in relation to the central rape sequence of *Irreversible*, followed by a sense of shame at this response, or relief that any arousal was only short-lived in the context of the prolonged and brutal nature of the assault (others express relief at not experiencing any unwanted arousal).⁵ In a case such as the hotel room sequence from *Import Export*, this might be a localized erotic stimulation relating to the spectacle of the unclad body, separate from its narrative context. It could go further, potentially, and involve an affirmation of the masculine domination embodied by Michael's abusive behaviour. The film provides specific grounds for assuming some such potential, in the sexual economy more generally, given the similarities between aspects of this sequence and what we have previously been shown being consumed more widely online. A parallel can clearly be suggested between Michael and the clients of the Ukrainian and other such businesses.

One option is to posit the existence of a distinct audience, akin to that established online within the film, for exploitative consumption of material of this kind. The most likely constituency for Seidl's film might be able to distance itself to a large extent from such a position, as part of the more general process of distinction marking based on class and other status markers usually involved in the choice to view such work. But the possibility also exists for a discomforting blurring of these distinctions, as is suggested by some of the responses examined by Barker. The viewer who would morally disavow such material can still be sexually stimulated to some extent by the images orchestrated for us by their diegetic and/or extra-diegetic directors. While the unnamed woman performs ostensibly to the orders of Michael in *Import Export*, the pro-filmic reality of the situation is at the behest of Seidl and ultimately for the viewer of the film (a parallel can be found in a sequence from a documentary about Seidl, in which we see him directing a sequence involving a naked woman trapped uncomfortably inside a small cage, the filming of a sequence from *In the Basement*⁶). It is for this reason that the filmmaker has been attacked by some critics as a voyeur, morally to be disapproved. Such criticism has been made in relation not just to this kind of sexual material but to his supposed portrayal of a 'poverty porn', indulged by middle-class audiences, in scenes such as some of those depicting blasted eastern European landscapes in *Import Export*.[7]

The sexual display offered by this film is framed critically in various ways: within the narrative world and, more broadly, within the realm of this kind of 'serious' or 'challenging' art film as a whole. Such frames are important shapers of how specific images are likely to be experienced. They also play a large part in determining who is likely to be viewing and in what manner. But framing of this kind is not all-powerful. If we watch a Hollywood-style action movie, for example, and are presented with the spectacular destruction of sympathetic forces for good, at one point in the narrative, we might still take pleasure from such a sequence at the level of the mounting of the spectacle itself, even if it is framed as a undesirable event in narrative-moral terms (such a contradiction might be more easily resolvable in most such cases, given the likely unspoken guarantee that moral restitution will eventually follow). This is not the occasion to get into detail on the long-standing debate about how far film (or other audiovisual media) can capture a pro-filmic reality that might directly be presented to the viewer, as a source of what has sometimes been seen as its particular potency as an effective and affecting medium. It is notable, however, that the figure most often associated with claims about the indexical nature of film, Andre Bazin, expressed a moral objection to any notion of including real sex in the cinema.[8]

Whatever is filmed is always inescapably framed and, thus, in some way shaped, mediated and interpreted. But filmed representation can also create direct affective responses, along with more cognitively grounded 'concern-based construals', as Plantinga and others argue. This can include direct sexual stimulation (even if such a notion might require qualification on the basis of socially learned gender behaviour) as well as taking other forms such as the often-cited example of the 'startle' response to sudden actions or noises.[9] If an *intention* to arouse is part of the definition often given to pornography, where this is the primary purpose, it remains the case that the representation of sex has the *potential* to arouse across a much wider spectrum of cinema, whether that representation be explicit and/or unsimulated or otherwise, or whether or not it is intended to be a source of discomfort.[10]

The question of the potentially direct impact of such material has been considered in relation to other films associated with a wider contemporary tendency towards 'extreme' and/or explicit representation of this kind in art cinema, including the French examples cited above in the Barker study (these are situated within the more assaultive or transgressive body of work examined by figures such as Lübecker and Grønstad, including more extreme forms of discomfort than are generally my subject). This is part of the production context of such films, within the economy specific to art cinema, to which I return below. One academic response to such productions, particularly that of Martine Beugnet, has been to emphasize their affective power as a material force in its own right, distinct from the presence of any narrative or thematic frameworks.[11] A broader body of analysis has stressed the importance of bodily or sensual levels of engagement with different kinds of film, including the work of Laura Marks and Vivian Sobchack.[12] Such discourses can become somewhat rhetorical in tone, as I have argued elsewhere in the case of Beugnet, but they offer a corrective to any tendency excessively to rationalize-away the sensually affective dimension of cinema.[13]

Sobchack, for example, offers a usefully balanced account of what she suggests is the simultaneous combination of bodily/sensual and rational/cognitive dimensions of engagement, a position in line with the mixture of the more and less cognitive facets of emotional experience suggested via theorists such as Plantinga earlier in this book.[14] Something similarly mixing a capacity for corporeal and intellectual engagement is the basis on which Grønstad establishes the particular ethical value of the aggressively confrontational and transgressive variety of post-millennial art cinema.[15] The point, in a case such as *Import Export*, is that rationalizing or morally justifying frameworks are unlikely ever to provide the sole basis of the experience of such material. The spectacle of the filmed naked or semi-clothed body is a real one in its own terms, with its own potency, even when clearly staged and strongly narratively and morally framed. This is a dimension of the material that becomes heightened in *Import Export* when it culminates in the woman giving what appears to be real, pro-filmic fellatio to Michael.

Moments such as the latter have potential to pull the viewer out of a focus at the level of narratively fictional material. The performer is not simulating the act of fellatio but really enacting the physical process in a substantial manner. This might prompt the viewer into extra-diegetic questions, beyond the framing of what one fictional character is doing to another, or to experience the kind of embarrassment at this level suggested in Chapter 1. The same might apply to the preceding material to some extent, but the situation appears to be changed, at least in degree, when it is clear that a real act of sexual contact, traditionally restricted to the realm of hardcore pornography, is involved. An uncomfortable question is potentially raised here about what exactly we are watching, in terms of what was involved at the pro-filmic level.[16] Is Anastasia Sergeyeva a professional actor being asked to do something that might be considered morally to be uncomfortably beyond the bounds of normal 'respectable' performance? Does she have a background in hardcore pornography, in which case the prospect might be some degree less disturbing to the viewer, at least in terms of any specific potential for the exploitation of the performer in this single instance. Or is she in reality a sex worker who has been hired for this task, and is thus doing something within her normal scope of employment, which might, again, seem less discomforting at the level of any question of specific exploitation of the performer in this case rather than in any other that is not used as part of a film, whatever broader political or moral evaluation might be made.

The latter is the case, according to Seidl, who says the limits of what would happen in the sequence had been agreed with Sergeyeva in advance.[17] The availability or otherwise of such knowledge to the viewer is likely to affect the manner in which such a sequence is experienced. The situation is in some ways akin to the source of controversy surrounding Vincent Gallo's *The Brown Bunny*, which featured an explicit and sustained act of fellatio performed on the director-star by Chloe Sevigny, although with differences including Sevigny's status as an already established indie regular; the viewer was, in this case, more likely to be aware of her status, but this was viewed by some as potentially undermining her professional credibility.

Discomfort of being implicated

My own experience of viewing the hotel room sequence in *Import Export*, socially situated as a middle-aged male heterosexual, is one in which I could not deny that some element of arousal is involved at times, along with the requisite moral disapproval. It seems notable, to me, that my first instinct is to want to deny this, and to phrase it in distantly academic terms, because it does not seem morally appropriate or comfortable to acknowledge. I cannot simply indulge in any pleasure that might result from the spectacle of the body posed in various ways during the scene, which later involves the woman being led to strip fully, in a more 'conventional' manner. Any such appeal is seriously undermined by the demeaning context and the unpleasant attitude of Michael but not entirely, whatever I would prefer to be the case. The result is the kind of discomfort that can arise more generally from uncertainty or ambiguity at the level of affective response, a quality offered by *Import Export* more widely, including sequences in which a droll or wry comedy accompanies uncomfortable material. This is the case, for example, in some of Olga's responses to what she experiences in the internet sex parlour and in scenes during a party at the geriatric hospital near the end of the film, although notably not in the hotel sex sequence.

If there is an apparent tension between potential arousal and a critical framework in which this should be disavowed, the possibility also exists for the element of erotic charge to heighten rather than undercut the force of the critique established via the surrounding moral economy. This is one suggestion from the audience study led by Barker. Many male and female viewers found some scenes of sexual violence arousing, but this was associated with greater condemnation of the violence 'because the arousal heightens awareness and involvement, and thus imaginative participation in the implications of the scene'.[18] Participants who were prepared to acknowledge finding aspects of the films arousing tended to be those classified by Barker and his team as 'embracers', who responded broadly positively to the work.[19] Viewers who dismiss such films because they are found to be unpleasant 'may well retain some uncomfortable memories from it', he suggests. 'However, precisely because these are uncomfortable, they are likely to be held at a distance. On the other hand, a person who is pleased, impressed, excited or aroused is likely to engage with the film more concentratedly, and will carry away impressions and memories which are more likely to be welcomed and absorbed.'[20] The latter sense of excitement or lasting impact can also result from viewing experiences that include a strong sense of discomfort, however, as is suggested in some of the responses seen in the previous and subsequent chapters of this book. This general proposition is found to be confirmed by participants in the study. Many wrestle with mixed levels of response to negatively framed sexual material. In the case of reactions to the prolonged rape sequence in *Irreversible*, for example, Barker says: 'We proffer very tentatively this proposition: *that it helps to have at least the experience of the possibility of arousal, in order to experience the horror of its uncontrolled expression.*'[21] In the case of responses that noted the sensually attractive nature of the rape victim immediately before the attack:

> Men's response to this was often to acknowledge the arousal, but double it with guilt at their awareness of what is about to happen to her. The arousal is not thereby simply negated, it is turned into something requiring self-scrutiny: how do you now feel about the way you felt? How do you feel about being made to feel this way.[22]

An initial bodily feeling of congruency with aspects of the representation of morally unacceptable activity, that is, might heighten the charge of the disjunction that follows or accompanies it, in a manner similar to the responses of excitement and/or repulsion considered by figures such as Hanich and Sobchack, as cited in Chapter 1. Those categorized as 'refusers', who rejected such films, were likely to discuss arousal in terms that projected such effects more easily onto others, rather than themselves,[23] a common feature in discourse of this variety more generally. It is always possible for some disavowal to be involved in any of these responses, but a number of significant potential trends are identified in this study of what some viewers report and discuss about their own responses.

One of the most powerful ways for films of this kind to make their points is, arguably, to put viewers into a position in which they might feel implicated in the dynamics that are the object of critique, in this case at the level of any uncomfortable sexual stimulation. In this respect, *Import Export* can be seen to be adopting an approach broadly similar to that attributed to Seidl's better-known Austrian contemporary Michael Haneke, whose work I examine in *Positioning Art Cinema*.[24] A process of distinction marking of the kind outlined in Chapter 1 is still likely to be strongly at work, however, in responses that illustrate this kind of dynamic, my own or those examined by Barker. I am compelled by my own positioning to believe that any even partial arousal I might experience is distinct from that which might occur for any posited viewer who did not also 'get' the critique but consumed such material comfortably and/or uncritically, even if I understand this formulation to be based on the projection of a questionable and almost certainly oversimplified 'negative other'. Likewise, those of Barker's respondents who admit to some feelings of arousal in examples such as the rape sequence from *Irreversible* also hedge this with various combinations of disavowal of such arousal or the use of such a response as part of the articulation of an experience of reflexive consideration of their own initial reactions.[25] To avow the admission of some arousal on the basis of this leading to a heightened complexity of response, of a kind that is a marker of the qualities of the cinema of discomfort, or a stronger way of internalizing the critical message, is another such characteristically intellectualizing, distancing and distinction-marking manoeuvre. To admit this is not to escape the issue but, I hope, to convey some sense of the potency and inescapability of such cultural dynamics as they inevitably shape viewing experiences of this kind.

Similar analysis can be offered of the framing of the sexual material in the sequences in the cubicles occupied by performers at the internet sex business. These also involve shifts between more or less direct forms of representation of sexual display. The first are witnessed quite briefly, the viewer sharing broadly the perspective of Olga as she glimpses the nature of the work of others while looking for her friend, Tatiana (Natalya Baranova). In the first case, the framing is akin to the part of the hotel sequence in which Michael appears at the extreme right of frame. Drawing back the curtain of one cubicle, Olga is positioned similarly, looking at a woman on her knees whose rear is presented to a computer monitor, and a presumed diegetic camera, while also effectively displayed at an angle only slightly away from that of Seidl's lens. As Olga peers into another cubicle, the camera initially moves with her but then presents the view of a woman's rear pointed more directly to the audience. The camera is positioned directly behind the monitor to which the performance is diegetically oriented. It then moves to the side, to follow Olga as she steps away. As Olga finds Tatiana, the camera moves from Olga to a position in front of and then partly alongside Tatiana, in mid-performance. A movement back to Olga is followed by a cut to a straight-on shot of Tatiana performing, the camera again in a position in line with that to which the performance is directed, although from a higher position. This set-up is held for somewhat longer before a cut back to Olga and the end of the scene.

FIGURE 8 *The machinery of online pornography: Olga watching a performance in* Import Export *(2007).*

Olga then watches another woman's performance, shot from approximately mid-way between a frontal and side-on angle, as she rubs her crotch and breasts: a position distinct from that of the webcam, but none the less revealing for that. Next we have a very different perspective on another performer, lying on her back with legs raised and masturbating, shown from behind the woman in this case, enabling us to see a low-fidelity version of the broadcast image on a monitor screen, along with the web camera beneath (Figure 8). Olga watches from a position behind one of the monitors. Any potential eroticism is undercut by a deadpan sequence in which Olga breaks down in laughter while being led by Tatiana through a sheet of recommended German phrases to use to clients.

The first performance of Olga that we witness is shot from a position closer to that of the diegetic webcam than any of those that have preceded it – at greater distance than would be likely for the online viewer, but with her naked rear aimed directly at the lens, with none of the monitor equipment included in the shot (Figure 9). Little is provided, that is, by way of visual mediation between film viewer and performance. This is also the most sustained of these sequences, accompanied by the hectoring tones of her client. Just sufficient distance is retained to avoid the kind of up-close detail that would be associated with hardcore pornographic display, but the film again seems wilfully to run the risk of blurring the lines between implied critique and its own acts of potentially audience-implicating sexual display. In this case, the main source of distancing mediation is the harshly unsympathetic voice of Olga's client, another orchestrator of sexual

FIGURE 9 *Less mediated sex: Olga's first online performance to camera in* Import Export *(2007)*.

performance from which the viewer is likely to feel separated. More overtly than in the hotel scenes, we are here being shown the *construction* of sexual performance of this kind, complete with its technological equipment, even if the source of instruction is similar to that provided by Michael. A different approach could clearly have been taken, one in which such an activity was represented without any sexual explicitness on the part of the film, as is the case in the example of the making of the porn film in *A Hole in My Heart*, cited in Chapter 1.

Discomfort of the reality of ageing

The discomfort offered by *Import Export* in the realm of sex is framed primarily in the context of performances and how these might be experienced by the viewer. Plenty of scope exists to question where the line exists, morally/judgementally, between sexual performance dictated within and beyond the frame of the diegesis and what the implications of these might be for the experience of the viewer. The question of performance, or its opposite, also looms large and in relation to issues of reality, fiction and the generation of discomfort in the parts of the film set in the geriatric hospital where Olga finds work as a cleaner. Events of the fictional narrative are set against the background of real institutions and their patients, a number of whom are witnessed in states of extreme age, infirmity and/or senility. The use of such elements is framed by Seidl, and many critical commentators, as part of a more general commitment to a blurring of lines between the fictional and the real, an approach often associated with the filmmaker's background in documentary. This is a tendency that extends more broadly across the film, including the sex sequences and the fact that the principals are played by nonprofessionals whose real lives appear not to have been entirely different from those of their characters.[26] The sequences in the geriatric hospital were shot in two real institutions, to which Seidl gained access and permissions, while the same is true of the internet sex premises. In this dimension, the work of Seidl can be situated within the broader realist strands of art and indie cinema, the claims to authenticity of which often include the staging of fictional material against real-world backgrounds. These include the canonical example of Italian neorealism and the basis on which it has been celebrated by critical commentators such as Bazin.[27]

As far as the hospital scenes are concerned, the film raises a number of uncomfortable questions for the viewer. It seems likely to be apparent to an uninitiated spectator that at least some of the patients – probably most – are real inmates, such is the seeming authenticity of their presence. We are confronted with a variety of uses of such footage. In some cases, direct interaction occurs between fictional characters and patients. In others, there is much less, increasing the impression of confrontation with the starkly discomforting spectacle of real people close to death. Where we see patients interact with fictional characters, we might be left wondering to what extent they are acting, or how far particular situations have been set up for the camera or not. The uncertainty this might involve is akin to that cited earlier in the case of a mockumentary such as *I'm Still Here*, although the stakes are raised considerably by the involvement of very old and vulnerable individuals situated within a context of ageing so much closer to one viewers are likely to be able to relate to themselves. Critical debate about the film frequently raises this issue, including the possible exploitation of those who might not have been capable of giving informed consent. I have not been able to ascertain through examination of materials such as interviews with the director whether or not any of the actual patients might have been coached for any of the interactions, although the impression created is that this was not the case. It is clear, however, that Schlager, the figure to whom this might apply most strongly, is not a patient, but performed by an actor, if not one of fully professional status, Erich Finsches having also taken a part in Seidl's *Dog Days* after appearing in an earlier television documentary.

The manner in which the scenes involving geriatric patients are handled can be considered in terms similar to those used above in relation to the sex sequences. Distinctions can be made between how far such material appears to be presented more or less directly to the audience, with varying degrees of orientation within or beyond the fictional world. The first sequence in the hospital begins by establishing the presence of Olga, as a new recruit being fitted with her uniform, having her details taken by a supervisor and then joining a procession of women pushing cleaning carts down a corridor the following morning. A cut is made to a wide shot of a female ward, in which three beds on each side recede towards large windows, a shot repeated on several occasions during the film. We hear one of the patients scratchily speaking lines from the poem 'T'was the night before Christmas'. Another mouths a nonverbal sound as Olga walks into the centre of the shot and away from the camera, mopping the floor. The shot is held for a while, the poetry recital continuing, before a cut to a position at the foot of one of the beds, Olga again coming into shot to wipe down its frame. The camera pivots around to favour Olga in the composition, her look directed towards the occupant of the bed.

The next cut takes us to a similar foot-of-bed position, this time that of a toothless woman whose head moves from side to side as she mouths a series of nonverbal utterances. We then have a shot of Olga moving, seemingly past this bed, although the background is blurry, following her to another bedside, where the camera shifts between positions that privilege first the occupant, then Olga, then frames the two together. Olga's attention switches from her work to the patient, who is speaking the words of a song. As Olga continues to clean the bed frame, the woman appears to notice her presence, but how far is not clear. As Olga moves away, the camera remains on the woman, who appears to be reminiscing. A cut is then made to Olga listening, looking at the women in a medium shot that frames her from just below the chest upwards. The camera, handheld, then turns back around to frame the woman in the upper half of the bed. A cut is made to Olga at the bedside of an additional patient, whose hands she is holding, another who is talking in a manner that suggests something less than full coherence (Figure 10). This is followed again by a mid-shot of Olga, framed from just below waist upwards, looking at the woman, from which the camera pans down to the bed, emphasizing the hand contact between the two. The next cut takes us to a medium shot of Olga combing the hair of another patient. It is at this point that the nurse, Maria, enters and criticizes Olga for making any such contact.

Our views of the patients throughout this sequence are clearly tied in to the narrative situation via the presence of Olga. Her response, one that suggests quiet concern, is part of the establishment of her character, while the general effect of our first experience of the ward and its inhabitants can be seen as an important element in any broader sociocultural interpretation of what the narrative implies, a dimension to which I return below. In a manner broadly similar to the framing of the sex sequences, what we see of the patients, and the discomfort this might generate in the viewer, is mediated quite strongly through the perspective of Olga. Most of the images of patients are positioned either clearly as her view or as something that reflects this more broadly, if not always literally, a familiar mainstream convention. But the viewer is sometimes confronted more directly with the

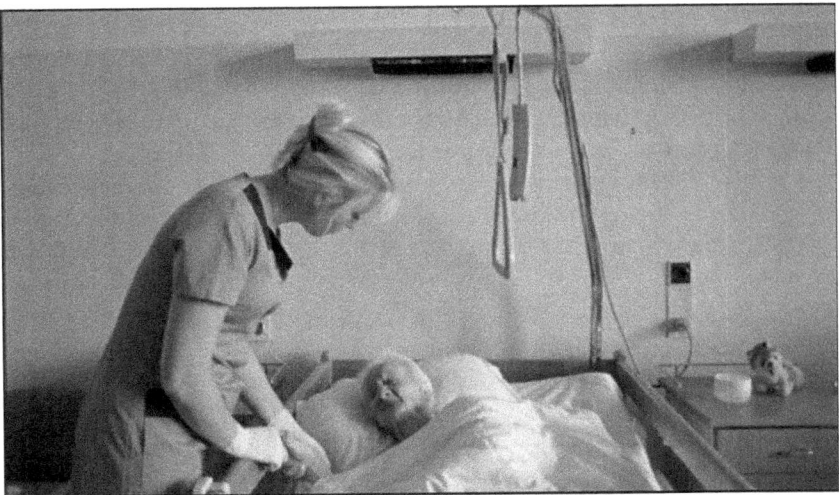

FIGURE 10 *Olga on the ward in* Import Export *(2007).*

potentially discomforting spectacle of these figures, either before or after the presence of Olga in the frame. We might also interpret much of the contact made between Olga and the patients as pro-filmic, at least as far as the experience of the latter is concerned. When she holds the hands of one of the women, for example, it might be without any consciousness on the part of the latter that this is being employed in a fictional narrative context. Any viewer awareness or consideration of this has potential to pull them out of the narrative frame, as might at times be the case with the sexual material examined above, to consider the potentially uncomfortable reality of the state of such individuals themselves, together with any discomfort that might be felt about their use within a film of this kind.

The entrance of Maria establishes the narrative frame more strongly, her superior attitude towards Olga fitting the broader sense of the injustice with which the latter is often treated. The much shorter sequence in which we first see patients on a male ward is also mixed with an element of fictional narrative-led material: Olga's introduction to the male nurse, Andi (George Friedrich), followed by his brief interaction with one of the patients. Our next visit to the ward is led by the movement of Maria, responding to a call from Schlager.

The establishing of this character has stronger narrative orientation, given his subsequent proposal to Olga, a development perhaps foreshadowed here by a preceding scene in which Olga's friend Natashka (Natalja Epureanu) complains about the behaviour of the 'paper husband' who has been her route to achieving residence in Austria. This effectively proves subsequently to wrap Schlager's presence more firmly into the fiction. Maria engages in conversation with Schlager, followed by a sequence with another male patient whose diaper she changes. Olga has a background presence during this series of interactions, largely off screen, as when we are shown the changing of the diaper, material that has no specific narrative import beyond the further establishment of the situation. This is another moment that seems liable to be read as largely unmediated, and therefore potentially more discomforting, pro-filmic reality, as far as the experience of the patient is concerned. Next we move to what appears to be a later moment, in which a general view of Olga cleaning is followed by a sustained conversation in a two shot with Schlegel, a Viennese who turns out to speak Ukrainian and sows seeds here for his later proposal.

Other sequences offer similar shifts between what might be interpreted as more direct or fictionally mediated perspectives on the patients. In one transition from the Pauli narrative back to the hospital, for example, we are given a male patient, shot from the end-of-bed position used in the female-ward sequence examined above, struggling to remove a tangled nightshirt. No cut to Olga or any other character follows and no one else enters the on-screen space. The next shot is a side view of the female ward, accompanied by a voice saying 'stinks'. This proves to be the toothless woman earlier seen making nonverbal noises, when a cut is made to her as viewed from a position at the end of her bed. One of the other women is then heard uttering a prayer, a cut showing this to be the patient who had been speaking the words of the poem and song earlier. Next, we see another of the women, from the same end-of-bed perspective as the previous two, whose words seem to devolve into an alliterative incoherence. The vocalizations of all three women can be heard, overlapping, throughout. We then have a medium head-and-shoulders shot of Olga, looking directly into camera with a largely blank expression, followed by further direct shots of each of the women in turn, the one who had previously been making the least vocal sounds now repeating the word 'death'. The following scene depicts Olga, apparently prompted by the discomforting nature of this experience, making a phone call home from the institution, to sing to her baby daughter, during which she breaks down in tears and hangs up.

In this sequence, the viewer is confronted significantly more directly with the uncomfortable spectacle of what appears to be the unadorned reality of senility and closeness to death. Any presence of Olga as a mediating figure is markedly absent from the initial series of shots, in which the viewer is left effectively to face such a prospect immediately and without the distancing offered by more substantial fictional framing (even if we might be encouraged to interpret them retrospectively as being implied to have been from Olga's perspective, thus motivating the expression in her look towards the camera). This is not to say that such a dimension might never be in play in a more conventional fictional modality. The presence of any very old performer, even a seasoned and familiar professional actor playing a clearly fictional character, might include some such extra-diegetic resonances, as can any actually performed activity in a film to some extent. More is likely to be at stake when the action or situation is of heightened nature, however, as with the non-performing presence of the extremely aged or those engaged in acts of sexual display. There is a parallel here, at opposite ends of the physical-health spectrum, between the potential experience of the presence on screen of the sexually inviting/attractive, as appealing or exploited, or any effect of discomfort that might be provoked (in the culture in which these films circulate) by confrontation with the reality of a state of near-death age and infirmity. That which might be defined or experienced as more extreme bodily repulsion or transgression is generally beyond the scope of the kinds of discomfort on which this book is focused. What seems more likely to be provoked by the hospital scenes, all the more so when relatively less mediated by the fictional frame, is a quieter sense of discomfort involved in having to confront the spectacle of a terrifyingly *ordinary* state of existence to which many of us, or our loved ones, are likely to be destined.

The narratives of the film end with moments that can be read as relatively hopeful, although perhaps only faintly so. Pauli has walked out on Michael from the Ukrainian hotel room. He tries and fails to pick up work locally and is last seen walking away from camera, hitch-hiking on a largely empty tree-lined road. While nothing specific is very positive about his prospects, he has at least escaped for now from what Michael seems to embody, and the movement away down a road is a trope generally associated with some kind of freedom. Olga is last seen sitting around a recreation table in the hospital, sustained laughter coming from her and the group of staff among which she sits, suggesting a spirit of resilience. The final images, however, are from the women's ward at night, entirely unmediated by the presence of any fictional characters and uncomfortably downbeat. A flat, distanced shot of four beds and their occupants on one side is followed by a similar, slightly closer shot of three beds on the other, to the accompaniment of quiet muttering sounds. The now-familiar long shot from the end of the ward follows, a series of voiced comments ending with of repetition of 'death, death, death' and a cut to silence over the initial titles (Figure 11).

Critical and other debate about *Import Export* has often revolved around its use of real geriatric patients, if anything more than the sexually explicit material. A question often raised, and clearly a major source of discomfort for some, is whether or not the patients are exploited by the film, either generally or on the grounds of what might be assumed to be the inability of some to have given any form of meaningful consent.[28] As far as the production process was concerned, Seidl has emphasized the care he says was taken during filming.[29] The main actors involved, playing Olga, Maria and Andi, apparently spent several weeks working in the two hospitals, to become integrated into patient routines and not an intrusive presence. Seidl says most of the inmates received no visitors, some effectively dying

FIGURE 11 *The reality of end of life: The final shot of the ward, with English subtitle, in* Import Export *(2007).*

of loneliness, and that this was a role effectively performed by himself and members of the cast and crew. This would underline any suggestion, for example, that it would be the performer Rak providing real comfort to the patient whose hands she holds as much as the character Olga behaving this way within a fictional context. The filmmaker expresses a commitment to allowing the patients to maintain their dignity, which I would suggest is generally the case as far as this is possible in what is in some ways inevitably a somewhat infantilizing experience, such as the male patient having his diaper changed on screen. A core aim, however, Seidl says, is 'to confront the audience with the truth. You have to show them the way things actually are'.

This is a rationale we might expect in such a case, one of the key bases on which major strands of art or indie film are customarily valorized more generally, particularly when it comes to the depiction of that which is likely to be discomforting to the viewer and, by implication, usually hidden from view. Seidl also fits into a broader art cinema context in expressing a commitment to the use of extended duration as a source of unembellished authenticity and specifically for the generation of discomfort. Without duration, he suggests, 'the audience wouldn't have that same uncomfortable feeling' produced by the film. He states explicitly: 'I want this to be uncomfortable.' Seidl discusses this in relation to the hotel room sex sequences. 'You have to find exactly the right length' of shot, he suggests. To cut away from the action too much is to weaken the likely impact. 'That means it must in some way torture the audience. It must be uncomfortable, but not so uncomfortable that they leave the cinema. They have to manage to stay there.'

It can be questionable to take at face value the statements of filmmakers, but this seems quite accurately to capture some of the key dynamics of the sequences examined above. *Import Export* dwells on difficult material, sufficiently so to establish substantial elements of pro-filmic reality texture that add weight to the narrative and its implications, and the discomfort likely to result from the combination of the two. But this is also qualified to some extent, through the employment of devices such as the presence of Michael in the frame in the sex sequence or Olga amid the geriatric patients. Such an approach is embodied in the style of the film more generally, one that moves between ironically distancing perspectives in some cases and others that are more mainstream-conventional in terms of inviting variable degrees of alignment or allegiance with the main characters. The latter is often achieved by a mobile, handheld camera that moves relatively close to characters, although not in an exaggerated manner or with the uncomfortably claustrophobic proximity found in examples such as the films of the Dardennes, as cited in Chapter 1. The balance here is slightly different from what we find in Seidl's documentary work, which is more strongly associated with the stylization that results from sustained static and frontal tableaux shots of his subjects. Such 'Seidlerian set pieces', as they are termed by Martin Brady and Helen Hughes,[30] are also found at times in *Import Export* and *Dog Days*, to which I return below, but are far from the dominant style in either case. The greater presence of such perspectives in his documentaries has sometimes led to this dimension being overstated in relation to his fiction features, the overall style of which creates a more complex structure of sympathy closer to that found in the films of Solondz.

Discomfort as social critique?

If *Import Export* is an example of a type of cinema that offers particular kinds and degrees of discomfort such as those explored above, we can best explain the existence of such work at the two levels suggested earlier in this book. It can be understood, on the one hand and perhaps most obviously, as a response to its social-cultural context, mediated by the particular concerns of the filmmaker(s), as a reflection of, and/or critical commentary on, aspects of its contemporary society. It can also be seen as a product of more specifically cinematic-institutional conditions of existence. I start here with the sociocultural, historical or political realm, one that is most often to the fore in explanations provided for the creation of work of this kind.

Import Export, along with other films by Seidl, seems quite clearly to present itself as a social critique, although typically one that does not offer any answers to the problems it appears implicitly to diagnose. As with the other works considered more briefly below, it can be seen as expressing, capturing or manifesting certain aspects of contemporary society, whether specifically Austrian or of broader provenance. The film can be read as a critique of certain prevailing conditions in the eastern European countries in which it is partly set, Ukraine and Slovakia, although this does not appear to be its main target. The aspects of these countries that are presented seem far from appealing in their general or sometimes extreme bleakness: the landscape of huge social housing projects and smoke-emitting industrial chimneys traversed by Olga on her daily walk to and from work, or the even more decrepit blocks of flats visited by Pauli and Michael in Slovakia. These perhaps risk being viewed as over-familiar clichés of 'grim' eastern Europe, particularly in the post-communist era, despite Seidl's expressions of affection for the countries of the east.[31] The film offers plenty that can be read as a critique of constructions of masculinity, as embodied by the posturing enacted at times by both Pauli and Michael, although this would seem to be of broader relevance rather than rooted solely in any of the territories in which the film is set. A more specific sense of social critique might be aimed at certain parts of Austrian society, as has often been suggested of Seidl's films more generally. In this sense, the films have been associated with others situated as constituting a 'New Austrian Cinema', although the term has also been taken to suggest something less particular to the country and a version of more widespread dynamics.

A number of Austrian factors have been associated with work that has been labelled in this or similar ways, especially in the context of a critique of certain forms of conservative, middle-class conformism, often within a national historical-cultural context. An example of the targeting of this social sector is found in the portrayal of the uptight woman who hires Olga as a cleaner, only to sack her without notice for no reason other than, perhaps, that Olga appears to be able to relax and play with her employer's children in a way the latter seems unable to do herself, at least from what we see. The woman is characterized with a cold (repressive?) and high-handed arrogance of a kind that would fit a broader critique of certain aspects of middle-class culture. A similar questioning of attitudes towards those of lower status seems to underlie Maria's meanness towards Olga, a response that seems heightened by jealousy at the latter's more conventionally attractive appearance. As Sathe notes, if the power of western characters to dominate those from the east includes the power of a dominating gaze in cases such as the hotel room sex sequence, the same applies to a large extent in the subjection of Olga to an empowered western gaze both in the internet parlour and subsequently in Austria.[32] This remains largely the case, even if both Pauli and Olga are granted some ability to fight back.

Other material offers a satirical approach to certain aspects of Austrian society, including the ludicrous pomposity of two be-suited training authority figures confronted by Pauli and Olga respectively: one recommending an attitude of 'flattery, obsequiousness and deference' to jobseekers, the other offering a self-importantly inflated emphasis on the importance of a menial office-cleaning post. A broader critique is implied by the scenes in the geriatric hospital, a cultural diagnosis of the process of locking away elderly relatives to die out of sight and apart from their families. Much the same can be said of what is represented more widely by the internet sex business, along with the more specific theme of exploitation of those in the east from the west. The latter applies to the activities of Michael in Slovakia and the Ukraine, both sexually and as part of a business that seeks to eke out profit from those in what appears to be a state of poverty, although on neither level do these enterprises appear very impressive. If the activities of Olga and Pauli can be seen as manifestations of broader neoliberal geopolitical dynamics, they are instances of how this affects those towards the lower end of the social scale. The fact that key decisions made by Olga, most notably the move to Austria, are not dramatized or discussed as such – we just see them happening, as fait accompli – encourages a sense that such events are to be interpreted as the products of inexorable wider forces rather than of individual freedom or agency.

In the Austrian national case, the contexts often suggested for critiques of the kind implied by *Import Export* and other artistic-cultural products range from unresolved Nazi-era guilt and the rise of the extreme right in politics in the late 1990s to specific traumatic events that drew attention to Austrian cultural production in the 2000s, such as the eight-year kidnapping of Natascha Kampusch and the even longer imprisoning of his daughter by Josef Fritzl. Added to such ingredients is an exploration by filmmakers such as Seidl and other artists of the state of the country in the wake of immigration that followed the collapse of state communism in eastern Europe, an issue sometimes framed in terms of Austria's past history as a more cosmopolitan melting pot or neutral state. This is the kind of conjunction of factors associated with what the *New York Times* critic Dennis Lim termed the Austrian film 'new wave', in an often-cited feature titled 'Greetings from the Land of Feel-Bad Cinema', an article that accompanied a showcase of recent works from the country by the Film Society of Lincoln Center in 2006.[33]

For Robert van Dassanowksy and Oliver Speck, in their introduction to a collection of essays titled *New Austrian Cinema*, the 'feel-bad' tag is a reductionist label for a broader new generation of work that had its beginnings in the late 1970s and came to wider attention two decades later, even if it might seem well suited to central aspects of the work of Seidl. As van Dassanowksy and Speck suggest, however, much of the material found in films associated with this movement has broader resonance than that provided by the Austrian context. The 'attacks of New Austrian Film are not aimed at a specific Austrian petit-bourgeois milieu', they suggest, but a more general mode of modern or postmodern western existence.[34] If these films capture a certain 'structure of feeling', to use the term employed by Raymond Williams, this is not restricted to the national context. The films discussed in the volume they edit, including three chapters focused on Seidl, 'do not deal with fascism because of Austria's arguably problematic relationship to its fascist past, but because they recognize that unfortunately nothing about this [situation] is truly exceptional'. The filmmakers involved 'are fully aware that Austria is not an exception but the rule'.[35] They add: 'What makes these films exceptional is the astuteness with which they analyse and represent an unexceptional and generalized postmodern condition.'[36] This is a realm similar in its potential breadth of application to the contemporary malaise identified by the sociological commentators cited in Chapter 1. Broader resonance of this kind can also be suggested for the more specific terrain of the border crossing movements around which *Import Export* revolves (even though no actual acts of crossing physical borders are shown), this having become a distinct topos within fictional art cinema and documentary in the period, from Austria and beyond. As Elżbieta Ostrowska and Johanna Rydzewska suggest, the image of the exploited migrant eastern European woman, in particular, became a feature of films from both east and west of the continent in the period after 1989.[37] A frequent basis for the valorization of works of art cinema more generally is the argument that they can combine a focus on the specific sociocultural factors involved in their place of origin with broader resonances of this kind.

From *Dog Days* to documentary

A wider domestic social canvas is offered by Seidl in *Dog Days*, which follows the experiences of a multitude of characters across a swelteringly hot weekend, set in a bland suburban landscape that includes a new housing development and a ubiquitous strip of anonymous out-of-town retail outlets (the later suggesting the kind of postmodern no-place evoked by von Dassanowsky and Speck). It is easy to assume much of this to imply a critique of such terrain, and its occupants, but the attitude of the film seems less clear cut. There are a number of apparent targets of criticism, including the oppressive bullying behaviour (or more bottled-up passive-aggression) of several male characters. One constantly berates his seemingly blameless girlfriend. A second is similarly obnoxious to his. A friend of the second forces the woman in this trio into meting out punishment to her abuser, in what constitutes little more than further male posturing and mistreatment. Another male is seen mostly in a state of discomforting and vaguely threatening brooding, still awkwardly sharing a house with his ex-wife, as she entertains a lover. The film includes sequences that are distanced and droll in their expression, including a number of the stylized tableau shots associated with the Seidl documentary style, particularly those depicting a variety of figures sunbathing in the heat; we see one couple lying incongruously next to a churning cement mixer. But this is not the dominant style. Like *Import Export*, the bulk of the film is shot unobtrusively, often with a moving handheld camera that creates more conventional forms of relative alignment with characters.

Some of what is shown is at least mildly bizarre, including one sudden cut into an orgy sequence. But, even here, the presentation tends to suggest its treatment as neutral and mundane material rather than implying critical commentary. One victim of violent abuse is seen beforehand, standing eating cold chicken in her underwear. Nothing very clearly marked seems to be signified by such a sequence. Its intention appears sympathetic rather than anything satirical but is left largely to the viewer to decide. In Plantinga's typology of types of alignment encouraged between viewer and characters, the work of Seidl occupies a position that shares some of the complexity of Solondz's *Palindromes*, although in a different manner. Much is viewed in a matter-of-factly observational manner that has potential for ironic/satirical distance but where this is not overtly marked and the resonance might be more mixed or ambiguous. Little is offered in the way of pointed subjective access to character. Non-diegetic music is generally absent in Seidl, a characteristic cinema of discomfort tendency to withhold clearer-cut emotional or evaluative cues. It is often almost *as if* the material were of a documentary status similar to that found in Seidl's non-fiction films, even where such figures are more narratively (and, of course, fictionally) located than is the case in the latter.

A similar lack of any overt interpretation is found in scenes in which the elderly Mr Walter (Erich Finsches) interacts with his housekeeper (Gerti Lehner), which includes her putting on dresses that belonged to Walter's deceased wife and later performing a striptease for him. Walter is not presented entirely sympathetically. We see him gardening, his stout figure clad in shorts, vest and braces cutting a somewhat comical figure as he tends an incongruously enormous hedge. He complains about the noise of the neighbours, eventually leaving his lawnmower running near the division between the two properties as a form of revenge. He hoards huge numbers of supplies, as if expecting an apocalypse, carefully weighing his produce at home and complaining at the supermarket if there is any discrepancy from the advertised quantity. He seems a far from progressive character, with his video-surveillance system and a large guard dog. He could easily be seen as a caricature of a certain kind of stereotypically 'traditional'/conservative Austrian figure. But the film tends to present him in generally neutral-to-sympathetic terms, despite any such connotations. The business with the housekeeper is handled in a manner that seems broadly designed to be touching rather than subjected to mockery or critique. The viewer is often left without any clearly marked indication of how to take this or other material in the film, a trait also widespread in Seidl's work in documentary.

If discomfort in *Dog Days* might often be a product of interpretive openness, the film also offers the uncomfortable prospect of implicating the viewer in one of its more disturbing developments. This can be seen as akin to the implication potentially involved in the viewing of the sex sequences in *Import Export*. One of the regularly recurring characters in *Dog Days* is a hitch-hiker (Maria Hofstätter). She is presented as a woman who clearly has mental health problems of some kind. Those who give her lifts are subjected to an almost unending verbal outpouring of questions and criticisms, many of them inappropriately personal, along with renditions of cultural trivia such as assorted 'top ten' lists, ranging from best supermarkets to most popular sexual positions. She seems to have a limited understanding of personal boundaries, often leaning in towards her drivers, uncomfortably closely, and breaching the bounds of usual social behaviour in activities such as going through the bags or wallets of others. She is a highly annoying character, to those she drives, many of whom become infuriated and angry, sometimes ejecting her from the car. She is also likely to annoy the viewer, designedly so, it seems. Towards the end of the film, another recurring character, Hruby (Alfred Mrva), appears without any basis to decide to pin the blame on the hitch-hiker for a wave of car vandalism he has failed to resolve. Having picked her up for a second time, he locks her in a basement. At least two of her supposed victims are then summoned to the location and left free to gain vengeance, which in one case is clearly implied to be of a sexual nature, probably rape. The impression is that those involved are taking out a variety of frustrations on the woman, but this might also appear extra-diegetically to be a kind of 'payback' for the serial irritation she is likely to have caused the viewer. This could leave viewers feeling uncomfortably complicit, vicariously, in some degree, for her treatment, notwithstanding the fact that the punishment is clearly incommensurate with any 'crime' of causing irritation.

Seidl's 'Paradise' trilogy also includes plenty of discomforting material that has sociocultural resonances, sexual and otherwise, again often highlighted by a neutral treatment that seems less to judge difficult characters than to leave the viewer to decide what exactly to make of them. These include distinctly awkward encounters in the first instalment, *Paradise Love*, between a middle-aged woman, Teresa (Margarete Tiesel), on a sex-tourism beach holiday in Kenya, and the local males with whom she gets involved. That Teresa wants to forge some relatively more meaningful connection with the hustlers seems understandable, on one level, but also to demonstrate a failure to appreciate the nature of the power relationship inevitably structured into such an encounter, a different and gender-reversed perspective on the commodification of sexual relations explored in *Import Export*. The film offers an uncomfortable representation, for the middle-class 'western' viewer, of the position of the tourist in 'exotic' places, sexually or more generally; of an underlying, and sometimes more overt, structural racism. The viewer is likely to share some of the discomfort caused to Teresa by the unwanted attentions of locals constantly seeking to sell something, or the way she is pumped for money on various pretexts by the men with whom she pairs. But this is combined with the knowledge that this seems an inevitable product of such a relationship, for which the Kenyan males can hardly be blamed. Distanced tableau-style shots are used quite frequently. These sometimes underline the inequalities of the situation, including those which highlight the division between tourists and the local vendors who stand the other side of a rope that fences them off from their would-be clients on the beach. But the film also offers sympathy for the experience of Teresa, as an individual who, although relatively empowered in this context, also seems a product of broader, social circumstances.

Paradise: Faith focuses on Teresa's sister, Anna (Maria Hofstätter), an evangelical Catholic who spends her vacation trying to convert immigrants to her faith. In some ways similarly to the figure of Mama Sunshine in *Palindromes*, although a far less warm character, Anna is likely to provide an uncomfortable source of allegiance for the typical arthouse constituency. When the paraplegic husband from whom she has become estranged turns up, a struggle entails between two unappealing characters: Anna, devout beyond what appears to be normal reason, having a relationship with Jesus that seems to cross over at times into the sexual, and Nabil (Nabil Saleh), a would-be source of patriarchal dominance. The third part of the trilogy, *Paradise: Hope*, features a queasily inappropriate relationship between a middle-aged doctor and Teresa's thirteen-year-old daughter, Melanie (Melanie Lenz), sent to a 'diet camp' while her mother is abroad. In this case, nothing explicit is shown and it is not clear how far things progress; such central questions are in this case left awkwardly unanswered. As with much of Seidl's work, the film features what could be seen as wry or dolorous distanced shots of the group of teenagers at the camp, particularly when engaged in various forms of exercise; but, again, the impression is less one of ironic distance or judgement than flat neutrality of presentation.

From a social-cultural perspective, Seidl's documentaries offer a broadly neutral impression at the individual level, similar to that often found in his fictions. The various frames he uses serve implicitly as vehicles for a broader window onto various parts of the contemporary social world: the movements between two communities across the Austria–Czech border in *Losses to be Expected* (*Mit Verlust ist zu rechnen*, 1992); people and their pets in *Animal Love* (*Tierische Liebe*, 1996); individual problems as elaborated through the medium of prayer in *Jesus, You Know* (*Jesus du weisst*, 2003); the vicissitudes of life as an aspiring model in *Models* (1998); the sometimes bizarre purposes for which some individuals use their cellars in *In the Basement*. Some of this material lends itself to a more obviously critical interpretation. The clearest such case is the figure who keeps a Nazi shrine in his basement, along with others in the same film who voice openly racist sentiments. But even here, the presentation is in a typically flat Seidl style that leaves us to bring the judgment to cases such as this or others that seem less clear cut in any moral economy, such as individuals who engage in consenting sadomasochistic practices. When we see the Hitler supporter framed in typical Seidl style with dummies in Nazi uniforms or other regalia on each side, this might seem like a tableau *designed* to criticize through its framing – if such an approach were not used so much more widely and often where no clear basis for any such critique is implied. In most cases, little if any blame appears to be suggested on the parts of the individual subjects, even the least sympathetic of which can be read as symptoms rather than causes of the situations in which they are depicted.

Animal Love embraces a considerable social range, from characters living on the margins to those with various degrees of comfortably middle-class status. What emerges often in cases such as this is a sense of people living lives of quiet desperation, as expressed in prayer in the one case or in the emotional needs projected onto pets in another. This implies a critique of the contemporary society in which they are set, whether national or more widely, but only in broad terms. These are presented as portrayals of situations rather than diagnoses of any potential causes. The style adopted by Seidl – absent any overt commentary, whether audio or through strategies such as montage juxtaposition – is not one that lends itself to more analytical investigation. Of the six established modes of documentary identified by Bill Nichols (poetic, expository, observational, participatory, reflexive, performative), Seidl's approach fits in some ways into the observational category, in the impression it creates of flat neutrality and the absence of the filmmaker from any overt presence on screen.[38] It also lacks any externally imposed commentary of the kind often found in the expository mode, which might situate the particular more explicitly within a wider social context. The footage that follows characters around their milieu, in a seemingly passive manner, accords with the qualities ascribed to the observational mode, one that stresses the non-intervention of the filmmaker. But this is not so for the many instances of staged tableaux, in which an act of intervention is explicitly involved in the arrangement of his subjects before the camera. These suggest the presence of a hybrid mode; the status in practice, as Nichols suggests, of most documentary films.[39] Where such staging implies the creation of editorial meaning of some kind, the films can be seen as operating in something closer to an expositional manner. This might be the effect of what Nichols generally terms 'strange juxtapositions' – found across Seidl's documentary and fictional work – that can be read as making a point rather than allowing events 'to unfold according to their own rhythm'.[40] The tableau style, particularly where the subjects look into the camera, might also create a reflexive dimension, signalling, if here only implicitly, the constructed nature of the documentary image as artefact.

There is plenty of potential for discomfort in Seidl's documentaries, often intensified by his distinctive formal approach. Characters sometimes look directly into the camera in silence for protracted periods, effectively returning the gaze of the viewer, as a number of critics, including Brady and

Hughes, suggest.[41] This can take the form of an implicit challenge to those who are looking in on their lives. In *Models*, a film that seems to mix real characters with some more constructed routines, a repeated confection is that the eponymous protagonists face the camera as if it is a mirror in which they are doing their make-up. The major device in *Jesus, You Know* is to have subjects praying towards the camera in churches (although not exactly into the lens, their gaze often shifting between a higher point, the location usually of a crucifix shown in reverse shots, or lowered, as customarily in prayer), another source of potentially uncomfortable intimacy. Discomfort can also result from the unexplained nature of some of the more passing routines. *Losses to be Expected* begins, for example, with a man dancing and then stripping naked to camera. Why, we have no idea at the time, or exactly later, although he turns up subsequently expressing his discontent with the conditions in which he lives, on the eastern side of the border. While the Nazi-supporting figure in *In the Basement* seems a clear object for critique, more disturbing in some ways, because we are left with no clear/familiar explanatory/condemnatory framework, is a woman who keeps a number of highly realistic baby dolls in boxes, bringing them out and putting them away to 'sleep' while talking to them as if they are real.

Elements of similarity can be found between some of the documentaries and the fictions. One character in *Jesus, You Know* seems to be a template for Anna in *Paradise: Faith*. The cross-border scenario of *Losses to be Expected* is very different from that of *Import Export*, but it permits the highlighting of some similar contrasts between standards of material life in east and west, although more explicitly in this case. The fictions have the feel of being more elaborated narrative scenarios that could easily have been built out of the kinds of real-world scenarios charted in the documentaries, which seems at least partly to have been the case. If *Losses to be Expected* has the most sustained character-narrative focus of the documentaries, elements of others could have similar potential; for example, two rather hapless male figures, almost Beckettian in their hats and coats, with an unruly new dog in *Animal Love*. A figure who opens but plays no further part in *Import Export* – repeatedly trying to start a motorcycle and sidecar without success, in a snowy landscape outside a bleak block of flats – could, meanwhile, easily have turned up as one of the drolly passing vignettes in one of the documentaries.

Producing and selling discomfort

If the films of Seidl, and others grouped under labels such as 'New Austrian Film' or the Austrian 'new wave', can be related to their contemporary social context, national or more broadly, they also remain products of particular film-industrial/artistic conjunctures. This can also be explained at both the local and more international levels. Von Dassanowsky and Speck trace the new wave that took on more concerted form in the late 1990s to what they term 'scattered beginnings' in the late 1970s, a period that involved the abandonment of commercial filmmaking after the collapse of the mainstream domestic industry by the end of the 1960s. If Austria was perceived as having missed out on the era of new waves that spread across other European countries in the immediate post-war decades, as they suggest, a new generation with very modest resources 'looked at styles abroad but found their vision and voice in critical topics set in recognizable circumstances'.[42] A limited revival of earlier practices of international co-production, primarily Austrian-German, led to a number of films gaining critical attention in Austria and beyond. State subsidy is usually a key component of cinemas of this kind in Europe, a contrast generally with the American indie sector. A new subsidy system was introduced and 'helped solidify the new growth to some extent', suggest von Dassanowsky and Speck, 'but it was and still remains among the weakest financial support structures in Europe'.[43] They add: 'With few traditional venues for distribution available, new companies and concepts such as the artist-run Sixpack Film (or sixpackfilm), which promotes short and experimental work, brought together a very disparate creative scene.'[44] The term New Austrian Film, they suggest, 'is thus one of convenience', as is often the case with such labels.[45] In summary, von Dassanowsky and Speck argue, this phenomenon

> grew organically from the uniqueness of the destruction of its cinematic parent [the previous commercial industry in Austria], from its resistance to official history and national image, and from the multicultural shadow that has always been a natural part of the internationality of this national cinema. Its categorization can only be found in its self-starting and casual collaboration, rather than in some overriding doctrine, in its ability to exist against all economic and market-driven odds, and in emerging critical sympathy to a multi-segmented and detached national film history/culture that has only recently been represented by archives, retrospectives, and research.[46]

A more established phase of New Austrian Cinema gained its international breakthrough, in this account, with Barbara Albert's *Northern Skirts* (*Nordrand*, 1999), which focuses on young women migrant characters in Austria.[47] By far the most prominent figure in the international circulation of such work is Michael Haneke, although his rise to higher profile was based at least partly on a movement from his Austrian beginnings to an orientation towards France (French language and stars, and international co-production) in films such as *Hidden* (*Cache*, 2005), as what appeared to be a more hospitable environment for such production.[48] The Austrian context of the films of Seidl and others has also to be understood within this wider, initially European but also broader international cinematic context, one that often includes a mix of domestic and international backing, sometimes precarious in nature. The budget for *Import Export*, for example, is said by Seidl to have been €2.1 million and 'getting the financing together was not easy.'[49] One subsidiser 'didn't give us enough money', which meant the costs had to be recalculated and shooting was delayed. Funds came from the Austrian Film Institute, the Vienna Film Fund and the state of Lower Austria. Additional support was provided by public service television networks, as is often the case for such films: the Austrian Broadcasting Corporation (ORF), Arte France Cinema (a Franco-German network focused on culture and the arts) and the German broadcaster, ZDF.[50] Also credited was an Austrian property company. The Austrian Film Institute and ORF are by far the largest domestic funders of films designed for theatrical release more generally, according to Mathias Frey.[51]

Reliance on such sources of funding is among other respects in which the Austrian situation can be seen as representative of wider trends for the cinemas of smaller nations, or those with smaller-scale film infrastructure, to depend on a close conjunction of local, national and international, regional and/or global networks.[52] Frey identifies three main production trends in recent Austrian cinema, only one of which, comedy, is rooted in an appeal to the domestic audience. The other two, documentaries and art films, including those designated as part of the 'feel-bad' tendency, rely primarily on their address to an international market.

The currency and potential for circulation of films such as *Import Export* exists largely in the framework provided by extra-national institutions such as the global festival network and certain kinds of internationally focused arthouse distributors, along with their appeal to critics. The film carries a key imprimatur of quality in this domain in having been part of the official selection at the prestigious Cannes Film Festival, a fact displayed in marketing materials and at the start of the film. *Dog Days* gained a similar status, having its premiere at the Venice Film Festival, another leading event, where it won the grand jury prize. Within this wider landscape, these films fit into a particular tendency at the time, and continuing since, for the appearance in such circuits of films that pushed beyond the usual contemporary limits of censorship/regulation, particularly in the depiction of explicit and/or unsimulated sexual material. If seen on its own, *Import Export* might appear extraordinary in some of the material examined earlier in this chapter; in this context it seems far less so, to the point of being to some extent contemporary art-cinema-generic. To say this is not to seek to denigrate or reduce such a film but to acknowledge its place within the particular set of norms encouraged by a specific conjunction of institutional forces.

The existence of the 'new extreme', as this broader phenomenon is often labelled, has been explained at both levels considered in this chapter: as a symptom of the broader sociocultural context and/or as a product of this more specific cinematic realm, as I discuss at greater length in *Positioning Art Cinema*. From the perspective of the industry, such films can be situated within a longer tradition of the sale of art cinema on the basis of its ability to go further in such directions than is usually possible for more commercial productions. A long-standing connection has existed between the 'art' of art cinema – and some indie production – and elements more often associated with the realm of 'exploitation', the latter chiefly involving selling products on the basis of notoriety derived from the use, or promise, of certain forms of sex, violence or related qualities. While academic analysis has offered various readings of the 'new extreme' or 'new brutality' film in terms of what it might say about issues such as sexuality in contemporary 'western' society, Frey provides a valuable corrective to any exclusive focus on this level in his consideration of the various institutional incentives that encouraged the production of such films in the period in question, as key parts of the broader culture of art cinema.[53] These include specific bases of appeal to stakeholders such as distributors, exhibitors and festival organizers, particularly as sources of 'scandal' and notoriety. The latter, in turn, is a valuable source of publicity, unpaid media coverage that can be of particular importance to a sector in which funding for marketing is usually limited. Such qualities reinforce a sense of art cinema offering space for transgression of cultural norms, one key basis of the broader valorization of art in cinema or elsewhere. Scope for such material was also created in some key markets by a liberalization of censorship regimes.

Frey also suggests similarly cinema-specific factors that help account for the existence of films located in the 'feel-bad' category from Austria. It is customary, he suggests, for this tendency to be explained in relation to particular traditions within the national culture, as argued above. This includes the citation by critics such as Lim of artistic work including the painting of Egon Schiele and Gustav Klimt and the writing of Thomas Bernhard and Elfriede Jelinek. While he agrees that such a case has some merit, 'a stronger claim, however, would embed these national-essentialist claims [...] into more concrete institutional frameworks'.[54] Efforts to situate such production at least partially in national terms need not be essentialist in nature, however, as is suggested by the approach of Von Dassanowsky and Speck, which also seeks to combine different levels of analysis. That some major strands of Austrian cinema are outward-facing and targeted towards the international art-cinema market is to a large extent explained for Frey by a lack of domestic demand for home-grown production, other than low-budget comedies, along with the shortage of sources of funding at the national level. This is a situation that applies to many varieties of art film, although Austria is considered to have one of the lowest levels of subsidy for a country of such substantial means.

Another specific institutional factor was the influence over the national film culture gained at a certain stage by key figures, especially Haneke, a situation in which, Frey suggests, 'a handful of role models wield a large amount of local authority', which 'can give rise to a master-apprentice phenomenon whereby a hegemonic style prevails'.[55] The industry in Austria is 'small and tightly networked', creating 'personal-professional constellations' within which the extreme tendency became an 'institutional aesthetic' in Austria, 'a feedback circuit that pervades education and national-cultural bodies'.[56] Teachers at the primary Austrian film school, The Filmakademie Wien, for example, included Haneke, with Seidl and Albert among its alumni, along with others associated with the 'feel-bad' approach. A certain kind of art cinema, in such a context, including the attitude of state or regional funding bodies, gained the status of 'an institutionally sanctioned, safe model with a record of success'.[57] Following such a model was a particularly effective way of jump-starting the careers of younger filmmakers, Frey suggests, citing as evidence work by Jessica Hausner, Ruth Mader and Anja Salomonowitz.[58] More generally, for a small national cinema such as that of Austria, as Frey puts it, as with some others, 'extreme representations of sex, violence, and sexual violence can function as comparatively attractive ways to elicit international attention from film festival programmers, journalists, buyers at distribution companies, and audiences'.[59]

If the feel-bad variety of Austrian cinema has potential to be viewed as an in some ways unrepresentative tendency, one that overemphasizes certain nationally focused negative clichés, this can also be seen as part of the broader dynamics of this kind of film economy. Certain examples of 'extreme' cinema from parts of Asia have been accused of promulgating negative 'orientalist' stereotypes, as Frey suggests. But, he argues, this is not simply something one-dimensionally imposed on filmmakers or others from outside, in the circulation of such films overseas. It can also entail what Frey terms a 'self-orientalization', a deliberate process of drawing on certain reductive stereotypes that are functional when it comes to the achievement of international recognition and sales, however regressive they might seem.[60] Something similar might apply, he suggests, in the maintenance of negative national stereotype in feel-bad examples of Austrian cinema, including the work of Seidl.

That the extreme or otherwise discomforting aspects of such films might be a major source of their currency in the international channels through which art cinema circulates seems to be without doubt. The work of Seidl is not as exclusively negative as some such writing suggests, however. A more sympathetic or at least neutral reading is also available in many cases, as suggested above, when such films are examined closely, if more at the individual scale than what is implied at a social level. It also remains important to qualify such notions through an understanding of the broader, *non*-nationally specific dimensions of many aspects of this material, the appeal of which might be as much on the basis of its resonance with contemporary existence beyond the borders of Austria as with the selling of a negatively framed national other.

Some of these varieties of the 'extreme' go beyond the focus of this book, in their more luridly staged and heightened forms of transgression, but they also include varied sexual dynamics such as those considered in both chapters so far. Whatever its other resonances, such material can be viewed as a source of a kind of 'thrill', or frisson, suitable for the target constituencies of such films: a 'respectable' or intellectualized equivalent of the sources of such affective responses offered by more mainstream films or particular genres such as horror. Any such qualities are given legitimacy, in this context, by their positioning as part of what is presented as a serious exploration or critique rather than the stuff of what might otherwise be dismissed as 'gratuitous' indulgence or 'cheap thrills'. Much of the critical debate about such films revolves around whether or not any such rationale exists, a point rejected by some journalistic critics in particular.[61] It is notable how relatively disproportionately contentious material of certain varieties is sometimes found in works from the art or indie sectors. This would include the presence of paedophilia in instances of indie cinema such as *Palindromes* and *Happiness*. We might imagine how different these films would be if broadly similar themes were explored but without the inclusion of specifically sexual material of these varieties in general, or in the explicit form it takes in some cases. The spectacle of age and infirmity in *Import Export* would not generally fit into this framework, given its lack of anything likely to be described as remotely 'lurid' or seductive in potential appeal, but it can be viewed as another form of extremity of representation in its own more quietly discomforting terms.

The potential commercial appeal of sexual content is confirmed by the choices made in some of the marketing materials for *Import Export*, many of which include the image of the naked Olga performing rearwards to camera from the internet parlour sequence. This appears in some of the poster artwork and DVD covers, either on its own or taking up the top half of combined images. It is also employed, along with some brief images from the hotel sex sequence, in trailers for the film, although here such material constitutes a much smaller proportion of the content overall. The region 2 DVD carries what is intended to be a warning, alongside the eighteen certificate, saying 'Contains strong real sex and very strong language', the first part of which might also be viewed as a selling point of its own in certain circumstances. 'Adult' certification has long served as one exploitable component of international art cinema.[62] That films which include explicit sexual content of the kind found in *Import Expert* can be subject to unwanted forms of appropriative consumption is demonstrated by the fact that images or footage also circulate in online pornography sites, put to a use uncomfortably close to that which is represented critically within the film.

Responses

Critical responses to *Import Export* were largely positive, despite the fact that it was reportedly greeted by some jeering during a press screening at Cannes.[63] The review aggregation site Rotten Tomatoes recorded an 84 per cent rating from journalistic critics, with twenty-seven out of thirty-two sampled responding positively and only five negatively.[64] The 'critics consensus' summary offered by the site confirms its status within the cinema of discomfort, making distinctions of the kind examined in Chapter 1: 'A grim and disturbing vision from Ulrich Seidl, makes for an uncomfortable and uncompromising picture of life, that is anything but comfy and pedestrian.' The Rotten Tomatoes 'audience score' is lower but still relatively high, at 75 per cent positive, from what is listed as a total of 1,625 'user ratings'. As with the previous chapter, I have sampled viewer responses from those who offer comments on the film in Rotten Tomatoes, along with the much smaller numbers from the two other sources used for *Palindromes*: twenty-two from the Internet Movie DataBase (IMDb) and eight from Amazon. com.[65]

The use of sexual images in the marketing materials is commented on by a small number of respondents. One IMDb reviewer is 'appalled at the poster of the movie', which is declared to be 'utterly misleading. The movie is not about sex, is about life and death.'[66] Another, atypically, takes an opposite approach, heading their response 'Long and Pointless' and suggesting that 'the main attraction here is the titillation suggested by the movie's poster, although it's not enough to sustain one's interest'.[67] One Amazon reviewer comments that the poster or DVD artwork could give the impression 'that this might be some kind of pornographic film but it is far from it'.[68] The director is credited here with being 'wise enough' to use explicit nudity 'to draw more people's attention to come and see his movie,' a positive interpretation of what is sometimes voiced by critics as a more cynical approach to the deployment of such material.

Another Amazon respondent focuses on the discomforting and non-titillating quality of such sequences in the film, which is suggested to take 'a prize for the amount of the un-sexy, most unpleasant and longest X-rated scenes ever filmed'.[69] They add: 'I guess if sex is not accompanied with love, desire or at least lust, it is very boring and uncomfortable to watch and makes a viewer guilty for the degradation they are forced to watch and makes them want to stop or fast-forward these scenes as fast as possible.' If that is what he intends, this viewer concludes, Seidl 'succeeded fully' in making them think of the serious issues raised by the film, although the discomfort involved was such that they would not want to watch it again. This is another example of what Berliner describes as appreciation of the level of 'interest' provided by the film – the cognitive challenge of having to think about serious issues – as opposed to any hedonic pleasure. One highly dismissive IMDb reviewer takes a very different tack, not appreciating what appear to be the intentions of the filmmaker, in suggesting that 'the absolutely horrendous sexual imagery [...] served no purpose but to poison the viewers [sic] mind and probably to excite the perverted director'.[70] For this respondent, the explicit nature of the material results in a lack of appreciation of any effective distinction from pornography, an indication of the difficulty that can be involved in how such material is understood: some of the images 'were like porn. In fact it was porn really.'

Positive respondents tend to highlight the social realist context of the film, one that in most cases obviates any associations with qualities such as the pornographic or the otherwise exploitative (no one admits to any component of unwanted sexual arousal of the kind discussed by some of the participants in the Barker study). This includes appreciation of its use of real locations and its generally bleak, hard-hitting nature, whether characterized generally or, in some cases, situated as a diagnosis of more specific geo-socio-economic issues. Terms such as 'disturbing', 'depressing', 'uncomfortable' and 'hard to watch' turn up in many user reviews, as might be expected, more often with positive than negative connotations. For those who embrace the film, to use Barker's category, the creation of discomfort is justified by the importance of the issues the film is seen as addressing and, generally, the manner in which it is done. Typical of the positive embrace of discomfort are the following phrases from Rotten Tomatoes reviews, suggesting that many viewers receive the work in the manner in which such films seem broadly to be intended: 'Deeply uncomfortable film, though compelling viewing'[71]; 'The film-maker approaches concepts like death, masculinity and poverty in an uncomfortable but above all HUMAN manner. Haunting'[72]; 'Avoiding grand cinematic gestures, the film forces us to view a reality that we'd rather not think too deeply about by pushing these issues [employment, immigration, poverty, the internet sex industry and others] far beyond the stage where they've made their point into an area that makes the viewer very, very uncomfortable indeed'[73]; 'often crossing the line between the comic and the uncomfortable with amazing results. I can't wait to see more from Seidl'[74]; 'left me a complete mess [...] utterly disturbing, but worth seeing.'[75] Some of these responses indicate the kind of exhilaration suggested by Berliner as part of an appreciation of what can make such work compelling and provocative of strong reactions. The language in which this is expressed sometimes suggests that the challenge the film presents occupies a position towards the limits of the coping potential of the viewer, in its generation of deep and sometimes unresolvable discomfort of the kind liable to leave a viewer 'a complete mess'.

Seidl faces occasional accusations of exploiting his characters or others who appear in the film, akin to the questions asked by some critics, although this comes from a small proportion of respondents. One Rotten Tomatoes reviewer declares *Import Export* to be a 'very problematic film'.[76] On the one hand, 'there is compassion' in the way the principals are portrayed: 'On the other hand there is an exploitative side to the way Seidl films the other people, a taste for the grotesque, a taste for the comic absurd that often comes across as condescending to its characters.' As this clearly film-literate reviewer notes, the scenes in the geriatric hospital 'are reminiscent of the mental ward in Titicut Follies', the controversial 1967 documentary by Frederick Wiseman. One IMDb respondent asks whether Seidl 'exploits his protagonists', answering in the negative but suggesting that 'everyone has to find his [sic] own answer' to the question.[77] A more negative reviewer on the same site accuses the film being 'essentially a wallow in some specific examples of life as survival into death and very little else'.[78]

For some viewers, the film's depiction of depressing material is too much and/or too sustained, going beyond a discomfort that is considered ultimately to be worthwhile or rewarding in its purpose. Some negative respondents find it 'boring', partly because of its length (135 minutes) and/or its relative lack of narrative drive, a common basis for the rejection of work from the arthouse sector.[79] One IMDb reviewer describes himself as 'open to dark films', thus establishing a certain position in the distinction-marking economy, but declares this to have been 'one of the most depressing, frustrating films I have ever seen'.[80] The director's declared aim to 'torture' the viewer seems to have worked in this case. The film's 'Long, long, long cut scenes of depressing or morbid circumstances (such as people suffering in palliative care, very raw)' are held for 'agonizingly long'. For this viewer *Import Export* crosses a line that seems to involve a loss of critical distance within the discomfort it produces: 'This film is not an exploration of existential depression – this film IS existential depression.' A Rotten Tomatoes poster has a similar response, suggesting that: 'If it's depression and discomfort you crave, then this is the movie that will take you there.'[81] The director's 'raw initiative and verisimilitude' are applauded but, for this reviewer, the film 'dearly lacks' any 'sense of hope and a path to redemption.' The opposite is suggested on this point by some respondents, however, more in keeping with my own reading. One Amazon reviewer, who describes himself as a 'natural cinephile' and makes a distinction-marking comment that the filmmaker has the courage 'to show reality and not meaningless "escapist-entertainment"' (a form of discourse found less frequently in these samples that those cited in the previous chapter) suggests that 'the message of the story is really one of hope and redemption'.[82]

Notes

1. Nikhil Sathe, 'Challenging the East-West Divide in Ulrich Seidl's *Import Export* (2007)', in Michael Gott and Todd Herzog (eds), *East, West and Centre: Reframing Post-1989 European Cinema* (Edinburgh: Edinburgh University Press, 2015), 72.
2. Geoff King, *Film Comedy* (London: Wallflower Press, 2002), 32–6.
3. Martin Barker, *Audiences and Receptions of Sexual Violence in Contemporary Cinema*, Report to the British Board of Film Classification, March 2007, accessed online at http://www.bbfc.co.uk/sites/default/files/attachments/Audiences%20and%20Receptions%20of%20Sexual%20Violence%20in%20Contemporary%20Cinema_0.pdf.
4. Barker, *Audiences*, 101.
5. Ibid., 152, for one of several such examples.
6. Constantin Wulff, *Ulrich Seidl: A Director at Work* (*Ulrich Seidl Une Die Bösen Buben*, 2014).
7. For examples of such accusations, see Martin Brady and Helen Hughes, 'Import and Export: Ulrich Seidl's Indiscreet Anthropology of Migration', in Robert von Dassanowsky and Oliver Speck (eds), *New Austrian Film* (New York: Berghahn, 2011), 219.
8. Andre Bazin, 'Marginal Notes on Eroticism in Cinema' in *What is Cinema?* Volume 2 (Berkeley: University of California Press, 1971). See discussion in Linda Williams, *Screening Sex* (Durham, NC: Duke University Press, 2008), 65.
9. Plantinga, *Moving Viewers*, 114.
10. For an extensive discussion of such issues, see Williams, *Screening Sex*.
11. Martine Beugnet, *Cinema and Sensation: French Film and the Art of Transgression* (Edinburgh: Edinburgh University Press, 2007).
12. Laura Marks, *The Skin of the Film: Intercultural Cinema, Embodiment, and the Senses* (Durham, NC: Duke University Press, 2000); Vivian Sobchack, *Carnal Thoughts: Embodiment and Moving Image Culture* (Berkeley: University of California Press, 2004). I discuss this issue at greater length in King, *Positioning Art Cinema*, chapter 8.
13. King, *Positioning Art Cinema*, 271. It is worth noting that Beugnet is writing about films that lean more towards the formally experimental and the foregrounding of their own materiality than is the case with those I examine.
14. Sobchack, *Carnal Thoughts*, 74.
15. Grønstad, *Screening the Unwatchable*.
16. For an account of similar issues in a number of other films featuring 'real sex' sequences, see Tulloch and Middleweek, *Real Sex Films*.
17. Interview with the filmmaker in Catherine Wheatley, 'Europa Europa', *Sight and Sound*, vol. 18, no. 10 (October 2008): 46–9.
18. Barker, *Audiences*, 3.

19 Ibid., 5.
20 Ibid., 9.
21 Ibid., 166. Emphasis in original.
22 Ibid., 182.
23 Ibid., 153.
24 See, in particular, the reading of Haneke's strategy by Catherine Wheatley, *Michael Haneke's Cinema: The Ethic of the Image* (New York: Berghahn, 2009).
25 See, for example, Barker, *Audiences*, 159.
26 For details, see, for example, both the cast background material and interview with Seidl in the film's press notes, available in English translation and German versions online at http://www.ulrichseidl.com/_filestorage/36/4e/folder-i-e.pdf.
27 For more on Bazin's approach to neo-realism, see King, *Positioning Art Cinema*, chapter 3.
28 See, for example, the discomfort expressed by Peter Bradshaw in 'Import/Export', *The Guardian*, 3 October 2008, accessed at https://www.theguardian.com/film/2008/oct/03/drama.importexport; a similar concern is expressed in an uncredited review, 'Import Export, Ulrich Seidl, 135 minutes (18)' in *The Independent*, 4 October 2008, accessed at https://www.independent.co.uk/arts-entertainment/films/reviews/import-export-ulrich-seidl-135-mins-18-951376.html.
29 The following detail and quotation are from an interview with Seidl on the region 2 DVD release.
30 Brady and Hughes, 'Import and Export', 219.
31 For a similar view, see Michael Goddard, 'Eastern Extreme: The Presentation of Eastern Europe as a Site of Monstrosity in *La Vie nouvelle* and *Import / Export*', in Tanya Horeck and Tina Kendall (eds), *The New Extremism in Cinema: From France to Europe* (Edinburgh: Edinburgh University Press, 2013), 88, and Sathe, 'Challenging the East-West Divide in Ulrich Seidl's *Import Export* (2007)', 67.
32 Sathe, 'Challenging the East-West Divide'.
33 Dennis Lim, 'Greetings from the Land of Feel-Bad Cinema', *New York Times*, 26 November 2006, accessed at https://www.nytimes.com/2006/11/26/movies/26lim.html.
34 Robert van Dassanowksy and Oliver Speck, 'Introduction: New Austrian Film: The Non-exceptional Exception', in von Dassanowsky and Speck, *New Austrian Film*, 2.
35 von Dassanowsky and Speck, 'Introduction', 3.
36 von Dassanowsky and Speck, 'Introduction, 5. Exactly what constitutes this condition is expressed in this account in rather sweeping 'high' theoretical terms, however.

37 Elżbieta Ostrowska and Johanna Rydzewska, 'Developments in Eastern European Cinemas Since 1989', in Rob Stone, Paul Cooke, Stephanie Dennison and Alex Marlow-Mann (eds), *The Routledge Companion to World Cinema* (Oxford: Routledge, 2018).
38 Bill Nichols, *Introduction to Documentary* (Bloomington: Indiana University Press, 2010), 31–2.
39 Bill Nichols, *Representing Reality: Issues and Concepts in Documentary* (Bloomington: Indiana University Press, 1992), 64.
40 Ibid., 41.
41 Brady and Hughes, 'Import and Export', 210.
42 von Dassanowsky and Speck, 'Introduction', 7.
43 Ibid., 8.
44 Ibid.
45 Ibid.
46 Ibid., 8–9.
47 von Dassanowsky and Speck, 'Introduction', 9.
48 A point I make in *Positioning Art Cinema*, 160. For more detail, see Wheatley, *Michael Haneke's Cinema*.
49 This and the following quotation is from an interview with Seidl by Karin Schiefer, 'Ulrich Seidl on Import Export', published on the website of Austrian Film Commission, June 2006, accessed at http://www.austrianfilms.com/news/en/bodyulrich_seidl_on_import_exportbody.
50 List of sources of support from press notes, at http://www.ulrichseidl.com/_filestorage/36/4e/folder-i-e.pdf.
51 Mattias Frey, *Extreme Cinema: The Transgressive Rhetoric of Today's Art Film Culture* (New Brunswick, NJ: Rutgers University Press, 2016), 143.
52 For just one example of a growing literature on such connections, see Mette Hjort and Duncan Petrie (eds), *The Cinema of Small Nations* (Edinburgh: Edinburgh University Press, 2007).
53 Frey, *Extreme Cinema*.
54 Ibid., 147.
55 Ibid., 148
56 Ibid., 147.
57 Ibid., 149.
58 Ibid., 148.
59 Ibid., 149.
60 Ibid., 150.
61 This is another issue I discuss at some length in King, *Positioning Art Cinema*, chapter 8. For sources on this and related debates, see Tanya Horeck and Tina Kendall (eds), *The New Extremism in Cinema* (Edinburgh: Edinburgh University Press, 2013) and Lindsay Coleman (ed.), *Sex and Storytelling*

in Modern Cinema: Explicit Sex, Performance and Cinematic Technique (London: I.B. Tauris, 2016).

62 For useful accounts of some striking historical examples of exploitation tactics in marketing, both in relation to ratings and more generally, which I also cite in *Positioning Art Cinema*, see, Lucy Mazdon and Catherine Wheatley, *French Film in Britain: Sex, Art and Cinephilia* (New York: Berghahn, 2013, 87) and Mark Betz, 'Art, Exploitation, Underground', in Mark Jancovich, Antonio Lazaro Reboll and Julian Stringer, (eds), *Defining Cult Movies: The Cultural Politics of Oppositional Taste* (Manchester: Manchester University Press, 2003).

63 Manohla Dargis, 'Seeking Dignity amid Brutality', *New York Times*, 30 July 2009, accessed at https://www.nytimes.com/2009/07/31/movies/31import.html.

64 *Import Export* entry on Rotten Tomatoes accessed 18 April 2018 at https://www.rottentomatoes.com/m/importexport/.

65 IMDb reviews accessed 18 April 2018, at https://www.imdb.com/title/tt0459102/reviews?ref_=tt_ql_3; Amazon reviews accessed 18 April 2018 at https://www.amazon.com/Export-Ekateryna-Rak/product- reviews/B002W1UIUW/ref=cm_cr_dp_d_show_all_btm?ie=UTF8&reviewerType=all_reviews.

66 Imdbidia, IMDb, 25 February 2011.

67 kenjha, IMDb, 29 December 2010.

68 Hee Chul Kwon, Amazon, 26 April 2016.

69 Galina, Amazon, 13 November 2011.

70 Maz Murdoch (asda-man), IMDb, 5 April 2012.

71 Martin F, Rotten Tomatoes, 3 October 2008.

72 Liam D, Rotten Tomatoes, 8 October 2008.

73 Noel M, Rotten Tomatoes, 23 April 2008.

74 Miles S, Rotten Tomatoes, 13 February 2008.

75 Patrycja M, Rotten Tomatoes, 2 January 2008.

76 X.T., Rotten Tomatoes, 6 August 2009.

77 herjoch, IMDb, 16 December 2007.

78 bob the moo, IMDb, 12 April 2009.

79 See for example, Maz Murdoch (asda-man), IMDb, 5 April 2012, also cited above on the status of the sexual imagery as 'porn'.

80 Scott Lanaway, IMDb, 2 July 2010.

81 Aston C, Rotten Tomatoes, 8 June 2008.

82 Carlos Romero natural cinephile, Amazon, 20 November 2012.

4

Weirdly discomforting: *Dogtooth* and the Greek new wave

With some exceptions, the discomforting experiences offered by *Palindromes* or the films of Ulrich Seidl are reasonably comprehensible to the viewer. Discomfort tends to lie in the nature of the on-screen material and/or in an ambiguity at the level of the emotional engagement encouraged or otherwise by the work. Discomfort can be heightened by a lack of any explanatory framework for awkward material, however, as seems particularly to be the case with the woman who tends to the baby dolls in Seidl's *In the Basement*. Nothing is provided here to rationalize her behaviour, even by establishing a clear basis in the markedly *ir*rational. *Dogtooth* (*Kynodontas*, 2009), the second feature directed by Yorgos Lanthimos and the principal example examined in this chapter, offers plenty that fits into the framework of discomfort already established in this book, including its own distinctly uncomfortable sexual activity. The film also leaves considerably more work to the viewer, however, to explain the strange activities of the family it depicts, as it becomes apparent that three young-adult offspring have been brought up without any contact with the world outside the high fence and hedges that surround their rural home. This offers an additional source of potential discomfort, at the cognitive level. *Dogtooth* is considered here alongside other manifestations of what became known as the Greek 'new' or 'weird' wave of the early twenty-first century, including *Attenberg* (dir. Athina Rachel Tsangari, 2010). As with the films of Solondz and Seidl, the character of such work can be explained through a combination of sociocultural and film-specific factors, both those particular to the national context and of broader resonance in each dimension.

Dogtooth establishes a sense of strangeness and alienation from any conventional idea of the normal from its opening sequence, in which we see a cassette tape being played that offers the 'children' surreally misleading definitions of familiar terms: 'a sea' is a leather armchair with wooden arms'; 'a motorway is a very strong wind', 'an excursion is a very resistant material used to construct floors' and 'a carbine is a beautiful white bird'. The general scenario of a son and two daughters being brought up in this strange manner, within a hermetic environment, emerges only gradually. The disturbing qualities of the film include the fact that it is hard, exactly, to place their position in the transitional period from later teenage youth to adulthood (they seem far too old to be taught vocabulary). Much specific detail remains for some time teasingly opaque at the level of a basic sense of what is happening and why. This includes, for example, the fate of what might be another son, who is implied later in the film to have escaped at some point before the start of the action. Early on, we see the present 'son' (Hristos Passalis), referred to only this way in the film, talking into the bushes of a surrounding hedge while cleaning his father's car, commenting at length on how he cleans the car better than the unseen object of his discourse. Why is not at all clear. We later see the 'eldest' daughter (Angeliki Papoulia) hurling cake over the fence. No explanation is offered, although the viewer is likely to surmise that someone sympathetic is assumed to be the recipient, real or imaginary.

That a belief has been inculcated in the young-adult children that some danger lurks beyond the garden is made clear – but not why – when the eldest daughter throws a toy plane through the gate during a struggle with her brother: the only way it appears to be recoverable is for the father (Christos Stergioglou) to get into his car and drive less than the length of the vehicle outside to pick it up by leaning down from the driver's seat. An explanation from within the world created by the parents is subsequently offered when the father decides to take advantage of the situation created when the son kills a cat in the garden. Splashing himself with red paint and slashing his clothes, he comes home from work to tell the children that their brother – the first time such a figure is mentioned – has been torn apart by a 'creature' like the one in the garden, 'the most dangerous animal there is', one that eats meat, the flesh of children in particular. If you stay inside, he declares, you are protected.

This is the first time we hear any overt rationale for their cloistered existence, although by this point it has become clear that the parents are concealing things from the children, such as a hidden phone used by the mother (Michele Valley) to alert the father to the situation involving the cat. It has also become apparent that they are otherwise cut off from the world by having a television that receives no broadcast signal, used solely to play home-video recordings that provide one of the high points of entertainment for the young people. A further part of the rationale provided to the children is revealed much later, when the father quizzes them on various matters that have clearly been drilled into them: a child is ready to leave home when one of their dogteeth (canines) comes out; only then is the body ready to face the dangers that lurk outside; to leave the house safely, it is necessary to take the car; they are ready to learn to drive only when one of their dogteeth grows again. Whatever their exact age and level of physical development, the trio are still clearly classed and treated as children within this rubric, and often act as such.

Other bizarre perversions of reality remain entirely unexplained, other than as products of the extreme variety of home education offered by the parents. When an aircraft crosses the sky, for example, and the mother throws another toy plane to be found by one of the children, it becomes clear they have been taught that the former is no more than the latter, its more substantial reality entirely occluded. This explains the puzzle provided by earlier moments in which we see unusual interest in planes passing overhead and why the toy plane featured earlier might be so valued; but it does not occur until some fifty minutes into the film. Everything that occurs within the world of the household appears to be used further to enforce the messages of compliance given to the children, although this, again, remains only implicit. When the father plays a recording of Frank Sinatra singing 'Fly Me to the Moon', for example, the singer is claimed to be their grandfather and the lyrics are mistranslated into Greek, line by line, as references to the family and the fact that the children are doing fine but need to try harder.

Flatness of tone

Some kind of satire on overprotective parenting might provide a rationale for material of this kind, the broader sociocultural context of which is explored further below. Any such reading has actively to be brought to the film by the viewer, however. The generally flat and neutral tone offers no overt signalling of such status, an absence of clear signposting typical of many examples of the cinema of discomfort. Most of the material is presented in a manner that suggests a matter-of-fact ordinariness, even that which is bizarre or in various ways uncomfortable, including a number of sex sequences. If the events are often strange and quietly unsettling, the visual style is generally low key. Much is shot in flat or relatively flat mid-to-long shots. At times this becomes akin to the distanced blank style identified by Sconce, including shots of the three siblings sitting facing the camera on a sofa; but, as was seen in the case of Seidl in the previous chapter, generally the style is less marked and not so overtly withdrawn. On one occasion, during a family-around-the-dinner-table scene, one of the stock tropes of blank style listed by Sconce, an element of wide-angle distortion of the background is apparent, in a repeated shot taken from behind the father. If used more often, such a perspective might be taken to signify something of the distorted world of meanings within which the children have been raised, but it is not. Other perspectives from around the table in the scene employ a similarly wide-angle lens, but in these cases the image is framed by the figures of family members in a way that does not provide the background effect of distortion at the extremes. The fact that the warped reality experienced by the children is generally presented in a non-heightened manner adds to the potency of the discomforting effect; the weird is presented and, it seems, experienced by the characters, as entirely normal.

There is much also in *Dogtooth* that has comic potential, another source of distance that could create a more evidently satirical effect and a clear offer of ironic separation for the viewer. But this is also subjected to the general style of flat, matter-of-fact presentation. Some of the events have a farcical quality in themselves, but not generally or strongly so in their mode of articulation. The business of driving the car so short a distance to pick up the plane appears ridiculous but is treated with a seriousness of attention by the characters involved, the father and son, with no specific intervention by the filmmakers to heighten any sense of the absurd or to invite an ironic mode of consumption. The material surrounding the cat attack has similar farcical potential. A cut from an apprehensive son to our first sight of the cat – small and docile – could be taken to signify the absurdity of his response. A more overtly comic dimension might be apparent in the manner in which he runs away, with a quirkily small-stepping gait; but his fear seems to be coded as real, as does that of the concernedly watching sisters. When we see the father 'explaining' the death of the other son, initially in a shot only at the height of his torso, with 'bloodied' and torn shirt, a cut to a fuller shot including his head creates a more clownish impression, splotches of paint covering most of his face and his hair standing up in dishevelment (Figure 12). Again, however, both his speech and the reactions appear to be taken entirely seriously within the diegesis. A separation seems clearly available in such moments between how the viewer might be encouraged

FIGURE 12 *Comical appearance but taken seriously in the narrative: The father after faking attack by a cat in* Dogtooth *(2009).*

to take some of this and how it is experienced within the narrative. There is space for ironic distinction-marking but this is not played up overtly, in formal or other terms. The film tends to maintain a broadly consistent sense of straight-faced middle distance from the action, one that leaves the viewer potentially unclear how exactly to respond.

The matter-of-fact mode of presentation is also a distinctive feature of the numerous uncomfortable sex sequences in *Dogtooth*. These begin with intercourse between the son and the one outsider granted admittance to the household, Christina (Anna Kalaitzidou), who works as a security guard at a factory of which the father appears to be either the proprietor or a senior manager. She is brought to the house, blindfolded on the way, and paid for providing sexual services to the son. The first such sequence begins with the incongruity of the father not just delivering Christina to the son's room, but removing a cover from his bed and adjusting his hair in readiness, the latter in one of a number of shots in which the heads of characters are positioned oddly, fully or partially cut off by the top of the frame. Left alone, Christina and the son strip in a perfunctory manner that characterizes all the sexual engagements in the film. They sit together naked, she clearly manipulating him by hand (although not explicitly visibly) to the point at which he is ready to lie on top of her and perform. Most of this is treated in a single, wide-angle long shot of a kind that heightens the general awkwardness of the affair, in typical cinema-of-discomfort style.

A further set of sexually oriented sequences involve Christina and the eldest daughter. Christina makes an offer of exchange to the latter, after it becomes apparent that the son has been unwilling to provide her with satisfactory oral stimulation. Christina proposes to trade a sparkly headband. The eldest responds with the choice of a pencil with an eraser on the end or a tape measure. The child-like nature of her level of engagement is underlined by the extent to which she seems impressed by the retractable mechanism of the latter. Christina drops her trousers and underwear, inviting the eldest to lick her in return for the headband. The latter complies, another act performed in an entirely flat, matter-of-fact manner. Christina asks if she is disgusted, to which the eldest replies in the negative. The impression is that, for her naïve state, this is an entirely unexceptional activity, not one in which anything out of the ordinary is at stake or that involves any boundary-crossing transgression of the kind that might usually be assumed in such a situation.

These qualities seem likely to add to the discomfort involved in the witnessing of such scenes, involving, as they appear to, an unequal exchange in which one, child-like party seems unaware of what is really involved in the activity into which she is led. This sense is underlined when the eldest subsequently proposes a similar exchange with her sister, who she asks to lick her on the shoulder; a location that implies no understanding, at this point, of the specific sexual dimension that was entailed with Christina.

On a later occasion, the youngest licks the eldest on the thigh while lying between her legs; that is, in a more suggestive position. The eldest directs her to another 'good spot' on her belly but a cut to the next scene intrudes before any indication is given as to whether or not this might have led to more overtly sexual territory. The overall movement of the narrative seems to entail a gradual awakening on the part of the eldest, but it is typical of the uncommunicative nature of the film for this potentially sexual dimension to be left open. A much later scene, discomforting in the characteristic absence of any explanation for something that involves such potentially inappropriate intimate contact, features the youngest licking her sleeping father's hand and chest.

The most discomforting sexual scenes in *Dogtooth* are none of these, however, but those involving the son and the sisters (we also see an instance of rather perfunctory sex between the father and mother; on another occasion, a uncomfortable cut is made from one scene straight into another in which one side of the screen is largely taken up by the images of a pornographic video being watched by the parents). Further exchanges between Christina and the eldest involve videotapes of Hollywood films, including *Rocky IV* (1985) and *Jaws* (1975), elements of which the eldest parrots and/or re-enacts afterwards. This is a major breach of the barriers erected by the parents. After its discovery, the father visits Christina's home and violently assaults her with a VCR machine, saying he hopes any children she has will have 'bad influences'. This is the only overt reference in the film to any rationale for the closeting of his own. He vows that no one else will enter the family house. The father ponders assigning Christina's duties to the eldest, subsequently suggesting that the son be allowed to choose. The next scene has the son being joined naked in the bath by both sisters (Figure 12). A highly uncomfortable sequence features the son very awkwardly feeling

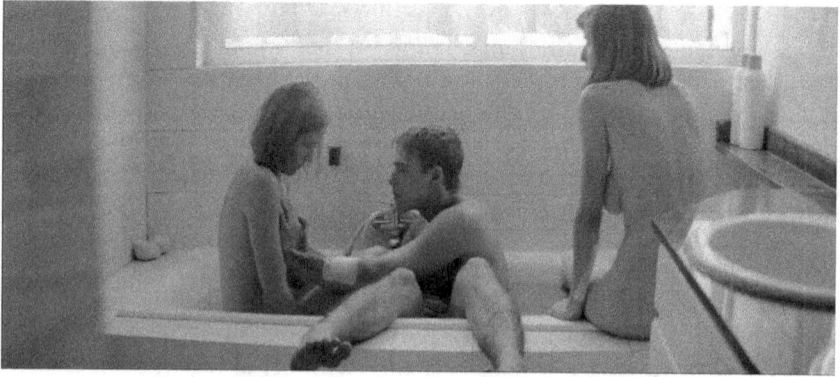

FIGURE 13 *Uncomfortable prelude to incest: The son choosing which of his sisters should be his next sexual partner in* Dogtooth *(2009).*

parts of the bodies of each sister in turn, in silence, the discomfort factor likely to be increased by the fact that the girls seem, from what we have seen up to this point, not to be sexually aware. This, again, is all treated as a perfunctory, matter-of-fact business rather than something that involves an apparent erotic or other interest on the part of the son. His decision is demonstrated at the start of the next scene, in which the mother is combing the hair of the eldest, now wearing make-up, preparing her to do what is implicitly framed to be her 'duty' and leading her to his bedroom door.

More distinctly uncomfortable and largely silent sex follows. The two sit together naked, in the now-obligatory awkward manner. He, inexpressive, puts her hand on his penis which she jerks. He feels her breast, in the perfunctory manner of the preceding scene involving both sisters. In a shift to a different angle, the discomfort potential is increased by the fact that we can now at times see her hand on his apparently erect member, previously obscured, introducing a dimension of 'real' sexual activity akin to that featured in *Import Export*. She lies back and full intercourse ensues; it is impossible at this point to tell if actual penetration occurs or is merely simulated, but the effect is one of strongly intimate realism either way. She appears uncomfortable at times, although nothing is said, her neck awkwardly resting on the end of the bed frame and the son roughly grasping one of her breasts. A departure from the generally plain and primarily mid-distanced style occurs in one shot towards the end, featuring her head, shoulders and upper body while the face of the son is framed to one side in a mirror. This seems to imply a more overt sense of alienated fragmentation in the experience. A jarring shift of tone occurs at the end of this sequence, as they lie in bed together, the eldest suddenly commenting: 'Do that again, bitch, and I'll rip your guts out. I swear on my daughter's life that you and your clan won't last long in this neighbourhood.' This is a line we might assume to come from one of the illicitly viewed films, although its origin remains unclear.

If much of the odd or bizarre material of *Dogtooth* is heightened in its potentially discomforting effect through being presented in a flat, matter-of-fact cinematic mode, a central motivation can be found for this approach. This activity seems to *be* matter-of-fact, ordinary, taken-for-granted reality for those involved. What might seem strange or uncomfortable to the viewer is presented as being simply the world into which the children have been inducted. No sense of shame or embarrassment appears to exist for the trio in the sexual activity in which they are involved, for the most part, at least, because they seem not to have been brought up with any reason to experience such feelings. The son seems simply awkward and lacking much in the way of sexual understanding, in relation to Christina, rather than, for example, embarrassed by having his father procure sexual favours for him. Likewise, all three seem, as far as we can tell, passively to accept that one of the girls has to replace Christina if that is what the parents decree, simply because their parents provide their only behavioural compass. No grounds are presented for any other interpretation. The eldest appears to have come to doubt their authority towards the end, however. As is typical of the film, it gives no specific or overt explanation for this. It could be the vicarious experience with the alternative world of Hollywood films, or the suspicions provoked by hearing her mother speaking on the phone, while listening at a locked bedroom door; or, her doubts might have been confirmed by being given no apparent choice but to have sex with her brother.

Characteristically, we are not provided with any scenes in which this is discussed; it just happens, as does everything else, as part of what appears to be the force of circumstances. The eldest eventually rebels, the film closing, indeterminately, on a shot of the boot of the father's car in which she escapes from the house. It is notable, however, that she remains committed to at least part of the parental creed, only leaving after violently knocking out one of her teeth.

For the most part the generally but not exaggeratedly flattened presentation seems broadly to reflect the world inside the film: the matter-of-fact status of the warped reality into which the children have been inculcated and, presumably, the habitual familiarity of the established routine of deception created by the parents. Even absent the children, for example, we never see the parents in any state of very heightened concern, other than on the discovery of the disappearance of the eldest towards the end, and even here this seems somewhat muted in the circumstances. If they have some reason to seek to secure the children in the manner they do, we never witness any articulation of this other than the passing comment to Christina. This is another characteristic art-cinema practice of narrative withholding. The parents are not presented as overtly monstrous and appear to be well-intentioned, if misguidedly so, as far as the viewer can tell. Apart from the incestuous sexual activity into which they are led, the offspring do not seem to suffer generally in any strongly exteriorized manner, and only to a limited extent is this clearly articulated even in this heightened instance. It is, again, the withholding of anything more clearly cut or explicitly condemnatory – any overtly articulated ground for moral disapproval at the individual level, for example – that adds to the overall impression of discomfort likely to result. The viewer is not given the relative comfort that might be provided were the parents overtly to be demonized rather than treated as if disturbingly ordinary.

A more stylized audiovisual approach is used on occasion, including some sequences that seem designed at least partially to evoke the experience of the children during various competitive play activities. These sometimes involve a shift from fixed to more mobile or unstable camerawork. One example features the son and eldest daughter pretending to sword fence in the garden, the camera mobile and an aestheticized effect created by sunlight refracted by water drops from a sprinkler and on the lens

FIGURE 14 *Aestheticized stylization: Water drops on the lens in the play-fencing scene, with English subtitle, in* Dogtooth *(2009)*.

(Figure 14). Non-synchronous sound is provided by the accompaniment of the father's educating voice referring to issues including triangle geometry and a multiple-choice quiz about the characteristics of the eyes of a dead fish. Some similar impressions are created by another sequence involving a game that involves the trio moving around in blindfolds. This features a handheld camera along with jumpy, discontinuous cutting and a rich French singing vocal that drops in and out of presence (from a source unexplained at the time). A sense might be created of the disorientation of the children although the style also contributes to that likely to be experienced by the viewer. Despite any implied sharing of perspective to some extent in these sequences, there is no real sense of emotional proximity or subjective access to the experiences of the three. Stylization has a distancing effect of its own here, resisting any more mainstream-conventional process of creating strong alignment or allegiance with the characters.

Something similar results from the occasional use of framing in which the heads of characters are cut off from the image, as in one instance cited above. This creates an off-kilter impression, a departure from basic framing convention, and constitutes a periodic denial of access to the facial expression that generally serves as the strongest source of potential sympathetic engagement; the 'emotional contagion' identified by Plantinga is generally absent from the presentation of events in *Dogtooth*. Another example occurs during a sequence involving the two daughters in a bedroom. At one point, the head of the youngest is out of shot and subsequently those of both, before they exit the frame, for no reason that appears specific to this particular sequence. The characters are generally presented in a flat and inexpressive manner that keeps the viewer at a distance. More mainstream-conventional regimes of continuity editing, such as the use of pairs of shots and reverse shots, are far from entirely absent but used sparingly and in a muted manner, denying the viewer the kind of closer dissection that might offer a stronger sense of access to interior emotional experience. Non-diegetic background music that might conventionally signal emotional responses or mood is entirely absent.

The faces of the three children are frequently blank or seem to express a sense of uncertainty. Their movements are sometimes a little awkward and their talk often seems halting, each on occasion having an almost mechanical and lifeless quality, although sometimes erupting in moments of sudden violence against one another. Their discourse shifts unsettlingly between the blank and the child-like earnest. The household environment increases such impressions, the interiors predominantly white and sanitized (contrasting with the verdant lushness of the garden). The pasty-faced brother and sisters are often clad in white, adding to a sense that they are some kind of scientific subjects – which, maybe, in a sense, they are, as a result of both the competitions set for them by the father and those they organize among themselves. In one of the latter, the sisters compete to see who will wake first after simultaneously inhaling a chloroform-type anaesthetic. This is another sequence that features their heads framed out of shot, at the start (Figure 15). A two shot follows, out of which each falls as they lose consciousness, leaving the frame empty before a cut that shows them lying on a bed in a sedated state that perhaps seems symptomatic of certain aspects of their lives.

When the son is talking to the imagined presence of his brother after cleaning the car, we are first kept at a distance in a long shot from behind his figure, dwarfed by the height of the bushes and fence. A cut to a close-up of his face follows, one that might more conventionally offer greater access to his feelings but here taken from a flat, side-on position that remains equally detached despite the greater proximity. The next shot is another from behind,

FIGURE 15 *Decapitation: Off-kilter framing of the two sisters in* Dogtooth *(2009).*

a view of his head and shoulders in the lower central part of the frame. In the terms used by Murray Smith, none of this creates a sense of either alignment or allegiance with character. The camera remains flatly behind or beside the son, aligned geometrically/artificially, rather than creating any impression of more organic attachment or sharing of perspective. In general, there is little in any of the character behaviour or the manner in which it is articulated to encourage the moral dimension of allegiance. No real sense of what any of the children stand for is created, beyond what remains a somewhat abstracted notion of the relative awakening and escape achieved by the eldest. A similar lack of access is provided to the parents, who generally seem equally semi-anonymous and indistinct. In one moment of quiet given to the mother, for example, when she is finishing a phone call with the father and then listening on headphones, the camera remains in a position largely behind her and to one side, refusing any access to her face at a moment that might otherwise be expected to provide some sense of her interior experience, as potentially another victim of what appears to be a regime of patriarchal dominance.

A further sense of dislocation and distance is created by sequences that overlap sound and images from different moments in time, in some ways akin to the more expressive material examined above. In one case, speeches made by the children to the 'dead' brother are layered over a sequence in the swimming pool that leads to the trio practicing mouth-to-mouth resuscitation, the images at times accompanied by a discomforting and coldly abstracting silence. The pool features in another example that temporally overlaps and shifts between the three competing to see who can hold their breath the longest underwater and the announcement by the father of a plan confected with the mother in which it is claimed that she will soon give birth to two children and a dog. The latter is accompanied, jarringly, by a halting learner's piano performance the source of which (from the son) is only belatedly revealed.

Allegories: From socialization to the family, neoliberalism and beyond

Dogtooth includes one uncharacteristically obvious reference to something akin to the process of strange education offered by the parents, in a discussion between the father and a dog trainer. The latter refers to dogs as being like clay, his job being to 'mould' them and show them how they should behave. The whole film can be taken as dramatizing an effort to do this with human offspring, the business about the dogtooth and fact that the father coaches the children to bark to ward off threats underlining the canine reference. How exactly we should interpret this in any more specifics is left entirely open, but it can be read at a number of different levels, more or less general in nature. The affordance the film offers for such interpretation, while leaving this generally implicit, is one of the potential bases of its appeal to the likely target constituency within the art-cinema sphere. At its most broad, it can be taken as a demonstration of the power of socialization, the process through which individuals are taught to internalize the norms of any particular society. One of the potentially disturbing implications of the film is its depiction of how readily what we might take for granted as meaning can be subverted or interpreted differently, from the significations of individual words to aspects of seemingly solid reality such as the existence of planes as something other than small toys thrown in the air. Also uncomfortable might be the routine and unquestioned nature of such understandings, and the fact that they are, specifically, created as a routine within a particular world. Viewers might be prompted to consider any ways in which the natures of their own learned realities might have a similar or analogical status, as is confirmed by some of the responses surveyed at the end of this chapter. *Dogtooth* has the broad potential to disturb on the basis of encouraging us to look again – afresh and anew – at that which is usually uncritically taken for granted, to defamiliarize aspects of the world, a quality often associated with works of 'higher' art more generally (one of the contexts for the valorization of artistic discomfort suggested by Aldama and Lindenberger, as cited in Chapter 1).

Interpretation of this kind can be made in very general terms or within the more specific sociohistorical contexts evoked via commentators cited in Chapter 1. If a key feature of the broad processes associated with the development of modernity, or with certain more heightened recent dynamics, is an undermining of traditional sources of meaning and authority, the world of *Dogtooth* could be read as one in which these are being created and shored up, defensively, at a microcosmic level, a key part of such cultural dynamics.[1] The parents offer a firmly bounded universe to their offspring, one that seeks both to limit and to reframe meaning. This entails an imposition of particular significations within the family and keeping the outside world at bay through the construction of a defensive enclave, the latter a process seen as typical of the response of the wealthier classes to the insecurities of neoliberal late modernity.[2] These dynamics are available for a range of sociocultural readings. The family could be read as offering an allegory of any kind of controlled society, in its attempt to contain its inhabitants and block access to external media. It seems no accident that a central source of fracture, and an impulse to rebellion, is provided by the videotapes viewed by the eldest. One marker of her apparently growing discontent is expressed during a celebration of the parents' wedding anniversary. The two girls dance, in an awkward style that seems as confining as their general upbringing. After the younger stops, pleading tiredness, the eldest transitions into a series of wilder and more expressive moves, including some distinctly recognizable to anyone who has seen it from the Hollywood production *Flashdance* (1983), implying that this was another title borrowed illicitly from Christina. *Flashdance* is one of a number of Hollywood features that celebrates the potential of dance to offer escape from overly restrictive regimes (another contemporary example is *Footloose* [1984]). Its choice here seems far from accidental, but the element of parallel highlights the difference between a particular kind of feel-good wish-fulfilment and the awkward uncertainties more characteristic of the cinema of discomfort.

The film is open to be read as a potential warning of the dangers of any form of isolationist or fundamentalist home schooling; or, as suggested above, as a commentary on overprotective parenting, or on power relations within the nuclear family more generally. In relation to controlling parents, it could also be interpreted in the context of Beck's notion of risk society or the critique of certain styles of parenting offered by Oliver James. The constant emphasis of the parents on threats that require the children to remain within their controlled environment can be taken as a cynical ploy to maintain their own power, akin to similar dimensions of the overstatement of certain supposed risks highlighted by Beck or others (some of the discourses surrounding the supposed 'war on terror', for example). It could also be taken as an invention motivated by other concerns about threats they perceive to be posed by external society; a version, if perverse, of more ordinary, real-world attempts to protect children from outside sources of harm. The world created by the parents, and the clinical quality of some of the imagery, could also be taken as a perverse manifestation of something like the realm of 'everyday social experiments' identified by Anthony Giddens as an outcome of the waning of tradition. If the family becomes viewed as a refuge in such a social-historical context, as Beck and Beck-Gernsheim suggest, this would be a good example of the double-edged nature of the situation. Where a contradictory pull exists between the potential for new freedoms and for the exercise of older inequalities, the scenario offered by *Dogtooth* is one in which the latter continue to prevail. It is certainly not a manifestation of the aspect of the social context evoked by Giddens that entails greater sexual freedom for young women – more like a dramatization of a reactionary response to such a situation, one that Giddens suggests involves increasing levels of male violence.[3] Characteristically, however, no such issues are articulated by the characters other than the one very minimal comment by the father and no clearly favoured interpretation is offered to the viewer.

The constant emphasis of the parents on individual competition among their offspring, with assorted disciplines, rewards and punishments, is another element that could be interpreted in such sociopolitical terms, as a version of one of the central dynamics of neoliberal capitalism. It seems clear the parents have succeeded in inculcating some such behaviours or values in their offspring, who devise unhealthy forms of contest seemingly on their own initiative (the sisters inhaling anaesthetic, all three preparing at the start of the film to see whose finger can bear the longest time under a hot tap). A connection can also be made between the general patriarchal context and the economic role of the father as proprietor or manager of the factory that constitutes the only recurrent location of the film beyond the family home, providing a class basis for the broader social situation of fenced-off bourgeois comfort and space within which to maintain control.

The relatively open allegorical potential of *Dogtooth* makes it a veritable cornucopia for anyone seeking explanations of these kinds. Such frameworks can be seen as offering ways, for those suitably equipped, of mastering and potentially reducing some of the discomfort it might otherwise engender. To shift the focus away from the immediate narrative world and onto a broader interpretive level is an example of the frame-switching process identified in Chapter 1. The film itself remains awkwardly resistant to anything more than the broadest of such readings, however, as far as any definitive interpretation is concerned. This can be taken as another of its credentials, as a work of art cinema that refuses too easily to be reduced to any narrowly particular or programmatic interpretation. Such a quality is a key measure of the subtlety often celebrated as a marker of this part of the cinematic landscape, while at the same time being a basis often for criticism from particular perspectives.[4] If we consider the film less in terms of specific social diagnoses but in relation to the more diffuse sense of capturing something like a prevailing structure of feeling of the kind identified by Raymond Williams, what it seems to offer is a quality the discomforting nature of which lies to a large extent in its reticence: in its refusal, generally, of elaborated or explicitly articulated sociocultural points of reference and the awkward distance it keeps the viewer from any sense of emotional involvement in material that seems as if it should, more conventionally, be accessible at this level.

Sociocultural readings of the film in the broad terms outlined above have been mixed with a multitude of interpretations more specific to the national context of this and other contemporary Greek productions, a combination of such perspectives available to all the examples examined in this book. In a widely cited article that helped to popularize the use of the term 'Greek Weird Wave' in some circles, *The Guardian* journalist Steve Rose asks, rhetorically, 'Is it just coincidence that the world's most messed up country is making the world's most messed-up cinema?'[5] This is a (somewhat hyperbolic) reference to the government debt crisis and subsequent austerity that hit the country around 2009, following the global financial meltdown of 2007–2008. If such work can be read in the context of the prevalence of neoliberalism, that is, this is a case in which its more punitive dimensions were being applied very visibly in this nation at the time. Although tempting, the assertion of a strict correlation between the two risks oversimplification, as plenty of commentators have suggested. Apart from any other complications involved in such relationships, which can be manifold, the production timing of

Dogtooth is such that it seems unlikely strongly to have been determined by events that did not reach their full scope until the year of its release.

When other films are included in the category, via auteurist links drawn across the outputs of individuals, some are dated considerably earlier, including Lanthimos's debut, *Kinetta* (2005). The timing of his follow-up to *Dogtooth*, *Alps* (*Alpeis*, 2011), would make such an argument more persuasive, in such practical terms, but less so the continuities in certain respects that can be identified across the three films. The timing of Tsangari's *Attenberg*, released in 2010, is another that would seem to complicate any such correlation, once writing and production time is taken into account. None of this is to doubt that these films, individually (with the exception of *Kinetta*) or collectively, lent themselves to be *interpreted* in this manner on release, however, whatever questions might be asked about causal links or intentions.

Dogtooth was widely received by critics, both domestic and overseas, within the 'crisis' context, Tatjana Aleksić suggests: as a critical treatment of some combination of Greek-specific or more general dimensions of the dysfunctional bourgeois family or the family or nation under siege from foreign influences.[6] As Aleksić argues, the film can be situated within the specific crisis narrative, in broad terms, but also offers a deeper assault on pathological family repression of a kind that can be considered to be fundamental to the institution rather than merely a case of an exception related to any particular moment. Mark Fisher makes a broadly similar point, reading the film as an exposé of the 'pathogenic' qualities of the nuclear family, the radical nature of which is suggested by its appearance in an era in which a conservative idealized notion of the family is seen as having gained a dominant ideological position.[7] As Fisher suggests, the mantra of the father – 'if you stay inside you are protected' – is 'the slogan of social conservatism, and it is as if Lanthimos is demonstrating what the ideal conditions for such conservatism would actually need to be.' He adds: 'The outside must be totally pathologized: the children have to become literally xenophobic, terrified of everything that lies beyond the limits of their "protected" enclave.'[8] If the film can also be interpreted as resonating with aspects of neoliberalism, this could also be seen as a version of Fisher's capitalist realism, albeit a critical variety.

Alex Lykidis interprets *Dogtooth* and other films from Lanthimos and Tsangari in the context of both the wider context of neoliberal capitalism and the specific impact of its regime on Greece, in the form of the debt crisis and the resulting imposition of austerity programmes under international pressure by the national government.[9] The approach here is to interpret various dimensions of such work as offering quite detailed and specific resonance with the prevalence of broader neoliberal phenomena, although any issues about actual causality are evaded. This includes, for example, a broad and rather loose reading of the film as an allegory of the systemic and anonymous violence of global capitalism being inflicted on Greek society and of the crisis of popular sovereignty resulting from the failure of the government to resist the neoliberal economic policies and resulting austerity dictated by the European Commission, the European Central Bank and the International Monetary Fund (IMF).[10] Lykidis also reads the use of language and internalized routine in *Dogtooth* and other examples in the context of the broader hegemony of depoliticized neoliberal technocratic discourse. In this interpretation, when compared with the manner in which disempowerment is thematized in Greek cinema in the earlier period of the 1980s, including the more overtly political and historically focused work of Theo Angelopoulos, the films of Lanthimos and Tsangari are said to 'signal a shift from orthodox Marxist to Foucauldian conceptions of power, with a greater emphasis placed on interpersonal relations in civil society rather the asymmetric power of states over their citizens'.[11]

As Rosa Barotsi argues, scope exists for the film's depiction of the family to be viewed in the local context of 'a familiar critique of an incestuous, corrupt Greek statism'.[12] This is a reading supported by the reported comment of Tsangari (an associate producer of the film) that the reason for the trouble being faced by Greek society and economy was that the country was run *as* a family. As Barotsi suggests, the film is open and non-specific enough in its allegorical potential to have been embraced from both the political left and right in Greece. Expressing caution about those such as Lykidis who have championed the film as offering a radical critique, she complains that *Dogtooth* fails to point the finger at anyone in particular at the political level.[13] To have done so, however, to be so specific in relation to the particular conjuncture, would seem likely to have robbed the film of many of its most powerful broader sociocultural resonances. It would also shift the nature of the film, variably, depending on how strongly this might be imagined to have been done, away from the direction of more characteristic arthouse prestige markers of subtlety and obliqueness. To argue for the merits of a more immediately political approach is legitimate in its own terms, but it might also be to ignore some of the more film-institutionally specific contexts that shape the production and circulation of work of this variety and its ability to achieve a wider international profile.

Something similar can be said in response to criticism of the film from Tonia Kazakopoulou, who argues that generally progressive aspects of the film are compromised by a stereotypical treatment of the mother figure, as a combination of nurturing and punitive; as complicit in the treatment of the children while lacking any real agency of her own.[14] Somewhat oddly, for me, Kazakopoulou complains specifically that the character is not committed either way, which might be read as a more productive ambiguity and challenge to such stereotypes.[15] Like Barotsi, Kazakopoulou seems to want the film to offer a more affirmative 'way out' for its female characters. A clash can be identified again here between an understandable desire, from this perspective, for something more actively positive within the diegesis and the institutionally structured imperative for the 'art' of art cinema to involve an approach that is more ambiguous, uncertain or discomforting. The latter can be seen as a function of the specific social location of the entire institution and the basis on which it is often valorized.

The international realm of art cinema is itself implicated in the neoliberal economy, as suggested in Chapter 1, the latter embracing global niche as well as mass-market consumption. Rosalind Galt makes an argument for the role of this kind of material as a potential form of resistance, however, to both neoliberalism in general and specific national debt crises of this kind. In a focus on the context of Argentinian cinema during the period of that country's decision to default on international loans in 2001, Galt develops the notion of a 'default cinema' as one of radical refusal in the field of representation.[16] This is a cinema that wilfully thwarts and unsettles prevailing narrative and other formal qualities, offering a broader 'disturbance of meaning' that includes a denial of clear national allegory or any direct, more realist treatment of the fallout from economic crisis. *Dogtooth* is cited in passing here, along with Galt's principal example, *Suddenly* (*Tan de repente*, 2002), as works in which sexuality is denaturalized, the 'perverse and the surreal is made to feel quite commonplace' and overall interpretive meaning remains opaque in the manner I suggest above.[17] What Galt terms 'default' cinema might overlap with aspects of other categories, such as 'art' and 'indie', but it has particular use here in the connection it encourages between certain kinds of refusals of conventional expectations and a specific socio-economic and cultural context, even where the latter is not addressed in any more overt manner.

The other commentators cited above examine *Dogtooth* alongside a number of other broadly contemporary Greek productions, including and beyond the work of Lanthimos and Tsangari. For reasons of space, consideration of others here is limited primarily to Tsangari's *Attenberg*, one of the other higher-profile examples at the peak of the 'weird' component of the time. It is worth noting, however, that plenty of discomfort is also to be found in Lanthimos' other Greek productions, *Kinetta* and *Alps*, the latter produced before the relocation of his career to take advantage of greater resources in English language productions starting with *The Lobster* (2015), *The Killing of a Sacred Deer* (2017) and *The Favourite* (2018). *Kinetta* and *Alps* both involve small groups of characters involved in disconcerting forms of acting or re-enactment. The former, sometimes shot in an uncomfortably close and unstable style, features a trio (a detective, a photographer and a hotel cleaner) who awkwardly restage violent crimes or murders. No rationale is supplied for such strange activity and the lines seem to blur disturbingly at times between real and pretend harm.

Alps focuses on a group of four who offer a service in which they act as paid stand-ins for the recently bereaved, supposedly to help with the grieving process, although it is not until nearly a third of the way through the film that the nature of the activity is made explicitly clear. The most discomforting scene in this case involves one who works as a nurse (Angeliki Papoulia) performing the role of a teenage girl tennis player who died after a car crash, the material slipping between her often halting acting and the occasional giving of instructions by the victim's parents. The camera here tends to stay close on the nurse, in a shallow focus that keeps the figures of the parents blurred most of the time, the source of an uncomfortably claustrophobic proximity to the protagonist. This is a role the nurse has taken on illicitly, outside the aggressively male-enforced rules of the group, a performance upon which she seems increasingly dependent. Both films present the viewer with disconcerting displays of acting that have potential to raise questions about the performed nature of real life or the films themselves, but in neither case with any explicit or rationalized basis for such dimensions. Among other notable examples is the deeply discomforting *Miss Violence* (Alexandros Avranas, 2013), the opening of which culminates in the suicide on her birthday of an eleven-year-old girl. The blank, underplayed style of what follows only much later leads to a moment of shocking confirmation that the explanatory scenario is one of ongoing sexual abuse of children, amid a regime of insidious paternal control.

Attenberg and modernity

The context of modernity and its dislocations that can be identified as a broad setting for elements of the cinema of discomfort, and for other works in the wider tradition of art cinema, is cited more explicitly as part of the backdrop to Tsangari's *Attenberg*. As Lykidis suggests, Spyros (Vangelis Mourikis), the father of the principal character, implies that Greece has suffered from a 'premature modernity' rather than a version of modernity more often considered to be 'belated' as a result of the country's peripheral location, in 'western' geopolitical terms, 'pointing out the folly of imposing external models of development onto societies without a regard for the local context.'[18] 'We built an industrial colony on top of sheep pens and thought we were making a revolution', Spyros states, his disillusionment, Lykidis suggests, 'a response to the deindustrialization that transformed his home town, Aspra Spitia, into a ghost town.'[19] The town, as Lykidis informs us, where Tsangari was born, was founded in 1960 as an experiment in modernist urban planning, its depopulation 'conveyed in *Attenberg* through intermittent montages of empty interior and exterior spaces [...] and long shots of the characters dwarfed by their surroundings'.[20]

This provides more overtly a sociocultural context for the narrative, the principal focus of which is on Marina (Ariane Labed), aged twenty-three, and her relationships with Spyros, who is dying from cancer, and her friend Bella (Evangelia Randou). Further allusion to the context of modernity is made by Spyros, an architect who is implied but not clearly stated to have designed the settlement and/or the sprawling nearby industrial plant for which Marina works as a driver. He is, he suggests, 'A toxic remnant of modernism ... of post- Enlightenment', happy to leave the twentieth century. The speech is delivered as Spyros and Marina stand on a rooftop looking down at Aspra Spitia, although the location's status as an embodiment of any negative connotations of modernity might not be very clear to viewers unaware of its identity. Shots of characters 'dwarfed' by large-scale surroundings are found but are relatively infrequent, the buildings of the town itself low-rise and white painted in a manner designed to resemble a more traditional Greek settlement. It is not overtly 'modernist' in appearance, despite its straight rows. Marina declares that she likes it: "It's soothing, all this uniformity', prompting a jocular response from her father that this is 'because deep down you're an optimistic bourgeois modernist'. The enormous nearby plant (Aspra Spitia was built to accommodate workers at an aluminium-processing facility) seems a more obvious signifier of any negative connotations of the modern, dominating its location between hills and the sea. A sense of industrial wasteland is also created in the closing images of the film, after Marina and Bella have scattered the ashes of Spyros in the sea. They walk across part of a vast red-earthed expanse, departing a scene that is held for an extended period up to and including the start of the credits, a vista comprised of large heaps of earth, tall chimneys, smoke, puddles and a constant traffic of heavy trucks.

The discomfort offered by *Attenberg* has something in common with that of *Dogtooth* and other examples examined above, most obviously residing in sequences of awkward sexual or sexually related activity, an arena in which the apparently naïve and under-socialized Marina is being schooled by Bella. The film opens with an extended sequence of extremely awkward open-mouthed kissing between the two, a spectacle as odd in its way as the sexual encounters of the Lanthimos feature (Figure 15). The effect is partly, at least, to defamiliarize so routine a procedure. 'I've never had something wriggling in my mouth before,' declares Marina. It is disgusting, she adds, making her want to throw up. As it becomes clear that Bella is attempting to teach her, Marina says she does not want to learn, suggesting a refusal to conform, although one set in what seems a far more benign, if distinctly odd, narrative context than the educational process in *Dogtooth*. Later scenes feature Marina kissing, again very awkwardly, and subsequently gradually engaging in sexual intercourse with a man she picked up and delivered to his hotel in the town, a figure unnamed in the film and identified in the

FIGURE 16 *Awkward kissing at the start of* Attenberg *(2010)*.

credits only as 'engineer' (played by Yorgos Lanthimos). During their most extended sexual intercourse, she offers a constant barrage of unsettling questions and commentary, sufficient to drive her partner to what seems an amused form of distraction. This, again, is a more benign and playful variety of the awkward sex trope so often at the centre of the cinema of discomfort.

If the film invites us, through Marina, to experience some aspects of sex as if they might be learned anew rather being taken for granted and familiar, and in which their more animalistic status might come more than usually to the fore, a key thread of *Attenberg* entails behaviour that involves the more direct mimicry of animal behaviour. After the opening kissing sequence, Marina and Bella drop to all fours, seemingly behaving like dogs, in a manner reminiscent of the defensive barking required of the children (and mother) in *Dogtooth* after the incident with the cat and the disappearance of the eldest. No rationale is provided for this at the time, although it seems spontaneous rather than enforced. A central reference point that emerges as the film develops (providing its title through a mispronunciation) comes from a number of nature programmes presented by David Attenborough, viewed by Marina and Spyros, including his famous youthful interaction with a band of gorillas. Father and daughter are prone to playful language games, one of which devolves into nonsense sounds and a sequence of sonic and gestural mimicry of the behaviour of apes. A later scene has Marina similarly aping the sounds and gestures of seabirds.

If language has become colonized by the technocratic-speak of neoliberalism, as he suggests, for Lykidis the play with language between Marina and Spyros 'signals their desire to escape the realm of ideology by focusing on word sounds rather than word meanings'.²¹ Whether this can really be interpreted at the level of such conscious intent or desire on the part of characters seems questionable, one of a number of points on which the argument of Lykidis seems to slide ambiguously between notions of what can be 'read into' texts such as this or what they might clearly or confidently be said to embody or reflect more directly themselves. Parts of *Attenberg* occupy a realm of non-verbal expression that can be interpreted in such a way, however. As Lykidis suggests, many scenes in the film take place in silence, any particular meanings left challengingly unexplained. The most striking sequences, punctuating the film throughout, feature Marina and Bella walking arm-in-arm in nearly matching dresses, wordlessly performing a range of odd and at times distinctly Monty Pythonesque 'silly walks', sometimes accompanied by assorted angular hand gestures, facial expressions and non-verbal utterances (Figure 17). No explanation for this activity is offered, but it seems to be another example of some kind of play across the lines of the human and the animal-like, the spontaneous and the regimented. These walks are situated along paths within the town, devoid of any signs of other inhabitants. They are distinctly quirky in nature but also tightly coordinated between the two women and so seemingly not a manifestation of anything entirely spontaneous in any disruption they might offer of the dominant sociocultural order.

In one interview, Tsangari suggests that the film presents humanity as 'the ultimate merger between animality and machine',²² as might be suggested here, a dimension that also seems to be picked up in the treatment of Spyros after death (a Greek ban on cremation means his wish to have his ashes

FIGURE 17 *Silly walks and gestures in* Attenberg *(2010)*.

scattered in the sea results in a machine-like bureaucratic routine of sending his corpse abroad to be processed). This formulation seems to leave out the middle territory of the socially constructed, however, and so marks a difference of emphasis from some of the central implications of *Dogtooth*. For the viewer, the weird walking sequences offer something that seems both appealing – they are amusingly deadpan and seem subtly subversive in broad terms, even if it is not quite clear why – but also puzzling and beyond easily immediate explanation. For Lykidis, again, these and other activities such as dancing – here and in other films by Lanthimos and Tsangari – 'reveal the desire of the characters to escape the social constraints of language', an interpretation he develops further in terms of Lacanian psychoanalytical theory.[23] Their potentially discomforting qualities also seem to escape reduction to any such clear cut theoretical explanations or assertions, however, another marker of the more abidingly ambiguous and unexplained status of such material in the cinema of discomfort. The more negative connotations are to the fore in Tsangari's next feature, *Chevalier* (2015), in which six men on a fishing trip enter into competition for almost every dimension of their activities, a scenario more akin to the unhealthy forms of sibling rivalry engineered by the parents in *Dogtooth*.

Making Greek waves

While the films examined in this chapter have most prominently been interpreted as a response to the Greek economic and social crisis of the early twenty-first century, their existence and qualities are also products of a particular cinematic context, both within and beyond the nation, in much the same way as those examined in other chapters. Whether in its 'weird' manifestations, especially in the work of Lanthimos and Tsangari, or more widely, a reasonably distinct 'wave' of art or independently oriented cinema can be identified in this period, a product of a conjuncture of local forces and the integration of their output with the global institutions of art cinema. Such labels can always conceal variety and give the impression that a group of films is more consolidated than might really be the case, as is equally true of consecrated examples such as the French *nouvelle vague*, but they can capture a sense of the relatively distinct nature of bodies of work produced in particular circumstances. As Maria Chalkou suggests, weirdness applies only to a minority of titles, more broadly applicable labels used at the time including 'Young Greek Cinema', 'Greek New Wave' and, in Greece itself, primarily, *Neo Elleniko Reuma* or 'New Greek Current'.[24] For Chalkou 'the new film trend', as she calls it, is marked by diversity but also a shared 'new gaze' and a 'new ethos' that constitute a clear break from the past of Greek cinema.

Thematically 'there is a shift away from history, ancient drama and issues of Greekness to the present reality, which is confronted with sharpness, irony, demystification and cold criticism, with the family and anxieties of identity as recurrent concerns.'[25] She identifies a diversity of style, 'from extreme naturalism and realism to the other end of the stylistic spectrum, while hybrid forms combining high art, popular elements and a variety of genres as well as playful narratives prevail'. There is also 'a clear shift in reference from canonical auteurs, central to the work of older Greek directors [the best known of which is Theo Angelopoulos], to more contemporary, diverse and often heterogeneous cinematic influences'.[26]

Beyond the individual efforts and talents of filmmakers such as Lanthimos and Tsangari, Chalkou identifies 'an exceptional revival in artistic, alternative and independent film' during the 2000s, a phenomenon attributable to broader changes in the Greek audiovisual sector.[27] These include the resurgence of a previously struggling domestic commercial film sector. A major engine of growth, Chalkou, suggests, was a dramatic expansion in Greek television, following the deregulation of broadcasting in 1989, accompanied by similar development of the domestic advertising and music video sectors. Rapid expansion in the 1990s and early 2000s created an increased demand for new technical and creative personnel: 'Young filmmakers and other film practitioners found systematic occupation and opportunities to develop their skills, in different fields of the industry.'[28] Such figures were given the opportunity quickly to master film techniques and new technologies while developing professional networks. Lanthimos is cited by Chalkou as 'the most representative example' of this new generation, having worked successfully in television, commercials, music and dance videos, theatre and on the ceremony for the 2004 Athens Olympics.[29] A key feature of this cohort, for Chalkou, was its movement between the art and more popular sectors, two domains she suggests were strictly divided in the mentality of the earlier art-oriented and state-funded New Greek Cinema of the 1970s and 1980s.[30] One example of such mutual relations is the financial support received by Lanthimos for *Dogtooth* from a production company, Boo, the prosperity of which at the time was based on commercials made by the director among others.[31]

Further background for the new generation of filmmakers suggested by Chalkou involves changes in domestic cinephile culture, including a greater international orientation following the broadening of the focus of the Thessaloniki Film Festival from 1992 and the establishment of alternative independent festivals, also with international scope, along with a more general opening up of the horizons of Greek film culture. 'This has led', Chalkou suggests, 'to the demystification of the "great masters" and radically shifted the point of reference of cinephiles and young film-makers alike to contemporary works and to a more playful and eclectic approach to cinema'.[32] Arthouse-oriented production in this period also sought more generally to make a break, at least partial, from the heavily bureaucratic and slow machinery of Greek public sector funding, along with various campaigns to change the system, one of which resulted in the creation of a new Hellenic Film Academy in 2009.[33] This is seen by Chalkou as part of a broader, new generational rejection of established, paternalistic and often corrupt bureaucracy.

A shift was made by many filmmakers to lower-budget production, Chalkou suggests, in some cases self-funded, often involving digital video (although this did not apply to Lanthimos' *Kinetta* or *Dogtooth*, both of which were shot in Super 16 mm) and an approach based on mutual collaboration and support. Hence, for example, the presence of Tsangari as associate producer on *Dogtooth* and Lanthimos as one of the producers and a performer in *Attenberg*. Tsangari co-founded the production outfit Haos Film while a student in the United States. The subsequent producer of films including *Kinetta*, *Attenberg*, *Alps* and *Chevalier*, the company is described by Tsangari as having the ethos of a cooperative, the members of which work flexibly rather than in fixed roles, a mode of operation with which she became familiar as a result of connections made with the American indie scene (including a chance encounter with Richard Linklater that led her to a small part in *Slacker* [1991]).[34] One marker of collaboration is, for example, the presence of Efthymis Filippou as writer or co-writer of most of the films to date of Lanthimos and Tsangari, a factor that seems likely to explain certain degrees of similarity within this body of work (and, of course, one that complicates any overly director-auteurist account of its nature).

Raising funds remained difficult, however. Following a 'modest but significant festival success' with *Kinetta*, Lanthimos funded *Dogtooth* through a combination of private (Boo) and public sources (the Greek Film Centre), according to Lydia Papadimitriou, just before the onset of the financial crisis.[35] Despite the greater success and profile of his second feature, however, he struggled to complete his third, *Alps*, receiving limited state funding from the Greek Film Centre and state television.[36] Tsangari's *Attenberg* was to have received funds from the Greek Film Centre, along with the European MEDIA programme, but had to replace the finance due to have come from the state once the crisis struck, turning instead to an internationally oriented private source, Faliro House Productions.[37] Such problems of funding contributed to the decision of Lanthimos to relocate to the UK and work in the English language, as a way to access larger-scale resources, a far from untypical move for a filmmaker who gains international recognition within the arthouse realm. For *The Lobster*, this included the use of stars such as Colin Farrell and Rachel Weisz. *The Lobster* retains a large component of the weird, set in a dystopian context in which single people are assigned to a hotel complex where they are given forty-five days to find a genuine romantic partner or face the fate of being transformed into a favourite animal of their choice (or, escaping to the woods outside, where people are only allowed to live as independent individuals and any sign of coupling is punished). Despite the bizarre nature of the latter concept, the film is in some ways more conventional than Lanthimos' earlier features, the nature of the immediate scenario being outlined much more clearly. Lanthimos has commented frankly on the financial advantage of having a central focus on romance, the film having been funded as an international Ireland, UK, Greece, France and Netherlands co-production.[38] *The Killing of a Sacred Deer* (a UK, Ireland, US co-production), is a distinctly uncomfortable and painful twist on the revenge thriller-horror subgenre, so again mixing characteristics that might be associated with Lanthimos and more commercial dimensions, also featuring the box-office power of Farrell and Nicole Kidman. Rachel Weisz also appears in his most high-profile film to date, *The Favourite* (2018), a production that offers a distinctive twist on the royal period-heritage format.

Crucial to the profile achieved by the internationally better-known examples of Greek art/indie film by Lanthimos, Tsangari and others in this period was their successful participation in the festival circuit, a more or less obligatory part of the life cycle of work from smaller nations or industries that gains broader arthouse circulation. *Dogtooth* achieved the major-league art-cinema credentials of a premiere at Cannes, among numerous other appearances, and the even higher profile that came with an Oscar nomination for best foreign language film. *Attenberg*, likewise, was screened at prestige venues including Venice, Toronto and Sundance. The pursuit of international profile of this kind was a deliberate strategy on the part of the producers, as Papadimitriou suggests, while the 'referential openness' and lack of much in the way of Greek-specific content made both films accessible to the international arthouse constituency.[39] The latter is an important point, making the films not seem dependent for their consumption on local knowledge and giving them the qualities of more general disturbing ambiguity often favoured within the domains of festivals and arthouse distribution. That the films were often located by critics within the context of the Greek crisis was not likely to undermine their broader resonance, given the extent to which what was happening in the country was clearly situated as part of the fallout from a wider, global process. The concept of the 'weird wave' had useful currency in this dimension, however much it might be questioned by the filmmakers themselves or the limited extent to which it might represent the wider independent Greek cinema of the period, as a marker of a distinct and identifiable tendency within the broader arthouse marketplace. However much it might directly have been reflected in the films examined above, the Greek financial and social crisis was almost certainly a major factor in the level of critical attention they gained, providing a strong interpretive angle at a time when Greece was in the international headlines.

Festival profile, probably as much as anything else, earned wider circulation for the best-known films of the Greek wave, although generally at the more marginal end of the business. In the United States, for example, it was some of the surviving smaller companies cited in Chapter 2 that distributed most of the early films of Lanthimos and Tsangari in the theatrical market: Kino International and its parent Kino Lorber for *Dogtooth* and *Alps*, respectively, and Strand Releasing for *Attenberg* and *Chevalier*. Each performed distinctly modestly in the United States, as might be expected for discomforting films with little in the way of higher-profile auteur associations. *Dogtooth* grossed $110,248 after opening in two theatres.[40] *Alps* took $16,057 after opening at the same scale. The theatrical gross for *Attenberg* was $24,036 in the United States, after opening on a single screen, with another $45,925 recorded for the international market, while *Chevalier* recorded $25,696, opening on three screens.

'What the hell did I just watch?': Responses to *Dogtooth*

Dogtooth is clearly a film that lends itself to appreciation by critics, with plenty of striking markers of distinctly unusual arthouse status, gaining a very high 92 per cent approval rating on the review aggregation site Rotten Tomatoes. Of sixty-three reviews included, fifty responded positively and only five negatively. The 'Critics Consensus' reported on the site is another that makes clear its discomforting status, concluding: 'It'll be too disturbing – and meandering – for some, but *Dogtooth* is as disturbing and startlingly original as modern filmmaking gets.'[41] The 'audience score' reported by Rotten Tomatoes is also high but, as is often the case for such films, significantly lower than that for critics, at 75 per cent, from what is said to be 10,009 user ratings. A summary of some user responses follows from among these, plus 153 from Amazon and 204 from the IMDb.[42] Some fall into broad patterns akin to those found in the previous two chapters. Many describe the film as 'disturbing', a substantial number declaring it to be the most disturbing or strange they have seen. The majority that describe the film this way do so as part of a positive response, although some are unsure what to make of it. One of the most frequent bases of justification for approval on this basis, as was seen in the case of *Palindromes*, is that what is disturbing is also 'thought-provoking', often staying in the mind for longer than usual after viewing.

This is another work of discomfort that has potential to generate strong levels of viewer interest, for those suitably oriented, rather than more hedonistic form of pleasure, but also to push towards and sometimes beyond the coping potential even of appreciative viewers. The capacity of cinematic material to continue to resonate after viewing is one of the markers of strong levels of interest identified by Berliner. One viewer sums the film up as 'An extraordinarily disturbing, thought-provoking picture.'[43] Another comments: 'This is a movie that disturbed, moved and fascinated me while I was watching it and made me think after having watched it.'[44] For some this includes explicit reference to the allegorical or similar qualities of the film, as a critique focused on issues such as the family, home-schooling and/or repressive religious or governmental ideological reinforcement either in general or in particular instances (the latter range from references to post-crisis Greece and North Korea to others who detect resonances closer to their own more ordinary lives, in the United States or elsewhere[45]). Some respondents revel in the experience offered by the film on this basis, although others are more ambivalent in their comments. There is quite widespread agreement, implicit or explicit, that this is the type of film that will appeal only to a certain kind of filmgoer, a constituency that appears to be over-represented, unsurprisingly, among those who have both seen the film and taken the time to post comments in such fora.

While some appreciators are unquestioningly celebratory of the discomforting qualities of *Dogtooth*, using language that suggests the kind of exhilaration identified by Berliner in the experience of meeting the challenge of difficult material ('disturbingly wonderful'[46] or 'made me cringe with delight'[47]), others are mixed in what they express, sometimes finding grounds for admiration more than for any kind of pleasure. This suggests a sharing of the bases on which such films are customarily valued, even if they are not actually enjoyed on such grounds in the manner suggested by those who revel more strongly in the challenge and discomfort offered by the film. It is useful to look at some of the ambivalent responses in more detail, to see how certain viewers wrestle with how to process such material, or how it exceeds the limits of their coping potential. One comments that there were many moments 'when I just didn't want to be watching what I was watching', especially the sexual material involving the siblings.[48] 'It's not a movie that will entertain you and you are sure to have zero fun watching it', this respondent adds, 'but it is extremely interesting if disgusting, creepy, disturbing, and repulsive. I watched the whole thing [clearly marked here as an achievement rather than taken for granted], and I'll say it is a well developed and made movie. I still didn't like it much.' Awarding the film just half a star out of the five maximum, he adds: 'In all honesty it deserves five stars because it is absolutely perfect at evoking the feelings it tries to evoke. I just can't give it anymore [sic] because I am so repulsed. Damn, this doesn't happen to me often, but this one did it. I have to respect it for that. Truly disturbing.'

'Truly disturbing' seems to suggest something that leaves the viewer unable easily to resolve their own response, rather than a recognition of the disturbing that can more readily be processed and pigeon-holed, positively or negatively, a potentially further-reaching form of discomfort. Something similar might be implied by those who say the film stayed with them for an unusually long time after viewing. Another reviewer has somewhat similar grounds for saying they are uncertain how to rate the film: 'It was kinda funny, but mostly weird and disturbing. I think it did what it meant to do really well, but not exactly sure what that was. Enter at your own risk.'[49] Again, to not be sure exactly what the film did, while still admiring it, seems to reflect an additional layer of discomfort generated by the presentation of a challenge that cannot entirely be met. Something similar is found from an admiring respondent who refers to being 'often confused over my own feelings' while watching the film: 'It truly touched a nerve in me, I am just trying to figure out which one.'[50] One headlines their review: 'Honestly don't know what to make of this' while another, who finds the film 'Strangely Compelling', asks: 'What the hell did I just watch?'[51] Another comments: 'Never have I felt so uncomfortable yet intrigued and satisfied by a film. There were moments within it that I definitely wanted to turn it off but I couldn't, I had to keep watching.' This viewer concludes: 'Saying that I got enjoyment out of this film would be difficult, it was more a sense of confused gratification at its content and outcome.'[52] For ten minutes after the credits rolled, one viewer reports that they 'sat there open-mouthed and glued to my seat, unable to control the myriad of feelings that had been stirred inside me while slowly realizing I had probably watched one of the greatest movies of the century'.[53]

A recurring refrain, in some cases citing a similar comment in a review by Roger Ebert, is that the film is like a 'car crash' in being hard to avoid looking at despite its disturbing nature. Some who make broadly positive comments report feeling guilty for watching the film or feeling bad afterwards, again suggesting its potential to unsettle in more than a passing manner.[54] One, whose review leaves open the evaluative opinion, comments: 'I left the movie feeling disgusted, squeamish and unsure about life.'[55] Another reaches for more colourful images through which to express the strength of their feelings, after saying they 'almost walked out on it several times, then applauded with tears in my eyes at the ending':

> If you like to be challenged to deal with the discomfort of emotion you feel when watching a stranger pick a scab on a bus while watching something that you can tell deep down is going to be rewarding in the long-run, or if you like to close your eyes and spin until you're dizzy, then take off your clothes and walk into public buildings to find out the reaction, then this is a must-see film.[56]

Strong qualifications, in other words, but ones that indicate the power of such a film to challenge and unsettle in a manner that suggests a heightened form of exhilaration.

Numerous appreciative viewers in all three samples offer a familiar distinction-marking articulation of this type, to the effect that this is a film for certain kinds of people but not for others. It is, variously, a film for those who like the bizarre, the weird or the disturbing, either generally or in the context of categories such as 'foreign' or 'European' films or work from the art or indie sectors more generally characterized. On the other side of this coin, it is very much 'not for the easily offended', as more than one puts it; or, in a more loaded phrasing, 'not for delicate sensibilities or lovers of fast action movies!'[57] The latter is a typical source of binary distinction marking in responses of this kind to art or indie cinema. As one comments, more neutrally than some participants in such discourse: 'Dogtooth is a film where the viewing experience is very much dependent on the sensibilities of the viewer.' In this case, this is one who says they found the film 'more satirical than disturbing', citing their enjoyment of 'the indie style of shooting, reminiscent of Submarine and Wes Andersen [sic] films'.[58]

A number of other cinematic reference points are cited by admirers, in their deployment of relevant cultural capital, the most common being the films of Lars von Trier and Michael Haneke. Such figures are also cited by some negative responders, however, what their names signify depending on the orientation of the viewer. As is usually the case in such samples, some of those who dislike the film explicitly reject what they see as an elitist adoption of work of this kind or what is viewed as excessive hype, the latter a quality marked by the positive consensus among critics and the Oscar nomination. For one, it is 'Definitely the type of movie snobs would sip wine to talking about how artistic and deep it is'.[59] For another it is 'typical art house bait' and 'for people who have a smug sense of superiority thinking I am clever that I do not watch blockbusters like the plebs'.[60] As was seen in the case of *Palindromes*, however, a number of those who express dislike for the film position themselves more generally as open to challenging or unusual works of art or independent cinema, signalling an antipathy to aspects of this particular example rather than to such categories as a whole.

Those who reject the film most strongly tend to find it disturbing but in a way that is not redeemed and characterized by terms such as 'sick' and 'disgusting' (including some who argue, like certain critics of *Import Export*, that the film is little more than pornography because of the sex sequences).[61] This demonstrates a discomfort that cannot, for such viewers, be translated into any more admirable qualities. The fact that discomfort itself sometimes seems to be used as a basis for positive valuation by others is challenged by one, in a manner similar to a response to *Palindromes* cited in Chapter 2. Before going on to criticize the film for weakness of narrative, this respondent asks, rhetorically: 'Are we really supposed to applaud this as an ingenious work of modernism simply because it's awkward and uncomfortable?'[62] Others adopt what often seems a default negative position for those who dislike such films, labelling it as 'boring' or 'dull', a verdict sometimes accompanied by a denial that *Dogtooth* has the power to achieve the status of anything really discomforting or disturbing.[63]

Notes

1. For another such account, see Jock Young, *The Vertigo of Late Modernity* (London: Sage, 2007).
2. See, for example, Keith Hayward, *City Limits: Crime, Consumer Culture and the Urban Experience* (London: GlassHouse, 2004).
3. Giddens, *The Transformation of Intimacy*, 3.
4. For a similar point in relation to the films of Michael Haneke, see King, *Positioning Art Cinema*, 171.
5. Steve Rose, 'Attenberg, Dogtooth and the Weird Wave of Geek Cinema', *The Guardian*, 27 August 2011, accessed online at https://www.theguardian.com/film/2011/aug/27/attenberg-dogtooth-greece-cinema.
6. Tatjana Aleksić, 'Sex, Violence, Dogs and the Impossibility of Escape: Why Contemporary Greek Film Is So Focused on Family', *Journal of Greek Media and Culture*, vol. 2, no. 2 (2016): 156.
7. Mark Fisher, '*Dogtooth*: The Family Syndrome', *Film Quarterly*, vol. 64, no. 4 (2011): 25.
8. Fisher, '*Dogtooth*: The Family Syndrome', 25–7. Another reading of the film that views it as, among other things, a critique of the traditional Greek family is Stamos Metzidakis, 'No Bones to Pick with Lanthimos' Film *Dogtooth*', *Journal of Modern Greek Studies*, vol. 32, no. 2 (2014) 367–92.
9. Alex Lykidis,' 'Crisis of Sovereignty in Recent Greek Cinema', *Journal of Greek Media and Culture*, vol. 1, no. 1 (2015).
10. Lykidis, 'Crisis of Sovereignty', 11. The terms 'systemic' and 'autonomous' in this account are taken from the work of Slavoj Žižek.
11. Ibid., 23.
12. Rosa Barotsi, 'Whose Crisis? *Dogtooth* and the Invisible Middle Class', *Journal of Greek Media and Culture*, vol. 2, no. 2 (2016): 181.
13. Barotsi, 'Whose Crisis?', 182.
14. Tonia Kazakopoulou, 'The Mother Accomplice: Questions of Representation in *Dogtooth* and *Miss Violence*', *Journal of Greek Media and Culture*, vol. 2, no. 2 (2016): 187–200.
15. Kazakopoulou, 'The Mother Accomplice', 191.
16. Rosalind Galt, 'Default Cinema: Queering Economic Crisis in Argentina and beyond', *Screen* vol. 54 (Spring 2013): 62–81.
17. Galt, 'Default Cinema', 64.
18. Lykidis,' 'Crisis of Sovereignty', 18.
19. Ibid., 18.

20 Ibid., 18.
21 Ibid., 15.
22 'On Solidarity, Collaboration and Independence: Athina Rachel Tsangari Discusses Her Films and Greek Cinema with Vangelis Calotychos, Lydia Papadimitriou and Yannis Tzioumakis', *Journal of Greek Media and Culture*, vol. 2, no. 2 (2016): 250.
23 Lykidis,' 'Crisis of Sovereignty', 16.
24 Maria Chalkou, 'A New Cinema of "Emancipation": Tendencies of Independence In Greek Cinema Of The 2000s', *Interactions: Studies in Communication & Culture*, vol 3, no. 2 (2012): 244.
25 Chalkou, '"A New Cinema of 'Emancipation"', 245.
26 Ibid.
27 Ibid., 247.
28 Ibid., 248.
29 Ibid.
30 For a brief summary of the earlier New Greek Cinema, see Lydia Papadimitriou, 'In the Shadow of the Studios, the State, and the Multiplexes: Independent Filmmaking in Greece', in Doris Baltruschat and Mary Erickson (eds), *Independent Filmmaking Around the Globe* (Toronto: University of Toronto Press, 2015), 120–1.
31 Chalkou, 'A New Cinema of "Emancipation"', 249.
32 Ibid., 255.
33 Ibid., 251.
34 Papadimitriou, 'In the Shadow of the Studios', 128.
35 Lydia Papadimitriou, 'Cinema at the Edges of the European Union', in Rob Stone, Paul Cooke, Stephanie Dennison and Alex Marlow-Mann (eds), *The Routledge Companion to World Cinema* (New York: Routledge, 2018), 184.
36 Papadimitriou, 'Cinema at the Edges of the European Union', 184.
37 Papadimitriou, 'In the Shadow of the Studios', 127.
38 Amir Ganjavie, 'Futureworlds: Talking with Yorgos Lanthimos about *The Lobster* (2015)', *Bright Lights Film Journal*, 19 May 2016, accessed at http://brightlightsfilm.com/talking- yorgos-lanthimos-lobster/#.W1w_FS3MzjA.
39 Papadimitriou, 'In the Shadow of the Studios', 124, 125.
40 This and the following figures are from the entries for the films on Box Office Mojo, boxofficemojo.com.
41 From the entry for the film at https://www.rottentomatoes.com/m/dogtooth.
42 Reviews accessed 6 August 2018: Rotten Tomatoes starting at https://www.rottentomatoes.com/m/dogtooth/reviews/?type=user&sort=; Amazon starting at https://www.amazon.com/Dogtooth-Christos-Stergioglou/product-reviews/B0048FQFFM/ref=cm_cr_othr_d_paging_btm_1?ie=UTF8&reviewerType=all_reviews&pageNumber=1; IMDb starting at https://www.imdb.com/title/tt1379182/reviews?ref_=tt_urv.

43 Michael T, Rotten Tomatoes, 26 April 2013.
44 Penelope Cappa, IMDb, 15 January 2011.
45 For an example of the latter, see Manal S, a response posted to both Rotten Tomatoes and the IMDb, 23 August 2016.
46 Sasha H, Rotten Tomatoes, 5 March 2015.
47 crizeene, Amazon, 1 May 2014.
48 Melvin W, Rotten Tomatoes, 21 July 2012.
49 Ed T, Rotten Tomatoes, 20 April 2016.
50 pgsev-1, IMDb, 21 June 2010.
51 MikesIDhasbeentaken, IMDb, 25 July 2011; billcr12, IMDb, 21 May 2012.
52 chloewinns, IMDb, 31 March 2018.
53 Manal S, Rotten Tomatoes and IMDb, 23 August 2013.
54 For example, respectively, Michael B, Rotten Tomatoes, 7 April 2011, and tony, Rotten Tomatoes, 10 April 2011.
55 William H, Rotten Tomatoes, 20 May 2011.
56 spencerra44, IMDb, 21 February 2011.
57 For the first formulation, see for example, 'Nuc Sub Veton, Amazon, 29 August 2016 and Bindy Sue Fronkunschtein, Amazon, 11 November 2013; the latter quotation is from Ian T. Webber, Amazon, 26 May 2011.
58 rbrogan3, Amazon, 30 September 2015.
59 Alyssa Brown, Amazon, 13 June 2018.
60 freemantle uk, IMDb, 27 November 2011.
61 See, for example, Katrina Janine C, Rotten Tomatoes, 10 August 2012.
62 Nick A, Rotten Tomatoes, 20 June 2011.
63 For one example of the latter, see iliaspart, IMDb, 10 February 2011.

5

Forces majeure and minor: From existential alienation to personal obligation in the films of Roy Andersson and Ruben Östlund

The cinema of discomfort comes in a number of varieties, both generally and, in some cases, within the same national context. The latter is the case for the examples examined in this chapter, from the work of two Swedish filmmakers, Roy Andersson and Ruben Östlund. The films of Östlund have some qualities in common with others considered so far and are broadly typical of the variety of internationally circulating art cinema that includes such discomfort among its prominent dimensions. Those of Andersson manifest a distinctly individual aesthetic, although their discomforting qualities include some more familiar dimensions. The fictional universe constructed by Andersson, particularly in the trilogy comprised by *Songs from the Second Floor* (*Sånger från andra våningen*, 2000), *You, the Living* (*Du levande*, 2007) and *A Pigeon Sat on a Branch Reflecting on Existence* (*En duva satt på en gren och funderade på tillvaron*, 2014), is a doleful, glum, grey and stylized world very much of its own, although it offers ready potential to be viewed as a commentary on the status of modern/contemporary alienated existence. Its scope ranges from the exaggeratedly bizarre to the humdrum, the sources of discomfort on occasion acute but more often lower key. The films of Östlund, including *Play* (2011), *Involuntary* (*De ofrivilliga*, 2008), *Force Majeure* (*Turist*, 2014) and *The Square* (2017), offer a more recognizable and familiar view of the world, generally and in terms of the usual parameters of contemporary European art cinema. Both provoke unease at least partly by leaving viewers in the characteristic cinema of discomfort position of having to decide for themselves how to interpret difficult or awkward material. In the case of Andersson, an aesthetic designed to encourage active viewing has been related explicitly by the filmmaker to a thematic focus on the dangers of passivity in the face of the plight of others, an issue also applicable to Östlund.

The strange, estranged world of Roy Andersson

The films of Andersson's trilogy are multistrand narratives, some threads of which are pursued across the length of a work while others are little more than passing vignettes. Their style is highly distinctive while their mood is generally dolorous. The world of the trilogy evokes some of the harsh realities of life but it is also a strange universe of its own, many inhabitants exhibiting a theatrical pasty-faced appearance and lines sometimes blurring between what is presented as diegetic reality, dream or nightmare. At their most unnerving, the films include material that is disturbing on a large scale. This includes the sacrifice of a young girl in the first film of the trilogy, *Songs from the Second Floor*. Culminating in an epic-scale social ritual, the event is preceded by sequences that show preparations that have a matter-of-fact quality, all the more so when the film is watched more than once and the viewer knows what is to come. Workmen are finishing off the arrangement of a pile of jagged rocks on the floor of a quarry. A dummy falls suddenly onto these from above. It is placed on a stretcher and examined by a doctor, a number of dignitaries watching from one side. Cut to a scene in a palatial room in which a young girl, identified as Anna (Helen Mathiasson), is being questioned by a woman and a seated group of elders. A couple standing in the background might be assumed to be her parents. The group, the woman tells the girl, has read all the books in the world and has the benefit of experience; but some things, she is told, are impossible.

There is no indication at this point exactly how this scene is linked to its predecessor, but we are then taken to a shot of what is clearly the top of the quarry, which immediately implies that all three are part of the same component of the film. A line of bishops stands to screen left, other figures in formal dress to the right and a large crowd is visible in the background. Just off the centre of the frame is a board that projects over the edge of the cliff, to which the line of figures in the middle-ground leads, suggesting a scene of imminent sacrifice. Into frame-right walks a white-coated doctor and the woman from the previous scene, walking half backwards, watching those who follow. Two adults – now more evidently the parents – come into frame with the girl in between, blindfolded and in a white dress. It is clear what is going to happen: that Anna is to be a sacrifice, for a reason that is not specified, and that we are to be presented with the spectacle of this awful event from a position of detached distance.

The trio walks slowly into mid frame, at which point the parents stop and hug the girl, who is then taken forward by another man. The pair moves on, again slowly, up to and onto the board. The man, holding the girl by the hand, lets her walk ahead, onto the overhang and up to the edge. A woman in a hat, attached to a tether held by another figure, follows onto the board, up to the girl, and quietly pushes her off. A brief disappearing scream from Anna breaks the silence in which the event has unfolded. The faint sound of crying is heard while the shot is held for some moments after the woman walks back onto firm ground. A hymn plays, broadcast through speakers mounted above the gathered crowd. As with the preparatory scenes, this is all presented in a distanced, matter-of-fact style that makes the material in some ways all the more discomforting than if the viewer were to be given closer access, for example, to the emotional responses of the parents to what they presumably know is to happen or to the event itself. A mainstream-conventional treatment would be likely to provide more in the way of outwardly expressed upset and disturbance of its own kind; but this is another example of the kind of discomfort that is rooted in the absence of any cinematic articulation, breakdown or emoting that would seem more commensurate with the disturbing nature of what is shown.

Another example of a heightened set piece of uncomfortable material is found in the third instalment, *A Pigeon Sat on A Branch Reflecting on Existence*, a sequence that appears to be a commentary on colonial violence although, characteristically, no unambiguous explanatory context is provided. This begins with a long shot of a large copper-coloured drum, the sides of which are fitted with numerous protrusions in the shape of the trumpet ends of brass musical instruments. To one side, a line of figures of semi-clad black African appearance are being led into the drum, tied together and disciplined with the use of a whip and a barking dog by a group of English-speaking soldiers in colonial-era uniforms. One of the victims is a woman with a crying baby on her back, who sinks to her knees at the entrance, leading to more cracking of the whip and brusque complaint from a soldier. The door is closed and one of the soldiers, quietly and methodically, while the framing remains unchanged, lights a fire beneath the drum. After a brief delay, the drum begins slowly to rotate on its axis and to emit a droning and downbeat form of brass-instrumental music. The experience of those inside is left entirely to the imagination of the viewer. While the nightmarish instrument plays, the soldiers standing to the side of the drum stand erectly, their look aimed primarily at the camera (Figure 18).

Eventually, a cut is made to a reverse angle showing a version of what we have been watching reflected in the wide, curtained glass of a building. The curtains are opened and sliding doors pulled back to reveal a group of figures in formal dress, mostly elderly, who emerge, drinks in hand, to gain

FIGURE 18 *Nightmare colonial 'musical instrument' in* A Pigeon Sat on a Branch Reflecting on Existence *(2014)*.

a better view of the spectacle as the music continues to play. What we are expected to make of this is again unexplained. That the view of the diegetic audience is much the same as that of the audience for the film has potential to add to the discomfort of the scene, implying some parallel between the two. The following scene features two salesmen of novelty goods who are a recurrently lugubrious presence in the film, Jonathan (Holger Andersson) and Sam (Nils Westblom). Jonathan says he had just thought of 'something horrible' in which he was involved. This provides scope to read the preceding sequence as located only in his imagination, the same actor appearing as one of the waiters serving wine to the viewing party. Sam asks if it was a dream, to which Jonathan replies that it 'felt like it had happened', which scares him, and that no one had asked for forgiveness. He does not relate the event itself, however, which leaves the connection less than explicit, while his comments imply something more than the work of idle fantasy. Any such interpretive context is absent for the first-time viewer during the drum sequence itself.

More typical of the trilogy, however, is a lower-key and more humdrum evocation of what might be termed, after Thoreau, 'lives of quiet desperation', although these are often situated within a broader but also unspecified context of foreboding and signs of social breakdown.[1] The films contain repeated mantras; blandishments that suggest a certain form of persistence in the face of a generally dismal fate. These include 'I'm happy to hear you're doing well', intoned flatly several times by different characters in *A Pigeon Sat on a Branch*, and the statement 'tomorrow is another day' in *You, the*

Living. Jonathan and Sam are a good example of the blend the films offer of that which is often awkward, uncomfortable or embarrassing to behold, if sometimes also a source of deadpan comedy. They are involved in what appears to be a hopeless enterprise, supplying shops with a dismal selection of cringe-makingly awful and dated novelty items such as plastic vampire teeth and a snaggle-toothed mask. Their sales pitch is weak, slow and painful to view and usually declined. The one store we see that stocks some of their items is failing and unable to pay the couple what they are owed. They live in cramped, bare-walled rooms, sometimes falling out with one another, arguing and niggling, but tied by a bond expressed by Sam when he apologizes at one point for being mean to Jonathan and declares the latter to be his only friend.

A Pigeon Sat on a Branch opens after the credit sequence with what a title describes as 'three meetings with death', each of which manifests the more humdrum variety of awkward or uncomfortable material. First, a portly middle-aged man, whose pasty face and balding head are typical of many inhabitants of the Andersson universe, dies from an apparent heart attack resulting from the exertion involved in so banal an act as trying to open a bottle of wine. His wife, visible through a doorway into a kitchen in the background, continues her activities, as oblivious to the drama as seems to be the incongruously jaunty lilt on the soundtrack, the latter a feature of much of the trilogy. The second involves an unseemly struggle, painful to watch, involving the adult offspring of an elderly women who lies in a hospital bed, close to death, attempting to remove from her grasp a handbag containing her jewellery and cash. The third is another vignette of low-key discomfort. A man is dead, having collapsed in the cafeteria of a ferry. Watching passengers are offered the food and drink for which the deceased has already paid: an awkward situation for the crew as they cannot accept payment for the same items twice. But who wants to take the shrimp sandwich and beer of a dead man? There is no strictly logical reason not to, but it might appear inappropriate. One man offers to take the beer, but otherwise an awkward silence reigns.

When not dying or facing other acute indignities, many of Andersson's characters are suffering in one way or another. Another tired and doleful failing businessman, Kalle (Lars Nordh) in *Songs from the Second Floor*, has set fire to his shop to try to profit from the insurance. He is subsequently talked into participating in another doomed business, selling crucifixes, an enterprise cynically sold to him as the chance of a lifetime, given the currency of the product in the run-up to the turn of the millennium. One of his two sons, Tomas (Peter Roth), is in a psychiatric hospital, having been driven 'nuts' by writing poetry, according to his father, although the son appears in some ways a more stable figure than Kalle himself. That the pain Kalle suffers has wider resonances is suggested in the sequence in which he is first seen: his soot-blackened figure travelling on public transport is surrounded by other passengers who break into song with a mournful operatic chorus, the tone of which is spread further as it continues to play over the start of the following scene in a café-bar.

Kalle is at one point followed by the ghost of another character, Sven (Sture Olsson), who had committed suicide. Kalle confesses to having been relieved when he heard of the death of Sven, to whom he owned money he would not be required to pay back. Another ghostly figure turns up and interacts with Kalle: an unidentified young Russian (Fredrik Sjögren) with a noose around his neck, who says he is trying to find his sister after they were both hanged by Nazi troops in Russia; the build-up to his own hanging, alongside the already dead body of his sister, is depicted in a scene that reconstructs a historical photograph.[2] The films move between moments of the relatively banal and material of this kind that is darker and more disturbing or bizarre. A man who appears to be a building worker in *You, the Living*, for example, recounts a dream in which he is taken to court and sentenced to death after destroying a tableful of 200-year-old china while failing at an attempt to perform the trick of pulling away the cloth and leaving everything in place. A psychiatrist, meanwhile, gives a speech to camera in which he bewails the hopelessness of his task, catering to people who are mean, egocentric and selfish. On occasion, characters admit to such qualities and obtain moments of insight, as in the case of one of the regular inhabitants of Limping Lotta's bar in *A Pigeon Sat on a Branch*, who identifies greed as the source of his own unhappiness. This is also the locus of one of the most warmly inflected sequences in the trilogy, a nostalgic flashback to wartime 1943 and an occasion on which the eponymous proprietor serves shots to members of the military, unable to afford the usual cost, for the price of a kiss. But there is much that suggests a heedless pursuit of futile objectives and lack of connection: a condition crystallized in one characteristic image in *You the Living* of a man running fast on a treadmill, but going nowhere, while ignoring the calls of his young son.

Stylized, static distance and the 'complex image'

Distinct formal qualities play a central role in the establishment of the particular varieties of discomfort found in this work. Andersson's is an idiosyncratic and often expressive variety of blank style. His camera usually remains static and distant from the action, with the characteristic effect of leaving much of the task of interpretation to the viewer. This includes both the cognitive and the emotional dimensions identified earlier in this book. The viewer is left to try to work out the significance of much of the material in the trilogy, including heightened instances of discomfort such as the sacrifice of the girl and the musical-drum sequence. The films offer various strands, more or less developed, but are reticent when it comes to any explicit articulation of what ties them all together. A broad thematic sense of social decline and/or crisis is evoked but never clearly explained. The sacrifice of the girl appears to be a response to some kind of threat. In the following scene, some of those involved in the ceremony are seen afterwards in a bar, where they have been drinking heavily. One dignitary vomits onto the counter. He comments: 'We have sacrificed the bloom of youth. What more can we do?', but no indication is given of exactly why this has been done.

References are made during the film to falling stock prices and a vast traffic jam that has not moved for eight hours. We see a large queue in an airport check-in area, individuals struggling with enormous piles of luggage. A character refers to escaping; but again, from what is not stated in any specifics other than that, for the privileged who can leave, 'a new day is dawning'. At the end of the film, in a desolate open space in the foreground of which the crucifix dealer is dumping unsold stock and cursing his stupidly for banking on such a 'dud product', Kalle is confronted by a slowly approaching group that includes Sven and the sacrificed girl. They are joined by many more previously unseen figures who rise up suddenly and disturbingly from the ground. 'What the hell is this', Kalle asks, voicing a question likely to be asked by viewers of the film. The group continues to move towards Kalle, the girl farthest to the front, but the film ends abruptly on a cut to black rather than offering any explanation. *You, the Living* ends with squadrons of heavy bomber aircraft appearing in the sky while an incongruously jolly tune plays on the soundtrack: another intimation of some kind of unexplained apocalyptic event.

The visual style favoured by Andersson involves long takes and stationary wide-angle framing. The latter creates a great depth of field, often combined with an angular recessive perspective and staging in layers of depth. Close ups are absent, as is any breakdown of sequences into the kind of analytical editing more characteristic of classical style. The closing scene of *Songs from the Second Floor*, for example, has the central group that approaches Kalle moving along a receding diagonal that runs into the distance. The airport check-in sequence, likewise, is an image that uses fake perspective and tromp l'oeil painting to give the impression of receding vastly into the distance (Figure 19). Andersson's vanishing points often create a triangular perspective, as is the case here, but, as Julian Hanich notes, they are sometimes rhomboid in composition.[3] This is a highly stylized aesthetic. The viewer is invited to explore such images in depth, often with varying planes of attention, such as those of the dying man and the woman in the kitchen near the start of *A Pigeon Sat on a Branch*. Andersson also joins his near namesake Wes Anderson at times in the use of horizontal or planimetric staging of centres of attention, although, as Hanich suggests, this also tends to include staging in layers of depth as well as width.

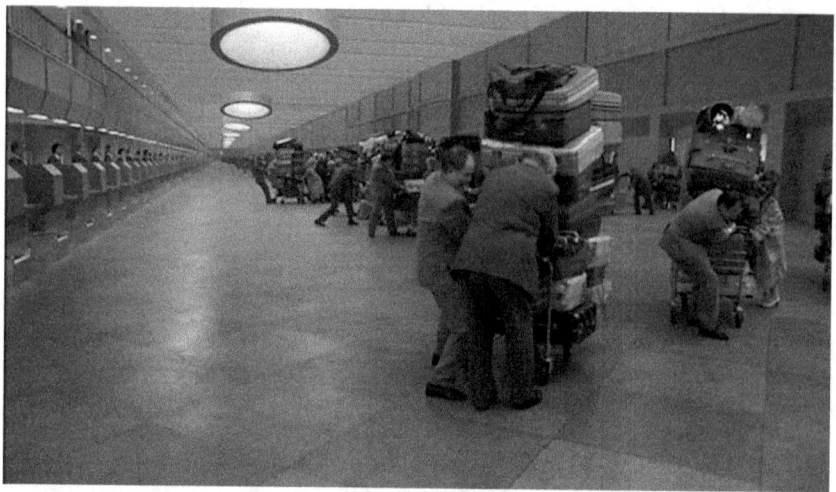

FIGURE 19 *Hyperbolically extended recession in the airport check-in scene in* Songs from the Second Floor *(2000)*.

The denial of certain kinds of broader explanatory information is to a significant extent a matter of narrative structure and content: the absence of any overt articulation of what ties together the various events and characters, along with the specific nature of what some of them might mean. Reticence at the level of emotional engagement is more closely related to the withdrawn visual style, as seen in the staging of the sacrifice of the girl. A more classically conventional handling of such material would be expected to offer perspectives close to those of the girl, her parents and/or those responsible for the event, to provide a more 'up close and personal' articulation of their responses and/or motivations. We are given some sense of the emotional impact on the participants in the scene that follows, but this remains distant and lacking a strong sense of close individualization that would represent a more thorough processing or working through of the material, which might make it at least relatively less discomforting to witness. Instead, we are left in many instances to come to terms with such content ourselves. The style employed by Andersson imposes a certain level of meaning in its own right, as was argued of blank style more generally in Chapter 1. Much of the dolorous gloom and deadpan humour that constitutes the dominant tone is rooted in a certain kind of flatness of presentation, including what sometimes appears to be a resigned and fatalistic acceptance of the disappointments of life. A withdrawn style contributes centrally to the creation of this impression, one that at times – if far from always – entails a flatness of response by the characters.

Andersson has argued explicitly for the merits of what he terms 'the complex image', which requires more active engagement by the viewer to apprehend what might be multiple layers of action or relative inactivity.[4] He cites the work of the French critic Andre Bazin, thus situating his preference within an established position in film studies generally and art cinema in particular: one in which the longer take has often been celebrated for precisely such a reason, in instances ranging from works of Italian neorealism to what more recently became known as 'slow' cinema.[5] As Andersson suggests, images of this kind can be 'demanding and provoking', the example he cites in his own work being from his short film *World of Glory* (*Härlig är jorden*, 1991). This involves a reconstruction of the Nazi practice of gassing Jewish people and others in diesel trucks, a forerunner of the death-camp gas chamber. We see a group of naked victims packed into the back of a vehicle, in a characteristic single-shot sequence. They are watched by individuals in civilian dress whose status, as bystanders or more active participants, is unclear. A young girl protests but is forced to enter, her screams audible as the door closes. A pipe is used to connect the exhaust of the vehicle to an opening in one of the doors. The engine is started and cries are heard from within as the truck moves off and drives around in circles in the near distance, presumably to allow enough time for asphyxiation.

This incident has some resonance with the drum sequence in *A Pigeon Sat on a Branch*. In Andersson's account, the use of the complex image in a case such as this is more powerful than a style that involves cutting to emphatic close ups, such as that employed by Steven Spielberg in his holocaust film, *Schindler's List* (1993). It is, he suggests, 'easier to see *Schindler's List* than to see this scene in my film'.[6] This is an explicit claim to, and celebration of, the qualities of a cinema of discomfort on the grounds that the 'experience lingers, one cannot leave it behind', as was suggested in some of the viewer responses to *Dogtooth* in the previous chapter. The implication is that it lingers in this way specifically because it has been less pre-processed and therefore remains harder to digest than if presented in a more classically conventional manner. Numerous other factors might also account for the different effects offered by these two approaches, but one is likely to be the greater onus put on the viewer by a more distant or complex form of image. This might include raising questions of our own responsibility for some such phenomena; as, for example, in the discomforting parallel between the position of diegetic and non-diegetic audiences in relation to the musical-drum spectacle in *A Pigeon Sat on a Branch*.

Hanich also argues for the discomforting effect of Andersson's style. This includes some instances in which he suggests the distanced aesthetic can perform an expressive function relating to the feelings of characters. One example is an early scene in *Songs from the Second Floor* in which Lasse (Sten Andersson) has just been fired from his job after thirty years of service, the kind of fate typical of that faced by many occupants of the Andersson world. He is on his knees begging his superior, Pelle (Torbjörn Fahlström), to relent. The scene occurs in a long corridor receding to a typically

FIGURE 20 *Embarrassing scene framed with characteristic receding depth in* Songs from the Second Floor *(2000)*.

Anderssonian vanishing point (Figure 20). As Pelle says there is nothing he can do and attempts to escape the highly awkward scene, Lasse clings to his legs and is dragged some distance along the floor. Pelle eventually frees himself and walks off, leaving Lasse prostrate, but he has to traverse the distance to the end of the corridor at the centre of the frame before either he or the viewer is spared a lingering state of uncomfortable embarrassment. The effect is heightened by the fact that the scene is witnessed internally by a number of others we can glimpse peeking through their narrowly opened office doors down the corridor. As Hanich puts it: 'The fact that Andersson uses a long take in deep focus and stages the scene in depth makes the scene all the more excruciating to watch.'[7] It is precisely this style, as he says, that allows the viewer to empathize with the discomfort of both figures. Pelle remains a source of sympathy for the viewer, as Hanich suggests, his objections to large numbers of redundancies having been expressed at the start of the film.

Social engagement

The engagement the filmmaker seeks in the complexity of the image is intended to carry over into any sociocultural issues raised by the material, as in the example of the Nazi atrocity. We are asked to think about the substance of what happened in a case such as this, including our own implication, alongside that of diegetic witnesses to the action, as seems more overtly the case in the staging of the musical-drum sequence. This is also identified as a key source of discomfort in the films of Andersson by Christopher Milden, who links the filmmaker's style to a tradition of European painting including the work of Pieter Bruegel the Elder.[8] For Hanich, what Andersson seeks is to prevent the viewer from being 'as inattentive, passive, apathetic as the bystanders in his films'.[9] What might be viewed as the freedom of the viewer to scan the image, in its depth or in the development of the staging of actions in various parts of the frame, can also be viewed, Hanich suggests, as a social or moral *obligation* to do so: to learn a lesson involving active and attentive observation of the world. If the films offer 'an existential critique of our modern life-world', as seems clearly to be the case in numerous ways, they also seek 'to involve the viewer more actively in the film [...] in order to counter this modern malaise'.[10] Style is therefore directly linked to a key theme within the work.

How such a malaise is conveyed can be viewed, as in the work examined in the previous chapters, at a combination of levels involving material that might be specific to the Swedish context and that which resonates more broadly. Ursula Lindqvist in this way situates the work of Andersson in a manner typical of the position ascribed to valorized sources of art cinema, describing *Songs from the Second Floor* as 'an art work intensely critical of both its immediate sociohistorical context – that of the small nation of Sweden – and of the state of humanity as a whole at the dawn of the second millennium'.[11] This appears to be a key basis of the wider arthouse appeal of films of this kind from smaller-producer nations. Much of the material of the trilogy seems to imply a broadly existential critique, part of what locates it solidly within the internationally focused tradition of art cinema. A general framework of this kind is explicitly announced at the start of *A Pigeon Sat on a Branch*, in a title that refers to the film as the final part of a trilogy 'about being a human being'. Kalle bemoans the fact that 'it is not easy being human'.

Incidents such as the endless traffic jam and those overwhelmed by their huge piles of luggage at the airport lend themselves to being read as images of existential entrapment or Sisyphean burden. Many of Andersson's characters have something like a Beckettian quality, in their whitened-faced and dourly clown-like appearance, and generally in seeking to drag themselves onwards, persisting through the seemingly endless or pointless trials of life. The use of whiteface implies, as Lindqvist suggests, their broadly equal status as archetypes of what it is to be human.[12] A more explicit reference point in *Songs from the Second Floor* is to the work of the Peruvian poet César Vallejo, to whom the film is dedicated in a title at the start. The dedication reproduces a translated line from Vallejo that encapsulates one of the primary sentiments expressed by the trilogy: 'Beloved be the ones who sit down', a valorization of the most ordinary, quotidian and wearied kind of activity. The passage that includes this line is voiced, unidentified, by the brother of the poet Tomas, Stefan (Stefan Larsson). This is a rewriting of the Biblical Sermon on the Mount, as Lindqvist notes, including other lines such as 'beloved be the one who wears a torn shoe in the rain / beloved be the bald man without a hat / the one who catches a finger in the door'.[13] As Lindqvist puts it: 'the poet replaces Christ's radical and divine declaration that the lowliest in society are the most blessed, with a humanist, and equally radical, declaration that we should love those whom society deems the least noteworthy on the basis of our common humanity'.[14] There are plenty of at least bald*ing* men in the trilogy, mostly without hats, along with those caught out in the rain, the latter especially in the apocalyptically storm-hit *You, the Living*, and one in *Songs from the Second Floor* with his hand stuck painfully in the door of a train carriage. Numerous additional artistic reference points are identified by Lindqvist and others, as part of the process of establishing the credentials of Andersson, including the writing of Celine, Strindberg and Goethe, the painting of Bruegel and Otto Dix and the films of Jacques Tati and Charles Chaplin.

Figures such as Kalle, Lasse, Pelle, Jonathan and Sam appear as representatives of the ordinary, the banal and the struggling that also constitutes a version of humanity in general. While most of the foregrounded characters are male, we can add to this list a number of women, including Mia (Elisabeth Helander) and Anna (Jessika Lundberg) in *You the Living*. The former is not the only character in this universe to comment on the difficulty of 'enduring this dammed existence', especially when deprived of the comforts of alcohol. The latter dreams of an idealized marriage to her fantasy hero, the rock star guitar-playing Micke (Eric Bäckman), an exception to the tendency for the sleep of some of those who populate these films to be disturbed by nightmares. Vallejo is echoed in the suggestion that it is at the level of the quotidian that what Lindqvist terms 'the most pressing social and existential questions of our age come into focus'.[15] Andersson has termed his approach 'trivialism', founded on a belief that 'the most important social and existential questions of our age come into focus in the most trivial, banal, and even absurd moments of everyday life'.[16]

Specific material within the films has scope to be read in these very broad moral or philosophical terms and also in some respects more particular to the contemporary period. The sense of a society on the edge of breakdown in *Songs from the Second Floor*, for example, can be read existentially but also includes a more specific indictment of neoliberal capitalism. This is particularly so in the scenes involving the crucifix businessman and his crass exploitation of a religious symbol for attempted economic gain and what he seems to have taught Kalle: that 'life is a market' and all that matters is buying something that can be sold for a higher price. The fallout of faith in such a concept is implied by the redundancies of which Lasse is only one of many victims. The film also draws on a sense of human guilt that can be situated locally or more broadly. The appearance of Sven, haunting Kalle, can be read as an embodiment of his personal culpability, for having gained through the suicide of the former. The figure of the hanged Russian implies a broader history of socio-historical guilt, as Andersson has suggested.[17] As Lindqvist puts it: 'This tragic stranger represents Kalle's, and mankind's, existential guilt for the horrors that humanity has inflicted upon itself.'[18] This is a discomforting phenomenon about which to be reminded, an implication magnified by the figures that rise up from the ground at the end of the film. In writing about *World of Glory*, Andersson draws on the concept of existential guilt in the philosophy of Martin Buber. This is paired with the argument of Georg Lukács to the effect that a period such as that of Hitler in Germany cannot be viewed as closed until society has radically overcome broader attitudes by which it was characterized, which is implied not yet to be the case.[19] A point highlighted by Dagmar Brunow is that the events of *World of Glory*, while alluding to something in the past, are presented in a manner that makes the setting ambiguous. The bystanders wear suits that appear contemporary and 'rather timeless', instead of being clothed in a manner that clearly evokes a period setting.[20] The viewer is thus denied the relative reduction of discomfort that might result from something established as historically distant, and so in which the world of the viewer is less likely to feel implicated.

In the musical-drum sequence from *A Pigeon Sat on a Branch*, the setting, the characteristics of the victims and the uniforms of the soldiers seem more clearly to situate the event as geographically and historically distant. The horror might, more comfortably, be put down to the specific historical practices of what can be viewed as a now (supposedly) alien world of colonialism. This is rather less clearly so, however, if we follow Brunow's lead and examine the clothing worn by the diegetic audience, at least some of which is far more modern than the nineteenth-century colonial era that is otherwise evoked. A particular institutional context is also implied in this case. The drum carries on its side the name Boliden, that of a Swedish mining company which faced a lawsuit after selling smelting residue to Chile in the 1980s, allegedly poisoning hundreds of people.[21] That the incident might be taken as an indictment of humanity more broadly is implied by the title that appears before the preceding sequence, 'homo sapiens', which could apply to this one as well. What follows is a distinctly discomforting scene in which a woman scientist talks on the phone (one of those to utter the 'I'm happy to hear you are doing fine' mantra), seemingly oblivious or inured to the suffering of a monkey on which painful experiments are being conducted.

The potential for a collapsing of historical distance in the experience of the material of *World of Glory* or other examples adds to the scope provided by the encouragement of the viewer more actively than usual to engage with the distant and complexly staged image. If viewers are urged to participate in this way, the ideal outcome is a Brechtian reflexive awareness of their own position, including their share in guilt that is both historical and relates to more contemporary matters. This might further be encouraged by a moment in *World of Glory* in which one of the spectators turns around and looks towards the camera. As Brunow suggests: 'His gaze can be said to address the audience as if to ask about his own as well as others' moral responsibility as bystanders to the killing.'[22] The same can be said of the gaze of the soldiers at the camera in *A Pigeon Sat on a Branch* and the implicit situating of the viewer in the same position as its diegetic audience. How far any such potential is actualized in viewers remains open to question, however, as I have argued more generally in relation to some celebrations of art cinema.[23]

The Nazi-related theme occurs in the trilogy with a mixture of more specific and broader resonances. The attempt of the building worker in *You, the Living* to perform the tablecloth trick is uncomfortable at what might be considered to be an ordinary, surface level, even if the sequence is framed as a dream experienced by the character concerned. It is painfully obvious to the viewer that he cannot possibly succeed, as he circles the table, weighing up the prospects and making what seem to be insignificantly tiny adjustments; so long is the table and so great the weight of piled-up china. When finally he launches into the act, the cloth slides down the length of the table, taking the crockery crashing to the floor with it. What is revealed is all the more discomforting, however: two large swastika symbols inlaid into the tabletop. It is, for Hanich, 'the Swedish bourgeoisie's unacknowledged involvement with the Nazis that Andersson lays bare here',[24] although no comment is made from within the diegesis and it is up to the viewer to make any such connection. If one aspect of Andersson's aesthetic is a general process of concealment and revelation, within the various dimensions of the complex and usually static in-depth image, as Hanich suggests, this is another instance in which the style is used to a more particular sociopolitical effect.

Andersson was one of the organizers of an exhibition, 'Sweden and the Holocaust' (2005–6), which offered a critical examination of what was seen as a form of passive Swedish collaboration with the Nazi regime during the Second World War, as opposed to its officially 'neutral' status.[25] This can be seen as a nationally and historically specific instance of the wider questioning, after Buber, of a failure to take responsibility for the fate of others. Sweden's formal neutrality enabled it to become the only Nordic country to prosper both during and immediately after the war, according to Lindqvist.[26] The exhibition also highlighted other issues, including the introduction of immigration laws that turned away asylum seekers from Germany, 'many of whom were later murdered in concentration camps'.[27] As well as having pointed resonance in continued debate in Sweden about such issues, Andersson's use of Nazi reference points can be related to the broader dimension of alienation within modernity, as addressed by a number of social commentators cited earlier in this book.

The plight of many of his dolorous but persisting characters can be viewed within this broader social context. *Songs from the Second Floor* is interpreted by Lindqvist, for example, as examining 'how human beings in Western society fumble towards meaning in a fragmented and nonsensical world'.[28] One of the more explicit instances is found in the comments of a military officer while stuck in a traffic jam during a taxi ride. He is on his way to visit his former commander-in-chief for a ceremony to mark the latter's 100th birthday and talks about the speech he has written for the event. He introduces imagery about life being a journey on a stretch of road. In order to travel, he adds, 'you need a map and a compass'. These are precisely the sources of orientation seen by some as having been lost in the conditions of either late modernity or the postmodern. 'And our map and compass are our traditions. Our heritage, our history', he proclaims. 'If we don't understand this, we're fumbling around in the dark.' His certainty is comically undercut when he asks the driver where they are and responds with a puzzled look when told they have only moved a few metres.

If this representative of an argument for the importance of heritage and history seems somewhat undermined by his own inability to map his location at this moment, a darker and more discomforting cast is given to his words during a scene that involves the aged general, during the ceremony in a rest home. A senior officer reads the speech, one that refers to the former commander as 'a representative of the safeguarding of our country, our traditions, our distinctive character and our history'. The general replies: 'My best to Goering!', adding 'Hoist the flags' and giving a Nazi salute, as the proceedings continue and a bugle is played. This might be taken to be the ranting of a very old man, but a disconcerting connection might also be made between such allegiances and a figure located as a representative of the kind of tradition and heritage to which appeal is often made in the face of the uncertainties of the modern or postmodern (in addition to any more specific allusion to wartime collaboration). A wider sense of such irrational appeal might also be implied in some of the background action visible behind the two occupants of the taxi on the way to the home. A procession passes of men and women dressed in business suits engaged in acts of flagellation, one seen earlier in the film that suggests a recourse to some kind of regressive superstition (akin to the sacrifice in *A Pigeon Sat on a Branch*) in the face of the falling stock prices and general decline of the country to which reference has been made.

A similar impression is created in a sequence from *Songs from the Second Floor* set around the boardroom table of what is described as the Economic Faculty council of experts, presumably an academic body. As one of the members tries to find an elusive document, a glass sphere is being passed around and examined by others. Why is not clear. The missing report relates to 'the long-term perspectives and strategies the council would like to propose to the government'. If he cannot find the long-term, the man suggests, the short-term ones should be in his file somewhere, but he cannot find those either. A shift from long- to short-term planning might suggest something of the state of anxiety-inducing destabilization diagnosed by Richard Sennett, implied here in the subsequent suggestion by the chair of the meeting that, in the absence of strategies, they focus on tactics instead. Throughout all this and after, the glass sphere continues to circulate. When the suited figures around the table stand up to look out the window after being told that (bizarrely) the house across the street is moving, a typical Andessonian moment of revelation within the frame shows the one person remaining seating, previously only partially visible, to be a woman in what now seems clearly to be the dress of a fortune teller, the sphere being her crystal ball. This is another intervention of the mystical/irrational in what appears to be an attempt to counter the instabilities of contemporary existence, either generally or that specific to neoliberal capitalism. Widespread concern about the value of shares also resonates with some of the critique offered by Sennett of what he diagnoses as a damaging obsession with short-term share prices, particularly when expressed by a company boss in *You, the Living*.[29] The executive says the business has a problem, like many others in this country and abroad: while it is doing well and profits are decent, the value of the shares is felt to be too low (he then promptly keels over and dies). The general sense of crisis or apocalypse evoked in the background to the trilogy might also, if loosely, suggest something like the 'risk society' identified by Ulrich Beck.

Another example of the collapsing of historical frames, one that has potential resonance with contemporary perceptions of crisis, occurs in the sequences in *A Pigeon Sat on a Branch* that refer to the Battle of Poltava, between Swedish and Russian forces, in 1709. Jonathan and Sam take refuge in a café-bar, to ask directions to the business of another customer who has failed to pay his bills. As they begin to go into the now-familiar routine involved in demonstrating their products, a horse carrying a military figure in period costume passes one of the windows, eventually followed, incongruously, by a full-scale procession of cavalry and infantry and the entrance into the premises of King Charles XII, seeking a drink and taking a fancy to a young male member of the staff. A strange mixture occurs of contemporary and period characters. The difference between the social norms of the two eras is marked by the forcible ejection of women from the establishment but closer continuity is implied when, later, some of the troops pass back in the other direction in a battered and wounded state after being defeated, a key historical moment that marked the end of the status of Sweden as a major power.[30] Women in the bar are now told they have been widowed and react with emotions that blur the temporal distinction between their era and the earlier time of national crisis and defeat.

In addition to its broader existential currents, *Songs from the Second Floor* appears clearly to be intended by Andersson as a critique of the specific toll taken by neoliberalism, both within and beyond Sweden. This includes, as in the trilogy more generally, a sense that the victims have often become distanced and alienated from one another, losing the sense of unity that might in the past have offered at least some compensations for social disadvantage (as in the case, perhaps, of the wartime solidarity indicated by the Limping Lotta number in *A Pigeon Sat on a Branch*). A loss of such collective spirit is a key component of the sociological diagnoses of modernity cited in Chapter 1. Andersson has referred to similar arguments in the work of the French sociologist Loïc Wacquant.[31] As Lindqvist suggests, critique can also be found in Andersson of key institutions such as the church and the health-care system, the latter a much-celebrated dimension of the established Swedish model of welfare capitalism, part of a consensual, corporatist system of the kind threatened, and elsewhere displaced, by the spread of neoliberalist regimes. This is a good example of a particular, national-specific, manifestation of the issues raised by the latter.

A priest to whom Kalle expresses his despair in *Songs from the Second Floor* offers no solace, only grumbles about his own financial situation, a response echoed by his deputy. Numerous scenes of the film are set in hospitals, but these appear to be either stretched (beds in the corridor) or lacking any indications of active care for the patients, with the exception of the expensive nursing home occupied by the elderly (and, we are told, very wealthy) general.[32] This might be taken as a reflection on neoliberal challenges to welfare capitalism, including the phasing out of some forms of psychiatric care reported by Lindqvist, or as a more general manifestation of the state of social malaise conveyed by the films. Some such material might be more accessible to Swedish than to the wider, international arthouse audience. Another locally specific detail identified by Lindqvist is the fact that the woman who pushes the girl over the cliff in *Songs from the Second Floor* is characterized in a manner recognizable as the figure of Sweden's Queen Silvia,[33] a detail that gives pointed resonance to what might otherwise seem a more abstract configuration. In the dimension of its critique specific to the national context, Andersson's work fits into a longer tradition within Swedish cinema of identifying a sense of something having 'gone wrong' either with the welfare state or more widely.[34] The existence of such forms of critique in this national context seems particularly notable, given the reputation of Sweden, along with other Nordic countries, as a state that has avoided the worst excesses of global neoliberalism.

Relational aesthetics and interpersonal responsibilities in the films of Ruben Östlund

Ruben Östlund is one of a number of Swedish filmmakers influenced by aspects of the Andersson style, including his use of a distant and detached camera and the creation of some scenarios in which uncomfortable parallels are created between viewers and those who witness questionable acts but often fail to intervene. *Involuntary* is widely seen as being indebted to Andersson, as a multistrand narrative that employs long takes and a static camera, although it unfolds in a world more recognizable than the stylized universe of his compatriot. The component scenarios include two teenage girls on a night of drunken behaviour; passengers on a coach, the driver of which refuses to continue their journey until one of them admits to having damaged a curtain rail in the toilet; a drunken male-bonding reunion, one member of which is forcibly fellated by another; tensions among teachers at a school, after one calls out a colleague for what she considers to be abuse of a pupil; and a dinner party and fireworks display during which the host is injured. *Play* follows the fortunes of three youngsters, two white and one of oriental appearance, who are more-or-less but not entirely forced into accompanying a group of black youths who eventually rob them, a situation that generates uncertainty about the nature of the likely outcome, accompanied by potential awkwardness for the viewer relating to the racial dimension. *Force Majeure*, the film that brought Östlund to wider international attention, revolves around the failure of a father figure to admit that he ran for safety, abandoning his family, in the face of an apparent threat from an avalanche. *The Square*, which further developed his status as a notable figure in the world of international art cinema, features the creator of a museum who becomes caught in a series of moral dilemmas against the background of works that explicitly highlight issues of interpersonal responsibility.

A sequence typical of one source of discomfort in the films of Östlund occurs on a tram in *Involuntary*, a setting revisited in *Play*. The two principal members of a group of drinking teenage girls are a noisy and uncomfortable presence for fellow passengers. They relentlessly pester one young man in a manner that is not unfriendly but clearly an invasion of his personal space. The viewer might feel a vicarious version of the annoyance experienced by this character or other passengers in the background. The preferred reaction of those involved in such incidents is generally to try to ignore what is happening, rather than to take the risk of embarrassment that might result from any attempt to intervene or resist, a feeling with which viewers are likely to be able to identify. Something similar occurs earlier in the film in the coach segment, when a group of youths behaves disruptively in the back seats (they prove not to be guilty of the damage to the toilet, however, as might have been expected, which is later revealed to have been done accidentally by an otherwise more centrally sympathetic passenger). Unlike diegetic witnesses, film viewers cannot really ignore, or pretend to ignore, such fictional behaviour, given that it is part of the material of the work they have presumably committed to watch. They are obliged to experience the more or less sustained vicarious discomfort likely often to result, if they are not to cease viewing. If a parallel of some kind can be found between the positions of diegetic and non-diegetic onlookers, as was seen above in some pointed instances in the films of Andersson, something similar applies in the more threatening-seeming scenario of *Play*, during which numerous witnesses to the situation (although not all) do little or nothing to intervene.

One scene in *Play*, on a tram, creates a dynamic similar to that of the equivalent sequence in *Involuntary*. Two of the black youths pester and mock another passenger, who is eventually obliged to follow instructions to sing loudly in order to end his ordeal; embarrassment seemingly is a price worth paying in this instance. No actual threat appears to be involved, which is less clearly the case with the young boys, but the experience is uncomfortable for the passenger and, presumably, for others who witness it without saying anything (one woman gets up and moves away early in the sequence). The persisting viewer is, of course, powerless to do anything and offered only the prospect of discomforting spectatorship.

The main narrative premise of *Play* has much potential for the generation of discomfort. At one level, it offers a source of conventional tension and suspense. The film clearly locates the three victims, one of which gives his age as twelve, as innocent, at least as far as this scenario is concerned, and the black youths, some of whom appear to be older, as being involved in some kind of bullying trick that seems likely to be a prelude to robbery or worse. Their encounter with the trio follows an earlier attempt we see with two other white boys, in a shopping mall; the fact that we see the routine repeated makes clear what was already largely apparent in the first instance: that what is involved is a carefully orchestrated scam. As in the previous incident, one of the group gains access to the phone of one of the boys, Sebastian (Sebastian Blyckert), and says it looks like one stolen from his younger brother. The routine involves a claim that they just want to have the phone seen by the victim of the supposed loss. The resonances of what this entails are more complex than a simple act of theft, in which one of the youths could easily have made off with the phone much earlier in the proceedings. The rightful owner is made to feel at least partly guilty by this ruse, particularly in the first incident, while those acting in a dubious manner at times claim the mantle of righteousness. They also seem to gain considerable pleasure from the power dynamics involved in the whole performance, a reversal of those they can be assumed usually to face on racial grounds, rather only to be seeking material gain.

The tricksters insist that Sebastian and his friends Alex (Sebastian Hegmar) and John (John Ortiz) go with them to see the supposed owner of the phone, a short distance away. The routine is extended when they are subsequently told they have to go further, which includes the tram ride. A question raised by these events is to what extent Sebastian, Alex and John are forced to do so, or pressured in a more insidious manner. The film implies some degree of complicity on the part of the boys, or at least the impression that they could have resisted more strongly much of the time, particularly when in the presence of passers-by (they ask for help from the staff in a café in which they take refuge at one point; the latter are not unsympathetic, but the senior of the two is reluctant to call the police). How this is experienced might be mixed up with a sense of guilt, diegetic or extradiegetic, relating to the racial dynamic.

From white liberal discomfort to moral complexity

The typical viewer of such a film, as a work that circulates primarily in the art-cinema arena, particularly in the international market, is most likely to be white, middle class and broadly liberal in values, and thus liable to be discomforted by what might appear to be an invidious conservative stereotype, in the image of a group of older and generally larger black youths picking on more vulnerable and mostly white counterparts. Played straight, this is the sort of scenario likely to be generated from a racist position, and so uncomfortable to liberal eyes, playing on deeply sedimented racist associations of the kind detailed by Robin Diangelo (not to mention its specific potential discomfort for any black viewer).[35] It might be argued that the younger boys could also feel some such difficulty: the racism that might be implied by any total distrust expressed on their part towards their assailants. The victims appear to be from middle-class backgrounds. We see the mother of one when the trio visits the office in which she works. A middle-class fastidiousness is implied in a moment when any marks that might have been created by the youngsters on glass office doors are wiped away after their departure; a small touch but one that creates a distinct sense of social location. Their assailants are more likely to be associated with a 'ghetto'-type landscape, a skate park and dilapidated blocks of flats, that forms one of the way stations on the journey (Figure 21). This creates further potential for discomfort on the part of the most likely constituency for the film. On the one hand, the film sets up a 'threat' narrative, although one that is uncertain in its degree of seriousness. On the other, it might encourage the viewer to feel uncomfortable with the racial and class allegiances such a scenario implies. The effect of the situation might be to play on and draw out in white liberal viewers the kinds of involuntarily-learned racist resonances (products of general socialization within structurally racist societies) that, as Diangelo suggests, they would prefer to disavow and to separate themselves from.

Figures such as the five boys and the drunken girls in *Involuntary* are disruptive presences. They cause awkwardness, discomfort and embarrassment, both for other characters within the diegeses and,

FIGURE 21 *Figures in an urban landscape in* Play *(2011)*.

potentially, for the viewer. The response to such figures for those of liberal sympathies is likely to mix scope for dislike and discomfort at one level, at certain aspects of their disruptive and unsettling behaviour, with a further dimension of guilty discomfort for the viewer who might prefer *not* to be led into such feelings towards those who are marked as from less advantaged social backgrounds, whether these involve race, a combination of race and class, or the seemingly lower-class character given to the behaviour and dress of the girls in *Involuntary*.

A degree of complexity and ambiguity is also developed in the ongoing relationships between some of the protagonists in *Play*. That one of the black youths in particular is merely playing the role of the 'nicer' and 'more reasonable' of the five-member gang seems initially to be clear (it is confirmed later, by an off-screen reference to having performed the role of 'good cop'). This is a key part of the ruse that helps achieve the compliance of the victims in the early stages, including his apparent arguments with others who take on a threatening guise. But there are also moments that suggest the possibility of a somewhat less exploitative or more innocent relationship between the groups. These include a brief discussion involving how the five know each other through being in the same football team; the encouragement given by all to Alex when he gets close to achieving the 100 press-ups he is told will be required for himself and John to leave, at one point when the groups have separated; and applause given to John when he is pushed into playing his clarinet. A binary division is also complicated by the fact that it is Alex, rather than one of the black youths, who pursues Sebastian when the latter attempts to run away after they move into a more rural landscape. It is also Alex who removes Sebastian's wallet and phone from the pockets of the latter, when the group proceeds into a routine in which their valuables are laid out on the ground, to be claimed by whoever wins a running race; another ruse on the part of the youths, the representative of which cheats by taking a short cut. The five youths end up effectively robbing the younger trio in this way, but this is, again, situated awkwardly, somewhere between more conventionally direct forcible theft and the outcome of anything that could be considered to be consensual.

A sense of moral complexity continues into later scenes in which one of the youths, now accompanied by a younger brother, is recognized by what appear to be two previous victims. Their fathers confront the youth quite vigorously, engaging in a scuffle and taking away a phone. What we are meant to make of this is uncertain. The adults have a reasonable case, in that they are seeking to tackle what appears to be serial criminality and that they also make the point that some kind of intervention might be good for the future of the perpetrators. Their response is questioned by a woman passer-by, however. She is warned not to get involved, and at one point pushed back, but goes on to make a case against the behaviour of the pair. One of the fathers himself seems to doubt the wisdom of their intervention, commenting that they went too far. The woman returns, saying she cannot let the incident go and will be reporting it to the police. She berates the two men for acting like vigilantes, criticizing them for harassing two young immigrants who lack the opportunities available to their own children. The liberal-minded viewer is likely to be somewhat torn here, or responses might vary. Both sides seem to have something of a case, but the way the two fathers act seems capable of uncomfortable resonance with the behaviour of the five youths. They might have right on their side, in that one activity has a criminal intent and the other does not, but much of what the woman says is likely to ring true. These exchanges make more explicit the difficulty of resolving the many ambiguous questions raised by the film.

Unlike Andersson, Östlund does not provide the certainty of a clear critique of non-intervention on the parts of passers-by, a few of whom do seek to do their best. This is the case with the café women cited earlier and the woman who challenges the two fathers, and another who joins her. One passenger on the tram does nothing during the various incidents, but afterwards approaches Sebastian and offers to testify as a witness if required. Viewers are invited, effectively, to consider what their own response might be to situations such as these, another source of potential discomfort (how many would be confident they would act in the right way, where this is clear?). *Involuntary* offers an indication of the price that might sometimes be paid. The teacher who calls out a colleague after seeing him forcibly detain and hit a misbehaving pupil seems likely to face ostracism from colleagues. In one of the final scenes she is in the staffroom, seated between two other teachers engaged in a conversation to which she does not contribute. At one point she asks one of the others to please look in her direction at some points rather than rudely to shut her out. Both reply to suggest no such intention was involved, and it is not easy to determine exactly what dynamic is at work: is she deliberately being left out, as part of the fallout of the earlier incident, or is she unduly sensitive in this case? The fact that we see only her, and the occasional hand of one of the others intruding into the frame but nothing of their bodies or faces, makes it all the more difficult to tell, one of many instances of restrictive framing of this kind in the film.

A more general and disturbing sense that individuals can be pressured into acting other than rationally is created in an earlier scene in the school strand of *Involuntary*, in which the same teacher is introduced. She has set up an experiment in which a pupil is asked to say which of two lines in an image is the longer. The girl correctly identifies a slight difference in the first example, but an arrangement has been made according to which the rest of the class has been prompted to disagree with her finding. The same happens again with two lines of more exaggeratedly different length. When she is shown the first one again, she hesitates and then changes her choice: a demonstration of the power of peer pressure, a phenomenon that can be applied in various ways to other aspects of these films, including the seemingly contradictory response of Olle (Olle Liljas) to the enforced sucking of his penis by his friend Leffe (Leif Edlund) in *Involuntary*. At first, it seems, he is highly upset, his wife arriving to drive him home after what she relates to have been a tearful late-night call; but he decides to stay and continues to participate in further drink-fuelled revelries.

Blankness and distance

Formal qualities such as the use of off-screen space in the school staffroom scene perform an important role in heightening sources of difficulty and discomfort in *Play*, in its rigorous maintenance of distance from the action. We find here another variety of blank style, if less theatrically heightened than that of Andersson, refusing to use the full cinematic means of leading the viewer towards a particular interpretation or emotional engagement with the events. As with other such examples, this involves both cognitive and affective dimensions. The detail of what happens is often obscured by the statically distant camera. In the tram sequence in *Play* considered above, for example, our viewpoint is from further up the aisle of the car, the action proceeding in a single long take. Nothing is done here, or elsewhere, to focus in on any close detail – of action or emotional engagement – that might indicate a more particular reading of events. When a group of older males enter the scene and a struggle ensues, it is far from easy to tell exactly what is happening. This, and a problem sometimes in determining which character is speaking, is heightened by Östlund's tendency to position some key action or comment off-screen, as in the position of the two teachers in the scene in *Involuntary* discussed above.

The general flatness of presentation in *Play* and elsewhere in Östlund's films denies the viewer any sense of close emotional access to the experience of characters. This is a dimension through which a more classically conventional presentation, involving an analytically edited breakdown of sequences, would be likely to provide clearer guidance to viewers, as suggested earlier in this book: both factual, on some occasions, but also and more importantly in terms of orientation at the level of alignment with character and the moral compass involved in questions of allegiance (issues addressed at greater length in Chapter 2). When Sebastian climbs high into a tree, for example, and refuses to come down, a classical articulation would be likely to provide close-up shots of his emotional state and/or shots from his perspective of the lengthy drop to the ground. Instead, the camera remains at its usual distance, Sebastian's figure relatively small, distanced and in no way favoured cinematically. If the character feels alone and vulnerable, the cinematographic presentation leaves him that way, as is generally the case in the film, rather than offering anything more up-close and warmly personal. This can itself be a source of discomfort for the viewer who might like to be positioned in a location of more unambiguous alignment and allegiance with either his perspective or any that does not remain awkwardly questionable at some level.

A similar style is employed in the key sequence in *Force Majeure* that opens a discomforting rift in the relationship between the central couple, Tomas (Johannes Kuhnke) and Ebba (Lisa Loven Kongsli) during a skiing holiday in the French Alps. The pair and their young son and daughter are being served lunch on a terrace with spectacular mountain views. An avalanche appears in the distance, apparently one of many triggered in a controlled manner in the resort, but it looms ever closer and seems about to engulf the terrace. As panic grows, Tomas is seen clearly to run away, towards the camera, manhandling another male as he goes (Figure 22). The screen is whitened out, but no damage proves to have been done, the terrace having been engulfed only by the 'smoke' generated ahead of the avalanche. As others, including the rest of his family, retake their seats, so does Tomas, saying nothing to explain his departure, a blankness reflected in the static distance maintained by the camera throughout. A cut is made to a sequence in which they return to their hotel in ski gear on a moving walkway: a shot from behind Tomas and Ebba, framed approximately mid shot to head-and-shoulders, and a similar shot of the children, Harry (Vincent Wettergren) and Vera (Clara Wettergren). Tomas looks back, with an uncertain expression, at Ebba; the children also look behind them in similar fashion, presumably at Tomas, but nothing is said. An uncomfortable silence reigns, broken only by the groaning noise made by the walkway mechanism, the sound of which

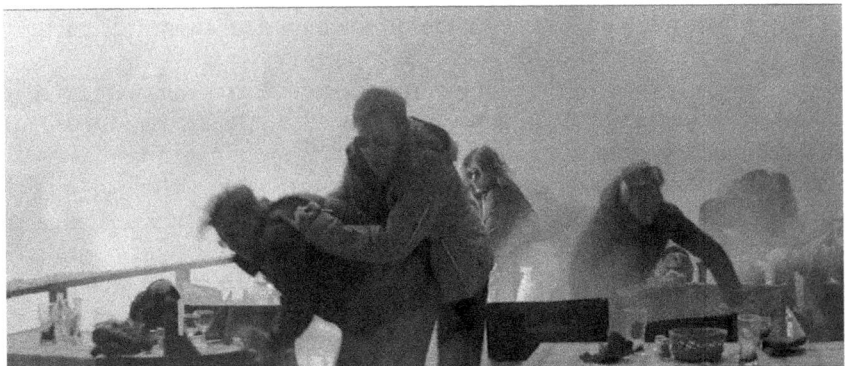

FIGURE 22 *Flight rather than fight: Tomas flees the apparently oncoming avalanche in* Force Majeure *(2014).*

seems to express the general state of awkwardness and unstated feelings. The absence of dialogue continues into the next shot, as they enter the hotel building, broken only by a sigh from Tomas when left alone.

The family is then seen walking down a corridor towards its room, Ebba striding ahead and Tomas lagging behind the children. Potential for comedy ensues, when Ebba insists that the children remain inside the room while the parents talk – the viewer understanding their sustained cries of objection at the presence of someone in the room, having seen a cleaner enter before the appearance of the family in the corridor. No clearly comic modality is established, however, leaving the tone awkwardly unclear. Tomas says his wife seems irritated. She says she is not and asks if she should be, but any opportunity to talk about the incident on the terrace is evaded, the issue left awkwardly looming but unarticulated.

Other major sequences of discomfort in *Force Majeure* ensue when Ebba brings up the question of the behaviour of Tomas, the level of awkwardness increased by the presence of witnesses. When she first confronts Tomas with his behaviour – running away and abandoning her and the children; and, exacerbating the situation, taking a moment first to pick up his phone and gloves – his response is one of flat denial. Repeatedly, he claims this to be a matter of differing perceptions, although the previously attentive viewer should be clear that Ebba's account is accurate. Östlund adopts a style that involves flatly framed two shots of two couples dining together: Tomas and Ebba and a woman met earlier by the latter, Charlotte (Karin Myrenberg), and her newly acquired partner for the night. At times, Tomas tries to laugh off the accusation. Laughter is also the first response of their companions, although this becomes attenuated or increasingly of the embarrassed variety as the discussion continues and Ebba expresses her incredulity at the response of Tomas. The entire sequence is characterized by a quiet, low-key form of discomfort, accompanied by sporadic moments of awkward laughter, particularly from the two witnesses.

In a subsequent scene the protagonists appear to agree on a version that acknowledges at least that Tomas was frightened, but the issue is opened up again, at a higher pitch, after another dinner, this time in their apartment and with another couple, one member of which, Mats (Kristofer Hivju), is an old friend of Tomas. On this occasion, Ebba is more outwardly upset, eventually crying, while Tomas looks distinctly, if blank-facedly, uncomfortable. Awkward silences pepper the sequence, this time organized through separate medium shots of each of the participants or listeners. The shooting style is some degree more mainstream-conventional, in moving closer in this way to capturing individual emotional expression, although that of Tomas remains primarily blank. Mats acts as mediator, suggesting that no one can tell how they might act in what appears to be a survival moment, when Tomas might not have been able to live up to his values. Ebba accepts this point but says he needs to admit what he did afterwards. Tomas maintains his line, that it is a matter of perceptions, until eventually forced to agree when shown evidence captured at the time of the incident on his phone.

In a later scene that takes place on the landing outside their room, Tomas at first seems to feign tears that become genuine and increasingly hysterical as he confesses to Ebba to hating himself for having done similar things before: lying, being unfaithful and even cheating when playing games with the children. His increasingly loud wails make Ebba the one feeling embarrassed, particularly at the potentially public nature of the display. As far as the main plot line is concerned, later events in the film seem to balance the equation to some degree between Tomas and Ebba. He takes charge when she loses her skis in a fog-bound run on their last day and it is Ebba who reacts in something close to blind panic when the incompetence of their coach driver on a precipitous mountainside road leads her to rush to the front and demand to be let out, leaving the children behind. The film ends with the family, along with the other passengers, grouped together walking down the road towards the camera, a sort of unity perhaps but uncertainly implied.

Personal relationships and social responsibility

The discomfort offered by *Force Majeure* is considerably less extreme in content than much of that found in the films examined so far in this book, including some of the examples explored earlier in this chapter. It is situated at the local level of relatively ordinary problems within personal relationships rather than anything more drastic or larger scale, although a thematic consistency can be found with other work considered above in terms of questions relating to personal responsibility. One implication, voiced explicitly on several occasions by Mats, is that individuals cannot always be held responsible for their actions; that, in certain conditions, the 'fight or flight' survival instinct takes over, with no time allowed for reflective action. As Ebba argues, however, there remains the issue of acknowledging this afterwards, which Tomas never fully seems to do even when given time for reflection. His 'breakdown' might be seen as a rather theatrical act of self-immolation, so broad in compass as to bypass the specifics of the case. If an initial discomfort might be offered by the failure of Tomas to respond to the avalanche threat in a more other-directed manner, a sustained variety is created by his continued denial of the facts, for which less justification seems present.

As Mats suggests, part of the problem with how we face up to such situations is the unrealistic model provided by conventional myths of heroism, an implicit critique of more comfortable fictional scenarios. The viewer is likely to want Tomas at least to admit what happened, to offer an appropriate response to what otherwise remains unresolved embarrassing behaviour, an issue addressed more generally in Chapter 1. Any such desire is frustrated by the film, even during his emotional outburst, the extremity of which is embarrassing to witness in itself and continues to deny any more reasonable articulation of his situation, as someone who acted instinctively in a manner that might not involve individual culpability. At the same time, his denial also has the ring of truth. Like some of the other incidents examined above, it has potential to pose to viewers the awkward question of how they might be likely to respond in a similar situation, both to the avalanche and to being confronted with the uncomfortable facts afterwards.

The issue of self-loathing or disappointment in one's own behaviour offers a point of contact with some moments in the films of Andersson. The latter include material that has more consistently overt social-political implications than is generally the case with Östlund, whether to do with a general sense of alienation or more specific critique of neoliberal capitalism. Social issues are also implicit in much of Östlund, however, including the uncomfortable play with racial or class distinctions in *Play* and *Involuntary*. *Force Majeure* raises issues relating to constructions of masculinity, for example. When Mats and his partner Fanny (Fanni Metelius) discuss the Thomas and Ebba situation, Fanny seeks to make clear that what is involved in abandonment of children in such situations is not a simple male/female opposition (even though she says she could not imagining abandoning children of her own). The issue, she argues, relates to different generational styles of masculinity. That the otherwise generally ameliorative Mats has characteristics in common with the more selfish Tomas seems all the more likely given how much a questioning by Fanny of what he would do in similar circumstances upsets his own equilibrium during a subsequent sleepless night.

Östlund has commented that all his films are about the broader social context of people trying to avoid losing face in difficult situations, a dimension clearly central to the behaviour of Tomas in *Force Majeure*.[36] There is a sense of fictionalized social experiment in works that set up dilemmas of this kind, akin perhaps, in the realm of representation, to the 'everyday social experiment' Giddens identifies in the intimate realm of relationships as a result of the undermining of tradition. The issue of saving face would include, for example, the coach passenger in *Involuntary* who refuses to admit to having broken the curtain rail, even when this was minor damage caused in an understandable manner when she grabbed for something to hold onto when the vehicle lurched. Once a failure to admit has been committed, the stakes are raised, in cases such as this, the more time passes. Something similar might be said of the plight of the three boys in *Play*: once they have gone along with the scam at the start, it becomes increasingly difficult to make a decisive refusal or attempted escape (it might also suit them not to test the boundaries of an ambiguous situation that might become more clearly threatening if they do). The social resonances of this material are likely to be strengthened for any viewer aware of the extent to which the filmmaker bases some of his scenarios on real-world evidence. *Play*, for example, was inspired by very similar crimes to those depicted, Östlund's research including interviews with some of those involved.[37]

Force Majeure also seems to establish a broader context of mechanization that might be read as an implicit social statement or a reflection on certain prevailing styles of relationship. The film is filled with moments in which the emphasis falls on the relentless rumblings of machinery, whether in the background or brought to the fore in scenes of otherwise silent awkwardness. This includes the walkway mentioned above and the sound of vacuuming that forms the backcloth to one of the exchanges between the central couple outside their room. Both seem to express aurally the discomfort of the scene, the underlying tensions that cannot at this point be voiced by the characters, a more outward manifestation of such qualities than is found in most of the work examined in this book so far. *Force Majeure* is interspersed with sequences that cut away from the character action to show large-scale mountain scenery, usually accompanied by the sound of controlled-avalanche explosions and the passage of a fleet of ploughs through the snowfields at night, the latter more than once intercut with the sound of electric toothbrushes as Tomas and/or Ebba perform their daily cleaning rituals.

During a quiet moment, when Ebba sheds tears while having a day of skiing on her own, away from the family, the soundtrack is filled by the persisting background clatter of chairlift mechanisms, variations on which are picked out on numerous other occasions. At one key moment of tension in the scenes involving Tomas, Ebba, Mats and Fanny a cut is made abruptly and disorientingly to a momentary point-of-view shot from the perspective of a drone that was seen being flown by Tomas earlier in the film, as the object is suddenly activated and nearly hits Mats. The mechanical background texture might be read as a comment about the mechanization of contemporary life, or lifestyles, or imply some kind of opposition between such devices and the natural world of the mountain and the apparatus through which attempts are made to tame and groom its surfaces (with the suggestion that this might be paralleled by the tension between social values and instinctive human response). Many of the intercut sequences of mountain scenery and other material are accompanied by bursts of a jarringly sudden and strident version of Vivaldi's 'Summer' from *The Four Seasons*, the effect of which is to increase the impression of cold detachment from the action.

A sense of broader implications at the level of monogamous domesticity is offered at another point, during a discussion between Ebba and Charlotte. Ebba challenges the merits of the lifestyle chosen by Charlotte, in which she and her partner have open relationships and she is enjoying a break from her children. Charlotte says she refuses to live in a way that involves gaining her self-esteem from her role within a single relationship or through being a mother. Does she realize what a provocation that entails, asks Ebba, suggesting what is at stake in the issues opened up by her husband's earlier flight from the family. A single moment of pressure, it seems, can open a rift in the whole basis on which many of our lives are predicated, an interpretation that adds to the discomfort offered by the film at a thematic level. This is another issue in which Östlund says some of his material was based on real-world sociological and psychological research. A broader social context is provided by his location of the events of *Force Majeure* within a consideration of historical shifts to an emphasis on the nuclear family, rather than larger family groups, or to individuals living on their own, material that again situates the fictional frame within larger social contexts of the kind outlined in Chapter 1. We need, Östlund suggests, 'to question the strong, fundamental beliefs that we have in the nuclear family, and where we are heading', issues with potentially uncomfortable resonances for many viewers.[38]

Issues of personal responsibility and questions relating to a loss of social solidarity, akin to those considered above in the films of Andersson, are more explicitly raised in *The Square* by some of the exhibits planned for the art museum curated by the central character, Christian (Claes Bang). 'The Square' of the title is a four-by-four-metre space declared to be 'a sanctuary for trust and caring' and within which are shared 'equal rights and obligations' to help one another. The creator is said to have been influenced by the real-world 'relational aesthetics' of the French art critic and curator Nicolas Bourriaud, which, the viewer is told, explores how people relate to one another within a social context. Östlund himself was involved in the creation of such a square at a design museum in 2015.[39] In perhaps a more general sense than that articulated by Bourriaud in the context of 1990s art,[40] 'relational aesthetics' captures a sense of what drives this and other work by Östlund. Having foregrounded this approach within the diegesis, *The Square* also develops its own manifestations. We see numerous individuals asking for help, many of them ignored.

Christian does what appears to be 'the right thing' early in the film, when he joins another man in coming to the aid of a woman who is shouting for help and that a man is trying to kill her. Most passers-by do nothing, but Christian helps the other to block the passage of the man who appears. They turn out to be victims of a scam, Christian afterwards finding his wallet and phone to have been stolen. When he, in turn, asks for help, trying to borrow a phone from by-passers, his appeal is rebuffed.

Christian subsequently embarks on a scheme to seek the return of his property. He is able to trace the location of the phone to an apartment block and collaborates with a junior colleague to draft a letter put through all of the doors of the building, in order to reach the perpetrator, threatening consequences if it is not returned via a local store. To his surprise, this works, in that the phone and wallet are returned, the latter still containing money. In his appreciation of this, he makes what appears to be a generous donation to a nearby beggar.

The enterprise proves to have unforeseen consequences, however, when Christian is pursued by a young boy who demands an apology to himself and his family, his parents having assumed him to be guilty of the theft after receiving their copy of the letter. This results in a number of awkward confrontations, the last of which ends with the boy falling down a flight of stairs outside Christian's apartment. Repeated cries of 'help' are heard immediately afterwards by Christian, although exactly what happens is less than clear. When he goes out onto his landing and calls out, he gets no reply, but the cries continue. The boy appears to have gone by the time Christian goes downstairs to search through trash to find the contact number the youngster had given him. Getting no reply, he sends a video message for the boy to show to his family, making what starts out as a full apology for his selfishness, carelessness and the prejudice he admits made him afraid to go knocking doors in the building in search of his belongings. As this develops, however, he says more about the problem being one of society rather than the individual. The latter may be true, and complicates the theme of personal responsibility, although it might also be read as a Tomas-like refusal to take due responsibility for his personal share. Christian seeks to follow up in person, but is told by a neighbour that the family has moved, leaving the issue uncomfortably unresolved, particularly as we are given no indication of how hurt the boy might have been.

The Square contains a number of scenes reminiscent of some in *Force Majeure*, in which Christian, in particular, faces potential embarrassment or loss of face by being confronted in public spaces. Notable examples involve the boy in his apartment stairway, an incident witnessed by Christian's children, and a challenge posed by an American journalist with whom he sleeps, Anne (Elizabeth Moss). Anne refuses to let Christian off the hook in a sustained interrogation focused on issues such as how often he sleeps with women he has just met and whether this is a power play on his part (this follows an awkward post-coital sequence in which Christian persists in trying to prevent Anne from taking his used condom for disposal, implying a lack of trust that he denies). Christian's discomfort is exacerbated by the presence in the background of the scene, set in one of the art gallery spaces, of a guard who seems to be straining to overhear. This sequence echoes some of those in *Force Majeure* in having the exchanges played out to the sounds of an exhibit in front of which they are standing: a pile of chairs that makes creaking noises, as if it is about to fall, and periodically emits a louder crashing-to-the-ground sound. The effect, as previously, is to offer what appears to be a symbolic/expressive rendition of the discomfort faced by Christian. The sequence also resembles Östlund's previous film in being shot largely in relatively close and conventional, head-and-shoulders single shots of each of the performers, albeit with the pile of chairs and an out-of-focus-view of the guard, near the edge of the frame, in those of Anne.

The Square provides fewer incidents of acute discomfort than some of the films discussed above, mostly offering low-key material such as struggles against the embarrassment that might result from problems being aired in public. There is one major set piece of discomfort, however (a second, although less heightened, involves the effect of a man who swears and makes noises, suffering from Tourette Syndrome, during a public talk given by an artist). A formal banquet at the museum is disrupted by a performance from an artist who does a convincing impression of an ape, a figure glimpsed previously on a screen in one of the gallery rooms. This is another overt treatment of the issue of interpersonal responsibility. In the introduction to the performance, to a background of 'jungle' noises, diners are warned that they will be confronted by a wild animal that will sense if they show fear. If they try to escape, it will hunt them down. But if they remain still, they might not be noticed and 'can hide in the herd, safe in the knowledge that someone else will be the prey'. The performer, Oleg (Terry Notary), appears, a physically imposing figure. Laughter is the principal initial response to his performative mannerisms as, for example, he quizzically inspects one woman diner. The line between normal performance and something more challenging begins to be pushed, however, as Oleg persistently confronts a male diner, who is eventually chased from the room. When Oleg jumps dramatically onto one of the tables, its occupants, along by now with most others in the room, sit with their heads down, fulfilling the introductory advice to hide within the herd (Figure 23). The sequence culminates with the line of acceptable performative behaviour seemingly crossed, Oleg's attentions to a women resulting in her hair being pulled. She asks repeatedly for help,

FIGURE 23 *Hiding in the herd with downcast eyes as ape-impersonation performance crosses the line in* The Square *(2017).*

including a direct address to a companion, but nothing is forthcoming. Oleg eventually pulls her violently to the floor and sits astride her, menacingly, shortly after which one man does intervene, then another, and then a whole crowd who pummel the performer, one shouting 'kill him'.

The sequence seems to offer a microcosmic version of much that is implicit in the work of Östlund and Andersson, a vision of a society that favours an individualistic 'law of the jungle', with supportive intervention only coming very belatedly and itself in this case in equally animalistic fashion. The broader social context is spelled out more explicitly by Christian as he shows his two young daughters elements of the exhibition in which 'The Square' is situated. This includes one room where another square is drawn, into which visitors are asked, trustingly, to deposit their wallets and phones. Christian relates a story told by his grandfather who, as a six-year-old, was sent out into the middle of Copenhagen to play alone, wearing a tag containing his name and address. At that time, Christian says, people generally trusted other adults to come to a child's aid, if needed, while today others would be more likely to be regarded as a threat. This is a clear articulation of the diagnosis offered by some of the social commentators cited above and earlier in this book, of a situation in which older forms of solidarity have been lost in the face of competitive individualism and/or neoliberalism.

The Square is likely to be a less discomforting film overall because it articulates such themes so explicitly, rather than leaving the viewer struggling to interpret the material, although the ape-performance sequence is left without any explanation for how far it went or what results from the assault at the end. It is relatively easy to apply interpretive frameworks to the film as a whole, a process that offers the viewer a greater prospect of mastery of the materials than is the case in some examples of the cinema of discomfort. Further such context is offered by some of the discussions surrounding the planned exhibition of 'The Square', including the comments of two youthful members of an advertising agency brought in to help with its promotion. They ask whether the exhibit has any sources of controversy or connections to current events likely to help get it noticed by the news media and/or to go viral on social media. Otherwise, they say, it is hard to gain any international attention, a point that might also apply to some forms of art cinema, particularly the more heightened sources of discomfort. A similar reflexivity can be found in Christian's point that what matters is the response activated in the audience, a key issue for both filmmakers examined in this chapter. The advertising duo eventually comes up with a provocative video, designed to spread online. It features a young blonde girl of homeless appearance who wanders into 'The Square' carrying a kitten and explodes: a parodic miniature version of the cinema of discomfort, perhaps (the film itself features a number of shots of homeless people or others begging on the streets, implying part of the wider background against which it is set). The controversy that ensues results in Christian's resignation, although he cannot seem to win in the public realm, the video facing widespread condemnation and the likely loss of a major sponsor while his departure leads to accusations of failing to protect freedom of speech.

Industrial bases

If *The Square* can be seen as a work in some ways similar to those featured within the film, in raising issues of individual responsibility for helping others, it also fits solidly within the established institution of art cinema. It status as a production of higher international note within this sphere was marked by the award of the Palme D'Or at the Cannes film festival. Other films by Östlund and the Andersson trilogy have also gained recognition within the international art-cinema sphere, although the latter's production base is as distinctly individual as the style of his work. Andersson's film career dates back to *A Swedish Love Story* (*En kärlekshistoria*, 1970), made with the support of the Swedish Film Institute (Svenska filminsituter, SFI), a body created to support national production in 1963. His second feature, *Giliap* (1975), was much less well received, leading to a gap of some twenty-five years during which he made commercials, in his distinctive style, and a handful of shorts including *World of Glory*. When he returned to features with *Songs from the Second Floor*, it was produced with an unusual degree of independence from the usual national or art-cinema institutions, Andersson having created his own production facility, Studio 24, to make his commercials. He had the unusual luxury of a permanently employed core crew and ownership of his own camera equipment, lighting and props, items usually rented on a film-by-film basis.[41] This gave him a rare degree of control, although difficulties were still faced in raising funds, especially for the first instalment of the trilogy.

The nature of *Songs from the Second Floor* was such that it did not lend itself to a conventional script, which led to the rejection of proposals to the SFI. As Lindqvist reports, a further batch of commercials produced in 1995 gave Andersson sufficient funds to self-finance a portion of the film, the first fifteen minutes, which could be shown to funding agencies. This more concrete demonstration of the work was screened for the SFI, which provided a grant of just under $1 million. Advance distribution funds from Sweden, Germany, Norway and Denmark made up the rest of the budget, a total of approximately $5.5.[42] The film won the Jury Prize at Cannes in 2000, the second highest laurel in the festival, a major boost to its status in the international market. *You the Living* screened in the festival's Un Certain Regard section in 2007 and was nominated for, but did not win, the Palme. *A Pigeon Sat on a Branch* was not accepted for the 2014 festival, which Lindqvist says had become Andersson's target venue for premiering his work. Östlund's *Force Majeure* screened that year in Un Certain Regard, winning the Jury Prize and, Lindqvist suggests 'setting up a friendly competition' between the pair.[43] Andersson received further consecration as an internationally significant art-filmmaker when given a celebratory season at the Museum of Modern Art in New York in 2009.[44]

Andersson's filmmaking methods remained distinctive, benefiting from the freedom he gained at Studio 24. Production of *Songs from the Second Floor* took four years, as closely documented by Lindqvist. This was partly because of breaks enforced by lack of funding, but the seven-year intervals between the subsequent instalments of the trilogy also resulted from the time he took to get the films exactly how he wanted, including the regular shooting of large numbers of takes and an almost exclusive reliance on non-professional performers. The majority of the footage was shot on purpose-built sets, sometimes elaborate and extensive, the design of which was the starting point for *Songs from the Second Floor* and is a key dimension of the distinctive Anderssonian universe. Studio 24 is one of a number of independent production companies established in Sweden since the turn of the century where, as Anders Marklund puts it, 'the commitment to personal vision is much greater than the films' budgets or the size of the audience'.[45] These include Plattform Produktion, co-founded by Östlund and co-producer of all four of his films examined above, and so another relatively stable basis of operations, if less distinctive in character than that of Andersson. That the production of work of this kind remains dependent on a wider range of sources of finance, as typical of the art-film sector more generally, is shown by even a glance at the lists of production companies credited for the work of the two filmmakers. These display a characteristic mix of national subsidies such as those provided by the SFI with other sources ranging from the Swedish public service broadcaster SVT to regional funding from EU bodies, co-production subsidies from other Nordic countries and investment from French and German film and/or TV sources.[46]

Notes

1 Henry David Thoreau, *Walden; or, Life in the Woods* (Garden City, KS: Anchor Books, [1854]1973), 11.
2 Ursula Lindqvist, *Roy Andersson's* Songs from the Second Floor: *Contemplating the Art of Existence* (Seattle: University of Washington Press, 2016), 136–7.
3 Julian Hanich, 'Complex Staging: The Hidden Dimensions of Roy Andersson's Aesthetics', *Movie: A Journal of Film Criticism*, vol. 5 (2014): 40.
4 Roy Andersson, 'The Complex Image', extract in Mariah Larsson and Anders Marklund (eds), *Swedish Film: An Introduction and Reader* (Lund: Nordic Academic Press, 2010).
5 For more on this background, see King, *Positioning Art Cinema*, chapters 3 and 4.
6 Andersson, 'The Complex Image', 177.
7 Hanich, 'Complex Staging', 47.
8 Christopher Mildren, 'Spectator Strategies, Satire and European Identity in the Cinema of Roy Andersson via the Paintings of Pieter Bruegel the Elder', *Studies in European Cinema*, vol. 10, nos. 2–3 (2013): 148, 152, 153. A similar connection between the tableau style and Dutch painters including Bruegel is made in relation to the films of Andersson and Joanna Hogg, subject of the next chapter, along with the Romanian filmmaker Corneliu Porumboiu, by Ágnes Pethő, 'Between Absorption, Abstraction and Exhibition: Inflections of the Cinematic Tableau in the Films of Corneliu Porumboiu, Roy Andersson and Joanna Hogg', *Film and Media Studies*, vol. 11, no. 1 (2015): 39–76, accessed at http://www.acta.sapientia.ro/acta-film/C11/film11-03.pdf.
9 Hanich, 'Complex Staging', 48.
10 Ibid.
11 Lindqvist, '*Roy Andersson's* Songs from the Second Floor', 18.
12 Ibid., 26.
13 Ursula Lindqvist, 'Roy Andersson's Cinematic Poetry and the Spectre of César Vallejo', *Scandinavian-Canadian Studies*, vol. 19 (2010): 201.
14 Lindqvist, 'Roy Andersson's Cinematic Poetry', 201.
15 Ibid., 207.
16 Lindqvist, '*Roy Andersson's* Songs from the Second Floor', 23. Andersson expands on this view in his director's commentary on the DVD release of *Songs from the Second Floor.*

17 Quoted in *Obsessions from the Second Floor (A Portrait of Roy Andersson)*, one of the extras provided on the Artificial Eye DVD release of *Songs from the Second Floor*.
18 Lindqvist, 'Roy Andersson's Cinematic Poetry', 219.
19 Andersson, 'The Complex Image', 276–7.
20 Dagmar Brunow, 'The Language of the Complex Image: Roy Andersson's Political Aesthetics', *Journal of Scandinavian Cinema*, vol. 1, no. 1 (2010): 85.
21 Joanna Dagliden, 'Interview: Roy Andersson: I'm Trying to Show What It's Like to Be Human', *The Guardian*, 28 August 2014, accessed at https://www.theguardian.com/film/2014/aug/28/roy-andersson-pigeon-sat-branch-reflecting-existence.
22 Brunow, 'The Language of the Complex Image', 84.
23 King, *Positioning Art Cinema*.
24 Hanich, 'Complex Staging', 48.
25 See Lindqvist, *Roy Andersson's* Songs from the Second Floor, 120; Brunow, 'The Language of the Complex Image', 85; for more detail, see David Stavrou, 'The Holocaust: Sweden's Complex Legacy', *The Local*, 26 January 2007, accessed online at https://www.thelocal.se/20070126/6214
26 Lindqvist, *Roy Andersson's* Songs from the Second Floor, 140
27 Stavrou, 'The Holocaust: Sweden's Complex Legacy'.
28 Lindqvist, 'Roy Andersson's Cinematic Poetry', 205.
29 Sennett, *The Culture of the New Capitalism*, 39–40.
30 Historical background from Jacob Field, 'Battle of Poltrova', *Encyclopaedia Brittanica*, accessed online at https://www.britannica.com/event/Battle-of-Poltava.
31 See Lindqvist, '*Roy Andersson's* Songs from the Second Floor', 123–4, and Loïc Wacquant, 'The Rise of Advanced Marginality: Notes on Its Nature and Implications', *Acta Sociologica*, vol. 39, no. 2 (April 1996): 121–39.
32 Lindqvist, *Roy Andersson's* Songs from the Second Floor, 149.
33 Ibid., 100.
34 See, for example, Anders Marklund, 'Introduction' to 'The New Generation of the 1960s' in Mariah Latsson and Anders Marklund (eds), *Swedish Film: An Introduction and Reader* (Lund: Nordic Academic Press, 2010), 241.
35 Diangelo, *White Fragility*.
36 Xan Brooks, 'Ruben Östlund: "All My Films Are about People Trying to Avoid Losing Face"', *The Guardian*, 11 March 2018, accessed online at https://www.theguardian.com/film/2018/mar/11/ruben-ostlund-the-square-interview-force-majeure.
37 Östlund, 'Director's Statement about Play', accessed online at http://comebackcompany.com/project/in-case-of-no-emergency/reader/?article=15.

38 Violet Lucca, 'Interview: Ruben Östlund', *Film Comment*, 21 October 2014, accessed online at https://www.filmcomment.com/blog/interview-ruben-oestlund/.

39 Jorg Heiser, 'Ruben Östlund: The Square Becomes What We Make Of It', *Frieze*, 2 March 2018, accessed online at https://frieze.com/article/ruben-ostlund-square-becomes-what-we-make-out-it.

40 Nicolas Bourriaud, *Relational Aesthetics*, English translation (Dijon: les presses du réel, 2002).

41 Lindqvist, *Roy Andersson's* Songs from the Second Floor, 50–1.

42 Ibid., 64.

43 Ibid., 151. Lindqvist is also the source of the preceding festival details.

44 Anders Marklund, 'Introduction' to 'Swedish Films and Filmmakers Abroad' section in Larsson and Marklund, *Swedish Film: An Introduction and Reader*, 307.

45 Anders Marklund, 'Introduction' to 'Production and Producers' section in Larsson and Marklund, *Swedish Film: An Introduction and Reader*, 323.

46 Full lists can be found in the 'Company Credits' sections of the entries for each of the films of Andersson and Östlund in the Internet Movie DataBase, IMDb.

6

A very English discomfort: Joanna Hogg

The films of Joanna Hogg continue a move seen in the previous chapter towards forms of discomfort in what are represented as increasingly ordinary social circumstances, as compared with some of the more heightened contexts found in earlier chapters. The examples examined here, principally Hogg's second feature, *Archipelago* (2010), offer quietly awkward and painful moments of interpersonal interaction, although situated within a very specific sociocultural domain at the levels of national and class formations. The sources of understated discomfort involved can be understood as having a distinctly English cultural location, a particular manifestation of which can be related to an upper- or upper-middle class social context. This also demonstrates some qualities in common with the examples considered above, however, including a tendency to heighten discomfort through the use of static and/or distanced shots, although not in the exaggerated or stylized manner found in Andersson. The aesthetic is one that increases discomfort through creating an impression of naturalistic verisimilitude at the level of performance, even if the social setting is one of privileged background and the style also quietly expressive.

Awkward dining

Archipelago includes a number of sequences that fit into the 'awkward dining' category from the repertoire of blank style identified by Jeffrey Sconce. One in particular offers resonances that seem distinctly English, their basis lying in what has been identified as a typical national source of discomfort. The scene occurs in a restaurant, to which the three principal characters have gone for lunch during a holiday in the Scilly Isles: the mother, Patricia (Kate

Fahy), and her two youngish adult children, Edward (Tom Hiddleston) and Cynthia (Lydia Leonard).

They are joined by an artist, Christopher (Christopher Baker), who is giving lessons during the holiday, principally to Patricia, and Rose (Amy Lloyd), employed to cook for the family group. Quiet but acute awkwardness and embarrassment ensue when Cynthia, who has been established as a less than entirely sympathetic figure, complains about her food. Anyone familiar with English cultural mores is likely to identify this as touching on a taboo area, the English being notorious for not complaining about such things; or, more precisely for not complaining to the source of whatever is at issue, rather than just grumbling to others in their party (I plead guilty to this tendency). The sequence is worth setting out in detail to capture the particular nuances of discomfort offered both within and beyond the diegesis.

Cynthia complains that her starter (guinea fowl) is not cooked properly, muttering also about having had to wait for twenty-five minutes. She asks her mother about hers, to which Patricia responds 'I ... I think mine's fine', slightly shaking her head. 'You don't have to say it's fine if it's not', responds Cynthia; 'I mean, we've paid so we can easily send it back.' 'It's fine', insists Patricia, while Cynthia emphasizes that hers is definitely not. 'Well ... shall we get ... somebody over', offers Rose, while Cynthia adds: 'it's actually quite dangerous to eat it like that, isn't it.' She goes on to add, more assertively: 'There's just no point in not complaining when you're in a restaurant the one day out.' Throughout this and what follows the others remain mostly in silence. Cynthia complains to the waitress, reiterating the point about it being 'actually quite dangerous'. Patricia, when asked, repeats that hers is fine, to which Cynthia replies 'you don't have to say it's fine, I'm sending mine back, so ...', at which point she is cut off by Patricia's: 'I've eaten some, it's fine.' Cynthia hands over her plate, clearly increasingly annoyed and asking for a word with the chef, again repeating her 'actually quite dangerous' formulation.

After the waitress leaves, Cynthia addresses the table with: 'You don't have to sit quietly and you don't have to look at me as if I'm making a massive scene, like "how embarrassing". It's not cooked properly, it's dangerous ... It'd be nice if I didn't sit here with everyone just in silence around me ... anyway.' Rose comments that she thinks Cynthia has done the right thing, if she's not happy: 'you know ... you have *the right*, as the customer, so...' Cynthia: 'Unfortunately, mum and Edward are just sort of allergic to any sort of complaining.' 'Well, you don't want to be ill', offers Christopher, quietly, in a conciliatory tone. Edward adds, slightly shaking his head: 'I'm sure you've ... I'm sure you've done the right thing.' The chef then arrives and informs Cynthia that guinea fowl is meant to be served slightly pink, at which she complains that it was also cold and again seeks confirmation from Patricia, who repeats that hers is 'fine'. After the chef departs, Patricia adds, quietly but cuttingly: 'It's actually rather good', which is followed by one of many characteristic silences. Cynthia says, condescendingly, to her brother: 'You can eat your soup, Edward; you don't have to sit there being moody', at which he gets up and walks out, adding to the general sense of discomfort all around.

The sequence offers a combination of sources of discomfort. At one level, its effect is likely to be based on audience recognition of a characteristic reluctance on the part of many English people to complain in such situations. It is at first not quite clear whether Patricia has any problem with her guinea fowl. When she repeats that it is 'fine' for the second time, the addition of 'I've eaten some' creates the impression perhaps that she is being excessively reticent, as if having started to eat a dish represents a commitment to its satisfactory nature (a not-untypical English attitude to such matters). Cynthia seems accurately to pinpoint the sense of discomfort experienced by the members of her family because of her insistence on what she sees as a legitimate right to complain and risk 'making a fuss'. Another level of awkwardness is added to the sequence by the position of Rose and Christopher, as paid employees who are presumably being treated to the meal. This seems to explain their more conciliatory approach, especially given the leading role Cynthia appears to have taken in arranging the event: it would not seem fitting for them to engage in the conflictual element of understated dysfunctional relationship that has already been indicated in the film, particularly between Cynthia and Edward.

Cynthia might be positioned as offering a more sensible and rational approach to matters such as complaining about food in restaurants than is often seen as the typical national norm. She makes Patricia and Edward feel uncomfortable within the fictional world, but the viewer might see this as an admirable demonstration of reasonable assertiveness. Cynthia seems generally to be characterized relatively more negatively in the film, however, and in this sequence. What could be taken to be reasonable assertiveness is situated as part of a needlingly snide presence with which the viewer does not generally seem encouraged to feel strong allegiance. There is a sense of her complaint being at least partly about egocentric self-assertion, in this context, for its own sake (it is also, seemingly inevitably, Cynthia who is the one who complains loudly after biting into a piece of lead shot when eating pheasant during a subsequent dining scene in the holiday house being rented by the group). For an English audience, at least, her response is also likely to create vicarious embarrassment for the viewer on the same basis it does for the rest of the table.

Sympathy vs. distance

Cynthia is often positioned as making what might seem to be reasonable points in themselves, but in a manner that seems grating and sometimes passively aggressive. Edward is generally the principal source of focalization in the film, likely to attract a greater degree of allegiance, although *Archipelago* also offers space for audience distance from and criticism of his position. Grounds might also be found for some sympathy with Cynthia, an understanding that she has personal troubles of her own, although unexplained, even if her attitude is one that remains likely to be irksome to many viewers. She is seen crying alone in her bed the evening after the restaurant scene, for example, and responds in what seems an excessively aggressive manner to the pain from the shot in her pheasant, getting up and leaving the table angrily in a way that suggests more is at stake than the immediate discomfort. Later, after dark, she returns to the house and shouts at her mother. Patricia's comment 'you don't have to be *so* angry' is met with an only semi-comprehensible screamed tirade that includes the suggestion that it is Patricia who should be angry (the latter probably a reference to the continued absence of the father from the holiday).

The entirety of this exchange, in an upstairs bedroom, occurs off-screen, the camera remaining downstairs with Edward, subsequently shifting to a shot of Rose, another presumably embarrassed witness to the aural spectacle. Plenty of evidence is provided to suggest that Cynthia is herself unhappy, even if no full explanation is provided (an explanatory scene was shot, Hogg reveals in her DVD commentary on the film, in which Cynthia was shown to have been upset after a recent split with a boyfriend she had hoped to be long term, but the filmmaker chose to omit it to provide more space for audience interpretation). In one of the sets of terms supplied by Plantinga to account for the stances offered by films towards fictional characters, we might not be encouraged particularly or necessarily to have a 'liking' for Cynthia while grounds are implied for sympathy on the basis of care and concern for someone who is suffering, whether or not liked.[1] Ambiguity of this kind, factual but also affecting the likely structure of allegiance that results, is a more general marker of the arthouse status of the production.

One indicator of the relative positioning of Edward and Cynthia that contributes to these dynamics involves their relationship with Rose. Edward seeks to establish a more fully 'human' level of contact, rather than treating Rose merely as a paid functionary, something against which Cynthia reacts negatively. In the first discussion we see of Rose, Cynthia makes the rather needling point that 'it must be quite a nice job, really: coming away, family, free holiday, nice bit of cooking, it's not' – before being interrupted by Rose's entrance into the living room where the three family members are sat. Her comments seem to imply a lack of recognition that Rose's is really a 'proper' job. As the latter is about to exit the room, Edward makes a point of asking whether she has had to come a long way, and seeking more than minimally obligatory details, during which Cynthia sits in silence, her body language exuding more than a faint sense of disapproval. After one dinner, the family trio sits at the table and Edward says it would be nice if they asked Rose to join them. Both Cynthia and Patricia demur, the former suggesting that Rose would probably prefer to eat on her own. She adds, in her typically snide manner towards her brother, 'you have your own friends; you don't have to make friends with the cook.' 'Darling, it's a job', says Patricia, Cynthia adding 'Oh my God', after Edward comments on the fact that Rose is doing the washing up on her own. Edward insists they could ask her to join them and that it would not be a 'huge thing'.

Cynthia and Patricia agree that he can invite Rose, concurring that she is 'very sweet', the former nodding, smiling and mock-laughing in what seems a patronizing manner. Edward says it does not matter, but calls out to Rose and then goes to join her in the neighbouring kitchen offering to help. Cynthia quips that she thinks he has a 'crush', adding: 'He's so ridiculous, burning martyr, sort of ... uh ... poor cook ... stuff', as Edward talks with Rose in the background. Patricia comments that 'he's just got too much ... empathy.' Cynthia responds that he is 'so annoying, though; it's always in such a sort of accusatory way.' Well', says Patricia, seeming not in full agreement, as Cynthia does an impression of one of Edward's earlier remarks. 'That's just Edward', says Patricia, as he re-enters the room, to clear the dishes, adding – maybe now more diplomatically, in his presence, when he asks what she means – 'caring about people's feelings'. After a moment of silence following his return to the kitchen, Cynthia gives out a sigh and what seems coded as a 'despairing' half laugh and adds: 'It's actually getting quite embarrassing now. I feel sorry for her.' Patricia concurs and they agree that Rose just wants to do her job.

For Cynthia and Patricia, it seems, Rose is simply hired help and should be treated as such. This does not imply behaving badly towards her, just an acceptance of the contract and roles involved. Edward appears uncomfortable with such an arrangement, implicitly seeking to question such role-based formalities and to offer Rose at least some degree of fuller participation in their activities on what would imply relatively more equal terms. This appears to be a noble aspiration in itself, although he might also be seeking more agreeable company than he finds with his family members, but it generates discomfort all around. The suggestion from Cynthia, with which Patricia agrees, that it is likely to be awkward for Rose herself seems entirely plausible as far as the post-dinner situation is concerned. Cynthia's attitude, as expressed in her comments and mannerisms, seems unduly hostile, however, perhaps indicating a defensiveness on her part; possibly, we might speculate, based on a level of guilt at the nature of what is effectively a quietly 'civilized' version of a master–servant arrangement. The relationship of this material to the specifically English dimension will be considered below.

This is another instance in which Cynthia might be considered to be right, at one level, including identifying a source of discomfort for other characters, while also portrayed rather negatively, perhaps cringingly for some viewers (myself included), in terms of her own attitude. Much the same happens in an earlier sequence in which she challenges Edward's decision to take time out from his employment; 'not a gap year', as he puts it, a period we later learn involves volunteering in Africa to teach safe sex with an AIDS charity. 'It sounds great', she says, clearly implying the opposite. 'Of course it's wonderful, what you're doing; it's really great', adding one of the little smiles that undercuts what she is saying. She goes on to suggest that 'actually' (a term that, in her use, tends to have a needling effect) he could have done this a few years ago, rather than being out of step with his generation: 'And then you could just get on with getting a job and, um ... working like the rest of us.' She then claims to be 'happy for you, you know, that you can be so cavalier with your future ... it's a luxury.' She suggests again that it is a 'wonderful choice' but he could have 'a bit more awareness that it's a luxury rather than a natural thing to do', speaking over protestations from her mother. In a later discussion during a walk, Cynthia continues to needle Edward, commenting on how he had been 'given the opportunity' in his previous job and was 'pretty set up': 'Pity you couldn't stick at it for just for a bit longer ... must be a bit embarrassing for Dad.'

Cynthia again seems to make some reasonable points, the viewer might be encouraged to conclude, especially when, later in the film, Edward expresses serious doubts about his own choice. Asked by Christopher what might be his alternative, Edwards says he might 'write' instead, which adds to an impression that he might be something of a naïve and privileged dilettante. It *is* a luxury for a figure such as Edward to take a year out to do voluntary work overseas, having been what would appear to be the beneficiary of nepotism in presumably a well-paying and secure job. That does not necessarily negate any benefit that might result, but it remains a position of class-based privilege. We might conclude again that Cynthia's problem with all this reflects, at some level, unhappiness with her own life circumstances, although these are not elaborated. If Edward represents an attempt to break out of his prescribed role, this might be discomforting for a sister who remains trapped within the confines of hers. Such interpretations rely on speculation, however, the film being characteristic of much of the cinema of discomfort, or certain kinds of art cinema more broadly, in its reticence about such matters. Edward's desire to transcend the employer–employee relationship with Rose can also be viewed as a luxury, a privilege granted only to those at the more powerful end of the scale. His desire to do so, at a personal level, might seem admirable in some ways, but also self-indulgent. The film offers potential for ambiguity in how any of this is interpreted and judged, but Cynthia seems overall to be presented more negatively and Edward more positively.

Detachment and understatement

Archipelago is filled with additional moments of awkward silence or stilted conversation that contribute to a consistent potential for discomfort both on and beyond the screen. Hogg joins some of the filmmakers considered in previous chapters in favouring static compositions, often combined with long shots, to heighten an impression of alienated detachment and to withhold any greater level of emotional or evaluative cueing. There is a general absence of formal encouragement of the 'emotional contagion' identified by Plantinga, in cases where close shots of faces are dwelt upon as a way to promote empathy with particular characters, or the intimate potential for subjective access identified by Smith.[2] As a form of realism, the style employed by Hogg is distantly or middle-distantly observational, as opposed to a verité style in which a handheld camera offers close and often unsteady proximity to character (the latter as found, for example, in the films of the Dardennes or some instances of English or British realism cited below).

The sequence in the restaurant examined above begins with a lengthy preamble of awkwardness in which some time is taken for the group to choose a table in the empty venue. Cynthia takes a lead role in orchestrating manoeuvres typically characterized by reticence on the part of everyone to express a clear preference. They eventually settle on one table and all sit down, albeit with some dithering about who should sit where, only to move to another; 'now ... the *next* choice', mutters Cynthia, as if to separate herself from the process. There are, it seems, too many options and too little willingness for anyone to commit themselves, an issue to which I return later in the context of distinctive English cultural characteristics. The whole process unfolds in a single long shot from one side of the room. For the first part of the complaint sequence, Hogg moves to a relatively closer but still long shot, from a perspective set back from the unoccupied head of the table. Cynthia and Christopher are on one side, Rose and Edward on the other and Patricia at the far end. Each is presented in a semi-silhouette effect created by the light coming through windows that open onto a scenic coastal view behind (Figure 24). Formally as well as in content, this is a manifestation of Sconce's 'awkward dining' trope.

Cynthia's initial complaints are expressed in this perspective, as are the responses of the others, within which her reactions and body language are signalled clearly enough, although not heightened by any moves closer to the character. The viewer is in a position akin to that of an uncomfortable witness sitting at a nearby table. A cut to a two shot of Cynthia and Christopher, viewed from approximately the waist upwards, is made shortly before the approach of the waitress to receive the complaint. This is taken as if approximately from the head of the table, rather than being a flat,

FIGURE 24 *Distance in initial shot of Cynthia's lunchtime complaint about her food in* Archipelago *(2010).*

head-on shot that would indicate a more strongly blank style. A single head-and-shoulders shot of Patricia is used at one point, just before Cynthia asks again if she wants to send her starter back, in which the mother looks less than comfortable and not in sympathy with her daughter. The use of a single shot might imply giving relatively greater weight to her perspective, but this is only a passing moment and not part of a more sustained formal privileging of any member of the group. The field of emotion constructed by the sequence, to use Murray Smith's term, remains relatively blank and withholding, as is characteristic of the film as a whole.[3] A return to the two shot is answered by a matching one, across the table, framing the blank expressions of Edward and Rose, as Cynthia asks to speak to the chef. A return to the initial long shot is made shortly afterwards, up to the arrival of the chef and his explanation. The two shot of Edward and Rose then indicates their continued silence, heads down, followed by further cuts between this and the two shot of Cynthia and Christopher. Edward then departs from one of the shots of himself and Rose, ending the sequence with the latter appearing discomforted. The development of the sequence emphasizes the 'sitting quietly' that Cynthia rails against, although it does so in a manner that itself remains relatively withdrawn. The viewer is, in characteristic cinema-of-discomfort style, denied any closer breakdown that might give a stronger indication of any of the particular emotional reactions involved or with whom the viewer should feel alignment or allegiance.

Static and long shots work to similar effect in many of the other sequences of discomfort offered by the film. The discussion about whether or not Rose

FIGURE 25 *Edward, in background, seeks more contact with Rose, to the annoyance of Cynthia, in* Archipelago *(2010).*

should be invited to join the group after dinner unfolds in an unbroken long shot at a slight angle to the table, with Rose visible through an open doorway, working in the kitchen behind, a space into which Edward moves when he offers to help (Figure 25). The fact that Edward leaves the foreground might appear somewhat to favour the perspective of Cynthia and Patricia, but this is the result of his change of place rather than any more active movement towards the other two that might indicate the offer of a stronger form of allegiance. The lunch scene that ends with Cynthia biting the lead shot is mostly presented in a long shot from square-on to one end of the table. Edward talks about the African context in which he is to work. He also expresses resentment to Cynthia about what appears to be her responsibility for his girlfriend not being allowed to join them for the holiday, just before which a cut is made to a two shot of Edward and his mother, on one side of the table, matched by an equivalent shot of Cynthia and Christopher, on the other side, broadly similar to the style employed in the restaurant. As in the previous case, little can be found here that implies the formal underlining of any particular offering of allegiance to one party more than another (even if the dialogue seems largely to favour the position of Edward). A return is then made to the longer shot from the end of the table. This persists until a return to two shots at the point where Cynthia expresses her pain and is resumed after her departure. The lunch-table sequence is preceded by another modified example of the blank-style tableau, in which the family members and Christopher are sitting in the living room, drinking. A two shot focused on a conversation between Patricia and Christopher (talking somewhat hesitantly, about children) is followed (although not immediately) by a longer shot of the foursome speaking rather desultorily (including a jokey impression by Edward of his father's voice) but finishing in a lengthy awkward silence emphasized by the sound of birdsong from outside.

Withdrawn distance also characterizes three sequences in which we see Patricia speaking to her husband on a phone situated close to a window, her figure silhouetted against the light and viewed through a doorway the other side of which the camera is located. From initially expressing how much she looks forward to his arrival, Patricia's response become increasingly annoyed by his continued absence, although characteristically understated. She describes things as 'not great', 'just a bit difficult' in the second conversation, shortly after the restaurant scene. In the third, she declares three times that she 'can't bear' the situation and puts the phone down. In a fourth that is not seen but forms the aural background to a shot in which Edward and Cynthia sit in discomfort at the dining table waiting for her, Patricia shouts angrily at her husband, eventually declaring her hatred for him. Hogg generally uses a combination of framing of this kind, which is more restrictive, and tableau shots to emphasize the awkward, often alienated relationships that prevail in her work. Like that of Andersson, her use of the tableau has been compared to the interiors of seventeenth-century Dutch art, and a tradition ranging across media from painting to photography, film and installation works.[4] As Ágnes Pethő suggests, the framing in images of Edward, such as his movement into a doorway better to hear the row between his mother and Cynthia, highlights his liminal status within the family, a similar position to that of the main protagonist of Hogg's debut feature *Unrelated* (2007), to which I return below.[5] The figure of the listening figure standing on the threshold is read by Pethő as an adaptation of the *Eavesdropper* series of paintings by Nicolaes Maes (c.1655) while the interiors of *Archipelago* are compared more generally with the nineteenth-century work of the Danish artist Vilhelm Hammershøi, the latter a source also acknowledged by Hogg.[6]

Comparisons of this kind with paintings are familiar markers of art-film status, as is the implicit reflexive commentary offered in *Archipelago* on its own cinematic strategies, via parallels with comments made by Christopher during his sessions with Patricia or other members of the family. When talking about his own impressionist-style land, sea or skyscapes, he speaks of their understatement, an approach that can also be applied to the film. He refers, for example, to seeking to 'evoke' the colour blue in one watercolour without using much blue paint and more generally attempting to approach his subject matter through 'intriguing tangent' rather than directly (Figure 26). This sequence is immediately followed by one in which Rose interacts with a fisherman who arrives in a small boat across windblown choppy water and comments that it is 'a bit of a breezy afternoon', to which she replies 'to say the least'; a clear example of understatement and its reflexive acknowledgement. Understatement and a tangential approach

FIGURE 26 *Reducing and abstracting: Christopher talks, reflexively, about his art in* Archipelago *(2010).*

characterize much of the material of the film, including many moments in which it leans towards a greater minimalism and what might be termed a poetic realism that seems expressive of character dislocation: lingering shots of the landscape or clouds; passages of silence or when the sound is that of birdsong or the wind; sequences in which very little happens or when the camera dwells on one figure or another towards the end of a sequence, often enabling whatever discomfort has been created to persist rather than being displaced by a cut into a new scene (for example, when we see Rose and then Edward in their bedrooms during and then after the shouting from Cynthia).

Christopher also talks about abstraction, which he defines as 'a reductive process, a way of simplifying, distilling, really', a quality that also seems embodied in such ways by the film. It evokes a whole world of conflicted relationships and damaged or uncertain life circumstances among the family members, but the bases of these remain largely unstated. Patricia's upset is, presumably, related to the absence of the father, and what this might signify more generally in their relationship, but none of this is spelled out. There is no direct discussion of the father, only the occasional instance of mockery of his upper-class intonation of certain phrases by Edward. Likewise, we have no indication of what ails Cynthia, other than a frosty relationship with Edward. The awkward exchanges appear to be indicators of much more that remains unsaid but is being evoked indirectly and tangentially. Ironically, one of the issues addressed most explicitly, through the presence of Christopher, is precisely this favouring of the understated.

Unrelated

Understated evocations of pain and discomfort also feature, if somewhat less centrally, in Hogg's first feature, *Unrelated*, set during another upper/upper-middle class holiday, this time a multifamily group staying at a villa in Tuscany. The principal character is Anna (Kathryn Worth), a woman aged in her forties who joins two families and their teenage children. She was meant to have been accompanied by a husband who remains absent and with whom Anna has a series of strained phone calls, similar to those in *Archipelago*. Rather than socializing with her friends, the closest of which is Verena (Mary Rosco), Anna spends most of her time with the group of four teenagers, particularly Oakley (Tom Hiddleston, in his feature debut), to the evident annoyance of Verena. She seeks, it seems, to regain a sense of her own youth, engaging in activities including drinking, dancing and swimming naked in the pool. This appears in some degree similar to the attempt of Edward in *Archipelago* to forge a relationship that crosses lines, if in this case it involves age groups rather than class. Her presence in the group is a source of some awkwardness, although a sense is created of warmth developing between Anna and the otherwise often sardonic Oakley. At one point, Anna invites Oakley into her room at night, to which he responds 'I'd better not.' This might be seen as avoiding the prospect of greater discomfort likely to result from any sexual liaison between the pair, the impression subsequently being created that he has his eyes on a neighbouring Italian woman instead.

The antics of the teenagers, accompanied by Anna, include crashing a car, presumably after drinking, an event that occurs off-screen; we see only the aftermath, a characteristic understatement, as the vehicle is being winched onto a truck. Anna is complicit in the covering-up of the event. Her relationship with the younger group is destroyed when Verena pressures her to tell what happened. The high point of discomfort in the film comes in the aftermath of the revelation. Anna witnesses difficult scenes in the house involving the adults Verena, George (David Rintoul) and their friend Charlie (Michael Hadley) and his son, Jack (Henry Lloyd-Hughes). These are followed by a sequence in which the others – and the viewer – share the painful experience of listening in embarrassed silence to a sustained loud and aggressive off-screen shouting match between George and his son, Oakley. The latter are indoors, the others dispersed around or in the swimming pool. Close shots are provided of each the listeners, but most of the sequence is rendered in a characteristically blank cinema of discomfort tableau-style long shot (Figure 27). Anna is subsequently exiled from the company of the teenagers. The symbolism of separation is clear when the party walks down a dusty road to visit family friends: the 'olds', as they are referred to, are at

FIGURE 27 *Listening to the off-screen shouting match in pained silence in* Unrelated *(2007).*

the front, the teenagers following together some distance behind, with Anna left bringing up the rear on her own.

Up to this point, Hogg employs framing that underpins the developing connection between Anna and Oakley, often paired visually together. An early encounter offers a variation from Sconce's 'awkward couple' shot, in which an initially uncomfortable relationship is figured through single head-and-shoulders shots of each in turn as they sit together. Anna's face is largely inexpressive. Her glance to screen left is matched by a cut to Oakley, followed by a return to her, averting her glance and lowering her lids before looking again in his direction. An extended silence reigns, creating a distinct impression of awkwardness. The camera eventually pulls back to a longer shot that situates the pair in something closer to the tableau style, one at each end of a sofa and a gap in between, although this is taken from a diagonal angle rather than from the straight-on perspective that would indicate a more flattened blank style. When the two engage later in a sustained and sincere conversation about relationships, including questions from Oakley about Anna's sex life and whether she wants to have children, such material is not rendered as a source of discomfort, despite its increasingly personal nature. The relative bond established between the pair is signified at this point by their presence together in a head-and-shoulders-scale two shot. The end of any connection between the two after the row between Oakley and his father is conveyed in single head-and-shoulders perspectives of each, intercut with double and single shots of the other three younger members of the group. It is in one of these that Anna says she is sorry and in another that Oakley declares that he has nothing to say to her. Oakley walks away from one of the subsequent shots, his abrupt shout of 'fuck off' occurring after a cut back to Anna, who also moves back away from the camera, similarly to underpin the fracture.

The approach of *Unrelated* is similar to that of *Archipelago*, a strong sense of verisimilitude being created by naturalistic dialogue and performance. The viewer is offered a position of eavesdropping on the exchanges of a group of generally not very appealing characters, with the exception of Anna. Individual moments of relationship tension or minor discomfort are used, as in *Archipelago*, to evoke a sense of broader but unstated background, the detail of which is often left open. Exactly what is wrong between Anna and her husband is not spelled out until late in the film, when the childless Anna opens up to Verena. She explains that she had been convinced she was pregnant, the apparent symptoms of which had turned out to be the onset of the menopause and so a marker of her inability to have children. This is a revelation of the kind resisted by Hogg in the case of Cynthia in *Archipelago*, one marker of the latter film's more withholding approach. *Unrelated* is also more closely oriented around the experiences of Anna than is *Archipelago* in relation to Edward, as is marked by the general rarity of any closer character shots in the latter, in which the very few framings at head-and-shoulders scale do not seem to favour any individual in particular.

A rather different element of discomfort can be identified in Hogg's third feature, *Exhibition* (2013), although it fits less clearly into the scope of this book. Featuring an often fractious or ambivalent relationship between a husband and wife pair of artists, about to move from their modernist designer-style London home, *Exhibition* is a more enigmatic work in which lines appear to blur at times between reality and dream or forms of performance art. It resembles *Unrelated* and *Archipelago* in its minimalist style, often lingering on patterns of reflection in the floor-to-ceiling windows of the house. *Exhibition* evokes a sense of the difficulty of sharing some conjunction of space and life-time, although the film takes an oblique and internal, psychological approach rather than highlighting the more explicit variety of discomfort found in its predecessors. A difficult relationship also features centrally in Hogg's subsequent film, *The Souvenir* (2019), the focus of which is on a young woman at film school. *The Souvenir* is in some ways a more elaborated and relatively more conventional work – it employs non-diegetic and diegetic music in a more standard manner than her earlier films, for example, including at one point the use of the narratively pointed Joe Jackson's 'Is She Really Going Out with Him' – although it remains understated, some key narrative events being rendered in an elliptical manner and the overall tone balanced between the sincere and the ironic.

Excruciatingly English: nationality and class

Most people just want to paint the view, comments Christopher during his observations about abstraction in *Archipelago*, as once did he. As you get older, he suggests, 'you want to say something with it.' So what might Hogg be 'saying', effectively, with her version of the tangential distillation of the relationships between her characters? *Archipelago* can be interpreted as painting a portrait of a very particular group of individuals, but their depiction also implies broader aspects of national and class identity. The forms of mostly understated discomfort it offers can be read as distinctly English in character, as well as having a more specific class accent within the wider national context. The same can be said broadly of *Unrelated*. To situate the films within an English framework in this way is not to embrace any idea of essential national 'character' or psychology but to locate it within what have been identified sociologically as an interconnected range of relatively distinct cultural traits. A useful measure against which to set the films of Hogg is the notion of Englishness outlined in the pop-anthropological work of Kate Fox, an account aimed at a broad rather than academic audience but founded on a substantial project of participant observation and interview- and survey-based research.[7]

Much of the material from *Archipelago* fits into the characterization of English culture offered by Fox, both generally and in some cases more specific to the particular class location. The focus here is distinctly on English culture rather than British or any of the slippage that often occurs between the two categories. ('British' has tended to be a more clearly distinct and separate category for those from Scotland, Wales and Northern Ireland than is often the case for the English, for a variety of historical reasons, particularly a tendency for 'Britain' as a construct to have served as a vehicle for English dominance.[8]) While the cinema of discomfort is generally a small-niche format, within the broader arena of cultural production, the kinds of qualities on which it tends to thrive are, according to Fox, far more normal and prevalent when it comes to English behaviour and attitudes as a whole. To be English, she suggests, is, for many, to exist in an almost constant state of awkwardness and actual or potential embarrassment. One of her primary conclusions is that English people suffer widely from social dis-ease: from a pervading sense of awkwardness and potential discomfort in the general management of social interactions. 'A tendency to awkwardness, embarrassment and general social ineptitude' is a key part of the 'grammar' of Englishness, she argues.[9] The English 'seem to have a greater potential for embarrassment than other cultures, to experience it more often, and to be more constantly anxious and worried about it', Fox suggests, in a study that includes cross-cultural comparison on various grounds.[10]

The presentation of the relationship sought by Edward with Rose can be understood directly within one of the dimensions of English discomfort analysed by Fox. Cultural signifiers of class location play a central role in much of what Fox examines, including an effort often to deny the realities of class difference and inequality. This is an issue that tends to be particularly acute for the middle classes, where small differences can loom disproportionately large, as has been argued elsewhere, including in the work of Pierre Bourdieu. As a form of upper- or upper-middle class realism, the work of Hogg can be situated as in some ways an English equivalent of the middle-class realism identified by Claire Perkins in some works of American indie cinema, as cited in the Introduction (its focus has much in common with the emphasis Sconce identifies in American 'smart' cinema on issues such as personal politics, communication and emotional dysfunction). A similar point is made about the films of Hogg by David Forrest, who argues that it is important to read her works as realist texts 'precisely because of this rejection of the mode's common thematic preoccupations' with working class themes or sociopolitical injustice.[11] They offer, for Forrest, a way of opening up the understanding of realism in British cinema to a wider range than he suggests has traditionally been favoured. In addition to a British context of realist cinema, Forrest argues, Hogg's films can be understood as examples of a broader movement 'in which a stylistic concern with everyday life transcends the need for an *explicit* focus on the "social" in realism'.[12]

Middle-class life is depicted here without functioning in any overt dialectical opposition to an unequally treated working class, as Forrest suggests is the case in examples of social-realist cinema such as the work of Ken Loach, but treated more as a terrain to be charted in its own right (it is notable that Christopher and Rose, the two figures employed by the family in *Archipelago*, themselves appear to be from clearly middle rather than lower class backgrounds). This might effectively entail a form of 'capitalist realism', Forrest concedes, to return to the concept from Mark Fisher drawn upon by Perkins: one that does not envisage any alternative to the universe of neoliberalism and that involves a shift of focus from the public to the personal realm, 'eschewing the potential of the realist address to intervene in debates around inequality and social justice, and instead occupying a narrative position which is domesticated; reflective; nostalgic, even'.[13] As Forrest argues, this can still be seen as functioning in a sociopolitical manner in a more oblique way, however, 'utilising a stylistic and sometimes *stylized* emphasis on the real as a site for the reflective exploration of everyday life'.[14] The latter might constitute 'a move towards realism as an aesthetic practice to be understood in relation to a far broader set of factors than the surface ability to document and reveal the mechanisms of capitalist injustice'.

To elaborate on these distinctions, we can start with a more widely prevailing notion of social realism that tends to focus on the lives of the markedly disadvantaged. The aim here is often to reveal to the rest of society the realities of those living on the margins, whether defined as working class or underclass (or in racial or any other terms); to put the lie to ideologies that ignore those in straightened circumstances or that blame them for their fate, and ultimately to spur social or political action. From this overtly political perspective, a portrait of upper- to upper-middle-class activity would be expected actively to show its role in the establishment or maintenance of structural inequality. To some extent, although within a more stylized fictional universe, elements of this can be identified in certain aspects of the films of Roy Andersson examined in the previous chapter. What *Unrelated* and *Archipelago* offer, instead, is a sense of the more banal, if also often painful, everyday texture of the lives of characters located in the upper-to-upper-middle-class social sphere. Their own internal relationships are explored. They might be found wanting, but variable bases of potential sympathy are also offered, without any indication of the impact on others that results from the unequal materialities that underlie the basis of their economic and social privilege. This might be deemed to be a more conservative realism, in effect, if not with the political intent that often underpins more obviously critical social realism. For Hogg, it would seem from her own reported comments, the world of the films is simply the one she knows best and wanted to capture in its own right rather than as specifically the representation of a particular class location chosen for that reason.[15]

This does not evacuate the films of any potential for political critique, however, as can be seen in the manifestation of English attitudes towards class found in *Archipelago*. The English middle classes are 'particularly uncomfortable' about class, Fox suggests, those located in the 'well-meaning upper middles' being 'most squeamish of all'.[16] This and her reference to the 'over-tactful' nature of such figures could be a description of Edward in *Archipelago*, in his attempts to establish a different kind of relationship with Rose (whether or not this includes any sexual dimension is not made at all clear in the film; at one point, he noses around in Rose's room, but to what end is not suggested; generally, the absence of any clear indication of whether or not any such relationship might develop – it does not – is a further element of potential discomfort for the viewer). What Fox terms the 'polite egalitarianism' widely found in the dealings of English people with those who serve them is a way of disguising orders and instruction as requests – not an expression of the true social relations involved but a way of masking class inequality.[17] Such hypocrisy is not viewed here as a deliberate attempt to mislead but as something deeply internalized as part of the culture, hence its applicability to what appears to be a genuinely well-meaning figure such as Edward. Seen in this context, the upper-to-upper-middle-class realism offered by Hogg has distinct potential to be interpreted in more critical sociopolitical terms.

The mannerisms and body language of the principals of the film can also be understood in the terms offered by Fox, whether in relation to class or Englishness more generally, the product of a form of performance that puts an emphasis on verisimilitude, as is the case also with *Unrelated*. Speech is often hesitant and as if improvised, a style that seems particularly able to capture qualities such as awkwardness or embarrassment (the production practice that encourages such an effect is considered below). English social squeamishness in areas such as not complaining tends to occur, Fox suggests, in 'barely visible nano-gestures, tiny facial twitches and minimalist coughs, sniffs and sighs' of the kind often manifested in particular by Leonard's performance as Cynthia.[18] Such responses, to which we might add some of the discomfort expressed corporeally by other characters, especially Edward, are seen as amounting to a distinctive English body language. Many examples can be found in *Archipelago* of a tendency towards a 'bland, insipid politeness'[19] at a superficial level of communication. This is generally concerned with the avoidance of giving offence rather than being sincerely meant in any specifics and might be seen as part of a typically middle-class English structure of feeling or expression. The main exception to this is some of the discourse from Edward or between Edward and Christopher, but it is exactly the 'earnestness' of the former – a quality identified by Fox as one especially disliked and considered to be embarrassing by the English – that tends to prompt icy responses from Cynthia. When Christopher engages sincerely in a discussion with Edward about his future options, it is notable that the earnestness of the exchange is combined with a very low-key hesitancy that seems more distinctly within the realm examined by Fox.

One of the central examples of behaviour examined above departs from the template suggested by Fox, but this might help explain its particular potential to generate discomfort on one basis. Cynthia's complaint in the restaurant does not fit any of the three different ways of dealing with exactly this situation outlined by Fox. These are: the silent complaint that remains unvoiced because of reluctance to create a scene, the response Cynthia attributes to Edward and Patricia; the apologetic complaint that displays its reluctance and is an example of what Fox sees as a widespread tendency of the English to apologize even when not at fault; and the loud, aggressive or obnoxious complaint. Cynthia actually, to use one of her preferred terms, makes a strong, direct complaint, mixed with additional complaining about the responses of the others. She thus departs from what Fox sees as the norm, this being the basis for the discomfort she causes the rest of the party and, potentially, the suitably attuned viewer.

The style of Hogg's work can also be interpreted as fitting into this broadly English context, understatement being another of the key characteristics identified by Fox and often more widely associated with national traits. Understatement is far from exclusive to English culture, its cinematic manifestations being found quite widely in art or indie films from many different locations. The point, as more generally in Fox's account, is that it tends to have a particular salience within English culture, to loom distinctly largely within the predominant cultural mix. *Archipelago* and *Unrelated* differ from such norms, however, in not relying greatly on another feature identified by Fox, ironic humour, which she views as a prevalent mechanism for the attempted management of difficult cultural encounters. The viewer is generally denied any clearly indicated ironic perspective that might offer a way of standing back from a sense of sharing the awkwardness typical of the fictional encounters (as is found, for example, in parts of *Palindromes*). This is itself a significant source of potential discomfort. The primary audience constituency for both films is likely to share a broadly middle-to-upper-middle class location, if not necessarily quite as privileged as that of the main characters, and thus to experience a discomforting sense of recognition (for English-based viewers, at least). That can be a source of satisfaction of its own, however, as is indicated by what Fox reports of some responses of readers to her book, in which she was *praised* for making them 'cringe with embarrassment'. 'Only in masochistic England', she quips, perhaps rather glibly in this case, 'would this be such a flattering compliment.'[20]

From modernity to gender

The account offered by Fox – one of the more persuasive as well as entertaining of many such attempts to dissect notions of Englishness – can also be linked to some of the broader themes relating to modernity encountered in previous chapters. The many minefields of potential discomfort and embarrassment Fox charts are situated within a context in which the English are diagnosed as being discomforted by excessive formality but also collectively incompetent to negotiate appropriate levels of informality in a comfortable manner; as manifested, for example, by familiar sources of awkwardness involved in the rituals involved in meeting and greeting others. The broader context evoked here is similar to that identified by Kotsko, as cited in Chapter 1, and other diagnoses of modernity invoked above. A loss of formal codes that existed in the 1950s is identified as a key source of awkwardness in areas such as clothing and greetings, for example: the latter from a standardly formal 'how do you do' to various phrases and physical fumblings in the arena of handshakes, hugs/touches and kisses. To some extent, the distinctly English traits identified by Fox can be situated as a local variant of the broader sources of awkwardness resulting from challenges to cultural traditions suggested by Kotsko or in versions such as Bauman's liquid modernity.

This seems a plausible reading, although Fox does not mention such contexts when she considers possible causes for the symptoms she diagnoses (which, as she makes clear, is not her primary objective). No clear cause can be identified, she suggests, rejecting 'reductive' traditional accounts, some of which are long-established, that have attributed English qualities, variously, to specifics such as geographically based insularity, climate or experiences such as having once had and then lost a world-leading empire. In all such cases, she suggests, other examples can be found of broadly similar phenomena in contexts where cultural outcomes have been different. That which seems relatively distinct to Englishness might be explained by a specific combination of such factors, however, and their particular inflections in this instance, even if the roots of what is taken to be English culture remain mired in a great deal of mythology and debate about its relationship to rival or overlapping notions of the 'British'.[21] If many of the qualities identified as distinctly English in particular forms are usually traced to a variety of earlier historical contexts, as is typical of the literature on this subject, some of those highlighted by Fox might be expected to be heightened in the conditions associated with late/contemporary modernity. The cultural terrain mapped by Fox is one in which uncertainties appear to generate risks at almost every turn, even if these are of awkwardness, discomfort or embarrassment rather than physical or environmental danger.

One response to such a situation suggested by Fox is the creation of particular arenas within which new or localized forms of agreed social ritual can provide means for the management of social relations, examples including sports, games and the formation of clubs for various leisure activities, and the particular salience of these to the English. The painting activity in *Archipelago* might be situated in this way, as a domain that provides its own structures for social interaction, creating an arena for some of the more sustained forms of discussion shown in the film.

We could certainly situate the characterization of Edward in the context of at least semi-untethered modernity. He appears to seek an escape from the habitual routine within which he is expected to perform: from his desire not to treat Rose solely as a paid employee to his break from the arc of a standard career pattern for a person of his privileged background (one we can presume to have included public school and an easy route into lucrative work). He is, effectively, another individual trying to engage in the kind of 'everyday social experiments' identified by Giddens as characteristic of contemporary modernity. This is another issue addressed in *Archipelago* through what appear to be presented as the sage-like, although hesitant, observations of Christopher. It is not so much what you do, Christopher suggests, as the intensity and conviction with which you do it; a view of the life-is-what-you-make-it variety. As he puts it: 'I mean, you just … by the conviction of your reality that you … you believe in, you make others believe in it … kinda-kinda make it up, really … and then … people get convinced and even you, oneself, gets convinced that that's …' Life is based, in such a view, on a kind of collective lived fiction, but there is not (or is no longer, if there were beforehand) any clearly defined path (at least, we might add, for those of comfortable means who are not forced into very limited options). As Christopher continues: 'there's not sort of one kind of ... hidden track that's there waiting for you. It's... you've just got to step into it. Whatever that is.' After a comment that relates this philosophy to the development of his own art he adds, in very Bauman-like terms: 'But it's not secure, is it ... it's not solid or anchored', to which Edward replies, characteristically, 'I'm just not sure.' A microcosm of this situation is the awkwardness surrounding the choice of table in the restaurant scene. Too many options are available, rather than any more clearly directed basis for making a choice. Coupled with the reluctance of any member of the party to be seen to be asserting a preference of their own, which might be taken as a form of passive aggression as much as anything else, this results in what does seem a characteristically English (or English middle-class) variety of indecisive discomfort.

While class location seems central to the qualities of her films, Hogg's work has also been interpreted as offering a distinctly feminist approach that can be seen as another dimension of its more broadly discomforting effect. Davina Quinlivan interprets *Exhibition* in contexts including the very particular notions of femininity found in the poststructuralist writings of Luce Irigary.[22] Ciara Barrett takes issue with what she interprets as an inherently 'phallogocentric' narrative within which she suggests Hogg's work has been positioned by many critics, particularly through comparisons with a tradition of male auteurs (phallogocentric, a term from post-structuralist feminist theory that combines 'phallocentric' and 'logocentric', suggests a conjunction of deeply embedded male and 'western'-oriented discourse).[23] As Barrett and some others stress, Hogg's work often foregrounds the painful experiences of women in particular, especially *Unrelated* and *Exhibition*, while the central male figure of *Archipelago* might be seen as himself to some extent a victim of patriarchal as well as class-based expectations.

Selina Robertson argues that Hogg's films 'represent a challenge to the dominant patriarchal order' by creating complex roles for women (and men) and through her collaborative creative process, the latter an issue to which I return below.[24] For Barrett, the films fit into the often denigrated category of melodrama through their focus (if not exclusive) on the experiences of women and also at the formal level, the latter both in departures from what can be seen as phallogocentric linear narrative structures and in the use of sound. Her realist aesthetic is combined with a version of the 'melos' of melodrama: traditionally, either music or a wider range of emotionally expressive devices. Non-diegetic music is absent from the bodies of the films, as is often the case in the cinema of discomfort, one of the ways in which the viewer is left without the comforts of the clear emotional guidance it often supplies. As Barrett suggests, however, Hogg employs a different kind of 'melos', in the use of unusually distinct background sound that lies somewhere between the naturalistic and the more foregrounded and expressive, as in the sound of birdsong or wind in *Archipelago* or the rumbling of chairs or doors in *Exhibition*. The sound design, identified by Hogg as a key dimension of her work, functions 'to highlight the isolation of her protagonists in space, and increasingly as an echo of their emotional states'.[25] Hogg confirms the intentionality of such practice, particularly the use of birdsong to provide a more subtle version of what might more mainstream-conventionally be offered by music, in her DVD commentary on *Archipelago*. The only music employed in the film, the location of which straddles diegetic and non-diegetic positions, is a song sung in the voice of Cynthia over the end credits, the lyrics of which Hogg suggests express some of the feelings towards her brother left unvoiced in the main body of the text.

Production, release and reputation

Like many of the examples considered in earlier chapters, the films of Hogg gained critical plaudits while existing on the margins, in some cases even those of the restricted arthouse sector. The budgets of her first three films were low for theatrically released features including professional performers. This is the result, it would appear, of the determination of the filmmaker to retain freedom to follow her own dictates following an earlier career working within the constraints of commercial television. *Unrelated*, *Archipelago* and *Exhibition* were shot on digital video to reduce costs, despite Hogg's declared preference for celluloid.[26] Budget figures are unavailable for *Unrelated* and *Exhibition*, with that for *Archipelago* put at £500,000, part of which is reported to have been contributed by a sympathetic Japanese businessman.[27] For her first film, Hogg had commented that she had 'very little money', as a result of which she had to do much of the post-production work herself.[28] She is reported to have been wary of the possible constraints associated with public funding,[29] although with the development of her reputation both the British Film Institute (BFI) and the BBC were involved in backing *Exhibition* and *The Souvenir*. The former received £430,194 from the BFI.[30] The latter received a total of £1,243,177 with a further £955,000 for its sequel, *The Souvenir Part II* (2020).[31]

Hogg's films can be situated within what has been identified as a resurgence of British art cinema from the 2000s. Although not mentioned by name, while *Unrelated* is cited in passing, Hogg seems to belong in the category of new British art-filmmakers identified in this period in a survey by Paul Newland and Brian Hoyle.[32] This remains the case even though her first two films do not appear to have benefited from funding from the since-disbanded UK Film Council, created in 2000 and cited by Newland and Hoyle as a key institutional factor in the emergence of what they term 'this new breed of film-maker', subsequently sustained in some cases through BFI funding of the kind Hogg obtained for *Exhibition*, *The Souvenir* and its sequel.[33] As Newland and Hoyle suggest, the filmmakers involved in this upsurge – which followed a decline in the 1990s, when support for British cinema shifted in a more commercially mainstream direction – do not fit into any single, clear cut narrative or approach. A variety of filmmaker backgrounds and styles are identified, from the careers of Steve McQueen, beginning with *Hunger* (2008), to those of figures including the film essayist Patrick Keiller, Lynn Ramsey and Andrea Arnold.

The work of Hogg is situated by Stella Hockenhull within a strand of poetic realism produced by British women filmmakers since 2000, including the work of Ramsey and Arnold along with others including Clio Barnard, Amma Asante and Samantha Morton.[34] Hockenhull follows Forrest in identifying in such work a tendency to focus less on the political dimension often associated with realism and more on the creation of a poetic aesthetic. Ramsey and Morton are associated with Hogg, in this way, in their use of landscape as a means of signifying internal crisis. Class location again remains more distinct in the work of Hogg, however, her films departing from the tendency identified by Hockenhull for this body of work to focus on the childhood or youth of figures from working or underclass backgrounds (as in examples such as *Ratcatcher* [Ramsey, 1999], *Fish Tank* [Arnold, 2009], *The Unloved* [Morton, 2009] and *The Selfish Giant* [Barnard, 2013]). A playful nod towards this difference is made in *The Souvenir*, the upper-class film-school protagonist of which, Julie (Honor Swinton Byrne), is at first ardently committed to making a film set in Sunderland, in which a young boy's relationship with his mother will provide a metaphor for the industrial decline of the region. The comment by one of her tutors that this is not rooted in her own background reads as an implied justification for Hogg's own focus on the territory with which she is most familiar. 'Why are they more real than me', asks Julie's irksome upper-class boyfriend Anthony (Tom Burke), when she talks about her characters, a questioning of class-based assumptions about realism, an assertion that she resists with the suggestion that everyone is equally real. While the national context is significant for work of this kind, often vital in terms of access to funding and important to some of the particular varieties of discomfort examined above, films such as those of Hogg need also to be seen as products of the broader arena of art or independent cinema, even if their distribution overseas has been limited, as is seen in some of the influences suggested by the filmmaker and other commentators cited below.

The naturalistic impression identified in Hogg's films above is the product of very particular production practices, involving varying degrees of scripting detail that leave considerable room for improvisation by the performers. Hogg has also mixed professional and non-professional performers, the latter bringing an extra level of verisimilitude, as in the case of both the artist (Hogg's own art teacher) and the cook in *Archipelago*. The protagonists of *Exhibition* are both non-professionals, the former punk singer Viv Albertine and the conceptual artist Liam Gillick. In the case of *Archipelago*, added intensity was created by the cast being required to live together for the duration of production, some two months, in the house in which much of the film unfolds. The narrative was shot mostly in chronological order, as is Hogg's customary practice, with the performers unaware exactly how certain events would develop.[35] For *Unrelated*, Hogg says she began with a fully developed script but largely discarded it during shooting and allowed the performers space to draw on themselves as well as their fictional characters.[36] Instead of a script, she says she wrote something closer to a short story or novella for *Archipelago* and *Exhibition*. The dialogue for the latter would be written the night before the shooting of a scene and given to the actors only an hour or so in advance of shooting: 'not enough time to memorize the line, but enough time for them to get the gist of what I wanted'.[37]

The scene in which Edward seeks to invite Rose to the dinner table in *Archipelago* was created entirely spontaneously by the cast, following the shooting of other material, according to Hogg's commentary on the DVD release. A preference for allowing such developments is one rationale for the use of longer shots. To move into close ups of the individuals would shift the overall valence of such a sequence, as I have suggested more generally, but would also be obviated by the practice of the filmmaker in this case because it would require replaying the action in a more detailed, pre-planned manner and so losing much of the spontaneous quality (this is not to say that multiple takes were not used for many scenes). During the restaurant sequence the non-professionals playing Christopher and Rose were not aware how it would play out, a factor that resulted in their discomfort being real, experienced by the performers themselves, rather than simulated.[38] The meal scene that climaxes with Cynthia's abrupt departure was repeated approximately eight times, although Hogg suggests that the real discomfort experienced by Christopher Baker in this case remained undiminished.[39] Spontaneity of performance is also encouraged by a general preference to avoid the full rehearsal of scenes.[40] Approaches of this kind contribute centrally to the naturalistic, halting nature of much of the dialogue in Hogg's films, a distinctly independent production practice of the kind that motivated her to continue working at the low-budget end of the spectrum.

Unrelated was greeted by critics as manifesting the appearance of what seemed to be a fully fledged auteur seemingly 'from nowhere', although feature and interview articles traced an earlier background that included film school and directing episodes of popular British TV series such as *Casualty*, *London's Burning* and an *EastEnders* special.[41] Hogg graduated from the National Film and Television School (NFTS) (an experience on which she presumably draws in *The Souvenir*), her entry having been gained through the shooting of a Super 8mm film made with a camera famously given to her by Derek Jarman. Her graduation film, which apparently was not well received at the NFTS, starred a then-unknown Tilda Swinton.[42] A period making music videos for artists including Alison Moyet was followed by more than a decade working in television until the move into independent production that led, after a lengthy period of development, to the release of *Unrelated*, this and her subsequent films drawing strongly on elements of her personal/family background. The film gained the quality credentials of a premiere at the London Film Festival, where it won the FIPRESCI international film critics prize.

Hogg won several other 'first film' or 'best newcomer' awards for *Unrelated*, her early works being widely received as distinctive within prevailing British cinematic traditions in their naturalistic approach to contemporary upper- or upper-middle-class material, along the lines outlined above.[43] *Unrelated* and *Archipelago*, the two works that defined her initial establishment as a new voice, gained the artistic consecration of being compared approvingly with films from established auteur figures from international art cinema such as Yasujiro Ozu, Robert Bresson and Eric Rohmer, while also being contrasted by many critics and feature writers with more familiar British or English tendencies to favour either lower-class realism or upper-class period nostalgia.[44] Hogg has cited as favourites the above three filmmakers along with others including her contemporaries Tsai Ming-Liang, Apichatpong Weerasethakul, Hirokazu Kore-eda and Nori Bilge Ceylan, some of the leading lights of the global 'slow cinema' tendency within which her work could also be included.[45]

While garnering positive reviews from many critics, Hogg's films to date were destined for limited theatrical release, as is typical of many of those examined in this book. The majority of the revenues of *Unrelated* and *Archipelago* were earned in the UK market, as might be expected: $154,463 in the case of the former, $491,598 for the latter (the number of screens on which they showed is not recorded in the source for this data, Box Office Mojo). *Unrelated* became the first release in the UK by a new London-based arthouse distributor, New Wave Films. *Archipelago* was handled by the established Artificial Eye, identified by Newland and Hoyle as one of the two companies to have played the primary role in sustaining the domestic distribution of postmillennial British art cinema in this period, along with Optimum/Studio Canal.[46] *Archipelago* followed *Unrelated* in having its premiere at the London Film Festival. No initial release was gained in the US market, the principal point of focus I have used in previous chapters as a measure of international reach. The first three films were given a showcase in the Emerging Artists series at the New York Film Festival in October 2013, which led to the US rights to *Exhibition* being obtained by Kino Lorber, one of the surviving small distributors highlighted in Chapter 1, also distributor of some of the work of Yorgos Lanthimos.[47] The company gave very limited openings to *Unrelated* and *Archipelago* in 2014, in the same month as the release of *Exhibition*. The resulting takings were minimal. *Unrelated* ran for twenty-one days on one screen, grossing just $4,529, while *Archipelago* took $7,791 over twenty-eight days, also in a single theatre. The US gross of *Exhibition* is put at $14,344 (I have not been able to find figures for its UK box office). *The Souvenir* marked a change of pattern in that its premiere was at the Sundance festival in the United States, where it won the jury prize. It gained US distribution from the noted indie outfit A24 along with a UK release by Curzon Artificial Eye, grossing a total of $1,713,707.

Hogg has herself commented on the ability of her films to generate discomfort, particularly as a result of their reticence. Viewers often want the 'blanks' filled in, she suggests: 'They feel very disoriented and uncomfortable with being given so much space to imagine themselves. So all those question marks that I've placed through the film can be discomforting.'[48] She does not set out to make people feel uncomfortable, she adds, but offers a familiar motivation for discomfort on the grounds of realism: 'I don't like easy solutions. I don't think life is like that.' Plenty of viewers of *Archipelago* reject the film for this kind of reason. A substantial proportion of those whose responses I have examined – from the Internet Movie Database, Rotten Tomatoes and Amazon – are highly negative, in terms familiar from many unsympathetic reactions to minimalist works of art cinema.[49] For many the film is dismissed for being 'boring' and/or uneventful, often in highly rhetorical terms ('the worst film I have ever seen', etc.). This is another example that strongly divides viewers, including a tendency for some rejectors to complain not just about the film itself but the positive responses of professional critics or others. A notable gap is found, for example, between the overall positive rating of the film on Rotten Tomatoes by critics (95 per cent) and that of 58 per cent from what is reported to be a total of 1,779 user ratings. Those who admire the film often engage in familiar distinction-marking gestures, with references to types of films they imagine might be preferred by detractors, while some rejectors follow a pattern also seen in other examples in previous chapters, in criticizing what is seen as the pretentious quality of positive reviews and in some cases commenting favourably on other examples of art cinema. Admirers often comment on the realistic quality of the film, either generally or with specific reference to the particular English/British class milieu, a number also identifying undercurrents of dry humour. To one, for example, the film is 'severe, understated, believably uncomfortable' and has 'buried deep, deep, deep down, a streak of humour thin and dry waiting to be discovered'.[50] Another admires the film for what is left unsaid, 'often excruciating moments of stillness and unease', and for the fact that the more 'intense/explosive' encounters are conducted off screen.[51]

Archipelago is another example of the cinema of discomfort that also generates mixed responses, further evidence of viewers sometimes wrestling to come to a single or fixed opinion. For one respondent it is 'a brilliant but utterly boring film.'[52] It is 'painful to watch but perfectly captures the dysfunction and the inability to focus on the essential of Britain's upper middle class today.' Unfortunately, this reviewer adds, 'the boredom wins out in the end', concluding with the kind of rhetoric employed by some of the strongest rejectors of the film: 'Don't watch this on a rainy day, you might want to go out and kill yourself afterwards.' For another the film displays, among other qualities, 'exquisitely uncomfortable writing' but is 'just too unpleasant to be as long as it is'.[53] While another respondent seems to admire the use of static wide and long shots, which at times 'really fuelled the tension and awkwardness of what was happening', she at other times 'almost screamed for closer shots', a strong expression of a desire for a more familiarly mainstream-conventional form of articulation.[54] This prompts another conclusion that suggests, ultimately, a heightened aversion to such material, the film being 'Not something I'd watch or even mention again.'

Notes

1. Plantinga, 'I Followed the Rules and They All Loved You More'.
2. Plantinga, *Moving Viewers*, 126; Smith, *Engaging Characters*.
3. Smith, *Film, Art, and the Third Culture*.
4. Pethő, 'Between Absorption, Abstraction and Exhibition'.
5. Ibid.
6. Director's commentary on Artificial Eye DVD release.
7. Kate Fox, *Watching the English: The Hidden Rules of English Behaviour*, second edition (London: Hodder and Stoughton, 2014).
8. For an account of the relative significance of notions of Britishness and Englishness at various moments in history and up to the 2000s, see Krishnan Kumar, *The Making of English National Identity* (Cambridge: Cambridge University Press, 2002).
9. Fox, *Watching the English*, 76
10. Ibid., 323.
11. David Forrest, 'The Films of Joanna Hogg: New British Realism and Class', *Studies in European Cinema*, vol. 11, no. 1 (2014): 64.
12. Forrest, 'The films of Joanna Hogg', 65.
13. Ibid., 66.
14. Ibid., 69.
15. See, for example, Rob Carnevale, 'Archipelago – Joanna Hogg interview', *IndieLondon*, undated http://www.indielondon.co.uk/Film-Review/archipelago-joanna-hogg-interview.
16. Fox, *Watching the English*, 112.
17. Ibid., 139.
18. Ibid., 127.

19 Ibid., 214.
20 Ibid., 273.
21 For a popular/journalistic account of some such issues, see Jeremy Paxman, *The English: A Portrait of a People* (London: Penguin, 1998). A more scholarly exploration of the history of change and continuity in notions of English 'national character' since the eighteenth century is offered by Peter Mandler, *The English National Character: The History of an Idea from Edmund Burke to Tony Blair* (New Haven, CT: Yale University Press, 2006). See also Kumar, *The Making of English National Identity*. For an examination of the diverse nature of components of Englishness and English cinema, see Julian Petley, 'The Englishness of British Cinema; Beyond the Valley of the Corn Dollies', in John Hill (ed.), *A Companion to British and Irish Cinema* (Hoboken, NJ: John Wiley, 2019).
22 Davinia Quinlivan, An Architecture of Light and Air, a Rhythm of Stillness: Absence in Joanna Hogg's Exhibition', ('Materialising Absence in Film and Media'), *Screening the Past*, 43 (April 2018), online.
23 Ciara Barrett, 'The Feminist Cinema of Joanna Hogg: Melodrama, Female Space, and the Subversion Of Phallogocentric Metanarrative', *Alphaville: Journal of Film and Screen Media*, 10 (2015), online.
24 Selina Robertson, 'Joanna Hogg, a Very British Outsider', in *The F Word: Contemporary Feminism*, 24 May 2012, accessed at https://thefword.org.uk/2012/05/new_review_hogg/.
25 Barrett, 'The Feminist Cinema of Joanna Hogg'.
26 Paul Dallas, 'Architecture of Desire: Joanna Hogg's Exhibition', *Cinema Scope*, 57 (Winter 2014), accessed at http://cinema-scope.com/cinema-scope-magazine/architecture- desire-joanna-hoggs-exhibition/.
27 Catherine Shoard, 'The Laugh-Out-Loud Nightmares of Joanna Hogg', *The Guardian*, 24 February 2011, accessed at https://www.theguardian.com/film/2011/feb/24/joanna-hogg-archipelago
28 Dallas, 'Architecture of Desire'.
29 See, for example, Shoard, 'The Laugh-Out-Loud nightmares of Joanna Hogg' and Robertson, 'Joanna Hogg, a Very British Outsider'.
30 Figure from *BFI Statistical Yearbook 2013* (London: BFI, 2013), 208.
31 Figures from the BFI at https://www.bfi.org.uk/film-industry/funding-awards (accessed February 2020).
32 Paul Newland and Brian Hoyle, 'Introduction: Post-millennial British Art Cinema', *Journal of British Cinema and Television*, vol. 13, no. 2 (2016): 233–42.
33 Newland and Hoyle, 'Introduction', 235.
34 Stella Hockenhull, *British Women Film Directors in the New Millennium* (London: Palgrave Macmillan, 2017).
35 Shoard, 'The Laugh-Out-Loud nightmares of Joanna Hogg'; Robertson, 'Joanna Hogg, a Very British Outsider'; Carnevale, 'Archipelago – Joanna Hogg Interview'. Hogg also talks about these production practices, including

some of the scripting issues considered below, in her commentary on the Artificial Eye DVD release.

36 Antonio Pasolini, 'Joanna Hogg', Kamera.co.uk, 18 September 2008, accessed at http://www.kamera.co.uk/joanna-hogg/, and Mark Lukenbill, 'Meet the Woman Who Discovered Tom Hiddleston, NYFF Emerging Artist Joanna Hogg', *Indiewire*, 8 October 2013, accessed at https://www.indiewire.com/2013/10/meet-the-woman-who-discovered-tom-hiddleston-nyff-emerging-artist-joanna-hogg-34161/.
37 Lukenbill, 'Meet the Woman Who Discovered Tom Hiddleston'.
38 Hogg commentary on Artificial Eye DVD release.
39 Hogg, DVD commentary.
40 Carnevale, 'Archipelago – Joanna Hogg Interview'.
41 See, for example, review by Peter Bradshaw in *The Guardian*, 19 September 2008, accessed at https://www.theguardian.com/film/2008/sep/19/drama1, and Shoard, 'The Laugh-Out-Loud Nightmares of Joanna Hogg'.
42 Among numerous examples of the retailing of these events, see Robertson, 'Joanna Hogg, a Very British Outsider' and Philip Sinden, 'Talent Issue – The Film Director: Joanna Hogg', *The Independent*, 29 December 2007, accessed at https://www.independent.co.uk/arts-entertainment/films/features/talent-issue-the-film-director-joanna-hogg-766033.html.
43 On the class dimension in particular, see Danny Leigh, 'Posh Pushovers: Why Do Films Squeeze Out the Middle Classes?', *The Guardian*, 25 February 2011, accessed at https://www.theguardian.com/film/filmblog/2011/feb/25/films-middle-classes-class-archipelago.
44 See, for example, Robertson, 'Joanna Hogg, a Very British Outsider'.
45 See, for example, Pasolini, 'Joanna Hogg'. For an academic reading of points of similarity and difference between Hogg and Ozu, see William Brown, 'Sparse or Slow: Ozu and Joanna Hogg', in Jinhee Choi (ed.), *Reorienting Ozu: A Master and His Influence* (Oxford: Oxford University Press, 2018).
46 Newland and Hoyle, 'Introduction', 236.
47 Lukenbill, 'Meet the Woman Who Discovered Tom Hiddleston'.
48 Ibid.
49 Sample accessed 6 August 2019, comprised of 44 reviews on the IMDb, starting at https://www.imdb.com/title/tt1527835/reviews?ref_=tt_urv; 76 on Rotten Tomatoes, starting at https://www.rottentomatoes.com/m/archipelago/reviews?type=user; 46 at Amazon.com, starting at at https://www.amazon.com/Archipelago-Tom-Hiddleston/product-reviews/B00NLV7HE2/ref=cm_cr_dp_d_show_all_btm?ie=UTF8&reviewerType=all_reviews.
50 'Early B', Rotten Tomatoes, 13 May 2012.
51 'LP', Amazon.com, 1 November 2014.
52 'Tom H', Rotten Tomatoes, 4 June 2011.
53 'Zoe S', Rotten Tomatoes, 19 November 2012.
54 'Ella H', Rotten Tomatoes, 1 June 2012.

7

The comedy of discomfort: Towards a conclusion

Elements of comedy occur in many of the films examined in this book so far, although their status is usually far from clear cut. Potential for comedy is often uncertain and mixed with qualities likely to provide awkwardness or embarrassment. Laughter provoked by parts of *Palindromes* is liable to be of a nervous variety, as suggested in Chapter 2, while comedy and pain are intermingled in moments such as Mama Sunshine's anecdote about the girl with no legs. A droll, flatly comic effect is created by some of the tableaux in the films of Ulrich Seidl examined in Chapter 3, but also often mixed with likely sources of pain and discomfort. Comic potential is also created in an example such as *Dogtooth*, particularly in the scenes surrounding the killing of the cat, as seen in Chapter 4, although again the operative modality is mixed and uncertain, the characters reacting to such events in what appears to be an entirely serious manner. The term 'hilarious' turns up in a considerable number of the reviews surveyed in Chapter 4 but often coupled with others such as 'strange' and 'disturbing'. A dry and flat deadpan comedy is found in the films of Andersson, mixed with a more tragic impression, while Östlund's *Force Majeure* and *The Square* offer sources of awkward diegetic laughter in material that remains largely uncomfortable. An underlying comedy, dry and understated, is also identified by a significant number of the viewers of *Archipelago* whose responses were examined in the previous chapter.

Comedy is a useful frame through which to bring together some of the themes of this book because of its more conventional employment as a source largely of comfort and the easing of what might otherwise be causes of tension and dis-ease. A comic modality of a broad kind tends to position on-screen material as essentially non-serious and non-consequential, implying that it should be taken lightly and not have great potential to become a source of discomfort. It might be for this reason that elements of comedy are sometimes played up in the marketing of the kinds of films examined in this book, whether or not combined with more serious qualifiers, in an attempt to widen the appeal of some titles. The front cover of the UK DVD for *Dogtooth*, for example, offers the appropriately balanced declaration that the film is 'brilliant, dark and disconcertingly funny', while some of the online respondents cited above complained at what they considered to be the misleading picking out of the isolated term 'hilarious', from a *New York Times* review, on the US version.[1]

I use the term modality here in the sense it which it is employed by Robert Hodge and David Tripp in their work on the implications of children's television.[2] Modality is employed in this sense, from linguistics, to suggest how particular kinds of texts work, implicitly or explicitly, to position their material in relation to notions of an ostensible external reality. Texts are coded to suggest varying degrees of reality/plausibility, ranging from signifiers of real-world authenticity found in formats such as news, documentary and some varieties of art or indie cinema, to markers of the more fantastical or unreal, often in complex shades and combinations. As I have suggested elsewhere, modality markers specific to broader forms of comedy establish a sense of distance from real-world seriousness or implications, although this can involve a wide range of variable degrees.[3]

In very broad slapstick, for example, little sense is created of characters facing real injury when subjected to violent physical attack. Art cinema and some forms of indie film are presented very differently, textual and extra-textual markers of serious modality suggesting that what happens on screen has implications that have importance and significance, both within and beyond the fictional world (that is, consequences for the characters but also implying something of pertinence to the real world).[4] A great deal of territory remains between these two extremes, however. Work positioned as broadly conventional comedy can also offer elements of discomfort or more diegetically consequential narrative material. The Laurel and Hardy short *The Music Box* (1932), for example, is farcical and unserious but offers an excruciatingly Sisyphean spectacle of the two clowns repeatedly trying to push a piano up a series of outdoor steps. Some forms of comedian comedy, or the antics of some performers – ranging from Jerry Lewis to the central character played by Ricky Gervais in the television series *The Office* (2001–2003) – are well-established sources of cringe-making embarrassment for some if not all viewers.[5] A format such as romantic comedy can also offer substantial basis for viewer alignment and allegiance with protagonists, the comic dimension being mixed with a dramatic or melodramatic modality, as in an example such as *Sleepless in Seattle* (1993). In cases such as this, the two modalities tend to work closely together and smoothly to be integrated.

Comic and other modalities can also clash, however, which brings us back to the territory of the comedy of discomfort.

A useful conceptual tool with which to pin down the specific mechanisms of any instances of comedy, or that which pushes at its borders, is provided by Jerry Palmer's notion of comedy as comprising a logic of the absurd.[6] Comedy, for Palmer, involves a particular balance between elements of the logical and the absurd. An element of absurdity marks out comedy as different from the non-comic norm. This often results from incongruity of some kind, another concept that helps to identify the bases of many varieties of comedy. Not all absurdity or incongruity results in comedy, however. To fall into the realm of comedy, Palmer suggests, the absurd needs to be mixed with a requisite quota of logic. Without sufficient logic, the result may be a variety of absurdity that lacks comedy. This is likely to be experienced more generally as nonsense (non-sense), odd, strange, weird or the sometimes capitalized and/or existential Absurd associated with certain artistic movements, particularly in theatre and literature. A certain degree of logical plausibility is required for comedy to result, in this account, a basis in reasonable possibility that is only rendered absurd up to a point, the exact nature of which can be examined in any individual instance. As I suggest in my book *Film Comedy*: 'Many forms of comedy-through-incongruity can be understood in this way. Substitution of objects often results in a form of incongruity in which implausibility outweighs, but does not entirely displace, plausibility.'[7] I cite the example of Chaplin's character seeming to eat his shoe in a celebrated sequence in *The Gold Rush* (1925). A shoe is not a suitable object for consumption, and so the act is absurd and unreal; yet the character is starving and acts *as if* the components of the shoe were edible, 'persisting in a sustained engagement that is logical in its own terms.'[8]

Mixing modalities

Comedy is bounded on either side, in this schema, by excesses of either absurdity or logic, although the exact parameters are likely to vary according to the orientation of the viewer. Too absurd and the result is a greater lack of sense, less likely to fall into the realm of comedy. Too logical and not enough difference from the norm is provided to provoke comic effects such as those based on incongruity or otherwise.[9] Excess logic is likely to result in the creation of a more serious interpretive modality that might entail a failure of comedy, if intended, and/or the production of responses including offence or embarrassment.[10] In the latter cases, the material might be taken more seriously than is intended, a frequent source of controversy over certain types of comedy. Such dimensions are not always so easily separated out, however. The examples already considered in this book involve a blend of potentially comic and more seriously discomforting material, often intentionally so.

The degree of discomfort on offer might seem to disqualify much of this from the realm of comedy, or any simple notion of comedy, but the seriously discomforting and the comic can coexist. The comic element might, in such circumstances, ameliorate awkwardness or anxiety, but it can also heighten the overall impression of discomfort that results, particularly if deployed in a manner that leaves the viewer uncertain how to take the material.

A central pleasure of comedy, in its more mainstream-conventional or clear cut usages, appears to be rooted in its function as a way of underlining the non-serious implications of the material in question. Comedy of this kind is, by definition, generally not meant to be taken seriously or to create substantial discomfort. It is, in this sense, the opposite of the type of cinema examined in this book: one of the archetypal forms of 'light relief' and 'entertainment' rather than 'heavyweight' challenge. This remains broadly the case even if, in practice, comedy is often mixed with more melo-dramatic components. An element of comedy is one way of allowing viewers to enjoy certain kinds of fictional activities without encouragement to worry (or to worry much) about any potentially questionable implications. This can be the case across the whole of a broadly comic text. Such a function is highlighted by the more proximate provision of scenes that offer specific *comic relief* from whatever tensions might be created by other material. The familiar comic one-liner that follows action sequences in certain varieties of action-oriented cinema is a good example. A joke made at such a point is a way of underlining that the preceding material, which might include assorted forms of destruction, is not meant to be taken too seriously.[11] Comedy of this kind might blur more generally into the texture of a work that mixes comic and relatively more serious modalities, or might be limited to isolated moments.

The comedy of discomfort is what can result when such modalities are blurred in certain ways, particularly when viewers are not given clear signals of how they are meant to respond: when it is unclear whether a moment of comedy marks a relieving distance from more serious implications or not; when the viewer might experience an irresolvable combination of the two. This is a specific variant of the broader tendency examined in this book for discomfort to be created by the reduction or removal of clear signifiers of tone or indications of preferred emotional response (in television comedy, a key element can be the absence of the prompt provided by a recorded laughter track). The comedy of discomfort, in my terms, can be seen in the context of longer traditions of tragicomedy in the arts, from earlier dramatic roots to the theatre and literature of the absurd that flourished in the 1950 and 1970s. The latter invites a response of both laughter and tears, often mixed or uncertain, also frequently interpreted in a context of a broadly modern or more specifically post–Second World War loss of faith in traditional sources of meaning.[12]

The relative balance between the comic and the more serious remains widely variable. Broadly mainstream comedy often includes significant elements of more serious or substantial modality as a matter of unexceptional routine, as suggested above. Shifts between the two can also be more jarring, even where comedy might still seem to defuse the impact of more serious material, as in examples such as Martin McDonagh's *In Bruges* (2008) and *Three Billboards Outside Ebbing, Missouri* (2017) or Bong Joon Ho's *Mother* (*Madeo*, 2009) and *Parasite* (*Gisaengchung*, 2019). To varying degrees absurdly awkward, farcical and comically exaggerated characters are sources of discomfort in many of the films of Mike Leigh, often rubbing up against that which seems more pitiful or tragic, in examples including *High Hopes* (1988) and *Secrets and Lies* (1996). Painful or awkward comedy is also found in television, particularly in niche channels, notable examples including *Curb Your Enthusiasm*, as examined by Kotsko, and *The Office*. I have written at some length elsewhere about the blurring of modalities in the mixing of certain forms of comedy and violence, the latter sometimes dark and disturbing.[13] In this concluding chapter, the emphasis is on the blending of elements of comedy and material that is awkward or discomforting in less heightened or extreme territory, in keeping with the general focus of the book. Two main examples are examined: *The Comedy* (2012), a low-budget American indie film directed and co-written by Rick Alverson, and *Tony Erdmann* (2016), written and directed by Maren Ade, a Germany/Austria/Monaco/Romania/France/Switzerland co-production that gained higher profile in the international arthouse arena. In each case, sufficiently awkward material is offered to make neither a clear cut case of comedy other than of a discomforting variety.

A comedy?

Whether or not Alverson's *The Comedy* merits the label it gives itself in the title is decidedly open to question. One of the primary sources of discomfort offered by the film is that the viewer is given little indication how exactly its material should be interpreted, particularly whether or not it should be taken in any way at face value, sincerely, or as an ironic presentation. The result, even more so than *Palindromes*, examined in Chapter 2, is a work the discomfort of which has potential to extend to, or be heightened for, many members of what might be taken to be typical indie-filmgoing constituencies. The principal character, Swanson (played by the comedy performer Tim Heidecker), is a singularly awkward, materially privileged white figure who participates in an orgy of cringeworthily inappropriate behaviour. Like a greatly exaggerated and looser-tongued version of Edward, in the latter's attempts to act in a more inclusive manner with Rose in *Archipelago*,

Swanson imposes himself with painful awkwardness on those who are paid to provide services, among other sources of inappropriate activity. He picks up a shovel and strips off his shirt, for example, to join a pair of Latino gardeners working on the grounds of the house next door to that of his wealthy father, whose lingering death he appears to be awaiting in a period of slacker-like limbo. He joins them briefly in their labour, initially without any comment, seemingly blithely unaware of the discomfort caused by this inappropriate and self-indulgent playing at the crossing of class and ethnic lines. When the owners of the house come by discussing the garden, he acts as if he is the chief of the crew, discomforting the couple by asking if it is OK for himself and the workers to use the swimming pool (which would be another transgression of lines), after which he wanders away.

Swanson provokes deep discomfort later in the film to a cab driver, in a similar act of self-indulgence, offering more and more cash until the driver is pressured by the absurdity of the amount (eventually $400) into conceding to his request to take a turn at the wheel. What is a passing indulgence to Swanson is, as the driver suggests, how the latter makes his living – not something suitably to be toyed with in so crassly insensitive a manner. The peak (or trough?) of such awkwardness comes in a sequence in which Swanson visits a bar in a predominantly black neighbourhood, asking if the business is hiring. He could attract a different clientele, he suggests, offering some 'diversity' by bringing his friends to visit and spend a lot of money, a comment that seems deeply inappropriate and is painful to witness. Swanson suggests he is trying to 'explore', to be 'cool', to get out of his own 'comfort zone', the latter something he manifestly provides for the likely viewer (Figure 28). Figures such as those in the bar stereotype *him*, he adds, this burst of inappropriateness being followed by the cringe-making question 'where your fuckin' bitches, man' and the observation that he wants to 'fuck some fuckin' black ass'.

Swanson makes some allusions to understanding that the locals work hard and have 'a lot of history', but this is all highly awkward, a manifestation of character likely to be deeply unsympathetic to the audience for such a film. Earlier observations with racist connotations are even more objectionable in themselves, if any of this is taken at face value. Many people from other countries, such as Bangladesh, do not have conscious thought, Swanson observes, talking to a woman at a party: an appallingly ethnocentric notion if to be treated at all seriously. Some deserve to have better lives than others, he adds, having been picked for such a fate by God. He is not a racist, he claims, there being 'black guys' who deserve it as much as white guys. He is not a Nazi, he subsequently declares, after suggesting that Hitler 'had ideas' and 'deserves a *little* credit', if the murder is taken out of the equation, for being 'like a male cheerleader for his own people', a figure whom he adds, incongruously, also suffered from horrible indigestion.

FIGURE 28 *Cringe-making: Swanson 'trying to get out of his comfort zone' in the bar scene in* The Comedy *(2012).*

How the viewer is meant to take such material is left open. It seems unlikely that many actual viewers of the film will believe such lines to reflect the opinions of the filmmakers, so strongly do they contradict the norms of the institutionalized indie sector. To laugh along *with* Swanson in some of his physical or verbal antics would be expected to be a highly uncomfortable position for most of those likely to see the film. To share in a joke is, effectively, to take on a position of complicity with the values it expresses, comedy being a fundamentally social phenomenon, creating what would in this case be likely to be an unwanted allegiance. It is for this reason that a dilemma is presented to the non-racist, for example, by any racist joke that might be considered to be funny, in its own terms (drawing on a wider racist substructure of ideas and attitudes), as well as being outwardly offensive. That such a combination of qualities is possible, rather than the one excluding the other by definition, is itself a discomforting prospect, liable to provoke rejection or repulsion. The latter seems most likely to be the dominant response to many of Swanson's routines in *The Comedy*, although an additional level of discomfort might result from the fact that the status of much of the material as intended comically remains unclear.

Is Swanson meant to be interpreted as an approximation of a rounded or broadly realistic character, a flawed individual who speaks and behaves in such a manner and poses a challenge to the viewer on this basis? This would give a logical dimension to his behaviour and seems more plausible a reading than one in which the viewer was expected to share his perspective, particularly given that many of his antics appear to be fuelled by alcohol. Other sequences create room for some sympathetic engagement, although this is understated, creating a moody, even at times mournful impression of his character. Plenty of scope exists, however, for such material to be read ironically, as a blank form of satire, tease or absurd pranksterism. Surely, we might think, this character is at least partly a wind-up, a provocation to the liberal-oriented viewer, founded on the assumption that such behaviour is well beyond the bounds of the acceptable for anyone who has been socialized into decent values?

Blurring lines between irony and sincerity

The lack of any clear answer to such questions remains a major source of the film's ability to discomfort, a quality it has in this respect in common with many others examined in this book. That this was the conscious intention of the filmmakers is suggested in the commentary on the DVD release provided by Alverson and Heidecker, the former describing the film as deliberately seeking to blur the line between the ironic and the sincere, with the intention of destabilizing the orientation of the viewer.[14] In certain respects Swanson could be imagined to function something like the caricatures depicted by Sacha Baron Cohen: blatant and often uncomfortable-to-watch provocateurs such as Ali G., Borat and Bruno, deployed to spur reactions from real-life individuals. The difference is that any such status is unclear in *The Comedy*, uncomfortably mixed with signifiers of more substantial fictional characterization, thus blurring the lines between any fictional-logical dimension (rooted in plausible character) and the absurd (over-the-top, ironic rhetoric). During the bar sequence, Swanson says he is 'trying to be honest' with the clientele, but is he? Is this a sincere attempt at engagement? Are his most crass comments meant to be ironic play? This seems probable in at least some cases but it remains difficult to tell. The fact that they could be interpreted as being intended this way by the character seems unlikely to lessen the discomfort of the occupants of the bar, or that experienced by the viewer. Similarly, Swanson tells the taxi driver that he respects him, but his conduct again suggests otherwise.

An element of parallel with figures such as those of Baron Cohen might be suggested by the fact that Swanson is performed by Heidecker, a comedian and comic actor, best known for work in which he is partnered with Eric Wareheim, who appears as one of his friends in the film. Heidecker and Wareheim perform as the duo 'Tim and Eric' in online and television series including *Tim and Eric Awesome Show, Great Job!* (2007–17) and the feature *Tim and Eric's Billion Dollar Movie* (2012). This is not 'a Tim and Eric movie', however, as Heidecker says, neither performing their existing varieties of comic personae in the film.[15] The established Tim and Eric recipe involves broad, zany, oddball and sometimes deliberately awkward material but in an unambiguously silly/absurd comic mode. Their characters and interactions with others in *The Comedy* draw more closely on their own personal qualities, according to the DVD commentary, although this is another area in which the location remains ambiguous. This dimension of the film is a product of a production practice akin to that employed by Joanna Hogg, in which only a brief outline script was apparently provided, without any dialogue, leaving the performers to improvise their routines within certain given parameters.[16]

Swanson's behaviour tends to provoke a mixture of blank bafflement, discomfort, anger or uncertain laughter from those with whom he interacts in the film. When he asks inappropriate questions of a male nurse tending to his father, the latter reacts blankly and without any comment. A similar, largely absent response comes from one of the gardeners. The taxi driver is clearly discomforted by the offer of money, increasingly so when asked to sit in the back of the vehicle when Swanson drives, subsequently provoked to a more outrightly angry reaction when the latter stops and tries to pick up a woman for sex.

Swanson's comments in the bar prompt reactions ranging from the appearance of impatience to bemused head-shaking and sceptical laughter. The woman with whom Swanson talks at the party responds with laughter that suggests a mixture of shocked amusement and disbelief within the diegesis akin to that likely to be experienced by the viewer. At another point he does a mocking, distanced impression from the perspective of a southern slave-owning family, making references to 'slave meat' and 'slave skin'. The silence of the woman to whom this is addressed, subsequently identified as his sister-in-law, appears to suggest a discomfort not assuaged by any acceptably comic dimension, as continues to be the case when he includes offensive sexual slurs. A shift then occurs into what seems a more sincere mode of engagement, as he begins to ask her about visiting his brother, who appears to be imprisoned, but this, too, leads into inappropriate sexual comments that drive her away.

Among various antics, Swanson and two of his friends behave in a boorish and obnoxious manner in the back of another cab. They sing loudly in an approximation of hip-hop style that the driver will not be getting a tip, because he does not have a radio able to play the music they request. Visiting a church, they extinguish prayer candles, slide up and down and clamber over pews and engage in mockery of religious style incantation. They act, that is, like overgrown (Swanson reports his age as thirty-five) spoilt adolescents. Worshippers are glimpsed in the church but only from behind, increasing perhaps the role of any discomfort experienced by the viewer in this case as stand-in for that located within the diegesis. There are some sequences in which the discourse seems more easily interpreted as part of a non-serious and more clearly comic-absurd routine, particularly when it involves Swanson and his friends rather than his interactions with others. An exchange in which he and another discuss the relatively greater cleanliness of poor people, ending with comments about the 'dicks' of hobos, seems clearly marked as a riff between two figures engaging in absurd banter as part of an implicitly contractual agreement, even if presented in a straight manner. This is a situation very different from many of Swanson's engagements with strangers (the character involved here is played by another comedian with whom Heidecker has worked elsewhere, Gregg Turkington, who performs under the stage name Neil Hamburger).

There remains enough in the film to encourage the viewer not simply to adopt a distanced, critical or ironic attitude to the material. Moments that seem to invite a more sincere engagement with Swanson, as an in some ways troubled or uncertain figure, include a later sequence in a hospital. He wanders part of the building, entering the rooms of two sleeping elderly patients. In the first, he just looks, rather blankly, at the woman occupant. In the second, he touches the face of an elderly man and carefully combs his hair, in what appears to be a sincere act of kindness and care. A nurse enters the room, assuming his presence is legitimate and indicating that he can stay. At this point it is Swanson, for once, who seems somewhat discomforted, glancing from one side to another in apparent uncertainty before remaining in the room. A quiet theme comes up on the soundtrack as the camera pans across a number of pictures of the patient's family on the wall, adding to the sense that something tentatively heartfelt is implied.

A more conventional piece of comic business follows soon after, when Swanson amuses a waitress at the restaurant where he has taken work as a dishwasher – a foray into employment he clearly does not need for financial reasons – by brushing his teeth and then applying the brush to his beard and attempting to insert it into his nose (earlier, he engages in more typically awkward banter with the waitress, although she gives as good as she gets in the encounter). *The Comedy* refuses to settle into a comfortable register overall, however, when we then join Swanson and the waitress on a yacht. A romantic mood is broken when she has a convulsive fit, during the quite sustained length of which Swanson watches her blankly. Eventually, a cut is made abruptly to him returning her to the shore and brief exchanges as they part. Whether or not Swanson's behaviour is appropriate here, or in the period that is omitted, is left open to speculation. The film does not take the opportunity that might more mainstream-conventionally be available to use this situation to underline any more positive approach to its protagonist.

Formal proximity

Formally, nothing is done to mark the material of the film as ironically intended. If anything, the opposite impression is created at this level. Alverson adopts an often close-shot, slightly unstable handheld visual style that tends to imply emotional proximity to character. Interactions are often shot at head-and-shoulders or closer scale in shallow focus, with backgrounds rendered blurry, an approach that implies broadly close alignment with the protagonists, including Swanson. This seems particularly to be the case in some lingering quiet moments that focus closely on his face and so have potential to offer the kind of emotional contagion detailed by Plantinga (an intensity of focus on his features is created by the blurring of background detail, as seen in Figure 28). His face tends to remain blank in such instances. This seems to lean towards implying an existential emptiness on the part of the character, and so a dimension of sincere engagement with what is figured as a personal-emotional experience, rather than the absence that might signify the deployment of a more shallowly absurd/ironic construct or caricature.

No use is made of the blank style more characteristic of many of the examples examined above or any other framing that might imply a more critically or ironically distanced attitude to the proceedings. While blank distance contributes to the creation of discomfort in many films, *The Comedy* demonstrates how it can also be generated by an unmarked form of proximity to such behaviour. If a closer visual articulation might offer a more thorough processing of the material, which might in many cases be somewhat less uncomfortable, as suggested in some instances above, any mitigation seems absent in a case such as this, in which the viewer is left without any other guidance on how exactly to take such awkward material. To bring the viewer closer, in this case, in broadly more mainstream-conventional terms, including the occasional use of music that contributes a moody or mournful impression relating to Swanson, is likely to generate discomfort on the basis of both awkward proximity and uncertainty of modality (although without the more pronounced discomfort of the heightened, claustrophobically excessive closeness found in some examples such as *Mother!* cited in Chapter 1).

Scope exists to read the central character of *The Comedy* not as a heartless and/or obnoxiously entitled figure (whether as monster or prankster) but as one whose social situation, although privileged, has rendered him directionless and lacking a sense of his proper role in life. This might explain his attempts – however inappropriate, cringe-making and lacking respect for others – to try out activities or forms of contact not typical for someone of his background, in some cases to attempt to forge what might be a genuine connection through participation. Swanson could be situated, in this sense, in the broader contexts of contemporary modernity evoked earlier in this book, lacking clearly defined or meaningful roots and experimenting, however crassly most of the time, with other ways of being. Grounds exist for such an interpretation, one strongly supported in Heidecker and Alverson's DVD commentary. Alverson refers to exactly this kind of undermining of traditional pillars such as family and religion, leaving many occupying 'an amorphous, ephemeral kind of place', in this case a specifically American-suburban version of the contemporary modernity theses outlined in Chapter 1.

The specific setting of the film in the Williamsburg neighbourhood of Brooklyn is relevant here, the area being known as a hotbed of gentrification and hipster lifestyle. This gives the location strong links to a prominent dimension of indie film culture, while also being bordered by zones including Greenpoint, with a large Polish American community, and Bedford-Stuyvesant, which has a substantial African American population. It is in the latter that Swanson has his encounter in the bar while one scene not included in the final cut involved an interaction with two elderly visiting Polish figures. In their DVD commentary, Alverson and Heidecker highlight a distinction between the cultural traditions of such populations and what the latter terms the 'flimsy, temporal' focus of the suburban American culture embodied by Swanson and his friends. No explicit grounds for any so specific reading are provided in the film itself, however, beyond the identification of the Williamsburg setting, another of the various ways in which it leaves the viewer to ponder what might be made of the material.

The tonal uncertainty of *The Comedy* is untypical of Alverson's other films of the time, which tend towards a more unambiguously sincere evocation of a quiet sense of character alienation. Poor-taste jokes also feature in *Entertainment* (2015), grimly delivered by a comedian (Greg Turkington) during a tour of bleak southwestern landscapes in a darkly moody film. A similarly sombre tone is found in *The Builder* (2010) and *New Jerusalem* (2011), each of which leans towards what can be seen as an irony-free existentialist dimension. The former focuses on what appears to be a failing attempt by its protagonist to build his own wooden cabin, pioneer-authentic style, in upstate New York. The latter features a figure recently returned from a support role to the military in Afghanistan, caught between the uncertainties of anxiety attacks that date back to his teenage years and the Christian dogma offered with sincerity by a co-worker. As works that exist towards the prickly-uncomfortable end of the indie scale, the films of Alverson can be located alongside others of the post-millennial period including those of Joel Potrykus, whose *Ape* (2012) is another to feature an awkward, struggling comedian. Further examples include Ronald Bronstein's *Frownland* (2007), a claustrophobic study in troubled central character unease, and Mary Bronstein's *Yeast* (2008), a similarly low-budget-oppressive feature, the maddening main protagonist of which is played by the director. Additional sources of often cringe-making discomfort are found in many of the films associated with the 'mumblecore' tendency of ultra-low-budget filmmaking from the mid-2000s onwards, particularly the work of Joe Swanberg and Andrew Bujalski.[17]

Pranks against neoliberalism in *Toni Erdmann*

If an element of provocative pranksterism might be involved in *The Comedy*, either by the filmmaker or Swanson or some combination of the two, a more overt variation is found in *Toni Erdmann*. The latter offers plenty of discomforting moments for its characters and/or viewer but is generally less challenging specifically because the process is more explicit and given an overt thematic connection with issues relating to the background of life within neoliberal capitalism. The two main protagonists are Ines (Sandra Hüller), a management consultant, and her father, Winfried (Peter Simonischek), a practical joker who is seeking to renew closer contact with his daughter while she is attempting to finalize a deal in Romania. Winfried's status as a prankster is established from the opening sequence, in which he leaves a delivery man uncomfortably bemused after claiming that a parcel is meant for his brother, whom he impersonates and claims recently to have been released from prison for sending mail bombs.

After the death of his dog, Winfried pays a surprise (shock) unannounced visit to Ines in Bucharest. He proceeds on numerous occasions to provoke discomfort for Ines and others by mingling at various events with those for whom she works either directly or indirectly. These include an important client, Henneberg (Michael Wittenborn), to whom Winfried jokes that he has hired a substitute daughter because Ines is hardly at home any more. Winfried is, from the perspective of Ines, a nightmare version of the embarrassing parent. Having supposedly gone home after one set of awkward encounters and difficult silences, Winfried reappears, bursting abruptly into the frame in one sequence in a 'disguise' consisting of a long-haired wig and buck teeth, the latter worn at times earlier in the film (Figure 29). From this point, Ines appears to remain uncomfortable and unhappy about his presence but also plays along to some extent, talking with him in his new character, that of a supposed businessman, consultant and life coach. Her patience is further tested, leading to additional bemusement, upset and exasperation, when Winfried-as-Toni manages to inveigle himself into conversations with her immediate boss, Gerald (Thomas Loibl). He also hides in her closet at one point, terrifying her on discovery, and handcuffs the pair of them together afterwards, without having the key, jeopardizing her attendance at an important meeting.

Discomfort is often generated within the diegesis by uncertainty about whether Winfried is being serious or not, although he quite often declares himself only to be joking, making this issue explicitly negotiated in a manner that is not the case in *The Comedy*. A clear thematic dimension is presented in the context of the excessive work ethic of Ines. Winfried's mission is to establish a more human level of contact with a daughter whose

FIGURE 29 *Winfried bursts into the frame in his Toni disguise, startling Ines, in* Toni Erdman *(2016).*

characteristic activity is constantly to be distracted from any other ties by the work-related demands coming via her phone or elsewhere. She has, it seems, almost no time for anything else, a topic on which he challenges her, at one point asking: 'Are you really a human?' In addition to any general implicit commentary about the pressures created by the contemporary workplace, this is put into a more specifically neoliberal capitalist context by the nature of the employment in which Ines is involved. The consultancy for which she works is advising a Romanian oil company to outsource its maintenance functions, a classically neoliberal process that, as she explains to Winfried, will result in the transfer of many workers to another company and their eventual redundancy. This is also situated within the specific context of the recent accession of Romania, a potential source of lower-cost labour, to the European Union, along with comments by Ines that champion the benefits of an 'international way of thinking' (that is, in this version, neoliberal globalization) that is less likely to benefit those on the margins. Ines recommends a strategy in which the consultants suggest a radical option of larger-scale outsourcing, in an attempt to get Henneberg to accept their more modest preference. This backfires, however, when Henneberg goes for the radical option. The implication is that the manoeuvering of Ines will be directly responsible for more job losses. The viewer is given a small portrait of the kinds of figures who will take the fall, in a sequence in which Ines and Winfried-as-Toni visit an oilfield that will be 'modernized' as part of the process and the latter has an encounter with one of the locals.

Ines is situated as an active cog in the neoliberal capitalist machine, even if her harried state can also be attributed to the demands of the corporate system on those involved in the implementation of its strategies (plus the specific pressures faced by a woman working in a strongly male-dominated business context). The structure of sympathy offered by the film seems evenly mixed between the two protagonists. The viewer is encouraged to share much of the awkwardness and discomfort experienced by Ines as a result of the behaviour of her father, but also to understand his motivation, if not necessarily his tactics. Winfried is unusual, among the work examined in this book, in being a primary source of discomforting behaviour the nature of which is given a sympathetic and purposeful rationale. The style of the film, with a generally slightly unstable handheld quality, does not favour one character over the other, often involving mid shots of the pair or editing that is generally equal in the establishment of positions of relative alignment and allegiance. A sequence in a bar after Winfried's arrival in Bucharest, for example, features the two awkwardly seated together in mid-shot scale, approximately from the waist upwards. Ines is unhappy, having in previous conversation with colleagues given away more than she should have done about the purpose of her work for the oil company. She is closer to the camera, in profile, while Winfried faces it, creating a broad equivalence of access: her greater proximity seems balanced by his fuller-face presentation. When Ines asks how long he plans to stay, Winfried says he has taken a month off work (as a school teacher). She look at him and then away, repeating the moves before pulling back in her seat. 'That was real fear', comments Winfried, his initially straight face breaking into laughter, after which silence is held for several beats. The viewer seems to be encouraged to have sympathy here for both: for Ines, on the basis of her preceding gaffe (if not necessarily what is involved in the outsourcing process itself) and the discomfort caused to her by Winfried; for him on the basis of his attempt to connect more closely with his daughter and the chasm implied by the comment about 'real fear'.

An element of some reconciliation is also implied, if tentatively. Ines appears on occasion to find her father's antics amusing, particularly in his incarnation as Toni. A significant moment of sincere emotional display results from one sequence that begins in a more characteristically discomforting manner, during a visit to the apartment of a woman to whom Winfried claims to be the German ambassador. Having introduced Ines as his secretary and pushed her into a distinctly uncomfortable participation in decorating an egg as part of an Easter ritual, Winfried raises the embarrassment stakes by declaring to the gathered company of strangers that he and Ines will perform a song for them. Ines stands in an initially sustained silence as Winfried cues her on piano to sing 'The Greatest Love of All', best known for its recording by Whitney Houston, to which he alludes. Any widening rift or refusal that might be anticipated recedes, however, as Ines begins to sing and continues with an increasing sincerity and commitment of engagement. In the context, her rendition gives the power ballad's potentially cheesy lyrics about 'learning to love yourself' a real emotional heft within the diegesis, and potential application to herself. After finishing to applause, she exits the apartment rapidly, leaving Winfried looking concerned, but the sequence implies a rare if indirect instance of outward emotional expression on her part.

What appears to be stronger evidence that her father has got through to her to some extent comes when Ines hosts a brunch party for her birthday. Her colleagues are invited, after Gerald asks her to do something to improve team spirit. A ready offering to sacrifice a personal occasion to such a corporate purpose appears to be another example of the dominance of her work over any private or family life. On the day, however, having initially answered the door to one guest while dressed only in her underpants, after struggling to remove a tight dress as the doorbell rang, she ends up declaring the event to be a naked party and only allowing attendance by those prepared to strip. Plenty of discomfort ensues for the two guests who subsequently arrive and stay, followed by the appearance of Winfried, now hidden in a startlingly absurd giant Bulgarian folk costume. Ines seems to have joined her father in what appears to be a provocative form of individual rebellion (even if recuperated by an initially discombobulated Gerald, who comments, approvingly: 'Hardcore! So hardcore!', Figure 30). Winfried leaves after not saying a word to reveal or confirm his identity, followed down the street by Ines, acting impulsively, it is implied, wearing only a thin robe, after which the two engage in a prolonged hug. In a subsequent scene back home in Germany, we discover that Ines has quit her job. This is a rebellion of sorts, the viewer having been shown earlier that Gerald went back on a promise

FIGURE 30 *'Hardcore! So Hardcore!'* Gerald's reaction to Winfried's giant Bulgarian folk costume during the nude party in Toni Erdman *(2016).*

that her period in Romania would be short-lived, although she has taken on a new two-year post in Singapore that sounds as if it is for a similar kind of enterprise.

In the final scene of the film, after the funeral of his mother, Winfried returns to the subject he has raised earlier of what makes life worth living. How are we supposed to hang on to individual moments, he asks, when the focus is often on getting things done? He recalls memories of Ines as a child but suggests it is impossible to do so in the moment itself. Ines reaches into his shirt pocket to don his buck teeth, also putting on an old-fashioned hat belonging to her grandmother. She smiles. Winfried goes to get a camera to preserve what seems a key moment of contact. She moves a little then stands still and wipes her eyes. The moment lingers, as do many in the film, and in the cinema of discomfort more generally, before she removes the hat and teeth and, it seems, the connection is lost. A mid shot is held, her face generally inexpressive, and a cut to black ends the film before her father's return. Winfried's speech is another sequence shown with characteristically even access to the two characters, this time in a series of alternating waist-upwards shots and reverse shots of their standing figures. His words might dominate but equal prominence is given to the expressions of each.

Toni Erdmann, then, offers a more overt processing of its material than is found in *The Comedy*. Acts of pranksterism and joking are marked as such, and put to work to explicit thematic purpose. We know Winfried is joking (even if the characters do not always), if sometimes with a more serious intent, and we know why. The film as a whole is, as a result, likely to be significantly less discomforting than *The Comedy*, giving the viewer a clearer steer on how to interpret both the on-screen activity and any wider social implications it might have, a quality it shares with Östlund's *The Square*. This is the case despite the fact that it does not offer anything close to a full reconciliation, even at the individual level, either between Ines and her father or Ines and her role within the neoliberal capitalist system. *Toni Erdmann* offers the viewer a clear sense of interpretive frames within which to situate its material, which makes it less likely to discomfort in a strong sense, even if these highlight difficult aspects of the contemporary lives of characters of a particular social status. The challenge of *The Comedy* is that of a greater overall awkwardness of modality and approach.

Neither film is really a comedy in a conventional or straightforward sense, as might be expected given their inclusion in this volume. Each includes plenty of material that might be taken to be joking at the diegetic level, although as we have seen this is less clearly signposted in *The Comedy*. How far any of the material in either is likely to generate a comedy response for the viewer is likely to vary, especially in *The Comedy*. The film has potential to generate disliking or offence for some; for its logic of the absurd to seem imbalanced on reception in favour of taken-seriously repulsion. This is the case for a minority of viewer responses posted in two samples I have examined, on

Rotten Tomatoes and Amazon (the largest basis on which it is rejected by those posting negative reviews is the familiar and less specific accusation from detractors of such films that it is 'boring' rather than offensive).[18] Some find the film comic, at least in parts, while the majority opinion among enthusiasts appears to be that the title is primarily intended ironically. A number of reviewers wrestle with their own responses, in a manner similar to that seen in some earlier chapters, particularly in balancing bases of admiration – such as a reading of the film as a critique of hipster culture or as a broader portrait of existential emptiness – with the degree of discomfort entailed by the process of watching. To cite just one example: 'Occasionally disturbing, sometimes unbearable, frequently painful, and almost always uncomfortable, Alverson has directed the equivalent of torture porn for the overly empathetic.'[19] It is, this reviewer adds, echoing one of the responses to *Archipelago* cited in the previous chapter, the definition of a 'one-time only film': 'I couldn't be bribed to watch it again.'

Toni Erdmann is a film *about* certain uses of comedy or joking as much as a comedy in itself, in the sense that Winfried offers a personal strategy of joking as an attempt to break through impersonal routines and establish new forms of individual contact. The viewer is liable to be divided in response: between any amusement prompted by his behaviour and sympathy for his goal, and the sharing of any diegetic discomfort that results on the part of Ines or others. This is not an issue generally addressed explicitly in reviews posted on Rotten Tomatoes and Amazon, although some of those who respond positively do so on the basis of qualities such as 'complexity' or 'subtlety', within which such a sharing of sympathies might be located.[20] As to where the film sits within the scale drawn upon above from Jerry Palmer, reactions vary entirely across the scale. Many find the film to be broadly comical while some reject it as entirely unfunny. A number suggest the film is 'weird' or 'bizarre' rather than comical, a judgment that is in some cases positive and in others negative. A substantial proportion of positive reviewers praise the combination highlighted in this chapter of the funny and the weird, strange, bizarre or the awkward and the uncomfortable.

In their mobilization towards a particular agenda, Winfried's pranks seem at times to combine a comic with something closer to a more disruptive absurdity, aimed if not at the challenging of neoliberal routines in themselves then at rescuing his daughter from total immersion in such a world. His wordless appearance in the giant Bulgarian costume has something of this less-comic absurdity, momentarily frightening to more than one character on first encounter. The further Winfried disguises himself – first teeth, then teeth and wig, then total disappearance into a faceless hairy giant – the more he perhaps succeeds in affecting Ines. The incongruity of the extreme outfit also has more immediately comic potential, however. It provokes general amusement rather than apparent disturbance among those who witness it when Winfried enters a park after leaving Ines at her apartment. The instant in which he makes his presence in the outfit known to a startled Gerald, behind whom he lurks, is at least one unambiguous laugh-out-loud moment in the film. If not likely to be as radically unsettling as *The Comedy*, *Toni Erdmann* offers its own sources of discomfort and irresolution.

Cruel optimism and the Berlin School

Toni Erdmann represents a return for Ade to overtly discomforting material akin to that found in her first feature, *The Forest for the Trees* (*Der Wald vor lauter Bäumen*, 2003), a lo-fi digital production that traces the painfully failed attempts of an idealistic newly qualified school teacher to make friends (effectively stalking a neighbour) or to control her classes. The central character, Melanie (Eva Löbau), appears to lack sufficient self-awareness, a source of much potential embarrassment for the viewer. Marco Abel suggests that the treatment of the relationship between the central young couple in Ade's second feature, *Everyone Else* (*Alle Anderen*, 2009), holidaying in Sardinia, indicates the damage inflicted by the contrary: their adoption of an ironic point of view as protection against the embarrassment that might result from more sincere engagement.[21] Both lack of distance from the self, in the one case, and ironic posturing, in the other, are seen as acting as a block to the achievement of sincerely desired connection. This is an impasse Abel situates within debates about the relationship between irony and sincerity, within the broader context of neoliberalism and post/modernism, considered in Chapter 1. *Toni Erdmann* might be read as a development from this position in its dramatization of a process of seeking to use an ironic stance as a way to provoke sincere engagement, although Lisa Haegele argues that a similar process is found in *Everyone Else*, contrary to Abel.[22] It is precisely through irony and performance, she suggests, that the couple are able to forge a deep emotional connection, particularly during an initially ironic feminized dance performance by the male character, Chris (Lars Eidinger), that contributes to the creation of their less gender-conventional relationship.

The relative fluidity of employment available to Ines in *Toni Erdmann* does not have the material precariousness faced by those on the receiving end of the neoliberal processes in which her work is implicated, as is suggested by her transition to another similar role at the end of the film. It might exact a price at the level of personal-emotional relations, however, as the film implies, akin to the contemporary condition diagnosed by Lauren Berlant as 'cruel optimism', another symptom of the world of neoliberal restructuring to add to those encountered in earlier chapters. Cruel optimism is, for Berlant, a state in which a desired object or goal (in this case, the success of Ines within the world of corporate strategy) is an obstacle to the flourishing of the individual.[23] This seems particularly applicable to Ines (the main film examples included by Berlant are from the work of Jean-Pierre and Luc Dardenne, in relation to figures at the lower end of the social scale, and Laurent Cantet, in a social sphere closer to that found in *Toni Erdmann*).

A connection between this concept and the films of Ade is made by Muriel Cormican, who argues that the filmmaker offers 'an aesthetic of embarrassment and awkwardness' that 'gives affective expression to cruel optimism'.[24] Discomfort, in this reading, is used to implicate viewers in the broader social context.[25] Berlant is also cited in relation to Ade by Hester Baer, in this case particularly what the former identifies as a 'situation tragedy' format that marks a departure from conventional forms of comedy.[26] In the more familiar territory of situation comedy, Berlant suggests, an individual 'whose world is not *too* destabilized by a "situation" that arises performs a slapstick maladjustment that turns out absurdly and laughably, without destroying very much'.[27] That is, what is involved here is a scenario in which the balance between the absurd and the logical remains within the scope of the broadly comic. In situation tragedy, by contrast, 'the subject's world is fragile beyond repair, one gesture away from losing all access to sustaining its fantasies: the situation threatens utter, abject unravelling.'[28] In the marriage between situation comedy and tragedy 'people are fated to express their flaws episodically, over and over, without learning, changing, being believed, becoming better, or dying'.[29] This formulation fails to note that repetition of character flaws without learning or change is also the basis of many classic instances of television sitcom, although usually within a comic modality that keeps at bay any such threat of more seriously coded dissolution.

The focus of these arguments is on Ade's female protagonists and they seem most strongly applicable to the cringe-making awkwardness of the central character in *The Forest for the Trees*. They appear less fully to account for the primary grounds of discomfort in *Toni Erdmann*, in which the main source of embarrassment and discomfort is rather different, in the deliberately provocative behaviour of Winfried. The emphasis of Cormican and Baer is specifically on the female gender politics of what is implied in Ade's approach, in her representation of white, middle-class women who fail or refuse to conform to certain norms enacted in more mainstream productions that present a neoliberal fantasy in which the goals of feminism are imagined sufficiently to have been achieved or be available at the level of supposed individual freedom. Both see this refusal as a source of discomfort for the viewer. For Baer, in the case of *The Forest for the Trees*, *Everyone Else* and other international examples including the films of Andrea Arnold and Kelly Reichardt: 'By creating discomfort and insecurity in the viewer, these films make palpable the paradoxes of neoliberalism.'[30] This might be arguable in broader terms, but I would suggest that discomfort also lies in the absence of any such explicit explanatory frame of reference, as is the case in some of the other cinemas examined in this book. If the palpable sense of discomfort might intellectually be read in relation to certain conditions of existence within the world of neoliberalism, it seems questionable whether any such connection is likely to be made by viewers of such work who do not engage in academic levels of textual interpretation. Neoliberalism might provide the context for an operative structure of feeling in such cases, along with other aspects of modernity evoked by the commentators cited above, but discomfort might be more likely to result from this *not* being clearly apparent to the majority of viewers.

In the case of *Toni Erdmann*, Cormican's broader point as far as discomfort is concerned might be extended from Ade's female characters to the behaviour of Winfried, although this is also open to question. The 'visceral effect' created by Ade's films, she suggests, 'is caused by the knowledge that this not only *could* be you but that it sometimes *should* be you.' She adds: 'We cringe because we recognize that we should be doing, perhaps sometimes, what these awkward characters are doing – refusing certain kinds of social interpellation, challenging certain social euphemisms, going off script.'[31] This, along with the account of Baer, is another version of the diagnosis of the production of discomfort as of critical social value, as seen in some arguments cited in Chapter 1. We might equally argue, however, that material that results in cringe-making discomfort for others – in this case including one of the principals, Ines, as well as the viewer – might have the opposite effect and tend to reinforce rather than to undermine social norms, as suggested more generally in Rowland Miller's analysis of embarrassment. The '*could* be you' evoked by Cormican seems if anything more likely to apply to the vicarious discomfort faced by the viewer, in response *to*, rather than in the enactment *of*, the refusal of more familiar-comfortable norms.

That is, in the throes of most of the moments of heightened discomfort, the viewer of *Toni Erdmann* might be more likely to feel with and for Ines, in her embarrassment, rather than with the perpetrator of the discomforting situation, even if the latter is given a broadly sympathetic rationale for his intervention. This might imply a vicarious sharing, in these moments, of her desire for the usual routine, and her ambitions, to be left uninterrupted (just as, in *The Forest for the Trees*, the viewer seems encouraged to crave some success for Melanie; some relief from the prevalent awkwardness of her failures in personal and professional life). The overall balance of sympathies might remain mixed, as I suggest above, but perhaps less so within the most awkward behaviour itself. How exactly this plays out might also depend on the extent to which any viewer is able to take active pleasure from the process of being discomforted or from having their own responses destabilized, as has been seen in some cases in previous chapters. Anyone who positively revels in the cringe of discomfort might be better positioned to experience such material as a source of critique to be embraced at this level – in the discomfort itself – as well as in more cognitive-rational interpretive terms, but this might not be a majority response even among the limited audience that exists for such work.

Ade's films can be situated in a broader German cinematic context, part of a second wave of what became known as the Berlin School of independent production. This is a movement, if loosely defined, that in some cases includes features in common with aspects of the cinema of discomfort (as well as broader art-cinema tendencies), including a favouring of flat, seemingly affectless modes of representation and openness to viewer interpretation.[32] Much of the work associated with the Berlin School, including the films of figures such as Christian Petzold, Angela Schanelec, Thomas Arslan, Christopher Hochhäusler, Valeska Grisebach and Ulrich Köhler, has been read as expressive of the lives of relatively ordinary characters under the alienating pressures created by contemporary neoliberalism, as experienced in the specific conditions of post-unification Germany.[33] It has also been situated in relation to similar tendencies in the wider arena of international art cinema, as in the case of Baer's reading of the films of Ade.[34] While including considerable variety, some of the work associated with the Berlin School entails characteristic art-cinema departures from the comforts provided by more classical/conventional cinematic regimes, as Abel and others suggest, although some of the filmmakers concerned, including Petzold, are noted for also working within more conventional genre frameworks.

Such departures include, for example, a refusal by Schanelec to use shot/reverse-shot style in the rendering of conversations that also feature the use of stilted language as an additional source of likely irritation to the viewer.[35] This is an example of the kind of frustration of familiar-conventional expectations at the formal level considered in Chapter 1, a denial of the variety of tension-reducing artistic practices identified by Arnheim. Notable examples are found in Schanelec's *Marseille* (2004). As the central character wanders through and observes the city, there are, as Inga Pollmann puts it, 'hardly any clues [to indicate] the spatiotemporal connection between shots', a source of likely disorientation for the viewer.[36] Her return to her home city of Berlin is, at first, entirely occluded in a cut from one shot to another. Commentators such as Abel and Lutz Koepnick interpret approaches such as this as further implicit sources of resistance to the demands of neoliberal regimes, a transformation imposed on the societies of both former East and West Germany, including their economy of more highly processed audio-visual attention.[37]

It is precisely at this formal level that Abel locates what he sees as the critical-political dimension of such work. The reality of contemporary life is not so much 'captured' by approaches such as those used by Schanelec, Abel argues, as *rendered sensible* through their effects on the viewer.[38] This includes an absence of more mainstream-conventional sources of cinematic comfort, as is more widely the case within various forms of art or indie cinema. The creation of discomfort can, indeed, be seen as a way of rendering sensible certain aspects of contemporary existence, having the potential to create bodily-experiential and emotional as well as cognitive effects that might have political implications without involving explicit engagement in such issues, the absence of the latter being a characteristic widely associated with the Berlin School. Abel's account is one of many analyses of art cinema that also claims a transformative impact on the viewer that might be more questionable, however, an issue I address more generally in relation to a range of such discourses in *Positioning Art Cinema*. Films of the Berlin School immerse the viewer in their images 'to affect us so that we may begin to resee and rehear – that is, to resense and rethink – our own relation to the world', Abel suggests.[39] The language in which this is expressed slips between that which often seems strongly determinist – for example, 'forcing viewers to engage the seemingly familiar as something unfamiliar'[40] – and partially more tentative suggestions such as the use of the phrase 'we may begin' in the quotation above. Some of the films included in this account might reasonably be said to have such potential at the textual level, in certain varieties of theoretical analysis, but a significant gap remains between this and any certainty we might have about actual transformative effects on viewers, collectively or individually.[41]

Ade's films are formally much more conventional than those of Schanelec and some of the others associated with the Berlin School that fit more strongly into the arguments of Abel. Their potential for discomfort generally lies more in character behaviour than audiovisual detachment or disorientation. They can also be located in a specific production context within the contemporary German industry, one that shares with some other examples examined above an emphasis on a small-scale, independent collective ethos that complicates any overly simplistic emphasis on the individual auteur filmmaker. Ade was co-founder of her own production company, Komplizen-Film, in 2000, through which she produced both her own work and that of many of her Berlin School contemporaries, one of a number of collaborative enterprises that offered particular support to women directors and producers in what remains a male-dominated wider film/media environment.[42] *Toni Erdmann* achieved far greater audience reach that most if not all other works associated with the Berlin School at the time, having premiered at the Cannes Film Festival, and enjoyed a high level of critical regard, the latter including a 93 per cent positive rating on the aggregation site Rotten Tomatoes. It possesses a number of the qualities requisite for critic and festival favourite status, having also gained the substantial publicity boost that accompanied an Oscar nomination for best foreign feature.

No consensus yet

The contrast between the industrial status of the two main examples considered in this closing chapter maps quite closely onto the differences in kind and degree of discomfort on offer in each case, further highlighting the importance of this dimension to the broader contexts in which such work is produced and made available for consumption. *Toni Erdmann* has awkward and challenging qualities, particularly when measured by mainstream standards, but distinctly less so than *The Comedy*. The latter has potential to create a more radically unsettling impression, including what many found to be queasily awkward sociopolitical resonances, less easily assimilated to more typical art or independent viewing positions. It offers more potential for the redoubling of awkwardness or the dwelling in discomfort advocated by Kotsko, as cited in Chapter 1, whether or not this appears as a form of social critique, or perhaps because any such judgement remains uncomfortably uncertain.

While the box-office performance of *Toni Erdmann* remained modest, a gross listed on Box Office Mojo of $1,479,387, that of *The Comedy* was a mere $41,113. *Toni Erdman* was distributed in the US market by the most art-cinema-leaning of the Hollywood studio speciality divisions, Sony Pictures Classics, opening in three theatres and achieving a maximum reach of 112. This is a position in the marketplace commensurate with its textual qualities; that is, at the smaller end of the larger institutional base constituted by distribution by a studio subsidiary. *The Comedy*, having had the benefit for its profile of a debut at Sundance, was opened in a single theatre by the smaller Tribeca Films, reaching a maximum of four, simultaneously being available via video-on-demand, an approach more typical of that used for smaller indie features.[43] The aggregate critical rating of *The Comedy* on Rotten Tomatoes is, unsurprisingly, much lower than that of *Toni Erdmann*, at 47 per cent positive. The website's 'critics consensus' text for the Ade film is that it 'pairs carefully constructed, three-dimensional characters in a tenderly funny character study that's both genuinely moving and impressively ambitious'. This might be taken to be a reasonably typical variety of arthouse endorsement for a film that can promise engagement in relatively mainstream-conventional terms within this sector.

It seems notable that no such verdict, either positive or negative, is offered for *The Comedy*. All that appeared in the equivalent section at the time of writing was the statement 'No consensus yet', which seems symptomatic of its more divisive status, even within the art/indie arena. The same can be said to some extent of many of the other films examined in this book, particularly in terms of the range of responses they generate from viewers. The production of potential for discomfort, at its strongest, tends, almost by definition, to be provocative and to resist consensus in broad terms. At the same time, however, like other products from the art and indie film sectors, the cinema of discomfort continues in many cases to offer more localized, critical and niche-audience consensus of its own: a comfort-with-discomfort for some that remains far from stable, as seen in some of the strained positive viewer responses cited in this book, but that offers an institutional basis from which filmmakers continue to offer discomfort, awkwardness and cringe-making embarrassment as sources of particular kinds of challenge, pleasure or mixtures of such experiences.

Notes

1. For two such examples in the Rotten Tomatoes sample, see Michael G, 30 January 2011, and Corey P, 1 February 2011.
2. Robert Hodge and David Tripp, *Children and Television: A Semiotic Approach* (Cambridge: Polity Press, 1986). What follows draws on my discussion of this in relation to comedy in King, *Film Comedy* (London: Wallflower Press, 2002).
3. King, *Film Comedy*.
4. See King, *Positioning Art Cinema*, 6.
5. See, for example, Steven Shaviro, *The Cinematic Body* (Minneapolis: University of Minneapolis Press, 1993), who suggests from the perspective of psychoanalytically based theory that to identify with a character such as those manifested by Lewis could be vicariously to face a distinctly uncomfortable prospect of schizophrenic fragmentation.
6. Jerry Palmer, *The Logic of the Absurd: On Film and Television Comedy* (London: BFI, 1987). For a longer account of this approach, see King, *Film Comedy*, 14–16.
7. King, *Film Comedy*, 14.
8. Ibid.
9. More background on theories of incongruity as a basis for comedy are found in King, *Film Comedy*, Introduction.
10. King, *Film Comedy*, 16.
11. For more on this, see King, *Film Comedy*, 172–9.
12. See, for example, Michael Bennett, *The Cambridge Introduction to Theatre and Literature of the Absurd* (Cambridge: Cambridge University Press, 2015), especially 11 and 19–20. Bennett identifies two major techniques used to create absurdity that overlap with some examples of the cinema of discomfort: a lack of exposition and a flattening of the narrative arc (19).
13. King, *Film Comedy*, 185–95.
14. 'Audio Commentary with Tim Heidecker and Director Rick Alverson', New Video Group DVD release, 2013.
15. *The Comedy*, audio commentary.
16. Ibid.
17. For more on mumblecore, see King, *Indie 2.0*, chapter 3.
18. The samples examined here are posted comments from a total of 4,434 user ratings on Rotten Tomatoes, starting at https://www.rottentomatoes.com/m/the_comedy/reviews?type=user, and 85 reviews posted on Amazon.

com, starting at https://www.amazon.com/Comedy-Tim- Heidecker/dp/ B009VS12L8/ref=sr_1_1?keywords=The+Comedy&qid=1559914259&s=gateway&sr=8-1, both accessed 7 June 2019.

19 David U, Rotten Tomatoes, 10 November 2012.
20 Samples are posted comments from a total of 6,196 user ratings on Rotten Tomatoes, starting at https://www.rottentomatoes.com/m/toni_erdmann/reviews?type=user, and 73 reviewers posted on Amazon.com, starting at https://www.amazon.com/Toni-Erdmann-Peter-Simonischek/product- reviews/B06X3W1DNZ/ref=cm_cr_dp_d_show_all_btm?ie=UTF8&reviewerType=all_revie ws, both accessed 7 June 2019.
21 Marco Abel, *The Counter-Cinema of the Berlin School* (Rochester, NY: Camden House, 2013), 270–2.
22 Lisa Haegele, 'Gender, Genre and the (Im)Possibilities Of Romantic Love in Derek Cianfrance's *Blue Valentine* (2010) and Maren Ade's *Everyone Else* (2009)', in Marco Abel and Jaimey Fisher (eds), *The Berlin School and Its Global Contexts: A Transnational Art Cinema* (Detroit, MI: Wayne State University Press, 2018), 69.
23 Lauren Berlant, *Cruel Optimism* (Durham, NC: Duke University Press, 2011).
24 Muriel Cormican, 'Willful Women in the Cinema of Maren Ade', *Camera Obscura*, vol. 33, no. 3 (2018): 108.
25 Cormican, 'Willful Women', 113.
26 Hester Baer, 'The Berlin School and Women's Cinema', in Abel and Fisher, eds, *The Berlin School and Its Global Contexts*.
27 Berlant, *Cruel Optimism*, 6.
28 Ibid.
29 Ibid., 176.
30 Baer, 'The Berlin School and Women's Cinema', 55.
31 Cormican, 'Willful Women', 115.
32 See Abel, *The Counter-Cinema of the Berlin School*, for a full account, although one that has very particular theoretical leanings of a broadly Deleuzian variety.
33 Abel, *The Counter-Cinema of the Berlin School*. See also Hester Baer, 'Affectless Economies: The Berlin School and Neoliberalism', *Discourse*, 35 (Winter 2013): 72–100.
34 See introduction and various contributions to Abel and Fisher, *The Berlin School and Its Global Contexts*, which identify parallels with numerous currents of art cinema from around the world.
35 Abel, *The Counter-Cinema of the Berlin School*, 116–21.
36 Inga Pollmann, 'The Forces of the Milieu: Angela Schanelec's *Marseille* and the Heritage of Michelangelo Antonioni', in Abel and Fisher, *The Berlin School and Its Global Contexts*, 164.

37 Lutz Koepnick, 'East of Berlin: Berlin School Filmmaking and the Aesthetics of Blandness', in Abel and Fisher, *The Berlin School and Its Global Contexts*, 223.
38 Abel, *The Counter-Cinema of the Berlin School*, 16, emphasis in original. Abel's approach is also taken up by a number of the contributors to Abel and Fisher.
39 Ibid., 20.
40 Ibid.
41 Abel's approach is based on a number of somewhat speculative/assertive theoretical foundations, especially the work of Gilles Deleuze and Felix Guattari, including central claims about the ability of film to affect viewers at the levels of their nervous systems. For one example, see Abel, *The Counter-Cinema of the Berlin School*, 60–3. Another connection between the claims made by Abel for such films and the broader context of a modern undermining of cultural norms, within which neoliberalism can be situated, can be made via Siegfried Kracauer's work of classical film theory, *Theory of Film: The Redemption of Reality* (Princeton, NJ: Princeton University Press, 1997, originally published 1960). This is a source sometimes cited in relation to the Berlin School, films such as those of Schanelec having some of the qualities of access to material reality valorized by Kracauer. The epilogue of Kracauer's book evokes the broader modern context in his suggestion that a return to the material and the concrete – such as that advocated in the films he considers to have qualities of the 'genuinely' cinematic – might offer a positive alternative what he views as the abstracting qualities of scientific discourse.
42 Baer, 'The Berlin School and Women's Cinema', 46.
43 Details from entries for each film on Box Office Mojo; also Peter Knegt, 'Tribeca Film Acquires Rick Alverson's "The Comedy"', Indiewire, 14 May 2012, accessed at https://www.indiewire.com/2012/05/tribeca-film-acquires-rick-alversons-the-comedy-47454/.

SELECT BIBLIOGRAPHY

Abel, Marco, *The Counter-Cinema of the Berlin School*. Rochester, NY: Camden House, 2013.

Aldama, Frederick, and Herbert Lindenberger, *Aesthetics of Discomfort: Conversations on Disquieting Art*. Ann Arbor: University of Michigan Press, 2016.

Aleksić, Tatjana, 'Sex, Violence, Dogs and the Impossibility of Escape: Why Contemporary Greek Film Is So Focused on Family', *Journal of Greek Media and Culture*, vol. 2, no. 2 (2016): 155–71.

Andersson, Roy, 'The Complex Image', extract in Mariah Larsson and Anders Marklund, eds, *Swedish Film: An Introduction and Reader*. Lund: Nordic Academic Press, 2010.

Arnheim, Rudolph, Arnheim, *Art and Visual Perception: A Psychology of the Creative Eye, The New Version*. Berkeley: University of California Press, 1974.

Audissino, Emilio, *Film/Music Analysis: A Film Studies Approach*. London: Palgrave, 2017.

Babbington, Bruce, and Peter, Evans, 'All that Heaven Allowed: Another Look at Sirkian Irony', *Movie*, vol. 34–5, (1990): 48–58.

Baer, Hester, 'Affectless Economies: The Berlin School and Neoliberalism', *Discourse*, vol. 35 (Winter 2013): 72–100.

Baer, Hester, 'The Berlin School and Women's Cinema', in Abel and Fisher, eds, *The Berlin School and Its Global Contexts: A Transnational Art Cinema*. Detroit, MI: Wayne State University Press, 2018.

Barker, Martin, *Audiences and Receptions of Sexual Violence in Contemporary Cinema*, Report to the British Board of Film Classification, March 2007, accessed online at http://www.bbfc.co.uk/sites/default/files/attachments/Audiences%20and%20Receptions%20of%20Sexual%20Violence%20in%20Contemporary%20Cinema_0.pdf.

Barotsi, Rosa, 'Whose Crisis? *Dogtooth* and the Invisible Middle Class', *Journal of Greek Media and Culture*, vol. 2, no. 2 (2016): 173–86.

Barrett, Ciara, 'The Feminist Cinema of Joanna Hogg: Melodrama, Female Space, and the Subversion of Phallogocentric Metanarrative', *Alphaville: Journal of Film and Screen Media*, vol. 10 (2015), online.

Bauman, Zygmunt, *Liquid Modernity*. Cambridge: Polity, 2012.

Bauman, Zygmunt, *Liquid Times: Living in an Age of Uncertainty*. Cambridge: Polity, 2007.

Bazin, Andre, 'Marginal Notes on Eroticism in Cinema', in *What Is Cinema?* Volume 2. Berkeley: University of California Press, 1971.

Beck, Ulrich, *World at Risk*. Cambridge: Polity, 2009.

Beck, Ulrich, and Elisabeth Beck-Gernsheim, *The Normal Chaos of Love*. Cambridge: Polity Press, 1995.

Bennett, Michael, *The Cambridge Introduction to Theatre and Literature of the Absurd*. Cambridge: Cambridge University Press, 2015.

Berlant, Lauren, *Cruel Optimism*. Durham, NC: Duke University Press, 2011.

Berliner, Todd, *Hollywood Aesthetic: Pleasure in American Cinema*. Oxford: Oxford University Press, 2017.

Betz, Mark, 'Art, Exploitation, Underground', in Mark Jancovich, Antonio Lazaro Reboll and Julian Stringer, eds, *Defining Cult Movies: The Cultural Politics of Oppositional Taste*. Manchester: Manchester University Press, 2003.

Beugnet, Martine, *Cinema and Sensation: French Film and the Art of Transgression*. Edinburgh: Edinburgh University Press, 2007.

Bordwell, David, *Figures Traced in Light: On Cinematic Staging*. Berkeley: University of California Press, 2005.

Bordwell, David, *Narration in the Fiction Film*. London: Routledge, 1988.

Bordwell, David, *The Way Hollywood Tells It: Story and Style in Modern Movies*. Berkeley: University of California Press, 2006.

Bordwell, David, and Kristen Thompson, *Film Art: An Introduction*, sixth edition. New York: McGraw-Hill, 2000.

Bourdieu, Pierre, *Distinction: A Social Critique of the Judgement of Taste*. London: Routledge, 1984.

Bourriaud, Nicolas, *Relational Aesthetics*, English translation. Dijon: les presses du réel, 2002.

Brady, Martin, and Helen Hughes, 'Import and Export: Ulrich Seidl's Indiscreet Anthropology of Migration', in Robert von Dassanowsky and Oliver Speck, eds, *New Austrian Film*. New York: Berghahn, 2011.

Brown, William, 'Sparse or Slow: Ozu and Joanna Hogg', in Jinhee Choi, ed., *Reorienting Ozu: A Master and His Influence*. Oxford: Oxford University Press, 2018.

Brunow, Dagmar, 'The Language of the Complex Image: Roy Andersson's Political Aesthetics', *Journal of Scandinavian Cinema*, vol. 1, no. 1 (2010): 83–6.

Chalkou, Maria, 'A New Cinema Of "Emancipation": Tendencies of Independence in Greek cinema of the 2000s', *Interactions: Studies in Communication & Culture*, vol. 3, no. 2 (2012).

Chion, Michel, *Audio-Vision: Sound on Screen*. New York: Columbia University Press, 1994.

Colebrook, Claire, *Irony*. London: Routledge, 2004.

Coleman, Lindsay, ed., *Sex and Storytelling in Modern Cinema: Explicit Sex, Performance and Cinematic Technique*. London: I.B. Tauris, 2016.

Cormican, Muriel, 'Willful Women in the Cinema of Maren Ade', *Camera Obscura*, vol. 33, no. 3 (2018): 103–27.

Crowley, John, *The Invention of Comfort: Sensibility and Design in Early Modern Britain and Early America*. Baltimore, MD: Johns Hopkins University Press, 2001.

Dahl, Melissa, *Cringeworthy: How to Make the Most of Uncomfortable Situations*. London: Corgi, 2019.

Dallas, Paul, 'Architecture of Desire: Joanna Hogg's Exhibition', *Cinema Scope*, vol. 57 (Winter 2014).

Diangelo, Robin, *White Fragility: Why It's So Hard for White People to Talk about Racism*. London: Penguin, 2018.
Donnelly, K.J., *Occult Aesthetics; Synchronization in Sound Film*. Oxford: Oxford University Press, 2014.
Fisher, Mark, *Capitalist Realism: Is There No Alternative?* Winchester: O Books, 2009.
Fisher, Mark, '*Dogtooth*: The Family Syndrome', *Film Quarterly*, vol. 64, no. 4 (2011): 22–7.
Forrest, David, 'The Films of Joanna Hogg: New British Realism and Class', *Studies in European Cinema*, vol. 11, no. 1 (2014): 64–75.
Fox, Kate, *Watching the English: The Hidden Rules of English Behaviour*, second edition. London: Hodder and Stoughton, 2014.
Frey, Mattias, *Extreme Cinema: The Transgressive Rhetoric of Today's Art Film Culture*. New Brunswick, NJ: Rutgers University Press, 2016.
Furedi, Frank, *Therapy Culture: Cultivating Vulnerability in an Uncertain Age*. London: Routledge, 2004.
Galt, Rosalind, 'Default Cinema: Queering Economic Crisis in Argentina and Beyond', *Screen*, 54 (Spring 2013): 62–81.
Gaut, Berys, 'Empathy and Identification in Cinema', in Peter French, Howard Wettstein and Michelle Saint, eds, *Film and The Emotions, Midwest Studies in Philosophy*, vol. XXIV. 2010.
Giddens, Anthony, *Runaway World: How Globalization is Reshaping Our Lives*. New York: Routledge, 2003.
Giddens, Anthony, *The Transformation of Intimacy: Sexuality, Love and Eroticism in Modern Societies*. Cambridge: Polity, 1992.
Goddard, Michael, 'Eastern Extreme: The Presentation of Eastern Europe as a Site of Monstrosity in *La Vie nouvelle* and *Import / Export*', in Tanya Horeck and Tina Kendall, eds, *The New Extremism in Cinema: From France to Europe*. Edinburgh: Edinburgh University Press, 2013.
Goleman, Daniel, *Emotional Intelligence: Why It Can Matter More than IQ*. London: Bloomsbury, 1996.
Gombrich, Ernst, *Art and Illusion: A Study in the Psychology of Pictorial Representation*. London: Phaidon, 1977.
Grønstad, Asbjørn, *Screening the Unwatchable*. Houndmills: Palgrave Macmillan, 2012.
Haegele, Lisa, 'Gender, Genre and the (Im)possibilities of Romantic Love in Derek Cianfrance's *Blue Valentine* (2010) and Maren Ade's *Everyone Else* (2009)', in Marco Abel and Jaimey Fisher, eds, *The Berlin School and Its Global Contexts: A Transnational Art Cinema*. Detroit, MI: Wayne State University Press, 2018.
Hanich, Julian, *Cinematic Emotion in Horror Films and Thrillers: The Aesthetic Paradox of Pleasurable Fear*. New York: Routledge, 2010.
Hanich, Julian, 'Complex Staging: The Hidden Dimensions of Roy Andersson's Aesthetics', *Movie: A Journal of Film Criticism*, 5 (2014): 37–50.
Hanich, Julian, 'Dis/liking Disgust: The Revulsion Experience at the Movies', *New Review of Film and Television Studies*, vol. 7, no. 3 (September 2009): 293–309.

Harold, James, 'Mixed Feelings: Conflicts in Emotional Responses to Film', in Peter French, Howard Wettstein and Michelle Saint, eds, *Film and The Emotions, Midwest Studies in Philosophy*, vol. XXIV. 2010.

Harvey, David, *A Brief History of Neoliberalism*. Oxford: Oxford University Press, 2005.

Hayward, Keith, *City Limits: Crime, Consumer Culture and the Urban Experience*. London: GlassHouse, 2004.

Hills, Matt, *The Pleasures of Horror*. London: Continuum, 2005.

Hjort, Mette, and Duncan Petrie, eds, *The Cinema of Small Nations*. Edinburgh: Edinburgh University Press, 2007.

Hockenhull, Stella, *British Women Film Directors in the New Millennium*. London: Palgrave Macmillan, 2017.

Hodge, Robert, and David Tripp, *Children and Television: A Semiotic Approach*. Cambridge: Polity Press, 1986.

Horeck, Tanya, and Tina Kendall, eds, *The New Extremism in Cinema: From France to Europe*. Edinburgh: Edinburgh University Press, 2013.

Hutcheon, Linda, *Irony's Edge: The Theory and Politics of Irony*. London: Routledge, 1994.

James, Oliver, *Affluenza: How to be Successful and Stay Sane*. London: Vermilion, 2007.

Kazakopoulou, Tonia, 'The Mother Accomplice: Questions of Representation in *Dogtooth* and *Miss Violence*', *Journal of Greek Media and Culture*, vol. 2, no. 2 (2016): 187–200.

King, Geoff, *American Independent Cinema*. London: I.B. Tauris, 2005.

King, Geoff, *Film Comedy*. London: Wallflower, 2002.

King, Geoff, *Indie 2.0: Change and Continuity in Contemporary American Indie Film*. London: I.B. Tauris, 2014.

King, Geoff, *Indiewood, USA: Where Hollywood Meets Independent Cinema*. London: I.B. Tauris, 2009.

King, Geoff, 'Introduction: What Indie isn't... Mapping the Indie Field', in King, ed., *A Companion to American Indie Film*. Chichester: Wiley Blackwell, 2017.

King, Geoff, *Positioning Art Cinema: Film and Cultural Value*. London: I.B. Tauris, 2019.

King, Geoff, *Spectacular Narratives*. London: I.B. Tauris, 2000.

Kiss, Miklós, and Steven Willemsen, *Impossible Puzzle Films: A Cognitive Approach to Contemporary Complex Cinema*. Edinburgh: Edinburgh University Press, 2017.

Koepnick, Lutz, 'East of Berlin: Berlin School Filmmaking and the Aesthetics of Blandness', in Abel and Fisher, eds, *The Berlin School and Its Global Contexts: A Transnational Art Cinema*, Detroit, MI: Wayne State University Press, 2018.

Kotsko, Adam, *Awkwardness: An Essay*. Winchester: O-Books, 2010.

Kracauer, Siegfried, *Theory of Film: The Redemption of Reality*. Princeton, NJ: Princeton University Press, 1997.

Kumar, Krishnan, *The Making of English National Identity*. Cambridge: Cambridge University Press, 2002.

Laine, Tarja, 'Jim Carrey: The King of Embarrassment', *Cineaction*, July 2001.

Lash, Dominic, *The Cinema of Disorientation: Inviting Confusions*. Edinburgh: Edinburgh University Press, 2020.
Lindqvist, Ursula, 'Roy Andersson's Cinematic Poetry and the Spectre of César Vallejo', *Scandinavian-Canadian Studies*, vol. 19 (2010): 200–29.
Lindqvist, Ursula, *Roy Andersson's* Songs from the Second Floor: *Contemplating the Art of Existence*. Seattle: University of Washington Press, 2016.
Lübecker, Nikolaj, *The Feel-Bad Film*. Edinburgh: Edinburgh University Press, 2015.
Lykidis, Alex, 'Crisis of Sovereignty in Recent Greek Cinema', *Journal of Greek Media and Culture*, vol. 1, no. 1 (2015): 9–27.
MacDowell, James, *Happy Endings in Hollywood Cinema: Cliché, Convention and the Final Couple*. Edinburgh: Edinburgh University Press, 2014.
MacDowell, James, *Irony in Film*. London: Palgrave Macmillan, 2016.
MacDowell, James, 'Notes on Quirky', *Movie: A Journal of Film Criticism*, vol. 1 (2010): 1–16.
Mandler, Peter, *The English National Character: The History of an Idea from Edmund Burke to Tony Blair*. New Haven, CT: Yale University Press, 2006.
Marklund, Anders, 'Introduction' to 'The New Generation of the 1960s' in Mariah Latsson and Anders Marklund, eds, *Swedish Film: An Introduction and Reader*. Lund: Nordic Academic Press, 2010.
Marks, Laura, *The Skin of the Film: Intercultural Cinema, Embodiment, and the Senses*. Durham, NC: Duke University Press, 2000.
Mazdon, Lucy, and Catherine Wheatley, *French Film in Britain: Sex, Art and Cinephilia*. New York: Berghahn, 2013.
Metzidakis, Stamos, 'No Bones to Pick with Lanthimos' Film *Dogtooth*', *Journal of Modern Greek Studies*, vol. 32 (2014): 367–92.
Middleton, Jason, *Documentary's Awkward Turn: Cringe Comedy and Media Spectatorship*. London: Routledge, 2014.
Mildren, Christopher, 'Spectator Strategies, Satire and European Identity in the Cinema of Roy Andersson Via the Paintings of Pieter Bruegel the Elder', *Studies in European Cinema*, vol. 20, nos. 2–3 (2013): 147–55.
Miller, Rowland, *Embarrassment: Poise and Peril in Everyday Life*. New York: Guilford Press, 1996.
Mirowski, Philip, *Never Let a Serious Crisis Go to Waste: How Neoliberalism Survived the Financial Meltdown*. London: Verso, 2014.
Mittell, Jason, *Complex TV: The Poetics of Contemporary Television Storytelling*. New York: New York University Press, 2015.
Newland, Paul, and Brian Hoyle, 'Introduction: Post-millennial British Art Cinema', *Journal of British Cinema and Television*, vol. 13, no. 2 (2016): 233–42.
Newman, Michael, *Indie: An American Film Culture*. New York: Columbia University Press, 2011.
Newman, Michael. 'Movies for Hipsters', in Geoff King, Claire Molloy and Yannis Tzioumakis, eds, *American Independent Cinema: Indie, Indiewood and Beyond*. Abingdon: Routledge, 2013.
Nichols, Bill, *Introduction to Documentary*. Bloomington, Indiana University Press, 2010.

Nichols, Bill, *Representing Reality: Issues and Concepts in Documentary*. Bloomington: Indiana University Press, 1992.

O'Neill, Deidre, and Mike Wayne, eds, *Considering Class: Theory, Culture and the Media in the 21st Century*. Boston: Brill, 2018.

Ostrowska, Elżbieta, and Johanna Rydzewska, 'Developments in Eastern European Cinemas Since 1989', in Rob Stone, Paul Cooke, Stephanie Dennison and Alex Marlow-Mann, eds, *The Routledge Companion to World Cinema*. Oxford: Routledge, 2018.

Palmer, Jerry, *The Logic of the Absurd: On Film and Television Comedy*. London: BFI, 1987.

Papadimitriou, Lydia, 'Cinema at the Edges of the European Union', in Rob Stone, Paul Cooke, Stephanie Dennison and Alex Marlow-Mann, eds, *The Routledge Companion to World Cinema*. Oxford: Routledge, 2018.

Papadimitriou, Lydia, 'In the Shadow of the Studios, the State, and the Multiplexes: Independent Filmmaking in Greece', in Doris Baltruschat and Mary Erickson, eds, *Independent Filmmaking around the Globe*, Toronto: University of Toronto Press, 2015.

Paxman, Jeremy, *The English: A Portrait of a People*. London: Penguin, 1998.

Perkins, Claire, *American Smart Cinema*. Edinburgh: Edinburgh University Press, 2012.

Perkins, Claire, 'Life during Wartime: Emotionalism, Capitalist Realism, and Middle-Class Indie Identity', in Geoff King, ed, *A Companion to American Indie Film*. Chichester: Wiley Blackwell, 2017.

Pethő, Ágnes, 'Between Absorption, Abstraction and Exhibition: Inflections of the Cinematic Tableau in the Films of Corneliu Porumboiu, Roy Andersson and Joanna Hogg', *Film and Media Studies*, vol. 11, no. 1 (2015): 39–76.

Petley, Julian, 'The Englishness of British Cinema; Beyond the Valley of the Corn Dollies', in John Hill, ed., *A Companion to British and Irish Cinema*. Hoboken, NY: John Wiley, 2019.

Pezeu-Massabuau, Jacques, *A Philosophy of Discomfort*. London: Reaktion Books, 2012.

Plantinga, Carl, 'The Affective Power of Movies', in Arthur P. Shimamura, ed., *Psychocinematics: Exploring Cognition at the Movies*. Oxford: Oxford University Press, 2014.

Plantinga, Carl, '"I Followed the Rules and They All Loved You More": Moral Judgment and the Attitudes Towards Fictional Characters in Film', in Peter French, Howard Wettstein and Michelle Saint, eds, *Film and The Emotions, Midwest Studies in Philosophy*, vol. XXIV, 2010.

Plantinga, Carl, *Moving Viewers: American Film and the Spectator's Experience*. Berkeley: University of California Press, 2009.

Plantinga, Carl, *Screen Stories: Emotion and the Ethics of Engagement*. Oxford: Oxford University Press, 2018.

Pollmann, Inga, The Forces of the Milieu: Angela Schanelec's *Marseille* and the Heritage of Michelangelo Antonioni', in Abel and Fisher, eds, *The Berlin School and Its Global Contexts: A Transnational Art Cinema*, Detroit, MI: Wayne State University Press, 2018.

Pye, Douglas, 'Movies and Tone', in *Close-Up 02*. London: Wallflower Press, 2007.

Quinlivan, Davinia, 'An Architecture of Light and Air, A Rhythm of Stillness: Absence in Joanna Hogg's *Exhibition*', *Screening the Past*, vol. 43 (April 2018).
Robertson, Selina, 'Joanna Hogg, a Very British Outsider', in *The F word: Contemporary Feminism*, 24 May 2012.
Sathe, Nikhil, 'Challenging the East-West Divide in Ulrich Seidl's *Import Export* (2007)', in Michael Gott and Todd Herzog, eds, *East, West and Centre: Reframing Post-1989 European Cinema*. Edinburgh: Edinburgh University Press, 2015.
Schatz, Thomas, *Hollywood Genres*. Austin: University of Texas Press, 1981.
Sconce, Jeffrey, 'Irony, Nihilism and the American "Smart" Film', *Screen*, vol. 43, no. 4 (2002): 349–69.
Sennett, Richard, *The Culture of the New Capitalism*. New Haven, CT: Yale University Press, 2006.
Shaviro, Steven, *The Cinematic Body*. Minneapolis: University of Minneapolis Press, 1993.
Shiner, Larry, *The Invention of Art*. Chicago: University of Chicago Press, 2001.
Smith, Greg M., 'Local Emotions, Global Moods', in Carl Plantinga and Smith, eds, *Passionate Views: Film, Cognition and Emotion*, Baltimore, MD: Johns Hopkins University Press, 1999.
Smith, Murray, *Engaging Characters: Fiction, Emotion, and the Cinema*. Oxford: Oxford University Press, 1995.
Smith, Murray, *Film, Art, and the Third Culture: A Naturalized Aesthetics of Film*. Oxford: Oxford University Press, 2017.
Sobchack, Vivian, *The Address of the Eye: A Phenomenology of Film Experience*. Princeton, NJ: Princeton University Press, 1992.
Sobchack, Vivian, *Carnal Thoughts: Embodiment and Moving Image Culture*. Berkeley: University of California Press, 2000.
Tulloch, John, and Belinda Middleweek, *Real Sex Films: The New Intimacy and Risk in Cinema*. Oxford: Oxford University Press, 2017.
Tulloch, John, and Deborah Lupton, *Risk and Everyday Life*. London: Sage, 2003.
van Dassanowksy, Robert, and Oliver Speck, 'Introduction: New Austrian Film: The Non-exceptional Exception', in von Dassanowsky and Speck, eds, *New Austrian Film*. New York: Berghahn, 2011.
Vogel, Amos, *Film as a Subversive Art*, originally published 1974, republished C.T. Editions, 2005.
Wacquant, Loïc, 'The Rise of Advanced Marginality: Notes on Its Nature and Implications', *Acta Sociologica*, vol. 39, no. 2 (April 1996): 121–39.
Wheatley, Catherine, *Michael Haneke's Cinema: The Ethic of the Image*. New York: Berghahn, 2009.
Wilkins, Kim, *American Eccentric Cinema*. New York: Bloomsbury, 2019.
Williams, Linda, *Screening Sex*. Durham: Duke University Press, 2008.
Williams, Raymond, 'Structures of Feeling', in *Marxism and Literature*. Oxford: Oxford University Press, 1977.
Wood, Robin, *Hollywood from Vietnam to Reagan*. New York: Columbia University Press, 1987.
Young, Jock, *The Vertigo of Late Modernity*. London: Sage, 2007.

INDEX

Abel, Marco 267, 270–1
Ade, Maren 2, 13, 253, 267–71
Albert, Barbera 139
Aldama, Frederick, and Herbert Lindenberger 47–8, 160
Aleksić, Tatjana 163
Alps 163, 165–6, 172, 174
Alverson, Rick 2, 253–60, 266
Á Ma Souer 113
American Pie 70
Animal Love 133, 134, 135
Angelopoulos, Theo 164, 171
Antonioni, Michelangelo 56
Apatow, Judd 54, 70
Ape 260
Apichatpong, Weerasethakul 243
Archipelago 13, 14, 219–29, 230, 232–3, 234–44, 253, 266
Arnold, Andrea 241, 268
Aronofsky, Darren 4, 29
Arnheim, Rudolph 21, 23, 24, 27, 47, 270
Arslan, Thomas 270
Asante, Amma 241
Attenberg 12, 149, 163, 165, 166–70, 172–3, 174
Auteur/authorship 4, 13–14, 174, 242, 243, 271

Babbington, Bruce, and Peter Evans 89
Baer, Hester 268–9
Baise-Moi 113
Barker, Martin 113–14, 116–18, 142
Barnard, Clio 241
Baron Cohen, Sacha 256
Barotsi, Rosa 164
Barrett, Ciara 239

Bauman, Zygmunt 8, 12, 55, 56, 58, 239
Bazin, Andre 114, 121, 189
Beck, Ulrich 8, 12, 55–8, 161, 196
Beck, Ulrich, and Elizabeth Beck-Gernsheim 57, 161
Berlant, Lauren 267–8
Berliner, Todd 22, 42–5, 59, 92, 93, 142, 175
Berlin School 270–1
Beugnet, Martine 115
Black Panther 24
blank style 8, 31, 34, 35, 38, 41, 75, 151, 186, 188, 203–4, 219, 226, 227, 231, 259
Blood Simple 87
Bong, Joon Ho 253
Bordwell, David 28, 31, 52
Bordwell, David and Kristen Thompson 20–1
Bourdieu, Pierre 10, 42–3, 49, 93, 234
Bourriaud, Nicolas 209–10
Brady, Martin, and Helen Hughes 127, 134–5
Breathless 27
Brechtian 68, 94, 193
Breillat, Catherine 5
Bresson, Robert 243
Brokeback Mountain 100
Bronstein, Mary 260
Bronstein, Ronald 260
Brown Bunny, The 98, 116
Brunow, Dagmar 193–4
Buber, Martin 193–4
Builder, The, 260
Bujalski, Andrew 260

286

INDEX

Cable Guy, The 38
Caouette, Jonathan 98
Carrey, Jim 38–9
Ceylan, Nori Bilge 243
Chalkou, Maria 170–2
Chevalier 170
Chien Andalou, Un 27–8, 56
Chinese 'Sixth Generation' 7
Chion, Michel 35
Citizen Ruth 83
class 1, 6–8, 10, 13, 25, 31, 43, 49, 55, 57, 58, 78, 80, 107, 108, 109, 113, 114, 128, 132, 134, 160, 162, 200–1, 207, 219, 224, 229, 230, 233–7, 239, 241, 243, 244, 245, 254, 268
classical film style 19–21, 23, 27–8, 29, 30, 31, 34, 41, 84, 187–8, 189, 204, 270
classical narrative 33, 34
cognitive approaches/cognitive engagement 2, 5, 11, 22, 33–6, 42, 44–6, 48, 52, 59, 65 n.116, 77, 92, 93, 115, 142, 149, 186, 203, 269, 270
Colebrook, Claire 53–4, 89, 90
comedy/comic 13, 38–9, 52, 54, 70, 79–80, 83, 92, 112, 116, 137, 185, 205, 249–68
Comedy, The 13, 253–61, 265–6, 267, 27
Cormican, Muriel 268–9
Cranz, Galen 17
critical responses/reviews by critics 12, 51, 84, 97, 121, 125, 136, 140, 141, 173, 240, 271, 272
Crowley, John 17–18, 48–50
Curb Your Enthusiasm 54, 253

Dahl, Melissa 51, 55
Dardenne, Jean-Pierre and Luc 3, 7, 29, 127, 225, 268
Denis, Claire 5, 98
Diangelo, Robin 55, 200
Dog Days 12, 107, 121, 127, 130–2, 137
Dogtooth 12, 17, 149–66, 167, 168, 170–8, 189, 249, 250
Donnelly, K. J. 23

embarrassment 1, 2, 11, 31, 36–9, 50, 67, 69–71, 78, 91, 95, 110, 115, 155, 185, 190, 198–9, 200, 205–7, 210, 211, 220–4, 230, 233, 236–8, 249–51, 261, 263, 267–9, 273
emotions/emotional engagement/affect 2–3, 5, 21, 246, 31, 34–6, 37, 40–1, 59, 63 n.69, 69, 71, 76, 77–8, 80, 85, 87, 88, 102 n.7, 114–16, 140, 176, 203, 226, 268, 270
Entertainment 260
Everyone Else 267
Evil Dead, The 87
Exhibition 232, 239–44

Favourite, The 165, 173
Filippou, Efthymis 172
film festivals 3, 9, 137, 138, 139, 171, 172, 173, 174, 213, 214, 243, 244, 271
Fisher, Mark 7, 58, 163, 234
Fishtank 241
Force Majeure 12, 181, 198, 204–9, 210, 211, 214, 249
Forest for the Trees, The, 267
Forrest, David 234, 241
Fox, Kate 233–8
Frey, Mathias 137–9
Frownland 260
Furedi, Frank 7, 56–8

Gallo, Vincent 98, 116
Galt, Rosalind 165
gender (*see also* Sex) 10, 39–40, 58, 108–9, 114, 132, 239, 267–8
genre 2, 4, 22, 23, 24, 26, 27, 33, 34, 39, 42, 89, 140, 171, 173
Giddens, Anthony 8, 12, 55–8, 161, 208, 239, 270
Giliap 213
Godard, Jean-Luc 27
Gold Rush, The 251
Gombrich, Ernst 21
Greek 'new wave', 'weird wave' 12, 149, 162–3, 170–4
Grisebach, Valeska 270
Grønstad, Asbjørn 5, 28, 41, 42, 114, 115

Haegele, Lisa 267
Haneke, Michael 3, 118, 136, 139, 177
Hanich, Julian 5, 26, 27, 28, 31, 32, 43, 45, 56, 62 n.63, 95, 117, 187, 189–91, 194
Happiness 87, 90–1, 94, 95, 97, 140
Harold, James 49–50
Hartley, Hal 9
Hausner, Jessica 139
Headless Woman, The 10
Hidden 136
High Hopes 253
Hills, Matt 25, 26, 43
Hochhäusler, Christopher 270
Hockenhull, Stella 241
Hodge, Robert, and David Tripp 250
Hogg, Joanna 2, 8, 13, 31, 219–45, 257
Hole in My Heart, A 28, 120
Holofcener, Nicole 9
Hong Sang-soo 10
horror 2, 4, 25–7, 28, 31, 32–3, 39, 41, 43, 45, 56, 95, 117, 140, 173, 193
Hunger 241
Hutcheon, Linda 54, 77, 89

Idiots, The 4
I'm Still Here 33, 53, 121
Import Export 11, 107–30, 132, 135, 137, 140–3, 155, 177
In Bruges 253
In the Basement 107, 113, 133–4, 135, 149
Intruder, The 98
Involuntary 12, 181, 198–204, 207–8
Irreversible 29, 113, 117–18
irony 6, 7, 11, 53–4, 59, 72–4, 77–82, 84–5, 87–91, 94, 110, 112, 127, 131, 133, 152–3, 171, 229, 232, 237, 253, 256–9, 260, 266, 267
Italian neorealism 3, 7, 121, 189

James, Oliver 7, 161
Jarmusch, Jim 9
Jesus, You Know 133, 135
Juno 79

Kazakopoulou, Tonia 164–5
Keiller, Patrick 241
Killing of a Sacred Deer, The 165, 173
Kinetta 163, 165, 172
Kiss, Miklós and Steven Willemsen 45
Koepnik, Lutz 270
Köhler, Ulrich 270
Kore-eda, Hirokazu 243
Kotsko, Adam 52–5, 56, 58, 70, 79, 107, 237, 253, 272

LaBute, Neil 6
Laine, Tarja 38–9
Lang, Fritz 50
Lanthimos, Yorgos 2, 12, 149–66, 167, 168, 170, 171–4, 243
Lash, Dominic 45
Lee, Spike 9
Leigh, Mike, 253
Lim, Dennis 129, 138
Lindqvist, Ursula 191–5, 197, 214
Linklater, Richard 172
Loach, Ken 234
Lobster, The 165, 172–3
Local Hero 35
Losses to be Expected 133, 135
Lübecker, Thomas 4, 5, 23, 41, 114
Lukács, Georg 193
Lykidis, Alex 163–4, 166, 168–70

M 50
MacDowell, James 60 n.12, 73, 78–9
Mader, Ruth 139
Manchester by the Sea 100
Marklund, Anders 214
Marks, Laura 115
Marseille 270
Martel, Lucrecia 10
Marx, Karl, and Friedrich Engels 56
McDonagh, Martin 253
McQueen, Steve 241
Middleton, Jason 52–3
Milden, Christopher 191
Miller, Rowland 36–7, 38, 50, 71
Minnelli, Vincente 89
Miramax 98–100
Miss Violence 166
Models 133, 135

modernism 3, 4, 47–8, 88, 166, 177, 232
modernity/late modernity 3, 17, 49, 51–8, 79, 107, 129, 160, 166–7, 181, 191, 194, 195, 197, 237–8, 252, 259–60, 267, 269, 275 n.41
Moodyson, Luke 28
Morten, Samantha 241
Mother 253
Mother! 4, 29, 259
music (or its absence) 21, 23, 24, 34, 35, 47, 72–3, 76–7, 79, 81, 87, 131, 158, 184, 232, 239, 240, 259
Music Box, The 250

Napoleon Dynamite 79
neoliberalism 3, 6–8, 10, 51, 55–8, 82, 129, 159–65, 168, 192, 196–7, 207, 212, 234, 261, 265, 266–70
New Austrian Cinema 128–30, 135–7, 138–40
New Jerusalem 260
Newland, Paul, and Brian Hoyle 240–1, 243
Nichols, Bill 134
Noé, Gaspar 5, 29
Northern Skirts 136
Nostalgia 30

Office, The 250, 253
Östlund, Ruben 2, 12, 181–2, 197–214
Ostrowska, Elżbieta, and Johanna Rydzewska 130
Ozu, Yasujiro 243

Palindromes, 9, 11, 67–100
Palmer, Jerry 251, 266
Papadimitriou, Lydia 172–3
Paradise: Faith 12, 107, 133, 135
Paradise: Hope 12, 107, 133
Paradise: Love 12, 107, 132–3
Parasite 253
Payne, Alexander 6
Perkins, Claire 6–8, 52, 53, 55, 56, 58, 82, 87, 107, 234
Pethő, Ágnes 215 n.8, 228
Petzold, Christian 270

Pezu-Massabuau, Jaques 19, 47–9, 54, 59
Pigeon Sat on a Branch Reflecting on Existence, A 12, 181, 183–7, 189, 191, 193–7, 214
Plantinga, Carl 24–5, 34–6, 40, 46, 51, 59, 78, 84, 88–90, 94, 109, 114, 115, 157, 222, 225, 259
Play 12, 181, 198–201, 203–4, 207–8
pleasure (in discomfort) 2, 10, 17, 24, 25–7, 32, 38–9, 41–6, 48, 52, 56, 59, 90, 92–3, 95, 114, 174, 269, 273
Pollmann, Inga 270
postmodern/postmodernity 3, 54–5, 107, 129, 130, 195
Potrykus, Joel 260
Prisoners 4
Pye, Douglas 36, 39, 79, 89

Quinlivan, Davina 239

race 1, 3, 53, 55, 67, 132, 133, 183–4, 198–202, 207, 235, 254–5, 257, 260
Raiders of the Lost Ark 35
Rambo: First Blood Part II 24
Ramsey, Lynn 241
Ratcatcher 241
realism 3, 6–7, 28, 40, 79, 121, 142, 155, 163, 165, 171, 189, 225, 229, 234–5, 239, 241, 243, 244, 255
Reichardt, Kelly 9, 268
Robertson, Selina 239
Rocha, Glauber 10
Rohmer, Eric 243
Romanian new wave 7

Salomonowitz, Anja 139
Sathe, Nikhil 111, 128
Saw franchise 42
Schanelec, Angela 270–1
Schindler's List 189
Sconce, Jeffrey 6–7, 8, 30–1, 32, 34, 35, 52, 53, 58, 59, 68, 72, 73, 79, 107, 110, 151, 219, 225, 231, 234
Secrets and Lies 253
Seidl, Ulrich 2, 8, 11, 31, 107–43
Selfish Giant, The 241

INDEX

Sennett, Richard 8, 55, 58, 196
sex 1, 4, 11–12, 31, 38, 40, 57, 66 n.142, 67, 68–73, 74, 75, 76, 87, 94. 97, 98, 108, 109–21, 122, 123, 125, 126, 127, 128, 129, 132–3, 137–42, 149, 151, 153–6, 161, 165, 166, 167–8, 175, 177, 224, 230, 231, 235, 257
Shiner, Larry 49
sincerity 78–9, 81–2, 231, 232, 236, 253, 256–60, 263–4, 267
Sirk, Douglas 89
Slacker 172
Sleepless in Seattle 250
Smith, Greg M. 34–5, 39, 40
Smith, Murray 74–6, 87, 88, 159, 225
Sobchack, Vivian 46–7, 115, 117
Soderbergh, Steven 9
Solondz, Todd 2, 6, 9, 11, 68–101
Some Came Running 89
Songs from the Second Floor, 12, 181, 182, 185–6, 187–8, 189–90, 191–3, 195–7, 213–14
Son of Saul 29
Souvenir, The 232, 240, 241, 242, 244
Spielberg, Steven 189
Square, The 12, 181, 198, 209–14, 249
Storytelling 91, 97
Suddenly, 165
Swanberg, Joe 260
Swamp, The 10
Swedish Love Story, A 213

Tan, Ed 39
Tarkovsky, Andrei 30
Tarnation 98
Taxi Driver 4
Three Billboards Outside Ebbing, Missouri 253
Three Women 4

Tim and Eric Awesome Show, Great Job! 256
Tim and Eric's Billion Dollar Movie 256
Titanic 24–5, 32, 35
Titicut Follies 143
Toni Erdmann 13, 261–9, 271–2
Trapero, Pablo 10
Tsai, Ming-Liang, 243
Tsangari, Athina Rachel 2, 12, 149, 163–74
Touchy Feely 6
Tulloch, John, and Deborah Lupton 58

Unforgiven 24
Unknown White Male 98
Unloved, The 241
Unrelated 228, 230–3, 235–7, 239–40, 242–3

van Dassanowsky, Robert and Oliver Speck 129, 130, 136, 138
viewer responses online 91–9, 141–3, 174–8, 244–5, 249, 265–6
Vogel, Amos 56
von Trier, Lars 3, 5, 177

Wacquant, Loïc 197
Warhol, Robyn 40
Weinstein Company, The 98
Welcome to the Dollhouse 67, 87, 97
Wellspring Media 96–101
Wilkins, Kim 8, 82
Williams, Raymond 6, 58, 129, 162
Wiseman, Frederick 143
World of Glory 189, 193–4, 213

Yeast 260
Young Adult 6
You, the Living 12, 181, 186–7, 192, 194, 196

www.ingramcontent.com/pod-product-compliance
Lightning Source LLC
Chambersburg PA
CBHW052214300426
44115CB00011B/1678